THE FIELD

Cultivating Salvation

The Collected Works of St Ignatius (Brianchaninov)—Volume 1

THE FIELD
cultivating salvation

The Collected Works of St Ignatius (Brianchaninov)—Volume 1

BY BISHOP IGNATIUS (BRIANCHANINOV)

Translated from the Russian by Nicholas Kotar

HOLY TRINITY PUBLICATIONS
The Printshop of St Job of Pochaev
Holy Trinity Monastery
Jordanville, New York

Printed with the blessing of His Eminence,
Metropolitan Hilarion First Hierarch
of the Russian Orthodox Church Outside of Russia

The Field
Cultivating Salvation

PRINTSHOP OF
SAINT JOB OF POCHAEV

An imprint of

HOLY TRINITY PUBLICATIONS
Holy Trinity Monastery
Jordanville, New York 13361-0036
www.holytrinitypublications.com

ISBN: 978-0-88465-376-9 (paperback)
ISBN: 978-0-88465-451-3 (ePub)
ISBN: 978-0-88465-453-7 (Mobipocket)

Library of Congress Control Number 2016951473

Cover Design and "Reflections" Artwork: Aubrey Harper – behance.net/aubreyharper

Contents

Part IV

Part V

Part VI

Introduction

Almost half a century has passed since our monastery published the first English translation of a part of the Collected Works of St Ignatius Brianchaninov, in 1968. The Fathers before us chose to publish the fifth volume from the Russian original first and entitled it in English as *the Arena*.

In the fifty years that have passed since then there have been profound changes in the geopolitical, economic and social environment in which we live our daily lives. But more fundamentally nothing has changed: God is the cause of our existence, and our elemental need is still to grow both in knowledge of Him and union with Him as the chief source of all our joy. To achieve this goal we must struggle to defeat our passions, even to lay down our earthly life for the greater life that is hid with Christ in God for all eternity.

We offer now *the Field* as a continuation of these themes, recognizing that the Field of battle may also be a place of harvest and great beauty. In this first volume of his collected work, St Ignatius shares with us many reflections on the beauty of the natural world that arouse within him a renewed desire for the much greater splendor of the heavenly kingdom. He shares with his reader in simple and direct terms the virtues we must cultivate and details how to combat the different kind of weeds that will inevitably seek to overwhelm us and keep us from the knowledge and love of God. Some of his advice is presented in the form of conversations between an Elder and his disciple or a layman and a monk. The questions posed help us to realize that many of the challenges we face today in seeking to live a godly life are not as unique to our own times as we sometimes think.

St Ignatius ends the main part of his text on a note of joy: Glory to God in all things! But he does not conceal his own spiritual struggles and physical infirmities that impact on these in his lament. Our hope in publishing this work is that notwithstanding one's own challenges the reader will be drawn to *the Field* and to renewed diligence in the cultivation of salvation.

Holy Trinity Monastery
Pentecost 2016

PART I

CHAPTER I

Emulating Our Lord Jesus Christ

"If anyone serves Me, let him follow Me," said the Lord.[1] Every Christian, through the oaths given at holy baptism, takes upon himself the responsibility of being a slave and servant of the Lord Jesus Christ. Every Christian absolutely must follow the Lord Jesus Christ.

Having called Himself the shepherd of the sheep, the Lord said that "the sheep hear his voice, and the sheep follow him, for they know his voice." [2] The voice of Christ is His teaching; the voice of Christ is the Gospel; following after Christ's earthly wanderings means completely following His commandments.

In order to follow Christ, one must know His voice. Study the Gospels, and through your life you will be able to emulate Christ.

Whoever is born in the flesh and receives regeneration in holy baptism, and then preserves the purity he has received in baptism with the help of a life according to the Gospels, will be saved. He will "go in" to a God-pleasing life on earth through a spiritual rebirth, and he will go "out" from this world in a blessed death, and in eternity he will "find" an eternal, expansive, sweet, spiritual "pasture."[3]

"If anyone serves Me, let him follow Me; and where I am, there My servant will be also. If anyone serves Me, him my Father will honor."[4] Where was the Lord when He said these words? In His humanity, united with His divinity, He was among people on earth in the midst of their exile and suffering, remaining in His divinity there, where He has been from the beginning without beginning. "The Word was with God"[5] and in God. This Word said of Himself: "The Father is in Me, and I in Him."[6] The one who follows Christ will share in His state. "Whoever confesses" with his mouth, heart, and deeds "that Jesus is the Son of God, God abides in him, and he in God."[7]

"If anyone serves Me, him my Father will honor." "To him who overcomes" the world and sin, who follows Me in this earthly life, in the life eternal "I will grant to sit with Me on My throne, as I also overcame, and sat down with my Father on His throne."[8]

Rejection of the world must come before following Christ. The latter has no place in the soul if the former has not yet been accomplished. The Lord said, "Whoever desires to come after Me, let him deny himself, and take up his cross, and follow me. For whoever desires to save his life will lose it, but whoever loses his life for My sake and the gospel's will save it."[9] "If anyone comes to Me and does not hate his father and mother, wife and children, brothers and sisters, yes, and his own life also, he cannot be My disciple. And whoever does not bear his cross and come after Me cannot be My disciple."[10]

Many approach the Lord, but few decide to follow Him. Many read the Gospels, find comfort in them, become inspired by their lofty and holy teaching, but few decide to model their actions according to the commandments of the Gospel. The Lord says to all who approach Him and desire to be joined to Him, "If anyone comes to Me," and he does not renounce the world and himself, "he cannot be My disciple."

"This is a hard saying," said even such people who appeared to be followers of Him and considered themselves His disciples: "who can understand it?"[11] This is how the word of God is judged by the wise of this world in the poverty of their discernment. The word of God is life, life eternal, true life. With this word, the carnal mind[12] is destroyed, since it is born from eternal death and supports eternal death in people. The word of God, for those dying from the carnal mind and those desiring to die from it, is "foolishness. But to us who are being saved, it [the Word] is the power of God."[13]

Sin has become so common to us as a result of the fall that it has absorbed all qualities, all intentions of our souls. Rejection of sin that has become part of the soul requires rejection of the soul itself. This kind of rejection of the soul is necessary for its own salvation. Rejection of the nature defiled by sin is indispensible to attain the nature renewed by Christ. When even part of a meal has been poisoned, all of the food is thrown away. The dish is carefully washed, and only then is more food put into it for serving at the table. Food that has been tainted with poison can be called poison itself.

In order to follow Christ, let us first renounce our own reason and our own will. Both the reason and will of our fallen nature are completely tainted by sin; they cannot be reconciled with the reason and will of God. Only he who rejects his reason makes himself capable of attaining the reason of God; only he who rejects the doing of his own will makes himself capable of doing God's will.

In order to follow Christ, let us take up our cross. The taking up of our cross is called the willing, pious submission to God's judgment, despite all sorrows that may be sent or allowed by God's providence. Grumbling and anger during sorrows and difficulties is a rejection of the cross. Only he who has taken his cross can follow after Christ—he is submissive to God's will, humbly acknowledging himself to be worthy of every judgment and punishment.

The Lord who has commanded us to sacrifice ourselves, to reject the world and to carry the cross gives us the strength to fulfill His commandment. He who decides to fulfill this commandment and tries to fulfill it immediately realizes its necessity. This teaching, which seems cruel to the superficial and erroneous point of view of the carnal mind, turns out to be most wise and full of good things. It calls the fallen to salvation, the dead to life, and those buried in hell to heaven.

Those who do not want to willingly renounce themselves and the world are forcibly obliged to do one and the other. When incorrigible and inevitable death comes, they have to leave everything that they loved behind. Their self-rejection at that point is so extreme that they are forced to throw off even their bodies, leaving it in the earth to rot and be eaten by worms.

Self-love and attachment to things fleeting and full of cares—these are the fruits of self-deception, blindness, spiritual death. Self-love is a twisted love for one's self. This love is insane and fallen. He who is full of self-love, passionate for fleeting pleasure, for sinful indulgence, is an enemy of himself. He is a self-murderer. Thinking to love himself and pamper himself, he ends up hating and destroying himself eternally.

Let us look around, we who are entertained, clouded, fooled by the world. Let us awake, we who have been enchanted by the world, denied our true self-knowledge by the world! Let us learn from the experiences happening constantly around us. That which happens around us will inevitably happen to us as well.

Did he who spent his entire life searching for honors take them with him into eternity? Did he not leave here on earth his bombastic titles, emblems of excellence, all the luxuries with which he surrounded himself? Did not this man go into eternity only bearing his deeds, his qualities developed during his earthly life?

He who spent his life gathering riches, who saved a great deal of money, bought huge tracts of land to own, established various businesses that brought in much profit, lived in chambers shining with gold and marble, rode around in magnificent carriages and horses—did he take all this with him into eternity? No! He left it all on earth, being content for the last need of the body with the smallest plot of land, in which all dead men are equally content.

He who spent his life in the pursuit of pleasures and enjoyments of the flesh, who spent time with friends playing games and other nonsense, who feasted at sumptuous banquets, is finally pushed away by necessity from his usual way of life. Soon comes old age, illness, and after them, the hour of the separation of the soul from the body. Then he will know, only too late, that serving one's passions and desires is nothing but self-deception that living for the pleasures of the body and sin is living without meaning.

Striving for worldly success—how strange, how monstrous it is! This search is frenzied. Hardly has worldly success been found when it immediately loses its value, and the search is renewed with new vigor. It is never happy with the present; it lives only in the future, wanting only those things it does not yet have. The desired objects attract the seeker's heart with the dream and hope of fulfillment. When the seeker is constantly fooled he rushes after more objects for the duration of his life, until unexpected death steals him away. How can one explain this seeking, which treats everyone like a soulless traitor yet still rules over all, still attracts so many? Into our souls has been planted the striving for eternal bliss. But we fell, and our hearts, blinded by our fall, seek in time and on earth that which exists only in eternity and in heaven.

The same fate that visited my fathers and brothers will visit me. They died, so will I. I will leave my cell; I will leave behind my books, my clothes, and my writing desk, where I spent many hours. I will leave everything that I needed or thought I needed during this earthly life. They will carry my body out of the cell where I live in anticipation of another life and country. They will carry out my body and give it up to the ground, which served as the beginning of man's body. The same fate will visit you, brothers, who read these words. You will die as well, leaving on earth all that is of the earth. Only with your souls will you enter eternity.

The human soul gathers qualities that coincide with its activity. As a mirror shows the image of the objects placed in front of it, so the soul becomes stamped with the impressions of its deeds and activities, of its surroundings. But while a lifeless mirror loses the reflected images when the objects are removed, the reasoning soul keeps these impressions. They can be wiped clean or removed by others, but this requires work and time. Those impressions that are stamped onto the soul in the hour of its death remain part of the soul forever, and a guarantee of either eternal blessedness or eternal suffering.

"You cannot serve God and mammon,"[14] said the Lord to fallen man, revealing before humanity that state into which he had been led by the fall. In a similar way, a doctor reveals to the patient his physical state, into which his disease has led him, and which the sick man himself cannot understand. As a result of our spiritual disease, we need timely self-renunciation and rejection of the world for our salvation. "No one can serve two masters; for either he will hate the one and love the other; or else he will be loyal to the one and despise the other."[15]

Experience continually confirms the justice of that outlook on the moral sickness of mankind, which the all-holy physician expressed in the mentioned quote, spoken with decisive straightforwardness—indulging sinful and vain desires always leads to obsession with them, and after the obsession comes slavery, which is death to everything spiritual. Those who allowed themselves to follow their desires and carnal mind became obsessed with them, enslaved by them, forgot God and eternity, and wasted their earthly lives pointlessly, dying an eternal death.

It is not possible to follow both your own will and God's will. From the actions of the former, the latter becomes tainted, useless. Thus, a sweet-smelling, precious myrrh loses its worth as it is mixed with even a small amount of foul-smelling liquid. Only then, God says through his great prophet, "you shall eat the good of the land" when you willingly hear me. "But if you refuse and rebel, you shall be devoured by the sword; For the mouth of the Lord has spoken."[16]

It is impossible to know the reason of God if one remains carnally minded. The Apostle said, "For to be carnally minded is death. The carnal mind is enmity against God; for it is not subject to the law of God, nor indeed can be."[17] What is the carnal mind? It is a way of thinking that has come about from the state into which people have been led by the fall, which directs them to act as if they were to live eternally on earth, raising up all that is temporary and prone to entropy, demeaning God and everything that refers to pleasing God, and taking away salvation from people.

Let us renounce our own souls according to the commandment of the Saviour, in order to find our souls! Let us willingly reject the tainted state into which we have been led by our willing rejections of God, so that we may receive from God the holy state of a human nature renewed by the incarnate God! Let us replace our will and the will of the demons (to which our will has subjected itself and with which our will has become aligned) with the will of God proclaimed to us in the Gospels. Let us replace our carnal mind—which we share with the fallen spirits—with the reason of God, shining out from the Gospels.

Let us renounce our earthly riches so that we are able to follow our Lord Jesus Christ! Renouncing earthly riches becomes possible only with a correct understanding of them. The Gospel provides us with the correct interpretation of dealing with substantial property.[18] When man accepts this correct interpretation, his reason inevitably realizes its truth. Earthly wealth does not belong to us, as those who have never thought about this erroneously believe. Otherwise, it always and forever would remain in our possession. But it changes hands constantly, thereby proving that it is given only for us to watch over temporarily. Wealth belongs to God; man is only the temporary caretaker. A faithful caretaker will follow exactly the wishes of the one who has entrusted the wealth to him. And we, temporarily ruling over the wealth given to us, must rule over it according to the will of God. Let us not use it as a means of indulging our desires and passions, as a resource for eternal perdition. Let us use it for the good of mankind, which lives in need and suffering; let us use it as a means for our salvation. Those who desire Christian perfection give away their wealth outright.[19] Those who wish to be saved must give alms according to their means, and must not indulge in excess.

Let us renounce love of honors and the praise of men! Let us not run after ranks and titles, or use dishonest and demeaning methods to earn them, deriding the laws of God, the conscience, the good of our brothers. Such means are most often used for the attaining of earthly glory. He who is infected and enslaved by vainglory, the insatiable seeker after human praise, is unable to believe in Christ. "How can you believe," said Christ to His praise-loving contemporaries, "who receive honor from one another, and do not seek the honor that comes from the only God?"[20] If the providence of God has given us earthly power and might, then let us use this to become benefactors of humanity. Let us reject the foul poison that is so dangerous for the human spirit—foolish and despised egotism that turns those infected with it into beasts and demons that become the scourge of humanity, evildoers against themselves.

Let us love the will of God more than everything else. Let us prefer it to everything else. Let us hate everything that is contrary to it with a righteous and God-pleasing hatred. When our nature, tainted by sin, rises up against the Gospel teachings, let us despise our nature by rejecting its desires and needs. The more decisive our righteous hatred, the more decisive our victory will be over sin and our nature, which is enthralled to sin, and the more swift and definite our spiritual triumph will be.

When family members become determined to distract us from doing God's will, let us direct our righteous anger against them like the anger that the lambs show the wolves when they do not pretend to be wolves themselves, nor do they protect themselves with bared teeth. "Behold, I send you out as sheep in the midst of wolves. Therefore be wise as serpents and harmless as doves."[21] This holy anger directed at our family consists of remaining loyal to God and not agreeing with fallen human will, even if these people are our nearest relatives. It is greathearted patience in the midst of insults hurled by them; it is prayer for their salvation, not evil words or actions, which reveal the anger of fallen nature. This is anger repulsive to God.

"Do not think," said the Saviour, "that I came to bring peace on earth. I did not come to bring peace but a sword. For I have come to 'set a man against his father, a daughter against her mother, and a daughter-in-law against her mother-in-law.'"[22] St John of the Ladder explains these words of the Lord thus: "He came to separate the lovers of God from the lovers of the world; the carnal from the spiritual; those who love praise from the humble-minded. God is pleased by this separation when it is done for love of Him."

The prophet called the earth the place of his wandering, and himself a wanderer and a pilgrim on earth: "For I am a sojourner with Thee," he said in his prayer to God, "and a pilgrim, as all my fathers were."[23] What an obvious and tangible truth, one that is forgotten by all in spite of its self-evidence. I am a stranger on earth—I entered through birth, and I will leave through death. I am a sojourner on earth—I was moved to it from Eden, where I defiled and sullied myself with sin. I will remove myself from the earth, from my temporary exile, into which I have been placed by my God so that I might reconsider, cleanse myself from sinfulness, make myself again able to live in heaven. For my stubborn, final brokenness, I should be eternally damned to the darkness of hell. I am a wanderer on earth—I begin my wandering in the cradle, finish in the grave. I wander in my ages from youth to decrepitude; I wander through various worldly circumstances and situations. *I am a stranger and a sojourner, as all my fathers were.* My fathers were strangers and wanderers on earth—they entered it through birth—they left it through death. There were no exceptions. No human being remained forever on earth. Even I will leave. I am already beginning my final journey, I am weakening in strength, I am submitting to old age. I will go; I will go from here according to the implacable law and the all-powerful command of my Creator and God.

Let us be assured that we are wanderers on earth. Only from this realization can we draw up a correct account of our earthly life. Only through this realization can we give our life the right direction and use it to attain blessed eternity, not for emptiness and worries, not for our destruction. Our fall has blinded and is blinding us! And only after a long time has passed are we forced to face the most obvious truths, which are so clear they need no confirmation.

When a pilgrim stops on his way in a house for pilgrims, he does not pay any attention to the state of the house. Why would he, when he is staying there only for a short time? He is content with only the basic necessities; he tries not to waste the money that he needs to continue his journey and to find housing in that great city to which he travels. He bears privation and lack of comfort with patience, knowing that they are only accidents to which every traveler is subject, and that undisturbed calm awaits him in the place to which he travels. He does not become attached to any object in his hostel, no matter how attractive such an object may be. He does not lose time doing unnecessary things—he needs all the time he can muster to complete the difficult journey. He is constantly deep in thought about the glorious capital city, the aim of his travels; the significant difficulties he will have to overcome and various things that could make his travels easier; about ambushes by robbers along the highways and the misery of those who were unable to complete the journey; and about the blissfulness of those who were able to complete it successfully. Having stayed in the hostel for as long as necessary, the pilgrim thanks the owner, and having left, forgets about the hostel or only remembers it in passing, because his heart was cold toward it.

Let us develop the same indifference to the world. Let us not foolishly waste our abilities of soul and body; let us not bring them as a sacrifice to the vain and fading world. Let us defend ourselves from attachment to the short-lived and material, so that the world will not prevent us from finding the eternal and heavenly. Let us defend ourselves from the indulgence of our insatiable and unquenchable desires, which only hastens a fall of monstrous proportions. Let us defend ourselves from excesses, being content only with what is necessary. Let us direct all our attention to the life after death, which will have no end.

Let us know God, who commanded us to know Him and Who allows us to know Him through His word and His grace. Let us attach ourselves to God during this earthy life. He offers us a most intimate union with Himself, and He gives us a certain amount of time to effect that union—our earthly life. There is no other time, except the limited time of our earthly life, when we could unite with Him. If it does not occur during this time, it will never occur at all. Let us become friends with the heavenly dwellers, with the holy angels and the reposed saints, so that they might accept us into the "everlasting home."[24] Let us also know the fallen spirits, those evil and vile enemies of the human race, so that we can avoid their traps and avoid living with them eternally in the flames of hell. Let the word of God be "a light unto my paths."[25]

Let us praise and thank God for the many benefits that He has given us, for the satisfaction of our needs, for our temporary home on earth. With a clear mind, let us contemplate the meaning of these benefits; they are but a pale imitation of the eternal good things. They imitate the eternal good things as weakly and ineffectively as a shadow imitates the object casting it. By giving us these earthly goods, God mysteriously tells us:

> My People! Your temporary sojourn is blessed with various, countless goods, which can capture and ravish the eye and heart, which can fill all your needs to excess. Imagine how much greater are the goods that will fill your heavenly home. Understand the boundless, unimaginable goodness of God, and, limiting yourselves to the reasonable use and contemplation of earthly things, do not act foolishly. Do not become enslaved to them, do not destroy yourselves because of them.

Using them as much as you need and require, with all your strength, strive to the attainment of heavenly good things.

Let us separate ourselves from any false teachings and activities. The sheep of Christ will not follow a strange voice, "but will flee from him, for they do not know the voice of strangers."[26] Let us come to know the voice of Christ, so that we may immediately recognize Him and follow His wishes when we hear Him. Having acquired yearning in our spirit for this voice, we will acquire estrangement from the voice of the stranger, which is imbued with a carnal mind of various manifestations. As soon as we hear this voice of the stranger, let us flee from him, like true sheep of Christ who save themselves from the stranger's voice by fleeing, by a stubborn refusal to hear it. Even to listen to it is dangerous; after listening comes enticement, after enticement—perdition. The fall of our forefathers began only with innocent heeding of the voice of a stranger.

Our Shepherd not only calls us with His voice, but also guides us with the example of His own life. He walks before His sheep. He commanded us to reject the world, to reject ourselves, to take and carry our cross, all of which He has already done Himself, before our very eyes. "Christ also suffered for us, leaving us an example, that you should follow His steps."[27] He deigned to take humanity upon Himself, and although He was born from a royal line, it was a royal line that had fallen to ranks of the lowest and commonest people. His birth occurred during the travels of His most holy Mother, who could not even find a place to lay Her head. He was born in a cave, where cattle were kept safe from the weather; the Newborn's crib was a feeding trough. No sooner had the news of His birth spread that a conspiracy was formed for His murder. The Child is already persecuted! The Child is sought to be exterminated! The Child flees from the ferocious murderers through the desert into Egypt!

The God-Man spent His childhood in submission to His parents, His adopted father and natural Mother, showing an example of humility to all people who are perishing in pride and prideful disobedience. The Lord dedicated His adult years to the preaching of the Gospel, sojourning from city to city, from village to village, never having His own home. His clothes were nothing more than a robe and cloak. While He announced salvation to people and spread divine grace on them, those same people hated Him, and tried many times to kill Him outright. Finally, they executed Him as though He were a convicted criminal. He allowed them to perpetrate the horrific atrocity that their hearts desired, because through the death of the all-holy, He wanted to redeem the criminal human race from the eternal curse and death. The earthly life of the God-Man was full of suffering; it ended with a doleful death.

In emulation of their Lord, all the saints entered into blessed eternity through the narrow and sorrowful path, denying all the glory and pleasures of the world, curbing the desires of the flesh with ascetic labors, and nailing their spirit to the cross of Christ, all of which, for fallen man, constitute the spirit of the commandments of the Gospel. They subjected themselves to various deprivations, evil spirits persecuted them, and their brothers oppressed them. Let us follow Christ and the hosts of saints who walk after Him, the God-Man, "who when He had by Himself purged our sins, sat down at the right hand of the Majesty on high."[28] He calls His followers: "Come, you blessed of My Father, inherit the kingdom prepared for you from the foundation of the world."[29] Amen.

CHAPTER 2

On Reading the Gospels

When you read the Gospels, do not seek enjoyment, do not search for exalted feelings, do not try to find brilliant thoughts. Seek instead to perfectly see holy Truth.

Do not content yourself with unproductive reading of the Gospels; strive to fulfill its commandments, read it with deeds. This is the book of life, and one must read it with one's life.

Do not think that these holiest of all books, the Four Gospels, begins with the Gospel according to Matthew and ends with the Gospel according to John. Matthew concentrated more on how to do the will of God, and his teachings are especially appropriate for those who are just beginning to walk the path of God. John explains the image of the union of God with man who is renewed by the commandments. This is only comprehensible to those who already have had success on the path of God.

When you open the Gospel to read it, remember that it will determine your eternal fate. We will be judged by it, and depending on how we lived in accordance to it, we will receive either eternal blessedness or eternal punishment.[1]

God revealed His will to a worthless speck of dust—man! The book that divulges this great and all-holy Will is in your hands. You can choose to either accept or reject the will of your Creator and Redeemer. Your eternal life or eternal death is in your hands. Consider how careful and wise you must be. Do not gamble with your eternal fate.

Pray with compunction to the Lord so that He will open your eyes to see the miracles hidden in His law,[2] the Gospel. When the eyes are opened, you will see a miraculous healing of your soul from sin, effected by the word of God. The healing of bodily sicknesses is a pledge of the healing of the soul, proof for the carnal-minded, for minds blinded by sensuality.[3]

Read the Gospel with the utmost reverence and attention. Do not consider anything in it unimportant or unworthy of study. Every iota gleams with the rays of life. Disdain for life is little more than death.

While reading about the lepers, the paralyzed, the blind, the lame, and the possessed that the Lord healed, remember that your soul, which is covered in the sores of sin and is in bondage to the demons, is like these sick men. Learn from the Gospel to believe that the Lord who healed them will heal you as well, if you will continually beg Him for this healing.

Acquire also a proper disposition to be able to receive this healing. Those who are capable of receiving it know their own sinfulness and are determined to leave it behind.[4] The proud, self-righteous man—that is, the sinner who does not see his own sinfulness—does not need the Saviour.[5]

Realization of sinfulness, an acknowledgment of the fall in which the entire human race exists, is a special gift of God. Ask for this gift, and you will better understand the book of the heavenly physician—the Gospel.

Try to integrate the Gospel into your mind and heart so that your mind will in a manner of speaking, swim in it, live in it. Then your every action will truly become evangelical. You can achieve this through constant reverent reading and study of the Gospels.

St Pachomius the Great, one of the greatest of the ancient Fathers, knew the Gospels by heart and, according to a revelation from God, imposed upon his disciples the indispensable need to learn it by heart. The Gospel thus directed them at every stage of life as their constant travel companion.

Even today, why should not the Christian parent beautify the mind of his innocent child through learning the Gospel, rather than befouling him or her with learning Aesop's fables and other trivialities?

What joy, what richness is to be found in learning the Gospel by heart! It is not possible to imagine the kinds of upheavals and sorrows that could happen in our earthly lives. The Gospel, if it belongs to the memory, can be read by a blind man, will accompany the prisoner to his prison, will speak with the farmer in the field watered with his sweat, will instruct the judge during his trial, will guide the merchant in the marketplace, and will give joy to the sick man when he cannot sleep or is overcome with loneliness.

Do not dare to interpret the Gospels and the other books of the Holy Scriptures on your own. The Scriptures were uttered by holy prophets and apostles, uttered not arbitrarily but according to the inspiration of the Holy Spirit.[6] How utterly mad, then, to interpret it arbitrarily!

Both the word of God and its interpretation are the gifts of the Holy Spirit. The Holy Spirit, who uttered the word of God through the prophets and apostles, Himself interpreted it through the Holy Fathers. This interpretation alone is accepted by the Orthodox Church! This interpretation alone is accepted by its true children!

Whoever arbitrarily expounds the Gospels and the entire Scriptures rejects the interpretation of the Holy Fathers and the Holy Spirit. Whoever rejects the Holy Spirit's interpretation of the Scriptures rejects, without any doubt, the Scriptures themselves.

And the word of God, the word of salvation, becomes for such brazen interpreters a double-sided sword with which they fatally stab themselves and so enter eternal death.[7] With it, Arius, Nestorius, Eutychius, and the other heresiarchs all killed themselves when they fell into blasphemy through their willing and brazen interpretation of the Scriptures.

"But on this one will I look: On him who is poor and of a contrite spirit, and who trembles at My word," says the Lord.[8] Even so must you be when encountering the Gospels and the Lord Who is present in them.

Leave your sinful life, leave your earthly passions and enjoyments, and renounce your fallen soul. Only then will the Gospel become understandable and accessible.

"He who hates his life in this world," said the Lord, a soul for whose fallen state the love of sin has become natural, even essential, "will keep it for eternal life."[9] For him who loves his fallen soul, for him who does not want to deny himself, the Gospel is shut. He reads only words, but the Word of life and the Spirit remain for him under an opaque veil.

When the Lord was on this earth with His most-holy body, many saw Him and yet saw Him not. What profit does a man receive when he sees only with the eyes of his flesh, which he shares with the beasts, but sees nothing with the eyes of his soul—his mind and heart? And today, many read the Gospels daily but at the same time never read it at all; they know it not at all.

St Mark the Ascetic said that the Gospel must only be read with a pure mind; it can only be understood as much as its commandments are fulfilled in deed. But even so, an exact and complete revelation of the Gospel's meaning is impossible to acquire by oneself. This is a gift of Christ.

The Holy Spirit, when He enters into His sincere and faithful servant, makes him a complete reader and true practitioner of the Gospel.

The Gospel is the image of the qualities of the new man, who is "the Lord from heaven."[10] This new man is God in essence. His holy race of people, those who believe in Him and are transformed in Him, He makes gods by grace.

You, who lie in the filthy and reeking bog of your sins, find your enjoyment in the Gospels! Raise your heads, look at the clear sky—there is your place! God gives us the dignity of gods; you who reject this dignity choose for yourself something else—the dignity of the lowest animals. Come to your senses! Leave that reeking bog, clean yourselves through the confession of sins, be purified through the tears of repentance, be beautified by the tears of compunction, rise up from the earth and ascend into heaven! The Gospels will lead you there. "While you have the light"—the Gospels in which Christ is hidden—"believe in the light, that you may become sons of light," who is Christ.[11]

CHAPTER 3

On Reading the Holy Fathers

The people you talk to and associate with have a great influence on you. Conversation and acquaintance with scientists result in new knowledge; with poets, in many exalted thoughts and feelings; with travelers, in much information about other countries, their manners and traditions. It is obvious therefore that conversation and acquaintance with a saint will impart sanctity. "With the holy Thou shalt be holy, and with an innocent man Thou shalt be innocent. With the elect Thou shalt be elect, and with the forward Thou shalt be forward."[1]

From this moment, during this short earthly life that the Scriptures do not even call life, but a pilgrimage, let us become acquainted with the saints. Do you want to belong in heaven and to its society; do you want to be a sharer of its blessedness? From this moment, begin to spend time with the saints. When you leave your mortal body, they will accept you as their own, as an acquaintance, as a friend.[2]

There is no closer acquaintance, no more intimate connection than the union of thoughts, feelings, and aims.[3]

Where there is oneness of mind, there must also be a symphony of emotions and success in the attainment of common goals.

Acquire for yourself the thought and spirit of the Holy Fathers through the reading of their works. The Holy Fathers have attained the ultimate goal—they have been saved. You also will achieve this aim according to the natural way of things. As someone who is one in mind and heart with the Holy Fathers, you will be saved.

The heavens have welcomed the Holy Fathers into their blessedness. Through this, it becomes apparent that the thoughts, feelings, and actions of the Holy Fathers are deserving of heaven. The Holy Fathers shared their thoughts, their hearts, and their actions in their writings. Thus, what invaluable guides to heaven are these writings!

All the writings of the Holy Fathers were composed by the inspiration or under the influence of the Holy Spirit. What miraculous consonance they all have! What incredible agreement! He who is guided by them has, without any doubt, the Holy Spirit Himself for a guide.

All the waters of the earth eventually pour out into the oceans, and it may be that the ocean is also the source of all the earth's waters. The writings of the Holy Fathers all come together in the Gospels; they all incline to teach us the correct keeping of the commandments of our Lord Jesus Christ; they all originate from one source and flow out into the same—the holy Gospels.

The Holy Fathers teach us how to approach the Gospels, how to read them, how to properly understand them, and what helps and hinders such a proper understanding. Thus, it would be wise for you at first to principally study the works of the Fathers. Once they have taught you how to read the Gospels, then these may become your primary reading.

Do not think it is enough for you to read only the Gospels without the writings of the Holy Fathers! This is a proud thought, a dangerous thought. It would be better if the Fathers lead you to the Gospels, as though you were their beloved child whom they raise and educate through their writings.

All who foolishly and proudly reject the Holy Fathers, who approach the Gospels directly with foolish brazenness and unclean mind and heart, fall into a lethal self-deception. The Gospel has rejected them, for it only accepts those who are humble.

Reading the writings of the Fathers is the beginning and end of all the virtues. From this reading, we learn the true meaning of the Sacred Scripture; we are inculcated in the true faith, the life according to the commandments of the Gospel; we acquire a deep reverence for them. In a word, these writings teach us salvation and Christian perfection.

As a result of the dearth of spirit-bearing guides in our times, the Holy Fathers have become the most dependable guides for those who desire salvation and Christian perfection.

The books of the Holy Fathers, according to the words of one of their number, are like a mirror—the soul who looks at them often and with attention will be able to see all of its deficiencies.

Again, these books are like a rich store of medical supplies—in them, the soul can find a lifesaving remedy for each spiritual illness.

St Epiphanius of Cyprus said in the *Alphabetical Paterikon:* "Only one look into these holy books inspires one to a pious life."

Reading the Holy Fathers must be a scrupulous, attentive, and constant activity. Our invisible enemy, who hates the voice of truth[4], especially despises the voice of the Holy Fathers. This voice denounces the lies of our enemy, his evil, and reveals his traps, his modus operandi. Thus, the enemy battles against the reading of the Fathers through various proud and blasphemous thoughts; he tries to plunge the reader into earthly worries to distract him from this salvific reading; he attacks him with depression, boredom, forgetfulness. From this battle against the reading of the Holy Fathers, we should see how effective this weapon is, and why it is so feared by the enemy. The enemy works without rest to snatch this weapon out of our hands.

Let everyone choose for himself the Fathers whose writings most correspond to his way of life. Let the hermit read the Fathers who wrote about hesychasm; let the cenobitic monk read the Fathers who wrote instructions for those who live in monastic communities; let the Christian in the world read those Fathers who wrote for the benefit of all Christians. Let each person, no matter what his calling, glean a fruitful harvest from the Fathers' writings.

It is absolutely necessary that the reading correspond to one's way of life. Otherwise, you will be filled with thoughts that may be holy, but may also be impossible to achieve in action, given your situation. This only results in a pointless exercise of the imagination and desires. Actual deeds of virtue appropriate to your mode of life will slip through your fingers. Not only will you become a fruitless dreamer, but your thoughts, constantly contradicting the actual reality of your life, will inevitably lead to confusion and lack of firmness in your actions, both of which will be detrimental to yourself and those around you. It is easy to fall away from the path of salvation into impenetrable roads and deep abysses if you read the Holy Scriptures and the Fathers incorrectly. This has already happened to many. Amen.

CHAPTER 4

On Avoiding Those Books That Contain False Teachings

Once again I address you, faithful son of the Eastern Church, with a sincere, good word. This word is not my own—it belongs to the Holy Fathers. All my counsels come from them.

Keep your mind and heart from false teaching. Do not even speak about Christianity with people who have been infected with false thoughts; do not read books on Christianity that were written by heretics.

The Holy Spirit accompanies all Truth. He *is* the Spirit of Truth. The devil accompanies and acts together with every lie. He is false, and the father of lies.

He who reads the books of a heretic immediately communes with an evil, dark spirit of falsehood. This should not seem strange or incredible to you—this is the unanimous opinion of the Holy Fathers.[1]

If your mind and heart are still a blank slate, let Truth and the Spirit inscribe on them the commandments of God and His spiritual teaching.

If you have allowed the tablets of your soul to be carved and written over with various opinions and impressions without ever wisely and carefully discerning who the writer was and what he was writing about, then sponge away things written by false teachers, purify your soul through repentance and rejection of all that is contrary to God.

Let the only writer of these tablets be the finger of God.

Prepare your mind and heart for this writer with purity, piety, and a chaste life. Then, through your prayers and your reading, the tablets of your soul will be inconspicuously and mysteriously inscribed with the law of the Spirit.

Only those religious books that are written by the Holy Fathers of the universal Orthodox Church are acceptable to read. The Orthodox Church requires this of her children.[2]

If you think otherwise, or find this command of the Church less authoritative than your own opinions or the opinions of others who agree with you, then you are no longer a child of the Church, but a critic of the Church.

Do you call me a one-sided, unenlightened rigorist? Leave me my one-sidedness and all my other deficiencies. I would rather be a deficient, unenlightened child of the Orthodox Church than an apparently perfect man who would dare to instruct the Church, who would allow himself to disobey the Church, to separate from it. My words will be pleasant to the true children of the Orthodox Church.

These true children know that whoever wants to acquire heavenly wisdom must first leave behind his own earthly wisdom, no matter how great it is, and to recognize its true nature—it is an attack on God.[3]

Earthly wisdom is war against God. It does not and cannot submit to the Law of God.[4] From the very beginning this was the case, and so it will remain until the end, when "the earth and the works that are in it will be burned up,"[5] including earthly, carnal wisdom.

The Holy Church allows the books of heretics to be read only by those whose thoughts and hearts have been healed and enlightened by the Holy Spirit, for such persons can always distinguish between true good and evil, which pretends to be good and wears a mask of good.

The great righteous ones of God, who know the universal illness of mankind, were afraid of the hell of heresy and falsehood, and thus, with all watchfulness, fled from conversations with people who were infected with false teaching and the reading of heretical books.[6] Seeing before their very eyes the fall into heresy of the most educated of men—including Origen, Arius (the lover of arguments), the great orator Nestorius, and many other wise men of this world—all of whom perished from self-assuredness and vanity, the Fathers sought salvation, and found it in the flight from false teaching, in total obedience to the Church.

Spirit-bearing Holy Fathers and teachers of the Church read the writings of blasphemous heretics only because they were forced to do so by the needs of the entire Christian world. With their powerful, spirit-filled word, they denounced the delusions of heresies that masqueraded as holy and pious teaching and revealed their hidden danger to all the children of the Church.

But you and I must protect ourselves from reading these books written by false teachers. Anyone who does not belong to the one Holy Orthodox Church, yet still dares to write about Christ and the Christian faith and morality, is a false teacher.

Tell me, how is it possible to allow yourself to read just any book, when every book that you read leads you wherever it wants and forces you to agree with everything that it requires of you and to reject everything that it wants you to reject?

Experience proves how dangerous the consequences of indiscriminate reading can be. Many different opinions can be found among the children of the Orthodox Church, many of which are incoherent, incorrect, and contrary to the teaching of the Church, even antagonistic to this holy teaching! All this is a result of the reading of heretical books!

My friend, do not be offended by my warning, which was inspired by a desire for your true benefit. Will not a father, mother, or kind teacher be afraid for an innocent, inexperienced child when he wants to be left in peace to walk into any room in the house, even where food may be placed together with poisons?

The death of the soul is worse than the death of the body. The dead body will rise again, and often the death of the body results in life for the soul. On the contrary, a soul killed by evil is a victim of eternal death. The soul can be killed by one blasphemous thought, even if it is subtle and unnoticed by the ignorant.

"For the time will come," warned the holy Apostle Paul, "when they will not endure sound doctrine, but according to their own desires, because they have itching ears, they will heap up for themselves teachers; and they will turn their ears away from the truth, and be turned aside to fables."[7]

Do not be fooled by the garish title of a book that promises Christian perfection to someone who can still only eat the food of babes. Do not be fooled either by the gorgeous binding or vivid pictures or by the beauty of the language or the alleged sanctity of the writer, proved only by many miracles trumpeted by him during his own life.

False teaching does not stoop before any lie, any fiction, to give its fables an air of authenticity, which makes it all the more effective in poisoning the soul.

False teaching is already, in essence, a lie. The writer has been deluded even before the reader.[8]

A book that is true—essentially beneficial to the soul—is a book written by a holy writer who is a member of the Orthodox Church and who is approved and accepted by the Holy Church. Amen.

CHAPTER 5

On the Commandments of the Gospels

The Saviour of the world, our Lord Jesus Christ, before He began to give us His all-holy commandments, said, "Do not think that I came to destroy the Law or the Prophets. I did not come to destroy but to fulfill."[1]

In what way did Christ fulfill the Law and the prophets? He sealed the foretold sacrifices in the prophets by bringing Himself as a sacrifice for mankind; He replaced the shadows and speculations of the Old Testament with the grace and truth of the New Testament. He fulfilled the foretelling of the prophets by accomplishing what they presaged. He supplemented the moral Law with such exalted instructions that the Law, though remaining unchanged, at the same time completely transformed as a result of the exalted nature of the new commandments, in the same way that a child, when he or she reaches adulthood, still remains the same person.

The importance of the Old Testament for a person can be compared to a will, which usually has all kinds of detailed explanations about an inheritance, including facts, figures, and plans for buildings. The New Testament is the inheritance itself. Previously, everything was described on paper; now everything is given in actual fact.

What is the difference between the Gospel commandments and the Ten Commandments of the Old Testament? The latter did not allow fallen man to fall further into an unnatural state, but at the same time it did not have the power to raise man to the state of sinlessness in which he was created. The Ten Commandments preserved in the person the ability to later accept the Gospel commandments.[2] The Gospel commandments raise us up to a sinlessness even higher than the one in which we were created—they make a person into the temple of the Living God.[3] Having made him the temple of God, they keep him in this grace-filled, supernatural state.[4]

The holy Apostles Peter and Paul fulfilled the law of Moses exactly, due to their special love for God.[5] The purity of their life's direction made them capable of believing in the Redeemer and becoming His apostles. Many obvious sinners, who in their sins resembled chattel and beasts, often became capable of faith after admitting their sins and deciding to bring repentance. Those least capable of faith were those sinners whose self-opinion and pride became similar to the demons, and like the demons, they refused to see their own sinfulness and repent.[6]

The Lord called His entire teaching and His entire Word "commandments."[7] "The words that I speak to you are spirit, and they are life."[8] They make the carnal man into a spiritual one. They resurrect the dead, and they make the descendants of the Old Adam into the descendants of the New Adam, the sons of men by nature into the sons of God by grace.

The commandment of the New Testament, which encompasses in itself all other commandments, is the Gospel itself. "The time is fulfilled, and the kingdom of God is at hand. Repent, and believe in the gospel."[9]

The Lord called His commandments "small" because of their simplicity and brevity, which makes them easy to fulfill for every person. But even though He called them small, He said that whoever breaks even one of them "shall be called least in the kingdom of heaven,"[10] that is, he will be bereft of this kingdom.

Let us fear this eventuality spoken of by Christ! Let us study the Gospels; let us find in them all of the commandments of the Lord; let us implant them in our memories for assiduous and constant fulfillment; let us believe with a living faith in the Gospels.

The first commandment given to people by the incarnate Lord is the commandment of repentance. The Holy Fathers insist that repentance has to be the beginning of a righteous life, and its very heart and soul for the whole length of it.[11] Without repentance, it is impossible either to confess the Redeemer or to remain in this confession of the Redeemer. Repentance is the recognition of one's own fallen state, which has made human nature defiled and shameless, and so constantly requires redemption. The Redeemer, Who is complete and all-holy, replaces the fallen man who confesses Him.

"Let your light so shine before men, that they may see your good works and glorify your Father in heaven."[12] At the same time, however, the Lord commanded His disciples to do their good works in secret and to expect to be hated and reviled by men.[13] How can we fulfill this commandment of God while still doing our good deeds in secret? We will only be able to fulfill both commandments when we have rejected our own self-seeking desire for glory, when we reject ourselves completely, and when we act only for the glory of God, according to the Gospels.

"As each one has received a gift, minister it to one another, as good stewards of the manifold grace of God. If anyone speaks, let him speak as the oracles of God; if anyone ministers, let him do it as with the ability which God supplies, that in all things God may be glorified through Jesus Christ, to whom belong the glory and the dominion for ever and ever. Amen."[14] God will glorify those who, having forgotten their own glory, only seek to glorify Him and help people come to know Him. "I will honor those who honor me."[15] "If anyone serves Me, him My Father will honor."[16] He who does all his good deeds in secret, only with the purpose of pleasing God, will be praised for the benefit of others by the mysterious workings of the providence of God.

"Unless your righteousness exceeds the righteousness of the scribes and Pharisees, you will by no means enter the kingdom of heaven."[17] The truth of the scribes and Pharisees contented itself with studying the letter of the Law of God without any corresponding study of the life according to the Law, so instead they led a life contrary to God's Law. As a result of their superficial knowledge, those who limit themselves to studying the letter of the Law fall into pride and conceit, as St Mark the Ascetic said in his fourth homily. This is exactly what happened to scribes and Pharisees of Christ's time. The commandments of God, which are essentially learned only by doing,[18] remained hidden from the Pharisees. The spiritual eyes, which are enlightened by the doing of the commandments,[19] were never opened for the Pharisees. Because of their actions contrary to God's Law, they acquired a false understanding of the Law of God, and the Law of God, which is supposed to bring one closer to union with God, ended up separating them from God and making them His enemies. Every commandment of God is a holy mystery; it is fully revealed only by following it and by how much one fulfills it.

The Old Testament forbade the evil consequences of anger, but the Lord forbade even the activity of the passion in the heart.[20] God Himself uttered the prohibition, and therefore it has a tremendous power. The passion weakens from only the remembrance of the short and simple words of God. This effect is noticeable with all the Gospel commandments. The Lord directed his first words against anger as the most serious sinful wound, the chief passion opposed to the two main virtues—love for one's neighbor and humility. Upon these two chief virtues is built the whole structure of the Christian life. Remaining in slavery to the passion of anger takes away a person's ability for any spiritual progress.

The Lord commanded to keep peace with one's neighbor with all one's strength.[21] The Apostle said, "If it is possible, as much as depends on you, live peaceably with all men."[22] Do not waste time trying to determine who is right and who is wrong, you or your neighbor. Instead, try to accuse yourself and preserve peace with your neighbor through your humility.

The law of Moses outlawed adultery, but the Lord prohibited carnal lust.[23] How powerfully this prohibition acts on our fallen nature! Do you wish to abstain from impure glances, thoughts, and fantasy? Remember these words when they begin to act in you: "Whoever looks at a woman" with his bodily eyes, or his mind, "to lust for her has already committed adultery with her in his heart."[24]

Between the bodies of the two genders there exists a natural attraction. This attraction does not always act equally; some people feel nearly no attraction at all to the bodies of the other gender, while others feel a very powerful attraction. The Lord commanded us to remain distant from those to whom we feel an especially strong lust, no matter how good their spiritual qualities may be, and no matter how necessary or beneficial we think they may be for us. This is the meaning of the commandment to cut off the right, offending eye and the right arm.[25]

The Lord forbade divorce, which was allowed by the law of Moses, except for those cases when the marriage was already broken by the lawless adultery of either partner.[26] Divorce used to be allowed for human nature lowered by the fall, but after the renewal of humanity by the God-Man, the law given to human nature in its pristine state was reestablished.[27]

The Lord reestablished virginity as a way of life, allowing the possibility of preserving it to those who desire it.[28]

The Lord forbade oaths. The Fathers correctly say that no one deserves less trust than he who often swears. In contrast, no one should be so completely believed as the one who always speaks the truth, even if he never utters an oath. Speak the truth, and you will not need to use an oath, which, as an offense against reverence, is a demonic action.[29]

The Lord forbade revenge, which was allowed by the law of Moses, and through which evil was paid back by evil. The weapon that the Lord gives us against evil is humility. "But I tell you not to resist an evil person. But whoever slaps you on your right cheek, turn the other to him also. If anyone wants to sue you and take away your tunic, let him have your cloak also."[30]

The Lord commanded us to love our enemies and to acquire such love, He told us to bless those who curse us, to do good to those who hate us, and to pray for those who cause us harm and persecute us.[31] Love for enemies gives the heart the fullness of love. In such a heart, there is simply no place for evil, and it becomes like the all-good God in its goodness. The Apostle Paul encouraged Christians to strive for this exalted moral state when he wrote: "Therefore, as the elect of God, holy and beloved, put on tender mercies, kindness, humility, meekness, long-suffering; bearing with one another, and forgiving one another, if anyone has a complaint against another; even as Christ forgave you, so you also must do."[32]

Perfect love for one's neighbor makes one a son of God by adoption.[33] The grace of the Holy Spirit is attracted to the person's heart and the all-holy love for God pours out into him.

The heart infected with anger and incapable of the Gospel commandment of love for enemies must be healed with those medicines indicated by the Lord—one must pray for one's enemies without condemning them, one must not speak evil of them, one must say only good things about them and do good to them as much as possible. These actions extinguish hatred when it inflames the heart and keep it constantly reined in and weakened. But the full rooting out of anger from the heart is only done by the workings of divine grace.

The Lord commanded those who give alms to do it in secret; those who practice prayer He commanded to pray in the solitude of their room; those who fast, He commanded to hide their fasting.[34] These virtues should be done only with the purpose of pleasing God and for the benefit of one's neighbor and one's own soul. Our spiritual treasure should not only be hid from the eyes of the world, but even from our own left hand.[35] Actions that praise men steal our virtues, when we do them openly and do not try to hide them; unnoticeably, we begin to find pleasure in pleasing people and in hypocrisy. The reason for this is the damaged, sinful state of our soul. As the diseased body needs to be protected from winds, cold, harmful food, and drink, so does the diseased soul need to be protected from all sides. When we preserve our virtues from being damaged by the praise of men, we also must preserve them from the evil that resides in us, which is our "left hand." We must not become distracted by vain thoughts and fantasies, with the joy and pleasure that vanity brings after the doing of a good deed, because this will take away the fruits of virtue.

The Lord commanded us to forgive our neighbors all they have done against us: "For if you forgive men their trespasses, your heavenly Father will also forgive you. But if you do not forgive men their trespasses, neither will your Father forgive your trespasses."[36] From these words, we see the obvious conclusion that a true sign of the forgiveness of our own sins is the state in our heart when we feel that we have definitely forgiven our neighbor all his sins against us. This state is created, and can only be created, by God Himself. It is a gift of God. While we remain unworthy of that gift, let us (according to the words of the Lord) examine our conscience before every prayer, and if we find remembrance of wrongs there, let us root it out with the already mentioned medicines—praying for our enemies and blessing them.[37] Whenever we remember our enemy, we must not allow a single thought about him except prayer and blessing.

To His closest disciples and followers, the Lord commanded voluntary poverty. "Do not lay up for yourselves treasures on earth, where moth and rust destroy and where thieves break in and steal."[38] "Sell what you have and give alms; provide yourselves money bags which do not grow old, a treasure in the heavens that does not fail, where no thief approaches nor moth destroys. For where your treasure is, there your heart will be also."[39] In order to acquire love for spiritual and heavenly objects, one must reject love for earthly things. In order to fall in love with the promised land, one must reject one's diseased fondness for the land of exile.

The Lord gave a commandment about the preservation of one's mind, a commandment for which people usually do not care, or even do not know about its existence, much less about its necessity and special importance. But the Lord, calling the mind the eye of the soul, said, "If therefore your eye is good, your whole body will be full of light. But if your eye is bad, your whole body will be full of darkness."[40] Thy "whole body" here means your entire life. Your life takes its chief qualities from the kind of mind-set that governs it. We strive toward a correct mind-set because it gives health, wholeness to our mind when it completely follows the Truth, not allowing any taint of falsehood to enter. In other words: the only mind that is healthy is one that wholly and completely follows the teaching of Christ, with the help and activity of the Holy Spirit. A greater or lesser turning away from the teaching of Christ proves a great or lesser disease of a mind that has lost its simplicity and become complex. Full turning away from the teaching of Christ is death for the mind. Then, the light stops being a light and becomes darkness. The actions of a person completely depend on the state of his or her mind. The actions coming from a healthy mind are completely God-pleasing; actions coming from a mind darkened by a false teaching, a mind that has rejected the teaching of Christ, is completely impure and foul. "If therefore the light that is in you is darkness, how great is that darkness!"[41]

The Lord forbade rushing about for the sake of the world's cares, so they do not dissipate us and weaken in us the essentially necessary desire to acquire the heavenly kingdom.[42] These useless worries are nothing else but a disease of the soul, an expression of its lack of faith in God. This is why the Lord said, "O you of little faith! Do not worry about your life, what you will eat or what you will drink; nor about your body, what you will put on."[43] Despise laziness, which is hated by God, and fall in love with work, which is loved by God. But on the other hand, do not fill up your soul with needless busyness, which is always extraneous and useless. In order to help you be firm in soul and zealous in the work of God and the labor of your salvation, God promised to give you everything needful for this life with His almighty right hand, that is, His divine providence.[44]

The Lord forbade not only judging one's neighbors but also condemning them,[45] except when there is a need to judge for the good of society. God gives this kind of judgment; without it good would run the risk of being confused with evil and our own actions could never be good and pleasing to God. This judgment is rarely found among people; but the kind forbidden by God is found among them constantly. The reason for this is because of their complete lack of attention to themselves, their forgetfulness of their sinfulness, their complete avoidance of repentance, and their conceit and pride. The Lord came to the earth to save sinners, and so he expects an inevitable admission of sinfulness from every person; judging one's neighbor is a rejection of this acknowledgment; it is an ascription to oneself of a false righteousness that produces only contempt and judgment of others. Such people are best called nothing other than hypocrites.[46]

The Lord commanded constant, that is, frequent and ceaseless prayer. He did not say that we must ask one time and then stop asking but told us to ask forcefully, without stopping—to ask God's promise to hear and fulfill the petition. "Ask, and it will be given you; seek, and you will find; knock, and it will be opened to you. For everyone who asks receives; and he who seeks finds, and to him who knocks it will be opened."[47] Let us ask with patience and constancy, rejecting our own will and reasoning, giving the all-holy will of God both the time and the space to act, ever expecting our petition to be answered. "And shall God not avenge His own elect who cry out day and night to Him, though He bears long with them?"[48] In other words, He will answer our petition, though He may wait a long time to fulfill it. The daily and nightly prayer with weeping of God's elect illustrates their constant, unstopping, ceaseless, powerful prayer.

One can judge the worthiness of one's prayer by its consequences. The Evangelist Luke said that God shall avenge His own elect, that is, He will free them from bondage to passions and the demons. The Evangelist Matthew says that "your Father who is in heaven give[s] good things to those who ask Him!"[49] The good things that "eye has not seen, nor ear heard, nor have entered into the heart of man."[50] Again, the Apostle Luke says: "How much more will your heavenly Father give the Holy Spirit to those who ask Him."[51] The reasons for our prayer must be spiritual and eternal, not temporary and worldly. The main and first prayer must be the request for the forgiveness of sins.[52]

As He raises us up to the doings of virtue, as He casts evil out of us, the Lord, who commanded us not to judge our neighbors and to forgive them all their transgressions against us, also commands us that "whatever you want men to do to you, do also to them."[53] We love it when our neighbors are condescending to our weaknesses and deficiencies, when they patiently bear offenses and insults from us, when they show us all kinds of condescension and do us favors. Let us be the same to our neighbors. Then we will reach the fullness of virtue, and our prayer will become correspondingly more powerful. The strength of our prayers is proportional to our goodness. "Judge not, and you shall not be judged. Condemn not, and you shall not be condemned. Forgive, and you will be forgiven. Give, and it will be given to you: good measure, pressed down, shaken together, and running over will be put into your bosom. For with the same measure that you use, it will be measured back to you,"[54] from the merciful and just God.

"Enter by the narrow gate; for wide is the gate and broad is the way that leads to destruction, and there are many who go in by it."[55] The wide gate and broad way are our actions done according to the will and reasoning of our fallen nature. The narrow gate is a life according to the Gospel commandments. The Lord, Who sees the past and future equally well, sees how few people will follow His holy will revealed in the Gospel commandments, choosing self-will instead of God's will, said, "Because narrow is the gate and difficult is the way which leads to life, and there are few who find it."[56] Encouraging and consoling his followers, He added: "Do not fear, little flock, for it is your Father's good pleasure to give you the kingdom."[57]

The Lord commanded us to live a temperate life in constant vigilance and watchfulness of the self because, on the one hand, the hour of God's visit to us is unknown, the time of our death, and the summoning to God's judgment. On the other hand, we do not know what passion may appear in our fallen nature, what snare can be set specially for us by the unsleeping enemies of our salvation, the demons. "Let your waist be girded and your lamps burning; and you yourselves be like men who wait for their master, when he will return from the wedding, that when he comes and knocks they may open to him immediately."[58] "And what I say to you, I say to all: Watch!"[59]

"Beware of false prophets," the Lord warns us, "who come to you in sheep's clothing, but inwardly they are ravenous wolves. You will know them by their fruits."[60] False prophets are always cunning, and so the Lord commands us to be especially careful with them. False prophets are known by their fruits—their manner of life, their deeds, and by the consequences of their actions. Do not be impressed by their effective speeches and sweet words, by their quiet voices, as if they were truly meek, humble, and full of love; do not be impressed by the pleasant smiles that play on their lips and faces, do not be fooled by their geniality and the servility that practically streams from their eyes. Do not be fooled by the kinds of rumors about themselves that they skillfully plant among people, those praises, loud names that the world willingly trumpets for them. Instead, look at their fruits.

The Lord said the following about those who listen to the Gospels and try to fulfill their commandments: they are the ones who "having heard the word with a noble and good heart, keep it and bear fruit with patience."[61] He warned his disciples that they would receive hatred from the world, persecutions, and attacks, and He promised to sleeplessly watch over them and protect them. He told them not to fear and be weak in faith, but rather to possess their souls in patience.[62] In constant reliance on God, we must bravely endure sorrows from passions coming from our fallen nature and from our brothers, the people who surround us, and from the demons, our enemies. For "he who endures to the end shall be saved."[63]

All you who are in the bitter slavery to sin, under the lordship of the cruel, stone-hearted Pharaoh, under the constant and painful blows of his servants who worship the idol of their own world-encompassing pride! You are called by the Saviour to spiritual freedom! He said, "Come to Me, all you who labor and are heavy laden, and I will give you rest. Take My yoke upon you and learn from Me, for I am gentle and lowly in heart, and you will find rest for your souls. For My yoke is easy and My burden is light."[64]

It requires self-denial, and so is called a "yoke," but it frees and enlivens the soul, and fills it with ineffable peace and joy, and so is also called a good and easy yoke. The yoke and burden are each full of meekness and humility, and they give these virtues to the one who follows the commandments. The habit of following the commandments makes meekness and humility natural qualities of the soul. Then divine grace pours into the soul with spiritual meekness and humility through the peace of Christ that surpasses wisdom.

All the commands of the Lord He condensed into two chief laws—the commandment to love God and the commandment to love one's neighbor. These commandments were described by Christ thus: "'Hear, O Israel, the Lord our God, the Lord is one. And you shall love the Lord your God with all your heart, with all your soul, with all your mind, and with all your strength.' This is the first commandment. And the second, like it, is this: 'You shall love your neighbor as yourself.'"[65] "On these two commandments hang all the Law and the Prophets."[66] A person becomes capable of loving God when he is full of love for his neighbor, but only prayer can raise him to the state where he strives with his entire being toward God.

The union of man with God is the reward for the fulfilling the Gospel commandments. When the disciple of Christ becomes healed of his hatred for his neighbor, and through the prayer of his mind and heart directs all the powers of his soul and body toward God, then he will come to love God. "He who loves Me will be loved by My Father, and I will love him and manifest Myself to him. My Father will love him, and We will come to him, and make Our Home with him."[67]

The one condition for remaining in the love of God and in union with Him also is the fulfillment of the Gospel commandments. Breaking them breaks the condition, and the breaker is cast out of the loving arms and from before the face of God into the outer darkness, into the realm of the passions and the demons. "If you keep My commandments, you will abide in My love. Abide in Me, and I in you. If anyone does not abide in Me, he is cast out."[68]

Brothers! Let us study the all-powerful and life-giving commandments of our great God, Creator, and Redeemer. Let us learn them assiduously, by word and by life. They are read in the holy Gospels, but they are known only as much as they are done in actual fact. Let us begin the battle against our fallen nature when it rises up against us and begins to fight back, not desiring to submit to the Gospel. Let us not be afraid if this war will be heavy and insistent. Let us rather strive for victory all the more insistently. Our victory must inevitably follow, for the war is commanded, but the Lord promises the victory. "The kingdom of heaven suffers violence, and the violent," that is, those who fight their own nature, "take it by force."[69] Amen.

CHAPTER 6

On the Gospel Beatitudes

Through the fulfillment of the Gospel commandments,[1] the soul is visited by senses that are contrary to our fallen nature, unknown to it. "That which is born of the Spirit is spirit."[2] And since the commandments of Christ are spiritual,[3] the senses created by them are spiritual ones.

What is the first emotion, or sense, that appears in the soul from the keeping of Christ's commandments? *Poverty of spirit.*

Almost as soon as the Christian truly desires to bring to fruition the inner and outer commands of Christ they become aware of their own damaged nature, which rebels and stubbornly acts against the Gospels.

The Christian, in the light of the Gospels, sees in himself the complete fall of humanity.

From this vision, naturally comes a humble self-assessment, which in the Gospels is called being "poor in spirit,"[4] or poverty of spirit.

Poverty of spirit is a Beatitude, the first in the Gospel Beatitudes, the first in the order of spiritual progress, the first spiritual state, the first step in the ladder of the virtues.

Every emotion and state belonging to the renewed nature is by necessity also a Beatitude, because each is the revelation of the heavenly kingdom in the soul as a pledge of salvation, as a foretaste of eternal blessedness.

The holy David said of poverty of spirit that "the sacrifice unto God is a contrite spirit; a contrite and humble heart God shall not despise."[5]

Poverty of spirit is salt for all spiritual sacrifices and whole-burnt offerings. If they are not salted with this salt, God will reject them.

Seeing one's own fallenness is already blessedness for the fallen man.

He who sees his own fall is capable of admitting the necessity for salvation and the Saviour, and he is capable of believing in the Gospels with living faith.

This state is a gift of grace, the action of grace, its fruit, and therefore it is blessedness.

A poor man naturally sorrows over his poverty.

Poverty of spirit thus naturally gives birth to the next Beatitude: *mourning*.

Mourning is the reverent cry of the faithful soul that sees its limitless sinful stains in the mirror of the Gospels.

Such a soul washes off these stains with holy water—its tears. The soul washes off these stains with holy sorrow.

Unutterable consolation, ineffable lightness pour out into the heart after the shedding of salvific tears for one's sins and fallenness, tears that have appeared as a result of poverty of spirit.

If, here on earth, reverent mourning gives such incomparable spiritual consolation, what sort of blessedness does it prepare for us in the life to come?

Christ uttered His judge's decision on those who reverently weep: "Blessed are those who mourn!"[6]

Did you commit a sin? Shed tears of sorrow.

Whoever is intent in a profound appraisal of himself, whoever sees himself defiled by countless sins, whoever considers himself worthy of eternal suffering and weeps as though already condemned for them, he barely sees the sins of his neighbors and easily excuses those deficiencies that he sees. From his whole heart, he gladly forgives all insults and offenses.

The state of a soul when all anger, hatred, remembrance of evil, and judgment has been rooted out is a new blessedness, a new Beatitude called *meekness.*

"Blessed are the meek,"[7] said the Saviour, "for they shall inherit the earth."

What is this "earth"? After the fall, God called Adam "earth," and in Adam, He has called me "earth" as well. "For dust you are, and to dust you shall return."[8]

Since I am dust and earth, I no longer have authority over this earth. Various passions have stolen it from me, especially the horrible anger that controls me and gives me pleasure. I even have no power of myself. Meekness returns this power to me and gives me authority over my inheritance, my "earth," which is my self, my body, my blood, and my passions. "The meek shall inherit the earth, and shall be refreshed in the multitude of peace."[9]

Having once again gained power over my "earth", I begin to desire heaven. I enter into a new state, which is created in me by grace. I begin to "hunger and thirst for righteousness" of God, not empty, human righteousness.[10]

The righteousness of God appeared to mankind through divine mercy and commanded us to become like God through perfect mercy,[11] not through some other virtue.

Mercy judges no man, loves its enemies, lays down its life for its neighbor, and makes a person-like God. This state is once again a Beatitude.[12]

The heart that is filled with mercy cannot have any thought of evil. All of its thoughts are goodness itself.

The heart that is moved only by good is a pure heart, capable of seeing God. "Blessed are the pure in heart, for they shall see God."[13]

What is a pure heart? One great instructor of monastics was asked this question. He answered: "It is a heart that, like God, is moved by a boundless feeling of mercy for all creation."[14]

The peace of God descends into a pure heart and connects the long-separated mind, soul, and body, re-creating man, making him a descendant of the New Adam.

The peace of God belongs to the saints of God. Through this holy peace, a Christian, having completed his repentance, makes peace with God, with all his earthly circumstances, with his neighbors, with himself. He becomes a son of God by grace.[15]

The peace of God is accompanied by the obvious presence of the Holy Spirit in the person, because it is the action and fruit of the Holy Spirit.

He who has acquired the peace of God in himself is capable of the other final Beatitudes—of patient suffering and of joy in persecutions, slanders, exile, and all other manner of evil.

He who has acquired the peace of God is not afraid of the waves of the sea of the world, because the consolation of grace has destroyed in his heart all appreciation for the things of this world—the sensuality, heaviness, and bitterness of the world.

Look at this great spiritual ladder of Gospel Beatitudes, and look at each step. How good it would be to stand at the top of this ladder; but truly blessed is the one who is even on the first step.

Jumps ahead are impossible on this ladder; one can only climb it one step at a time.

Divine grace leads one up this ladder. It leads him to the next step not when he thinks he is worthy, but when grace admits his worth.

Those who are worthy of climbing to the next step are the humble.

Do not invent Beatitudes for yourself. Proud and stupid self-conceit can invent all manner of blessedness for a person, and he will fool himself during the course of his entire life, flattering himself, and so he will deny himself any true good things either on earth or in heaven.

Seek poverty of spirit. Striving after this virtue is allowed and even encouraged. It is the foundation and giver of all other Beatitudes. When the foundation is weak, then even the one on the highest step of spiritual progress will fall down, and often he is killed by the fall.

Poverty of spirit is found by the study of the Gospels, by keeping its commands, by measuring one's own actions by the standards of the Gospels, by forcing one's own heart to courageously endure insults, and by self-accusation and prayer for a heart that is broken and humbled.

God rejects the petitions of the proud. He does not answer petitions that are unnecessary for us, but when His creature begs an essential and beneficial gift, He sends it from his bottomless treasure troves.

God's most essential and useful spiritual gift for man is *poverty of spirit.* Amen.

CHAPTER 7

Truth and Spirit

Do not be deceived by the self-assurance and teaching of those deluded by their own self-worth, who, contrary to the true faith and divine tradition, insist that truth can be revealed in one's heart without words and can direct you by itself according to some indeterminate and unclear action. This is the teaching of falsehood and its followers.[1]

The signs of this false teaching are the following: murkiness, vagueness, self-deception, and their accompanying dreaminess and physical and emotional pleasure. It is effected subtly by vanity and sensuality.

Fallen mankind must approach holy Truth through faith; there is no other way. The Apostle teaches us: "So then faith *comes* by hearing, and hearing by the word of God."[2] The word of God is Truth.[3] The commandments of the Gospel are Truth.[4] But every man is false.[5] All this is witnessed by the Sacred Scriptures. How can one who is false speak the word of holy Truth?

If you want to hear it, this spiritual voice of holy Truth, you must learn to read the Gospels. In them, you will hear the Truth; in them will you see the Truth. The Truth will reveal to you how far you have fallen, your bonds of self-delusion, with which the soul of every person not renewed by the Holy Spirit is invisibly tied.

Are you ashamed to admit that you are a fallen proud man, proud even of your fall, that you must search for truth outside yourself, and that its entry into your heart must come from the hearing and other senses? But this is the inarguable truth that reveals just how far we have fallen.

Our fall is so profound, so frightening, that the word of God assumed human nature so that all people could be converted from disciples of the devil to disciples of God and the Truth; so that they could be freed from slavery to sin by the mediation of the Word and the spirit of truth and be taught all truth.[6]

We are so crude, so sensual, that it was necessary for holy Truth to be submitted to our bodily senses. We required not only the sound of His words but also the healing of the sick, palpable miracles with water, on trees, and on bread so that we, convinced with our earthly eyes, might at least glimpse the Truth. This is how dark the eyes of our soul have become!

"Then said Jesus to him, 'Unless you people see signs and wonders, you will by no means believe.'"[7] With such words, the Lord warned the sensual people who asked only for healing for their bodies, not even suspecting that their souls were in an incomparably worse state and so required incomparably more healing for their souls from the heavenly physician, rather than for their bodies.

And a certain man admitted to the Lord that signs viewed with his earthly eyes brought him to faith, to spiritual vision. "The man came to Jesus by night and said to him, 'Rabbi, we know that you are a teacher come from God; for no one can do these signs that you do God is with him.'"[8] And this man was very educated.

Many saw the Saviour with their eyes, saw His divine power over creation in His miracles; many heard His holy teaching with their ears, heard the very demons who witnessed of Him, but still did not know Him, hated Him, even dared to commit the most frightening of crimes—deicide. How profound, how frightening is our fall, our darkness.

It seems to me that it is enough to read one chapter of the Gospels to come to know God speaking in them. "You have the words of eternal life," our Lord and God, who revealed Himself to us in the humble form of a man, and "we have come to believe and know that You are the Christ, the son of the living God."[9]

Truth Himself tells us: "If you abide in My word, you are My disciples indeed; and you shall know the truth, and the truth shall make you free."[10] Study the Gospels, and He will tell you the unfeigned, holy Truth.

Truth can also speak inside a man. But when does this happen? It happens when "you are endued with power from on high,"[11] and "when He, the Spirit of truth, has come, He will guide you into all truth."[12]

If anyone begins to hear the internal voice of Truth before the obvious descent of the Holy Spirit into the heart (a state of visible sanctity), if anyone thinks he hears inside himself the guidance of Truth, his pride is lying to him; he fools himself. More likely, he hears the voice of the one who said in Eden: "you will be like God."[13] And such a voice seems to him the voice of Truth!

This is a great joy—to come to know the Truth from the Gospels and the Holy Fathers, and with the guidance of such reading to enter communion with the Holy Spirit residing in the Gospels and the Holy Fathers.

I am not worthy of the joy of hearing the Truth directly from the Holy Spirit! I am not capable of this! I am not able to withstand Him, to guard Him in my heart, which is not ready, not fully grown, not strengthened. The wine of the Spirit, if it were poured into my heart, would make it burst and would spill out,[14] and so my all-good Lord, having compassion for my weakness, shows His long suffering[15] and does not offer me, a babe, the strong spiritual meat for food.[16]

The centurion admitted that he was unworthy to accept the Lord into his home, and asked that only the all-powerful word of the Lord come into the house and heal his young servant. The Lord praised the faith and the humility of this centurion.[17]

The sons of Israel said to their holy deliverer and lawgiver, speaking from the proper understanding of the greatness of God, an understanding that gives birth to a comprehension and knowledge of the insignificance of man: "You speak with us, and we will hear; but let not God speak with us, lest we die."[18] These humble and salvific words are appropriate to every true Christian. Such a Christian is protected from spiritual death by this compunction of heart. This spiritual death seizes those who are deluded by their own pride and impudence. In contrast to this true Christian, this spiritual Israelite, the self-deluded madman cries out in his insanity:

> The sons of Israel once said to Moses: speak thou with us, and we will listen; may the Lord not speak to us, lest we die. But this is not my appeal to you, O Lord! Does not Moses or another of the prophets say to me: speak to me, O Lord God, who gives inspiration to all the prophets. You alone, without any of them, can teach me completely
>
> He is unworthy of God, unworthy of emulation, who, complete with his foulness and uncleanness, his foolish, proud, delusional self-worth, thinks he is in the embrace of the All-pure, All-holy Lord; who thinks he has Him in himself and speaks with Him, as with a friend.[19]

"Great and terrible is He over all them that are round about Him," says the Scripture;[20] He is frightening even for the highest of the heavenly hosts. The six-winged Seraphim fly around His throne, praising Him constantly in wonder and awe of the greatness of God, and close their fiery faces with their wings of flame. This is what the seer Isaiah saw.[21] O man! Cover yourself piously with humility.

It is enough if the word of God, the Truth, comes into the home of your soul through hearing or reading, and thus heals the young servant—that is, your heart—who is still a youth in reference to Christ, even if in your body you are already silver with age.

There is no other way to the Truth! The Apostle says, "How shall they believe in Him of whom they have not heard? And how shall they hear without a preacher? So then faith comes by hearing, and hearing by the word of God."[22] The living bearers of the Holy Spirit have all fallen silent. The Scriptures spoken by the Holy Spirit alone declare the Truth.

Faithful son of the Orthodox Church! Hear the advice of a friend, advice that might bring you salvation. Do you want to definitively know the path of God, to walk along this path to eternal salvation? Learn the holy Truth in the Holy Scriptures, especially in the New Testament, and in the writings of the Holy Fathers. In addition to this, you will inevitably need to toil and purify your life, because only those who are pure in heart can see God. Only then will you become, in good time, when and how the Lord wills, a disciple and bearer of holy Truth, a communicant with it and its Giver—the Holy Spirit. Amen.

CHAPTER 8

Faith and Works

"Repent, and believe in the gospel," we are told by the Gospel.[1] What a simple, true, and holy command! We must repent, leave behind our sinful life, before we become capable of approaching the Gospels. In order to accept the Gospel, we have to believe in it.

The Apostle Paul considered the essence of the preaching of Christ to be the message of repentance and faith. He testified to everyone, both Jews and Gentiles of, "repentance toward God and faith toward our Lord Jesus Christ."[2]

The Gospel, as the revelation of God, is higher than any achievement, remaining inconceivable for fallen human reason. The inconceivable wisdom of God is only conceived by faith, because faith can accept everything that is impossible for reason and that even contradicts reason. Only the soul that willfully rejects sin and directs all of its willpower and strength to divine good is capable of faith.

"I have come as a light into the world," said the Lord.[3] This light came to the Jews clothed in flesh; before us, he stands clothed in the Gospels.

This light comes before us, "that whoever believes in Him should not perish but have everlasting life. He who believes in Him is not condemned; but he who does not believe is condemned already.[4]

Who does not believe in the Son of God? Not only he who openly, assuredly rejects Him but also he who, while calling himself a Christian, leads a sinful life, rushes around after pleasures of the world, whose god is his stomach, whose god is gold and silver, whose god is earthly glory, who honors earthly wisdom, antagonistic to God, as god himself. "For everyone practicing evil hates the light and does not come to the light, lest his deeds should be exposed. But he who does the truth comes to the light, that his deeds may be clearly seen, that they have been done in God."[5]

Without self-denial a person is not capable of faith; his fallen reason fights against faith, demanding an answer of God in all His actions and proof of His revealed truths. The fallen heart wants to live the life of the fallen, which faith strives to mortify. Flesh and blood, ignoring the constant presence of death all around it, wants to live its own life—the life of death and sin.

This is why the Lord told all who desire to follow Him with living faith: "If any one desires to come after Me, let him deny himself, and take up his cross, and follow me. For whoever desires to save his life will lose it, but whoever loses his life for My sake will find it."[6]

The fall has become so assimilated to the essence of all mankind that rejection of the fall has become tantamount to rejection of our very life. Without such self-denial it is impossible to acquire faith, which is the pledge of the eternal, blessed, spiritual life. Whoever wants to enliven the passions of his heart or body and to gain pleasure from them, whoever wants to enliven his fallen reason, he will fall away from faith.

Living faith is walking into the spiritual world, the world of God. It cannot exist in a person who is nailed to the cross of the world, ruled by flesh and sin.

Faith is the door to God. There is no other door to him: "without faith it is impossible to please [God]."[7] This door opens only slowly before the one who purifies himself with constant repentance; it is open widely only before the pure heart; it is shut for the lover of sin.

Only through faith can one approach Christ; only through faith can one follow Christ.

Faith is a natural quality of the human soul, planted in man at the creation by the merciful God.[8] This natural quality is chosen by God during the course of redemption as the branch through which to graft grace back onto fallen man.

God wisely chose faith as the tool of mankind's salvation, for we perished by believing the flattery of the enemy of God and mankind. A long time ago, the noise of his evil words was heard in Eden, and our forefathers listened and believed, and were cast out of Eden. Now, in the land of our exile, their descendants hear the voice of the Word of God, the Gospels, and once again those who listen and believe in it can enter paradise.

You who do not believe! Turn away from your lack of faith! Sinner! Reject your sinful life! Wise man! Deny your false wisdom! Turn to God! With your goodness and lack of evil, you will become like children, and with childlike simplicity you will believe in the Gospel.

Dead faith, or confessing Christ merely out of unwilling necessity, is something that the demons are capable of! Such faith will only add to a person's greater condemnation at the judgment of Christ. The unclean spirit cried out to the Lord: "Let us alone! What have we to do with You, Jesus of Nazareth? Did you come to destroy us? I know who You are—the Holy One of God!"[9] Faith in the Gospels must be living; one must believe with the mind and the heart, confess the faith with one's lips, and express and prove it with one's life. "Show me your faith without your works!"[10] Thus, the Apostle James addresses the one who boasts of his dead faith, with only the bare knowledge of the existence of God.

"Faith," said St Simeon the New Theologian, "in the full sense of this word contains in itself all of the divine commandments of Christ. It is stamped with the assuredness, that there is not a single part of the commandments that has no meaning, that all of them, until the very last iota, are the life and reason for eternal life."[11]

Believe in the dogmas that are declared by the Gospel, learn and confess them exactly as the Orthodox Church does because it alone has contained the purity and completeness of the Gospel's teaching.

Believe in the sacraments, established by the Church by the Lord Himself, and preserved by the Orthodox Church in all their fullness.

Believe the holy, life-giving, evangelical commandments, whose correct fulfillment is only possible within the true Church, whose fulfillment is called by the Father the active faith of a Christian.[12]

The dogmas contain theology given by God Himself. Therefore, rejecting the dogmas is nothing less than blasphemy, while perverting the dogmas is another form of blasphemy, called heresy.

The mind that has yet to be purified by repentance, still wanders in the darkness of the fall, and is not enlightened and led by the Holy Spirit. The man who dares to reason about God with his own sickly mind and from the darkness of his own pride, always falls into error. Such error is nothing less than blasphemy. We can know God as much as He has revealed Himself to us in His great mercy.

Through the sacraments of the Christian Church, the faithful are led to union with Divinity, which is the essence of salvation, the stamping of faith with the actions of faith, the full reception of what was once only the pledge of eternal good things.

He who rejects the devil, sin, and the world for the sake of faith in Christ dies to the life of the fallen nature, in which he existed before in unbelief and sinfulness. By being submerged in the laver of baptism, he is buried for this life; he comes out of the baptistery already born for the new life, the life in Christ.

Through baptism, the Christian is betrothed to Christ, he is clothed in Christ. Through the communion of His Holy Mysteries, he is united with Christ. Thus, through the sacraments, he becomes wholly Christ's.

He who is baptized into Christ already does not live as though he were the source of his own existence, but lives like one who has taken the fullness of his life from another Being—Christ. The Apostle Paul tells the Christians: "You are not your own, for you were bought at a price. Your bodies are members of Christ. Therefore glorify God in your body and in your spirit, which are God's."[13]

Through the fulfillment of God's life-giving Gospel commandments, a person's union with Christ is maintained. Otherwise, no member of Christ could remain united to Him, as one who acts in His will, through His reason. Both the will and the reason of Christ are expressed in the Gospel commandments.

It is normal for every creature to act, in its inner and outer life, according to its nature. Thus, the one who is clothed in Christ, the new man, naturally thinks, feels, and acts as Christ thinks, feels, and acts. To be led by thoughts and emotions of the old man, even if they are superficially good, are unnatural to the new man.

The guide of a Christian must be the Holy Spirit in the same way as the guide of the old man was the flesh, blood, and the evil spirit. "'The first man Adam became a living being.' The last Adam became a life-giving spirit."[14] All the thoughts, feelings, and actions of a Christian must flow from the Holy Spirit, not be his own, fallen, according to the nature of the Old Adam. You will achieve this when you completely align your life with the commandments of the Gospels, according to the holy words of the Gospel: "The words that I speak to you are spirit, and they are life."[15]

The Orthodox faith in Christ, sealed with the mystery of baptism, is alone sufficient for salvation, without deeds, when the person has no time to do them, because faith transforms a person into the likeness of Christ while deeds change him only to the likeness of Christ's actions.

But during the course of the earthly life, good deeds are necessary. Only those deeds are considered good in a Christian that serve to fulfill the Gospel commandments, through which his faith is fed and lives, through which his life in Christ is supported, because the only true Doer of Christianity is Christ Himself.

The baptized person has no right to act according to the inclination of his heart's feelings, which depend on the influence of the flesh and blood on the heart, no matter how much such feeling may seem to be good. He only should accept those good deeds that the Spirit and word of God inspire him to do, because such deeds belong to the nature renewed by Christ.

"The just shall live by faith."[16] True faith in Christ is the only way to salvation, but this faith must be living, expressed through the entire being of a person.

The holy Apostle James demands this living faith of a Christian, when he says that faith without works is dead, that faith is accomplished by works.[17]

This common activity of deeds and faith accuses other faith that secretly and criminally hides away in the heart of man.

When he praises the deeds of the Patriarch Abraham, St James praises the deeds of his faith—the bringing of his son as a sacrifice according to the command of God, a deed completely antithetical to our very nature, which we call good. The strength to do this was given by faith, and the deed expressed the strength of faith. That is how the Apostles James and Paul interpret the actions of Abraham.[18]

Those who give a high value to the so-called good deeds of our fallen nature are blind. These deeds have their value and honor within time and among people, but not before God, before Whom "they have all turned aside; they have together become unprofitable."[19] Those who rely on the good deeds of our fallen nature have not come to know Christ, they have not understood the mystery of redemption, and they are snared in the traps of their own false reasoning, raising up against their own half-dead and vacillating faith, the foolish asking: "Is God so unfair that good deeds done by heretics and idolaters will not be crowned by eternal salvation?" These so-called judges extend the incorrectness and weakness of their own argument to the judgments of God.

If good deeds according to the feelings of the heart would give salvation, then the incarnation of Christ would have been a pointless act. The redemption of mankind through the passion and the cross would have been unnecessary, and the gospel commandments would be meaningless. Thus, obviously, those who believe that good deeds done in our fallen nature are enough for salvation destroy the meaning of Christ and reject Christ Himself.

The Jews were unlawful enemies of faith because they demanded from the faithful only superficial ritual acts of the Old Testament. In the same way, the sons of the God-hating world lawlessly require those who believe in Christ to fulfill good deeds according to the reasoning and feelings of our nature because they do not know Christ in a mystical, yet essential, way.

The one who believes in Christ holds a drawn sword against the emotions of the heart, and he forces his heart, using the sword of obedience to Christ, to cut off not only obvious sinful inclinations but even those desires that seem to be good but in their essence contradict the Gospel commandments. And this means all actions of man that are inspired by the fallen nature.

These apparently good deeds inspired by fallen nature grow the person's *ego*, destroy faith in Christ, and are antagonistic to God. The works of true faith destroy a person's selfishness, uniting him to Christ and increasing faith yet more.

"If you confess with your mouth the Lord Jesus and believe in your heart that God has raised Him from the dead, you will be saved. For with the heart one believes unto righteousness, and with the mouth confession is made unto salvation."[20]

True living faith, even if a person only confesses it with his lips, brings him salvation. It gave salvation to the thief on the cross; it gave salvation through repentance to many sinners in the last minutes of their life.

It is so important, so necessary to confess the heart and soul's beliefs with the mouth of faith, that the holy martyrs of all ages of Christianity, starting with the apostles of Christ, considered it better to suffer terrible and prolonged suffering, to pour out their blood like water, rather than utter a rejection of Christ, even if only with the lips without the agreement of the heart.

God requires of man only *living, true faith* for salvation. Like a pledge of salvation and eternal blessedness, it must be more precious even than life for the Christian.

Martyrdom was the fruit of true knowledge of God, given by faith.

Martyrdom was a deed of faith. Those who highly value the fallen nature of man blaspheme this deed. In their blindness, they call this great-hearted, most holy labor given by God to man a result of insanity!

Every thought of the God-given dogmas is so important that the holy confessors, like the martyrs, witnessed the Orthodox confession of the dogmas by long sufferings and streams of their own blood.

As important as faith is the work of salvation, so correspondingly heavy are the sins against faith. Every one of these is a mortal sin—that is, they result in the death of the soul—and after them comes eternal perdition, eternal sufferings in the pits of hell.

Lack of faith is a mortal sin; it rejects the only means to salvation—faith in Christ.

Rejection of Christ is a mortal sin; it denies the one who rejects Him the living faith in Christ, revealed and contained in the confession with the mouth.

Heresy is a mortal sin; it contains blasphemy in itself and infects the one who is far from true faith in Christ with blasphemy.

Despair is a mortal sin; it is the rejection of an active, living faith in Christ.

Essentially important in the work of faith is the confession with the mouth. During his work of faith, the great lawgiver of the Hebrews, the God-seer Moses only uttered a word with some taint of doubt in it, and he was denied entry into the promised land.[21]

The disciple of a certain Egyptian desert dweller, in his simplicity during a conversation with a Jew, only barely uttered a false word about Christianity, and the grace of baptism left him.[22]

Church history tells us that in the first centuries of Christianity, during the times of persecutions, some pagans uttered the confession of Christ flippantly, with the desire to mock Christians. When they were suddenly overwhelmed by the grace of God, they immediately turned from hardened pagans to zealous Christians, and ended up sealing that confession, which was first uttered as a blasphemy, with their blood.[23]

Suffering and dying for the Gospel commandments is also a deed of living faith in Christ, a form of martyrdom.[24] This form of martyrdom belongs mostly to holy monks.

Inspired with living faith, the holy monks, like Abraham, left their homeland and the house of their parents. Like Moses, they preferred suffering for Christ over earthly pleasures; like Elijah, they chose the desert and caves for their dwelling place; and though they were half-naked, they saw the promises of heaven with the eyes of faith.

In their deserts, far away from people, far away from the pleasures and business of the world, they entered the fray against sin, they cast it out of their actions, their thoughts, their emotions, and the Holy Spirit descended onto their pure souls, filling them with grace-filled gifts. Living faith in Christ and in the Gospels gave them the strength to withstand this battle against sin, making them vessels of the Holy Spirit.

Faith is the mother of patience, the mother of courage, the power of prayer, the instructor toward humility, the giver of hope, the ladder to the throne of love.

Faith in Christ, revealed and confessed both visibly and invisibly through the keeping of Christ's commandments, contains an invincible pledge of salvation, and to those who leave the world in order to completely dedicate themselves to this evangelical work, it gives Christian perfection.

In those who have attained Christian perfection, strengthened faith, with the help of the Holy Spirit, looks very clearly at the promises of God, as if seeing and feeling eternal goods already in this life. And sometimes it truly is, according to the teaching of the Apostle Paul, "the substance of things hoped for, the evidence of things not seen."[25]

Those who have been enriched with living faith in Christ change with respect to the visible world and the earthly life. The law of death, fading, and termination in all perishable things of the earthly world becomes apparent to them; earthly priorities, as short-lived, become in their pure vision completely insignificant.

Those who have been enriched with living faith in Christ fly through all sorrows and difficult circumstances as if they had wings. Those who are satiated with faith in the all-powerful God do not consider difficulties to be arduous, do not feel the pain in diseases. They consider God to be the only doer in the universe, and they have made Him their own through their living faith in Him.

He who believes in Christ, even if he dies the death of sin, will resurrect through repentance.[26] And we see many saints who fell from the heights of holiness into the abyss of heavy sins, with the help of faith and the repentance inspired by it, later rise up again to the heights of purity and holiness.

Despair is an accuser of hidden lack of faith and selfishness in the heart—he who believes in himself and trusts in himself will not rise up from sin with repentance; only the one who believes in Christ, the eternal Redeemer and Physician, will rise again through repentance.

"Faith comes by hearing."[27] Listen to the Gospels that speak to you and the Holy Fathers who explain the Gospels. Listen to them attentively, and little by little, living faith will settle within you, which will require you to fulfill the Gospel commandments; for this fulfillment, you will be rewarded with the hope of inevitable salvation. Faith will make you a follower of Christ on earth and His co-inheritor in heaven. Amen.

CHAPTER 9

A Scattered Life and an Attentive Life

The sons of the world consider distraction to be innocent, but the Holy Fathers consider it to be the beginning of all evil.[1]

A person who is entrenched in his scattered way of living has a very superficial and shallow appreciation of all things, even the most important ones.

The scattered man is usually inconstant—the emotions of his heart are lacking in depth and strength, and so are feeble and short-lived.

As a moth flutters from flower to flower, so the scattered man passes from one earthly pleasure to the next, from one useless activity to another.

The scattered man lacks love for his neighbor—he sees his neighbor's suffering with no twinge of sympathy and very flippantly lays intolerable burdens on others.

The scattered man is profoundly affected by sorrows, since he never expects them; he always expects pleasures.

If the sorrow is heavy, yet short-lived, the scattered man quickly forgets it in the noise of his constant distractions. A long-lasting sorrow destroys him.

The scattered way of life itself turns on the one who is devoted to it—sometimes it becomes boring to him, as to one who has never acquired any real knowledge or impressions, he descends into a deadly, profound depression.

The scattered life, so dangerous in essence, is especially harmful in the doing of God's work, in the work of salvation, which requires constant vigilance and attention.

"Watch and pray, lest you enter into temptation,"[2] said the Lord to His disciples.

"I say unto all, Watch!",[3] He said to every Christian, consequently to us as well.

He who leads a scattered life directly contradicts the commandment of the Lord Jesus Christ with his very life.

All the saints assiduously avoided distraction. Constantly, or at the very least as often as possible, they concentrated their thoughts within themselves, paying attention to every movement of the mind and heart, directing these according to the commands of the Gospels.

The habit of vigilance over the self protects one from an absent way of life, especially in the midst of loud worldly pleasures that surround one from every side. The attentive man remains alone within himself even in the midst of a crowd.

Having learned for himself the importance of attention and the harm of scattered thoughts, Abba Agathon said, "Without forceful vigilance over ourselves we will not progress in a single virtue."[4]

It is foolish to waste our short temporal life (given to us to prepare for eternity) on earthly concerns alone, on satisfying our insignificant, endless, insatiable desires and passions, frivolously rushing from one perishable pleasure to the next, forgetting about or only sometimes remembering about imminent, majestic, and terrifying eternity.

God's work—this is obvious!—should be examined and studied with great reverence and attentiveness; otherwise, a person will be unable to consider it, or to learn of it.

That great work of God, the creation of man, and the renewal of man after the fall through Christ's redemption, should be studied in great detail by every Christian. Without this knowledge, he will never know and be able to fulfill the calling of a Christian. Knowledge of the great work of God cannot be acquired while leading a scattered life!

The commandments of God are given not only to the external man, but more so to the inner man. They encompass all the thoughts and emotions of a person, all his subtlest movements. Living according to these commandments is impossible without constant vigilance and profound attentiveness. Vigilance and attentiveness are impossible in a scattered way of life.

Sin,—and the devil who wields it as a weapon,—sneaks quietly into the mind and heart. A person must be constantly on guard against his invisible enemy. How will he stand guard when he is devoted to his scattered thoughts?

The scattered man is like a house without doors or locks—he can protect none of his treasures, which are all stolen by thieves, murderers, and prostitutes.

A scattered life, full of the cares of this world, makes a person weak and stupid, just like a person who eats and drinks too much.[5] Such a person is stuck to the earth, busy only with vain and temporary matters. Serving God becomes a secondary matter to a scattered man; to him, the very thought of such service seems to him wild, murky, and intolerably heavy.

An attentive life lessens the effect of physical emotions on a person, while sharpening, strengthening, and forming the influence of spiritual emotions. A scattered life, in contrast, has a soporific effect on the spirit—it feeds on the constant activity of physical emotions.

It is useless for the scattered man to call his scattered way of life harmless! He is only proving the depth of his own sickness, which has taken him over completely. This sickness is so profound, it dulls the fine emotions of the soul so that the infected soul does not even recognize its diseased state.

Those who desire to learn attentiveness must reject all empty activity in their lives.

Private and social responsibilities are not considered part of the scattered life—distraction is always connected to a waste of time or activities that are so meaningless, they can very correctly be considered a waste of time.

Useful earthly work, especially service to one's country done with conscientious diligence, does not prevent the development of attentiveness to oneself. In fact, it helps to form it in the first place. Even more useful are monastic obediences, when they are fulfilled in the proper manner. An active way of life is a perfect way to acquire vigilance over oneself, and this path is recommended by the Holy Fathers for all who want to learn self attentiveness.

Attention to oneself in solitude brings priceless spiritual gifts, but such solitude is possible only for men of mature spiritual age, who have long labored in piety, at first learning attentiveness during an active life.

Other people are a great help to a person striving to learn attentiveness in an active life, because they remind him of how he constantly loses attention. Being a subordinate is the best way to become attentive—no one teaches attentiveness to the self as much as a strict manager.

As you do your work among people, do not allow yourself to waste time in empty words and foolish jokes. If you do clerical work, avoid flights of fantasy. Soon, your conscience will become sharp; it will begin to show you every time you lapse into scattered thoughts, since each lapse is a breach of the Gospel law. Amen.

PART II

REFLECTION

The Sea of Life

I see before my eyes a majestic sea. This is the north of Russia, where it is most often cloudy and stormy, even though sometimes it is quite glorious. O wide and deep sea! You attract my thoughts and eyes. I look for a long time at this sea. There is no variety in this display, but my glance and my thoughts cannot be torn away from it, as if they were sailing along this wide sea, as if they were submerged and drowning in it. What incredible inspiration is contained in this sea! What fullness I feel in my soul when the eyes are satiated with contemplation of the sea! Let us look, dear friends. Let us look at the sea from our monastery window, the monastery that has been placed by God's providence at the shore of the sea.

Beyond this sea is a different sea—the capital of the powerful North. Its view is magnificent across the water from the banks of the sea, where St Sergius's hermitage stands. This sea is a part of the famous Gulf of Finland. Its wide, crystal, silvery waters are bounded by Kronstadt, beyond which the limitless waters bleed into the never-ending sky.

The holy David once praised the "great and wide sea also, wherein are things creeping innumerable, both small and great beasts. There go the ships: there is that Leviathan, whom Thou hast made to play take his pastime therein."[1] The words of David have a mystical meaning, explained by the Holy Fathers. The sea is the world; the countless beasts and fish with which the sea is filled are the people of all ages, nationalities, and callings, all of whom serve sin; the ships in general are the Holy Church, and in particular the true Christians who overcome the world. Leviathan, the great serpent that lives in the sea, is the fallen angel who was cast out of heaven to the earth.[2]

The Holy Church sails along the waves of the sea of life for the entirety of its existence, for the centuries, millennia that it will endure. While it belongs to the world by virtue of its existence in the world, it does not belong to it in spirit, as the Lord said to the Church through its apostles: "you are not of the world, but I chose you out of the world."[3] According to your bodies and needs, you belong to the world but according to your spirit, you are foreign to the world, because you belong to God, Whom the world has despised.[4]

The Holy Church sails along the waves of the sea of life but remains above them because of the divine teaching that contains in its heart true knowledge of God and of man, of good and evil, of the visible and invisible world, of the earthly and temporary world, and of the spiritual and eternal world. All true Christians in all the world belong to this one true Church, and keeping its teaching in fullness and purity, they make up that armada that sails over the sea of life, never submerging into its murky depths.

Every true Christian sails on the waters of the sea of life on his way to eternity. There can be no permanent home on the sea of life, only a life of wandering. There is nothing constant on the sea of life, nothing that would remain the personal property of a man forever, even beyond the grave. Only a man's good deeds and sins accompany him into eternity. Naked he entered this earthly life, but departing he is without even his body. The slaves of the world, the slaves of sin do not see this, only the true Christian does. He can be imagined as a great ship that is filled with many different spiritual treasures, constantly gaining more of them along the way. The world cannot contain such riches—they are too great. They are so precious, that all the riches of the world are nothing compared to them. And so the world is envious of these riches; it lives and breathes hatred on those who acquire them.

This ship, despite its good construction and large size, is constantly in danger of winds, storms, underwater rocks, and shoals. Every Christian, even though he has put on Christ, must complete his earthly wandering amid many dangers. All who wish to be saved, without exception, will be persecuted.[5]

The ship embarks and stops along the way only for short rests, only in direst need. And we also must strive to reach heaven and eternity with all our strength. Let us not allow our hearts to be enamored of anything temporal! Let not our "soul be bowed down" by the self-deception that works in our hearts and in the world surrounding us! As a result of our fall, "our soul is bowed down into the dust," it has become enamored of all fading things, "our belly," our spiritual essence, "cleaveth unto the ground,"[6] instead of striving toward heaven and to eternity. We will bear our earthly work and responsibilities as burdens laid on us by God, we will fulfill them as though before the gaze of God, with a clean conscience, with eagerness, always ready to give account of our work to God. May our sinful intentions and goals not defile or steal away this God-given work! We will fulfill even our earthly work with the goal of pleasing God, and so it will become heavenly work. Let our essential and most important work be the service of God, the desire to become one with Him. To serve God means constantly being mindful of God and His commandments and fulfilling these commandments in all our actions, whether obvious or in secret.

The ship is guided by the helmsman—he constantly thinks about the final shore, where all the passengers must disembark. He constantly worries about being driven off course on the wide open sea that has no marked roads. Either he looks at the sky and its stars, or to his instruments and compass, using them to direct the ship. The person is thus guided by his mind. The sea of life also has no marked roads—everywhere there are potential ways for the Christian to travel. No one knows what the future holds, whether in one day or in a single hour. More often than not, we encounter events that are unforeseen and unexpected. You cannot rely on the constancy of your helping wind—sometimes it pushes you along, but more often it suddenly turns into a contrary wind or a fierce storm. Every way is a potential path for the Christian—he believes everything that happens to him does so according to God's will.

For a Christian, even a contrary wind can be helpful because submission to the will of God helps him remain peaceful, even in the most difficult and bitter circumstances. Our mind must constantly strive toward the spiritual heavens—the Gospel—from which the teaching of Christ shines forth like the sun in the earthly heaven.[7] It must constantly keep watch over the heart, over the conscience, over the person's inner and outer activity. May this helmsman always strive toward the blessed eternity, remembering that forgetfulness of eternal blessedness leads to eternal misery. May the mind keep the heart away from passionate attachment to the care-filled and perishable world, from coldness toward eternal things, from preference for the fleeting over the true and essential. May he look into the conscience often, as if to his compass, so that he does not choose a way that is contrary to the indications of the conscience. May he guide all the person's actions along God-pleasing lines, so that the far shore of eternity will open its gates and allow entry to the ship that is laden with spiritual treasures.

Let us not be afraid of the storms on the sea of life. The crests of its waves reach as high as the sky, its troughs to the very depths, but living faith will not allow a Christian to drown in the ferocious waves. Faith wakes up the sleeping Saviour, Who, in a mystical sense, is depicted in the Gospel account as sleeping only while His disciples sail over the sea of life with lack of faith. Faith calls out to the Saviour with fiery prayer from the humble heart, from the heart that suffers for the sinfulness and weakness of mankind, the heart that asks help and deliverance, and receives it. The Lord and master of all creation rebukes the winds and the sea and restores great silence to the water and the air.[8] Faith that is tested by the winds of the storm feels itself strengthened, and with new enthusiasm and courage it prepares itself for new labors.

Let us not trust the apparent calm of the sea of life. This calm is a false calm, for the sea is fickle. Let us not allow ourselves to fall asleep in laziness, for the ship may unexpectedly run aground on invisible rocks or unexpected shoals and be damaged beyond repair. Sometimes, an apparently innocent little cloud appears that suddenly begins to churn out winds, thunder, and lightning, and once again the quiet sea boils in a frightful storm. Our life is filled to the brim with sorrows, temptations, and miseries. Even our helmsman, the mind, sometimes loses his way and takes our whole life along with him down the wrong path. Our heart distracts us when it inclines to the fulfillment of its own fallen desires, when it leaves the path of God's will. Sin attacks us, both the sin we were born with and the sin that acts on us as a result of countless temptations that surround us on all sides. The world pushes us off course because it serves vanity and death and tries to force everyone else to serve its fallen masters, sometimes with kind words, sometimes with outright persecution. Our enemies, the fallen spirits, stand in our way, as do those who are ruled by them. Even our friends become hindrances, whether they know it or not. In all these circumstances the Lord commanded us to be constantly vigilant, to practice virtue, to shield ourselves from sin by the word of God, prayer, faith, and humility.

Who are the great beasts that play in the great expanse of the sea of life? I would wish no one to be like these denizens of the sea, who have only one joy—the darkness of the depths, densely covered with water, where the rays of the sun dare not penetrate. There they live, there they remain, leaving only occasionally for the hunt, to support their miserable life through the murder of numerous victims. Their fierce glance cannot abide the light. These beasts in the psalm are symbolic of the kinds of people who are great according to their abilities, knowledge, riches, and political influence, but, alas, their souls are in total bondage to vanity and death. Their hearts and minds are directed exclusively to the search for earthly glories and pleasures. They have drowned in the sea of life, only rushing after the fleeting, the evanescent, the ghostly.

The Scriptures say that they pass "through the paths of the seas."[9] How strange are these paths! They disappear behind the one who passes, and the traveler has no signs by which to determine the direction of these paths. Thus, earthly success knows not what it seeks; once it finds what it has sought, it is as though it no longer needs it, and once again it desires and seeks something new. The light of Christ's teaching is heavy and intolerable for the sons of the world. They run from it into their dark, soundless pits—into distractions, into various earthly pastimes, into carnal pleasures. There, in their moral darkness, they live their earthly life with no spiritual, eternal goals. Such people are not even worthy to be called human, even in the Scriptures: "man, being in honor, understood it not; he shall be compared unto the brute beasts, and is become like unto them."[10] A human being is one who can come to know himself, said St Pimen the Great.[11] He is one who has understood his meaning, his calling, his worth.

The *small beasts* of the sea are people who are not especially gifted or rich or powerful, but even in such a state, they still serve vanity and sin. They do not have the means to commit great and loud iniquities, but they take part in the crimes committed by the great beasts, pushed by their blind, angry self-will. As much as it is their power, they commit sins along with the great beasts. They wander through the sea of life without consciousness or purpose.

Leviathan, the great serpent, "is king over all the children of pride,"[12] is the fallen angel who abides in all who are filled with hatred and evil. He acts as much as possible in secret so that his actions, being noticed by only a few, will be the more dangerous and fatal. His slaves do not feel the chains that bind them from hand to foot, calling their bondage freedom and the greatest joy. True Christians mock this serpent, clearly seeing his traps with their mind, destroying them with the power of divine grace that has illumined their souls.

Let us be like those ships that sail straight and true along the sea! A good part of this ship is submerged under the water, but never completely, as are the fish and other creatures of the sea. It is impossible for the ship sailing over the sea of life not to get wet, but neither should it go completely under the waves.

The sea is full of innumerable beasts. What can we say about them? The name itself says it all. Miserable is the lot of those whom the word of God has deprived of the name human and given instead the name of animals. How much more miserable then, are those whom the all-holy Word, the Judge of the universe, has stamped with the name "beasts." They do not live and find pleasure in the waters, but in the foul and dirty bogs to which they are cast out even by the waves of the sea, where all foulness is cast out, where the bodies of the drowned come to rest, murdered by the pirates of the sea of life.

My brothers! My friends! I stand with you on the shores of the sea; I look at the sea, striped in different bands of color. Beyond the sea is another sea, with sparkling golden domes and spires. . . .

In the meantime, in the Church of God, the choir sings the majestic, symbolic hymn: "Beholding the sea of life surging with the flood of temptations, I run to Thy calm haven, and cry to Thee, Raise up my life from corruption, O Most Merciful One."[13]

CHAPTER 10

On the Snares of the Prince of This World

With the sign of the holy cross I lead you, brother, to a spiritual vision. Our guide will be the great Father among the saints, Anthony the Egyptian desert dweller.

Through the power of divine revelation, he once saw the traps of the devil that were set all over the world to lure mankind into perdition. Having seen that there were an infinite number of these snares, Anthony implored the Lord with tears: "Lord! Who can avoid these traps and attain salvation?"[1]

I contemplate these traps of the devil. They are set both outside and inside a person. One net is tightly bound to another. In some places, these nets stand several layers deep; in other places, the traps are set over great pits that lead to the most convoluted nets, from which deliverance seems impossible. Seeing these numerous nets, I begin to cry bitterly. Involuntarily, I also ask the question of the blessed desert dweller: "Lord! Who can be delivered from these nets?"

Traps intended for my mind are set in various books that pretend to be illuminating but instead contain the teachings of darkness, written under either the overt or implicit influence of the devil, from the source of the fallen reason, damaged by sin, " by the trickery of men, in [their] cunning craftiness"[2] as the Apostle said; writers, who are "vainly puffed up by [their] fleshly mind."[3] My brother, whose salvation I desire, can also become a trap for me, leading me to damnation, when his mind is caught in the nets of false teachings and so-called wisdom. My own mind is stamped with the fall; it is enveloped in murk, it is infected with the poison of lies. My own mind, fooled by the prince of this world, lays traps for itself.

Even in Eden, the mind tried to acquire knowledge without wisdom and attentiveness, and the knowledge proved to be lethal! After the fall, it became even less discerning, even more careless. Brazenly, it drinks the cup of poisoned knowledge, and so even more confidently it destroys in itself the taste and desire for the divine cup of the knowledge that gives salvation.

So many snares are prepared for my heart! I see crude ones and subtle ones. Which are to be considered the more dangerous? I do not know. The hunter is skilled, and whoever escapes the crude nets often falls into the subtle ones. But the end of the hunt is the same—perdition. The nets are hidden in all manner of ways, with unsurpassed skill. Sinful falls are hidden in all triumphs; the desire to please people, hypocrisy, and vanity are hidden in all attempts at virtue. The darkness of self-deception and demonic delusion is hidden behind a spiritual, heavenly mask. Passionate love, often sinful, hides behind the appearance of holy love. The false, sinful sweetness of fantasy pretends to be spiritual joy. The prince of this world tries every possible means to keep a person in his fallen state; and this is enough, even without heavy sins, to make a person distant from God. Crude, obvious falls into sin are very easily substituted with the prideful thoughts of a Christian who is content with the so-called virtues of fallen nature and self-deception. Such a Christian separates himself from Christ.

How many snares are laid for my body! It is in itself such a snare! How terribly the prince of the world uses it! Through the body and its shameful inclinations and desires we become like the dumb cattle. What an abyss! What separation from the likeness of God! Into this deep abyss, so far from God, we plunge ourselves when we give in to crude, carnal lusts, called by a name appropriate to their sinful heaviness—"falls into sin." But the more subtle carnal sins are no less destructive. For their sake, a person stops caring for his soul and forgets God, heaven, eternity, and the calling of mankind. The prince of this world tries to keep us in constant diversion, darkening us through the pleasures of the body!

The emotions, the doors into the soul through which the soul communicates with the outside world, are constantly led by the devil into fleshly pleasures and their inextricable bonds. In famous concert halls, loud music expresses and arouses various passions; these passions are depicted on the stages of theaters. People are led in all possible ways to these pleasures of deathly evil. When drunk with these pleasures, a person forgets about the divine goodness that saves him, the blood of the God-Man that redeems him.

This is but a weak description of all the traps that are set by the prince of this world to catch Christians. Does not even this weak description make us shudder, does it not make us ask the same question: "Who can escape these traps?"

But I have not yet finished painting the terrifying picture! Once more, my brush is inspired to continue painting, led by the word of God.

What does the word of God say? It foretells of events that are already happening before our eyes, a prophecy of the last times, when "lawlessness will abound, [and] the love of many will grow cold."[4] The word of God, more immovable than the heavens and the earth, tells us that in the last times, the snares of the evil one will increase, as will the number of ensnared.

It is true! I look at the world, and I see that the snares of the devil have increased, especially when compared with the times of the early church. They have increased a countless number! The number of books containing false doctrine has increased; the number of minds that contain and teach others false doctrines has increased. The followers of holy Truth have diminished to an absolute minimum. More and more people honor so-called virtues that are openly pagan, contrary to one's very nature, which is disgusted by them. The understanding of Christian virtues has diminished, and I do not even begin to speak of the dearth of their actual practice. A carnal life is preferred; the spiritual life is disappearing. Pleasures and cares of this world eat up all our time; we have no time to remember God. And all this becomes not just a free choice but a requirement, a law. From abounding iniquity shall the love of many become cold, and this abounding iniquity makes ever fewer the number of those who would abide in the love of God if it were not for the pervasiveness of evil and the increasing snares of the devil.

The sorrow of St Anthony was warranted. How much more should a Christian mourn our own times when he sees the snares of the devil? The sorrowful question is essential, in fact: "Lord! Who of us humans can avoid these snares and receive salvation?"

The answer to the righteous desert dweller was: "The one who is humble-minded will avoid these traps, and they will not even be able to touch him."

What a divine answer! How it removes all doubts from the heart, how well it describes in only a few words the surest method of victory over our enemy, a way of destroying and tearing apart his convoluted nets, which he has woven over many millennia of hateful experience.

Let us barricade our mind with humility, not allowing it to strive unscrupulously wherever it wishes, carelessly gathering information; but rather preventing it, no matter how interesting or attractive it seems. Let us guard it from the temptation of the false teachers who hide under the sheep's clothing of the Christian faith. Let us humble our minds through obedience to the Church, laying down all thoughts that aim to take God's place. The narrow path of obedience to the Church is difficult for the mind at first; but it leads the mind to the width and freedom of spiritual wisdom, contrary to everything the carnal mind has to say. Let us not allow our mind to read spiritual literature written by anyone other than the writers of the true Church, which the Church has witnessed to be true vessels of the Holy Spirit. He who reads holy writers doubtlessly takes part in the grace of the Spirit who lived in them and spoke to them; but he who reads the works of heretics, even if they are called saintly by the heretical assemblies to which they belong, takes part in the spirit of delusion. For disobedience to the Church, which is pride, he falls into the snares of the prince of this world.

What about our heart? Let us graft a branch of a fruit-bearing olive to this wild olive tree, let us graft into it the qualities of Christ, let us teach it evangelical humility, let us force it to accept the will of the Gospels. When we see our heart's constant disagreement with the Gospels, its constant contradiction, let us see in this contrariness, as we would see in a mirror, our own fallenness. Let us weep for our sins before the Lord, our Creator and Redeemer, let us us feel the pain of salvific sorrow. Let us remain in this sorrow until we see our healing. "A contrite and humble heart God shall not despise."[5] God is our Creator and our great Master. He can re-create our heart and make it into a heart that constantly calls to Him with tears and prayers, a heart transformed from a lover of sin to a lover of God.

Let us guard our senses, not allowing them to be the channel for sin to enter into the cell of the soul. Let us rein in our curious eye and our curious ear. Let us place a heavy bond on the apparently small tongue, which can wreak such tremendous havoc. Let us humble the irrational desires of our body with temperance, vigilance, ascetic labors, frequent remembrance of death, and attentive, constant prayer. Bodily pleasures are so short-lived! How foul is their inevitable end! In contrast, the body that is shielded by abstinence and the safeguarding of the senses, purified by tears of repentance, and sanctified by frequent prayer, mysteriously transforms into the temple of the Holy Spirit, making all the attacks of the enemy futile.

Humility avoids all the snares of the devil, and he cannot even touch it!

Amen.

CHAPTER II

The Pharisee

Brothers! Let us look into the way of life of our Lord God and Saviour Jesus Christ. We will see that He was never offended by the sins of others, no matter how heavy those sins might have been. Also, there is not a single example in the Gospels of the apostles being offended by the sins of others. However, the Pharisees were constantly tempted by the sins of others; they were offended even by the most perfect Lord, the incarnate God. They were offended so often, that they even condemned Him as a criminal and delivered Him to be shamefully executed. They crucified the Saviour on a cross between two thieves! It should be obvious from this that being offended at the sins of others is a serious spiritual disease. With discernment, one must carefully watch over one's heart and mortify any temptation in it to judge one's neighbor. Only the Gospels teach this.

The Gospel is a holy book! As the sun is perfectly reflected in a pure spring, so the Gospels reflect Christ. He who wishes to see Christ must cleanse his mind and heart through repentance! In the Gospels he will see Christ, the true God, the Saviour of fallen mankind. He will learn from the Gospels the qualities a disciple of Christ must acquire, as he is called to learn meekness and humility from the Lord Himself. In this virtuous emulation of God, he will find blessed peace for his soul.

Segment 1

There was a time when the Lord entered the house of a certain publican named Matthew, transforming the tax collector into an apostle, and the incarnate God reclined at the table with sinners. The Pharisees, seeing this, were offended. They asked the disciples of Jesus: "Why does your Teacher eat with tax collectors and sinners?"[1]

Tell me first, Pharisees, why do you call these men sinners? Would it not be more appropriate to call them blessed angels, cherubim, because God Himself deigned to recline with them? Would it not be better to say, "We are sinners as well! Accept us, merciful Jesus, let us approach your feet. You have preferred these sinners to us, O Knower of hearts and true judge! You have reclined with them. It is obvious: our sins are heavier in Your sight than theirs. You have reclined with them; allow us at the very least to fall at Your feet."

But there is no sweet fragrance of humility in these dark, so-called righteous men, who are filled only with the treasures of the fallen human nature, the fabricated truth of the world, the truth of demons. They blatantly judge the Lord, they judge the sinners accepted by Him, sinners made righteous by the choice of God. They reject the Lord, saying: "your teacher," thereby making it clear that they do not accept Him as "our teacher."

The Lord's answer is the same for all their actions tainted by spiritual disease. This answer is a terrible condemnation and rejection from the face of God intended for everyone who considers himself to be righteous according to the definition of men, especially when this righteousness is accompanied by the judging of one's neighbor. "Those who are well have no need of a physician, but those who are sick. But go and learn what this means: 'I desire mercy and not sacrifice.' For I did not come to call the righteous, but sinners, to repentance."[2]

Once, on a Sabbath day, the Lord was walking with His holy disciples and apostles through fields covered in wheat. The disciples were hungry and began to tear off the ripe heads with their hands and clean off the stalks to reach the seeds, which they then ate. The Pharisees, seeing this, said to the Lord: "Look, Your disciples are doing what is not lawful to do on the Sabbath!"[3] The Lord, reminding them of David and the priests, the first of which broke the Sabbath incidentally, the others according to the law, again repeats His terrible admonition: "But if you had known what this means, 'I desire mercy and not sacrifice,' you would not have condemned the guiltless."[4]

This temptation is so atrocious, so evil! It pretends to keep to the law with obsessive correctness, but it destroys the essence of the law. O blind and dark Pharisee! Can you not understand that the Lord tells you: "I will have mercy"? When you see the shortcoming of your neighbor, have compassion for him—that is your duty! The weakness you see in him may become your weakness tomorrow. You are only tempted because you are proud and blind! You fulfill only some of the eternal rules of the law and become so impressed with yourself! You despise and judge your neighbor, who breaks the law in some trifling way, yet you do not notice them doing great, secret virtues that are pleasing to God, because such secret virtues are foreign to your proud, cruel heart. You have not searched your own heart enough. You have not seen yourself, and so do not consider yourself a sinner. Because of this, your heart is not broken;it has not been filled with repentance and humility. Because of this, you have not understood that you need God's mercy and salvation as much as everyone else. It is a terrible thing, not to consider yourself a sinner! Jesus rejects those who do not acknowledge their sinfulness: "I did not come to call the righteous, but sinners, to repentance."

How wonderful it is to admit one's sinfulness! He who considers himself a sinner is allowed access to Jesus. What blessedness—to see one's sins! What blessedness—to see the depths of one's heart! Whoever looks into his heart will forget that there are sinners on this earth other than him alone. His neighbors will all seem to him pure and spotless and angelic. Looking within himself, scrutinizing his own stains of sin, he becomes convinced that the only way he can be saved is by God's mercy. He is a slave, not only because he breaks the commandments of God, but also because he does not fulfill them enough, because his fulfillment is better called a perversion of the commandments. Since he needs mercy in abundance, he pours it out on those surrounding him. He has mercy only for all his neighbors. "But go and learn what this means: 'I desire mercy and not sacrifice.' For I did not come to call the righteous, but sinners, to repentance."

Our merciful Saviour and Lord Jesus Christ, while not rejecting those who seemed to be publicans and harlots, also did not forget the Pharisees. He came to heal man of all his sicknesses, among them Phariseeism, which is difficult to heal precisely because this disease considers itself and declares itself to be in a state of blooming health. It rejects the physician and his medicines; it wants instead to fix the diseases of others. It tries to take the barely visible speck out of the gentle eye of another by smashing it with heavy logs.

A certain Pharisee invited the Lord to dine with him. "And He went to the Pharisee's house, and sat down to eat."[5] It seems that the Pharisee, although he had zeal and a certain faith in the Lord, accepted him with a measure of calculation and self-importance due to his own position as a righteous man. If he had not, what was there to prevent him from running to meet the divine Visitor, to reverently fall at His holy feet, to place his soul and heart as a carpet for His feet? This was not done; the Pharisee missed this blessed opportunity to honor the Saviour as the Saviour. A certain woman of that city, a well-known prostitute, seized this chance. She hurried to the house of the Pharisee with a bottle of sweet-smelling myrrh, entered the room where the dinner was served, and began to wash the feet of the Saviour with her tears and dry them with her hair. She kissed the feet of the Saviour and anointed them with myrrh.

The blind Pharisee did not see the virtue that was being performed right before his eyes, an action that condemned his coldness and the deadness of his own heart. Temptation and judgment began to slither in his heart. He thought: "This man, if He were a prophet, would know who and what manner of woman this is who is touching him; for she is a sinner."[6] Why do you belittle God, calling Him a mere prophet? Why do you call her a sinner when she worships God better than you? Be afraid, and be silent, for the Creator is before you! To Him alone belongs judgment over His creation. It is the same for Him to forgive a sinner's debt of five hundred or fifty denarii. He is all-powerful and eternally generous. As usual, the Pharisee does not calculate this fact! Seeing the five hundred denarii debt owed by his neighbor, he pays no attention to his own fifty, does not even consider it a debt, while the divine court proclaims that both of them should pay nothing, since both of them equally need forgiveness for this debt. "And when they had nothing with which to repay, he freely forgave them both."[7]

A deficiency of humility, characteristic of Phariseeism, is extremely harmful to spiritual growth. While those who fall into serious sins bring zealous repentance in brokenness of heart, forgetting the whole world and seeing nothing but their sin, the Pharisee allows his glance to wander. His own sin seems insignificant to him and attracts no attention whatsoever. He remembers his several good deeds and places all his hope in them. He sees the sins of others; comparing them with his own, he acknowledges his own to be slight, excusable. The more his own righteousness grows before his eyes, the smaller grows divine justification, which is given in abundance to those who repent. This, in turn, weakens and eventually destroys the feeling of repentance completely. With the diminishing of this sense of repentance, all spiritual progress is stunted, but if it is destroyed, the person is hurled off the path of salvation to the path of self-opinion and self-deception. He is bereft of the holy love for God and for his neighbor. "Her sins, which are many, are forgiven, for she loved much. But to whom little is forgiven, the same loves little."[8]

He who is infected with the disease of Phariseeism ceases all spiritual progress. The soil of his heart's field is rocky, it brings no harvest. The spiritual harvest requires a heart that is harrowed by repentance, softened by compunction, and irrigated by tears. Lack of progress is already a serious sickness! But the harm brought on by Phariseeism is not limited by the fruitlessness of the soul. The death-dealing infection of Phariseeism is usually accompanied by the most pernicious consequences. Phariseeism not only makes a person's good deeds useless but it even makes them into evil deeds, counting them toward his condemnation before God.

The Lord illustrated this in the parable of the publican and the Pharisee, both of whom were praying in the temple of God.[9] The Pharisee, looking at himself, sees no reasons for repentance, no need to feel compunction in his heart. Quite the opposite! He finds reasons to be pleased with himself, to pat himself on the back. He acknowledges his fasting, his almsgiving, but he misses those same sins that he sees or searches for in others. I say "searches for" because this temptation has very big eyes—it sees sins in the neighbor that he does not even have, sins it invented for itself, led ever forward by evil. The Pharisee, in his self-deception, praises God for his sinful state. He conceals his self-aggrandizement, and his pride conceals itself from him under the mask of gratitude to God.

Glancing only superficially at the Law, he seemed to be a true fulfiller of the Law, a God-pleasing man. He forgot that the commandments of God are quite far-reaching, and before God, even "the heavens are not pure."[10] God does not desire sacrifices, not even whole-burnt offerings, when a heart that is broken and humbled does not accompany them. The Law of God must be planted in the heart in order to bear the fruit of true, blessed, spiritual righteousness. This righteousness appears only when the person begins to feel poverty of spirit.[11] The vain Pharisee dares to thank and praise God: "God, I thank You that I am not like other men—extortioners, unjust, adulterers."[12] He lists all the most obvious sins that are visible to everyone; but he speaks not a single word about the passions of the soul—pride, hypocrisy, hatred, envy, evil. And these are the decorations of a Pharisee! They darken and kill the soul, making it incapable of repentance! They destroy the love for one's neighbor and give birth to the temptation of cold pride and hatred. The vain Pharisee dares to thank God for his good deeds; but God turns away from him; God utters against him a terrible condemnation: "Everyone who exalts himself will be humbled."[13]

When Phariseeism ripens and takes over the soul, its fruit is horrifying. There is no lawlessness too base for such a person. The Pharisees dared even to blaspheme the Holy Spirit. The Pharisees dared to call the holy of God a man possessed. The Pharisees allowed themselves to say that the incarnate God, Who came to the earth as a Saviour, was dangerous for the social welfare, for the way of life of the Jews. And what was the purpose of all this convoluted reasoning? It was to satisfy their insatiable lust for blood, to bring a sacrifice of blood to their own envy and vanity, all the while hiding behind the mask of fairness, nationalism, the law, and religion. They killed God! Phariseeism is the most frightening of poisons; Phariseeism is the worst of spiritual diseases.

Let us try to draw the image of the Pharisee, taking our inspiration from the Gospel, so that everyone who looks at this terrible, beastly perversion may carefully keep himself, according to the words of Christ, from the "leaven of the Pharisees,"[14] the thoughts, rules, and makeup of the Pharisee.

The Pharisee, contenting himself with the fulfillment of the external rites of religion and the accomplishing of some visible good deeds (that are done even by the pagans), slavishly serves the passions while constantly trying to hide them. He may not even see or understand the passions within himself while they make him completely blind to God and all of His teaching. Recognition and acknowledgment of the activity of the passions is given by repentance, but the Pharisee is beyond any sense of repentance. How can the heart that is drunk on itself ever humble itself, how can it ever break and feel compunction for its sins? Since he is incapable of repentance, he is incapable of seeing the light of God's commandments, which illumine the eyes of the mind. Even though he reads the Scriptures, even though he reads the commandments in them, they slip away from his glance, and he replaces them with his own reasoning, no matter how stupid, ugly, or foolish it may be.

What can be stranger or more foolish than the reasoning of a Pharisee as mentioned in the Gospel? The Pharisees say that "whoever swears by the temple, it is nothing; but whoever swears by the gold of the temple, he is obliged to perform it."[15] The Pharisee, ignoring the fulfillment of the commandments of God (which are the essence of the Law), strives to slavishly follow all external trivialities, even if these obviously contradict the commandments. God's holy commandments, in which is life eternal, are left unattended by the Pharisees, completely forgotten! The Lord said to them: "You pay tithe of mint and anise and cumin, and have neglected the weightier matters of the law: justice and mercy and faith. You blind guides, who strain out a gnat and swallow a camel."[16]

The most deeply rooted of all spiritual passions is vanity. This passion more than all the rest masks itself before the heart of man, giving him pleasure that is often confused with the consolation of the conscience, or even consolation from God. And it is exactly this passion that ferments the Pharisee. He does everything for the praise of men—others would witness his love for fasting, his almsgiving, and his prayer. He cannot be the disciple of the Lord Jesus, who orders his followers to reject the praise of men, to go the way of humiliation, want, and suffering. The Cross of Jesus is a stumbling block for the Pharisee. He needs a messiah who looks more like Alexander the Great or Napoleon, with the triumphant glory of the conqueror, with trophies and booty! The mere thought of heavenly, spiritual glory, of the glory of God, of eternity—all these are impossible for his soul, which slithers along the earth in the dirt and corruption.

The Pharisee is a lover of money. His heart is where his treasure is. There is his faith, there are his feelings, his hopes, his love! With his lips and the tip of his tongue he professes faith in God, but with his heart he rejects Him. He never feels the living presence of God, he never sees the providence of God, and he does not know from experience what the fear of God is. His heart has no room for God or for his neighbor. He is all earthly, all carnal, completely in thrall to spiritual passions, being moved by them, ruled by them, led to every possible sin. He lives and breathes exclusively for his self-love. Within this soul stands an idol—the *Ego*. This idol is offered constant incense and sacrifices. How can such a soul combine service to the all-holy God with service to the foul idol? This soul is in horrifying delusion, in terrible darkness, in frightening numbness. It is a dark cave inhabited only by ferocious beasts or even more ferocious thieves. It is the tomb, decorated on the outside for the physical eyes, so easily fooled, but inside filled with dead bones, stink, worms, everything that is unclean and despised by God.

The Pharisee, being far from God, has a need to appear to be a servant of God before the eyes of men. Being filled with all manner of sins, he has a need to appear before people as a man of virtue. While he strives to satisfy his passions, he has a need to make his deeds appear good. The Pharisee needs a mask.

He has no desire to be truly virtuous and pious, only desiring to be considered by people to be such a person. This is his hypocrisy. Everything in him is a lie, an invention! His words, actions, his entire life are nothing but constant lying. His heart is a dark hell filled with all passion, sins, and never-ending suffering. It is this hellish heart that turns on the neighbor with all manner of offenses and judgment. The Pharisee, trying to remain righteous in the eyes of the world, is the child of Satan in his soul. He grasps at several qualities in the Law of God and decorates himself with them to fool the inexperienced eye into not noticing that he is the enemy of God. The Pharisee judges his neighbor not for evil or sin or for the breaking of the Law. No! How can he condemn evil when he is evil's friend? His arrows are aimed instead at virtue. But, in order for his aim to be true, he slanders virtue, calls it a great evil, and kills the slave of Christ, whom he hates.

Pharisee! You are leading an innocent to execution for a crime that you invented! You are worthy to be executed, worthy of all punishment! Are you emboldened by the fact that the slave of Christ, in emulation of his Master, drinks the cup of suffering in silence? You miserable person! Be afraid of this greathearted and mystical silence. In this moment, the servant of Jesus is silent for the sake of Jesus, but at the dread judgment, Jesus will speak out for him; He will accuse the lawless one and will send him into eternal suffering. The Pharisees even invented crimes for the very incarnate God-Man! They condemned Him to be crucified. They paid the price of His blood, but pretended not to understand Him.

The Pharisees have committed the worst crime possible on this earth. They were always faithful—and they remain faithful—to their demonic calling. They are the chief enemies and persecutors of true Christian virtue and piety, not ashamed even by the worst depravity. The words of Christ echo against them:

> Serpents, brood of vipers! How can you escape the condemnation of hell? Therefore, indeed, I send you prophets, wise men, and scribes: some of them you will kill and crucify, and some of them you will

> scourge in your synagogues and persecute from city to city, that on you may come all the righteous blood shed on the earth, from the blood of righteous Abel to the blood of Zechariah, son of Berechiah, whom you murdered between the temple and the altar. Assuredly, I say to you, all these things will come upon this generation.[17]

The words of the Lord were proved true and continue to prove true. Those who are infected with the leaven of the Pharisees remain in implacable war with true followers of Christ. They persecute them, either openly or hiding behind slander. They hunger and thirst for their blood.

Lord Jesus Christ! Help Your servants. Let them come to know You and to follow You, You who are "led as a lamb to the slaughter, and as a sheep before its shearers is silent, so He opened not His mouth."[18] Let them see You with the pure eyes of their mind and, suffering in blessed silence as if before Your face, let them be enriched with the gifts of the Spirit, let them feel the Spirit inside their hearts. For it is the Spirit who tells Your servant that it is impossible to be Yours unless one drinks of the cup of suffering that You chose to be Your lot and the lot of those who are near You.

Segment 2

The Lord spoke many commandments in the Gospels, all of which lead the person to thoughts and emotions that are opposite to soul-killing, man-hating Phariseeism. These commandments destroy the very foundation that Phariseeism is built upon. "Beware of the leaven of the Pharisees," [19] said the Lord. One of the evangelists explains that, by the words "leaven of the Pharisees," the Lord meant the teaching of the Pharisees (Matthew), which another understood it to mean their hypocrisy (Luke). These are one and the same—from their hypocrisy comes their way of thinking and their teaching. And vice versa—the teaching and way of thinking of the Pharisees encourage the formation of the hypocrite, who fears no sin, who respects no virtue, who hopes to hide any and every sin, to excuse and justify it, and to replace all virtue with its pale imitation.

The Lord told His disciples to be direct in their behavior, sincere, and founded on holy wisdom, not justified by evil. Their behavior must shine with pure virtue and heavenly beauty in order to attract the eyes and hearts of all men:

"Let your light so shine before men, that they may see your good works and glorify your Father in heaven."[20]

The Pharisees, conversely, desire only to appear righteous and take pains only to show themselves off as servants of God before the society of men, before the mob, which can rarely discern the truth. Even today, we see that Pharisees bend themselves over backward to make their deeds (superficially virtuous) shine as brightly as possible before men. At the same time, they mask their crimes with fancy words such as political expediency, justice, choosing the lesser of two evils, and other justifications that come so readily out of the heart filled with evil.

The Lord forbids such behavior in no uncertain terms: "You are those who justify yourselves before men, but God knows your hearts. For what is highly esteemed among men is an abomination in the sight of God."[21] The Pharisees tried to cover their spiritual passions and their consequent fruits with self-justification. The spiritual passions, shaded and protected by justification, usually grow very deep roots in the soul, becoming a tree that covers with its leaves all the deeds of a person. In other words, the passions enter into his thoughts, his emotions, and all his actions. St Pimen the Great said, "If a person helps his sinful will with justifications, he will become depraved and will perish."[22]

A man who first seeks glory in the insignificant, fickle, unstable opinion of other men, not virtue in the sight of God, is incapable of understanding the Christian faith, to accept it into his heart, because such a heart must acknowledge its own sinfulness and confess that sin openly. The Lord said to the Pharisees: "How can you believe, who receive honor from one another, and do not seek the honor that comes from the only God?"[23]

The Lord takes from His disciples all food for vanity. He wants the altar of the heart to be purified of that foul idol and from everything that applies to such idol worship. The Lord commands us to do all our good deeds in secret. Even almsgiving and fasting must be done in secret! Even our prayer must be spoken in the inner room of our heart. Our good deeds not only must be hidden from people but from our own selves, so that their praises may not wither our soul, and that our heart itself may not praise us, becoming an adulterer with vanity instead of a faithful spouse of humility.

"Do not let your left hand know what your right hand is doing."[24]

Not only this, but the Lord also commands us to reject ourselves in this short earthly life, to put away all justifications, all so-called truth in favor of the Truth of the Gospels. What is this Gospel Truth? It is suffering; it is the cross! This is what the Saviour calls His disciple to do! This is what distinguishes the elect! This is what divides the wheat from the tares! "And he who does not take his cross and follow after Me is not worthy of Me. He who finds his life will lose it, and he who loses his life for My sake will find it."[25]

Brothers! Let us lay all earthly ideas of honor, offenses, affronts, unfairness, human laws, and human justice at the foot of the Cross. Let us become fools for Christ! Let us turn our cheeks for more blows! Let us bury our earthly dignity with dishonor. Let us give up our constant cares for our earthly riches; may all of this be carried away by the wind! Let us not spare our bodies in either our ascetic labors or our unintentional suffering! Let us learn holy silence from the Lord Jesus Christ, which is the highest theology and oratory, amazing even to the angels! He, the incarnate God, was not treated fairly by the world. Why should we expect otherwise for ourselves? Let us reject the fairness of the world for the Cross of Christ! Let us not be as the beasts, who attack and wound their hunters. Let us emulate the Lamb of God here on earth during our short wandering in this life, and He will give us His likeness in eternity, where our blessedness will have no end or limit. Even here, in the earthly exile, the faithful disciple of Jesus is visited by the Holy Spirit, the comforter, who breathes into his soul the unutterable blessedness of the future life. This will lighten his suffering; this will give him invisible, holy consolation and joy that does not depend on other people or circumstances. Before these joys, all earthly pleasures are insignificant, even lawful ones.

The main characteristic of a hypocrite—the first arrow, so to speak, that he aims at his neighbor—is judgment. The reasons these hypocrites have for judging others is often invented and falsified, only an apparent rationale for their evildoing, which they have long planned and justified in advance. This temptation of judging others is part of our original infection passed on by the sin of Adam, and no matter how well-intentioned a person is in his striving for salvation, this sin is a sign of a spiritual sickness of especial magnitude and stubbornness. This disease acts against repentance, which is required for our purification. This temptation is an infected assessment of the failings of others, when these failings begin to take on gargantuan, horrific proportions in the imagination. This temptation is a child of self-love that roots itself into the soul, a love that is foreign to the love of one's neighbor and the proper kind of love for oneself. The Lord likens this disease to a log. By comparison, all the sins of all our neighbors are mere specks:

> Judge not, that you be not judged. For with what judgment you judge, you will be judged; and with the measure you use, it will be measured back to you. And why do you look at the speck in your brother's eye, but do not consider the plank in your own eye? Or how can you say to your brother, "Let me remove the speck from your eye"; and look, a plank is in your own eye? Hypocrite! First remove the plank from your own eye, and then you will see clearly to remove the speck from your brother's eye.[26]

You must forcefully distract yourself from judging others, guarding yourself with fear of God and humility. In order to weaken and (with God's help) completely root out this temptation from your heart, you must descend into yourself with the light of the Gospels, search out your own failings, and scrutinize your own sinful inclinations, movements, and states. When our own sin becomes the object of our search, then we will have no time to watch after the sins of others and notice them. Then all our neighbors will truly seem wonderful and saintly; then every one of us will admit himself to be the greatest sinner in the world, the only sinner in the world; and only then will the wide gates of true and effective repentance open for us.

St Pimen the Great said, "We and our brothers are like two different pictures. If a person, looking at himself, sees his own failings, then in his brother he sees perfection. If he seems perfect to himself, then he will find all manner of failings in his brother."[27]

The greatest saints of God took special care to see themselves as sinners, and sinners so foul, that the sins of others, either great or small, would seem to them forgivable and insignificant. St Sisoes said to Abba Or, "Give me instruction."

"Do you trust me?" asked Abba Or.

"I do," answered Sisoes.

"Go and do as I do."

"What do you do, Father?"

The elder said, "I see myself as worse than all other people."[28]

"If a person reaches such a state," said St Pimen the Great, "which is described by Apostle Paul thus: 'to the pure all things are pure',[29] then he will see that he is worse than all creation."

A brother asked Abba Pimen, "How can I imagine that I am worse than a murderer?"

Pimen answered, "If a person reaches the state indicated by the apostle and will see a person who committed murder, he will say, 'that man killed once, but I murder myself every day.'"

The brother reported St Pimen's words to another elder. The elder answered him, "If a person reaches such a state of purity and sees the sins of his brother, then his righteousness will make that sin disappear."

The brother asked again, "What is this righteousness?"

The elder answered, "Constant self-accusation."[30]

Here are the true listeners and doers of evangelical law! Having routed all judgment from their hearts, they became filled with holy love for their neighbor, pouring out compassion on all, and even healing sinners with that compassion. It was said of St Macarius the Great by the Fathers that he was a god on earth. This was the power of his compassionate bearing of the burdens of others. Abba Ammon, constantly watching over himself and accusing his soul in its deficiencies, reached profound humility and holy simplicity. He so loved his neighbor that he no longer saw any evil in him; in fact, he completely forgot about the existence of evil! One time, someone brought a young woman who was pregnant out of wedlock to him for judgment since he was a bishop. They said to him, "A certain person did this to her, and you must lay a heavy penance on them both."

Ammon, having made the sign of the cross over her belly, told them to get six towels for her, saying, "When her time to give birth comes, it may be that either she or her baby will die, and they must be buried in something."

Those who accused the girl said to him, "What are you doing? Lay a penance on them!"

He answered, "My brothers! She is near to death! What else can I do to her?" And he released her.

Another time, Abba Ammon visited a certain monastery to share a repast with the monks. One of the brothers of that place had fallen into sin—a woman visited him regularly. This became known to the other brothers; they were upset and, after discussing this together, they decided to expel the brother from his cell. When Bishop Ammon visited, they asked him to come with them to inspect the brother's cell. The guilty monk heard about this and hid the woman in an inverted wooden barrel. Abba Ammon knew this and, for God's sake, covered the sins of his brother. When they all came to the cell, Abba Ammon sat on the barrel and ordered the others to inspect the rest of the cell. The cell was thoroughly searched, and the woman was not found.

"What is this?" said Abba Ammon. "May God forgive you your sins."

After this, he prayed and ordered all the brothers to leave. As he was leaving, he took the accused monk by the hand and said to him with love, "Brother! Be attentive to yourself!" In this way, St Ammon avoided judging anyone and at the same time healed sinners by softening their hearts with his mercy, leading them to repentance.

As much as the Lord leads us away from the pit of judgment and condemnation, as much as true slaves of the Lord avoid this pit, so much does the devil lead us into it, covering it with various justifications. One of these demonic justifications is immoderate zeal, which is assumed to be holy zeal for piety. St Isaac the Syrian has this to say about such zeal:

> A person who is led by irrational zeal will never attain peace of thought. Whoever lacks this peace, lacks joy. If peace of thought is complete health, and zeal is contrary to this peace, then he who has this evil zeal is terribly ill. O man! While you imagine that you are aflame with a just zeal against the sins of others, you are destroying the health of your own soul! Labor, labor for the health of your soul! If you wish to heal others, then understand that the sick need attentive patience more than strictness. In addition, at the same time that you do not help your neighbor, you yourself become seriously ill. Such zeal in a person is not a sign of wisdom, but of spiritual sickness. It points to a lack of spiritual wisdom and great ignorance. The beginning of divine wisdom is silence and meekness, qualities of a great and strong soul that appear in the soul only when one bears the burdens of others.[31]

The sin of judging others is a very easy way to destroy oneself spiritually, and so the devil loves not only inspiring envy and prideful thoughts, which are always joined by actively putting down one's neighbor, but also sets obvious traps to catch those who are not attentive to their passion of judging others. Abba Pimen said:

> The scriptures say, "Speak the things your eyes see."[32] But I suggest that you do not speak even of those things that you have felt with your hands. One brother was fooled in this way once. It seemed to him that another monk had sinned with a woman. For a long time he battled with himself, but finally, having approached them, he kicked them with his foot and said, "haven't you had enough already?" But it turned out that what he imagined were human bodies were nothing more than bunches of wheat. This is why I say to you, don't accuse, even if you feel something with your very hands.[33]

The sin of judgment is so repulsive to God that He is even angered and turns away from his righteous ones when they allow themselves to judge their neighbor. He takes from them the grace of the Holy Spirit, as we see in many examples preserved by Church writers for the good instruction of Christians. No righteousness gives one a right to judge a sinning brother, because God can give that brother true righteousness that is far more established and real than anything that we are capable of on our own. We can only be righteous in the Truth of God, but when we judge our neighbor, we reject the Truth of God, replacing it with our own, which is the definition of Phariseeism. The one who judges another usurps the role of God, who alone has the right to judge His creation and to judge the living and the dead on the last day.

The wondrous John the Sabbaite said of himself:

> When I lived in the desert not far from the monastery, a certain brother came to visit me. I asked him, "How do the fathers and brothers live?" He answered that they were doing well, thanks to my prayers. Then I asked him about one of the monks about whom a certain evil rumor was being spread. He answered me, "Believe me, father, this monk continues to live as he did before." When I heard this, I said, "Oh!" and immediately fell down in a stupor. I see myself standing before Golgotha in Jerusalem. Our Lord Jesus Christ was standing on Golgotha between the two thieves. I began to fall down to bow before him. At that moment I saw the Lord speak to the angels who were ministering to Him, and He said to them, "Cast him out, for he is an anti-Christ. Before My just judgment, he has also passed judgment on his brother." As the angels were pushing me away, I lost my *mantia,* and the angels kept it. Immediately, I came to myself and said to the monk visiting me, "This is an evil day for me." He asked me

> what I meant, and I told him about my vision, adding that the loss of the *mantia* meant that the protection of the Lord was no longer over me. From that day, I went into the deep desert and wandered there for seven years, never eating bread, never entering a house, and never speaking to anyone. After this time I once again saw the Lord. He returned my *mantia* to me.[34]

Brothers! Let us be attentive to ourselves! Let us try to purify ourselves not only from fleshly passions but from spiritual passions as well—vanity, lack of faith, envy, anger, love of money, and other such illnesses that apparently act only in the soul, without the body's participation. Actually, they do have an effect on the body, but only a subtle one that many do not notice at all. When we become vigilant and purify ourselves of these passions, we will slowly begin to love our neighbor, and this love will gradually weaken and destroy the desire to judge others. Let us constantly remember that there is no God-pleasing truth outside of poverty of spirit. Let us justify others and judge ourselves so that God will give us His grace and mercy, which He gives only to the humble and merciful. Amen.

CHAPTER 12

A Christian and His Passions

A certain great ascetic said, "We must endure our own deficiencies in the same way as we bear the sins of others, and to be condescending to the soul's sicknesses and incompleteness. At the same time you must not become lazy, but rather must be zealous in the work of improving and perfecting the self."[1]

"Don't become angry or shocked when you see in yourself the working of some passion. When a passion rises up in you, fight against it, trying to rein it in and root it out with humility and prayer."[2]

The confusion and shock we feel when we find the action of a passion in us is proof that the person has not come to know himself.[3]

In the light of the word of God, let us look at how we relate to our passions and weakness in order to gain a correct understanding of ourselves, and, based on this proper self-knowledge, we may be able to have control over ourselves.

Every person is conceived and born in sin.[4] Consequently, passions or sinful diseases of the body and soul are typical of our fallen nature.

But the passions are unnatural to our untainted human nature in the way that it was created. The passions are also unnatural to renewed human nature; they are only natural to fallen nature. Just as the symptoms of a disease of the body follow from a given ailment, sickness and death are natural to our body, which has lost its immortality and the qualities of eternity. Before our fall, immortality was natural to our body, and disease and death were unnatural.

Passions are also called sins in the general meaning of the word. When the Apostle Paul speaks of sin that dwells in man,[5] he means "sin" to be the general infection of evil in the whole human nature, in other words, passions. This state is called also a *carnal* state and a state of death.[6]

Before the redemption of human nature by our Saviour, mankind could not fight against passions. They forced him to listen to them; they lorded over him against even his will. With the help of holy baptism, the Christian himself casts off the yoke of sin; he receives the power and ability to fight against the passions.[7] Thus, the redeemed man, the renewed man, who has been settled in the spiritual Eden, the Church, is also given freedom. With his free will, he can act against the passions and defeat them in the Lord, or instead be subjected and enslaved to them. Thus, also in the earthly Eden, a choice was given to the first man—to be obedient to God's commandment or to break it.

Every time you resist the insistent desires of the passion, they weaken in you. Constant resistance destroys the passion. Every time you fall to the passion it becomes stronger, and constant enjoyment of the passions makes you their slave.

A Christian's struggle with his passion must reach the levels of crucifying the flesh with its passions and lusts.[8] In experienced spiritual warriors, it must reach even to the spilling of blood—give your blood and receive the Spirit, say the Fathers.[9] This means that only he who suffers in his body through willing or unwilling labors is capable of withstanding the sinful desires of the flesh, to suppress and silence them in himself. The body that is coddled and pampered is the house of the passions.

The God-Man who suffered and was crucified for us requires his followers and disciples to emulate his sufferings, to sacrifice all that is temporary for the eternal, all that is perishable for the undying. We must be disciples and followers of the God-Man by our very lives!

Ascetic labors are necessary for a Christian, but the labors themselves do not free a person from his passions. Only the right hand of the Almighty can free him, only the grace of the Holy Spirit.

Suppressing and mortifying the flesh through good works done with a careful following of the Gospel commandments gives a Christian true humility. True humility consists of complete self-denial, complete loyalty to God, and constant service to God. Such humility attracts divine grace into the soul. Divine grace, having illumined the soul, gives it spiritual senses, and the passions—these sinful feelings and desires of the flesh—end up powerless.[10]

The effect of the passions that please the carnal man is heavy and painful for the spiritual man. He is filled with revulsion for them. Even the smallest appearance or arousal of passions cause him to flee from them as though they were hungry, wild animals or a murderer. The spiritual man runs to the haven of prayer, to the protection of the teachings of the Gospels, to the cover of God.

The soul that has not fulfilled the Gospel commandments and the body that has not done good deeds of virtue are not capable of becoming the temple of divine grace, the temple of the Holy Spirit.

The essence of ascesis is found in the fulfillment of the commandments. He who refuses to deny his body through work, fasting, vigils, and prayer, instead giving power over himself to his carnal mind-set, which feeds and encourages the passion, cannot become the doer of the divine commandments.

Only death can completely free even the saints of God from the influence of sin. The passions have no shame—they can even appear inside a person on his deathbed. Even on the deathbed one must never stop being watchful over oneself. Believe in your body's dispassion only when it lies in the coffin.

The passions, which remain in the Christian, constantly force him to be on guard, constantly call him out to battle, and in so doing end up helping his spiritual progress. Thus evil, through our bad intentions, works for good, because of the all-wise Divine providence.[11]

The heavy and massive millstone crushes the grains of wheat into flour, making tough, hard wheat good for baking bread. The heavy battle with the passions crushes the heart of man and his proud spirit, forcing him to acknowledge his own fallen state by vividly revealing these passions within him. It forces him to recognize the necessity of redemption; it destroys his trust in himself and transfers all his hope to the Redeemer.

We must believe that the seeds of all passions are contained in the ancestral sin and that we have been born with an inclination toward all forms of sin. Thus, we must not be shocked by the appearance of any passion within us as though it were something unusual or strange.

Because of the unique characteristics of each body and soul, because of the effect of one's environment and the particular set of circumstances surrounding each life, a particular passion acts the most obviously in one person, and a different passion acts prominently in another person. One person is inclined toward love of money, another eats too much. One is inclined toward carnal lusts, another thirsts for the useless honors of the world. Whoever has not entertained a particular passion should not think that it may not uncover itself in his heart later, when the time is more appropriate for its ripening.

One must therefore be constantly ready to battle against all the passions. One must be especially vigilant against the passions that appear more often than others, those that most bother the particular person.

Passions that are natural to our corrupted human nature differ greatly from passions that each person willingly cultivates in himself. The strength of the latter is incomparably greater than the former. But repentance, that all-powerful medicine, adequately treats all diseases in the one who desires to use it.

In spiritual warfare, one must first arm oneself against the foundational passions. The sins that come as their consequence will wither and die on their own. He who has rejected carnal pleasures, the glory of men, the gathering of riches, a scattered life, will not fall to the sins of anger and sorrow. He will not be affected by either pride or envy. Instead, he will walk without hindrance along the path of the commandments of God toward salvation, toward the complete knowledge of God that is only open to those with a pure heart.

The leader of all passions in this war is unbelief. It opens the doors of the soul to love of money and power, to carnal lusts, to anger, depression, and the pinnacle of these evils—despair.

The door into the soul for every Christian virtue, consequently, is faith.

The passions live secretly in people who lead a scattered, inattentive way of life. For the most part, such people are content with their passions and do not notice them. For the most part, they excuse them, while sometimes even considering these passions to be the purest, most exalted virtues.

Only the true Christian, who constantly watches over his heart, who studies the Law of God day and night, who tries to fulfill the commandments of the Gospel with assiduity, can see his passions. The more he is purified and progresses spiritually, the more he sees his own passions. Finally, the eyes of the mind that is healed completely by the Gospels see the bottomless abyss of the fall of man. The Christian sees the full effects of this fall in himself because he sees his passions. The passions are the badge of the sinful, death-bearing disease that has struck all mankind.

Into what kind of a state will a man be led by the proper appreciation of his own passions, his own fall? Sorrow over his sins, bitter, inconsolable tears. No earthly joy can stop or console this sorrow. Only divine grace can stop it occasionally, giving the weeping and ravaged heart hope in salvation, spiritual consolation, and heavenly joys, flowing from the peace of Christ.

Into what kind of a state will a man be led by the revelation of the effects of the passions? Such a man will be inspired to begin a forceful battle against the passions. The ascetic of Christ increases his prayers, his fasting, his vigils, his prayers on bended knee; and showing his calamitous state to God, he begs for mercy with his silent compunction and the pain in his heart. "But when they troubled me, I put on sackcloth, and humbled my soul with fasting, and my prayer shall turn into mine own bosom. As one weeping and mourning, so I humbled myself."[12]

How do the passions appear? They show themselves in thought, fantasy, and sinful desires. Thoughts and fantasy sometimes unexpectedly appear before the mind, sometimes they approach it silently like a thief, and sinful desires similarly appear in the heart and the body. Sinful thoughts, mental images, and feelings incline a person to sin in actual act, or at the very least, to enjoy and feel pleasure in his slavery to sinful thoughts, fantasy, feelings, and to sin in his imagination and emotions.

The Christian ascetic must reject not only sins of action but also sins of imagination and sins of emotion. Every passion becomes stronger each time one finds pleasure in it and fulfills its illicit demands, even in the imagination. A passion that is committed in actual deed or has been planted into the soul and tended over the course of many years becomes the person's master. A long time is needed, a bloody battle must be waged, and God's special mercy and help is required to cast off the yoke of the passions, either from a single fall into a serious mortal sin, or from illicit, willful enjoyment of sin in the secret spiritual bridal chamber, which is dedicated to Christ.

It is impossible for the passions that live inside a person to not be revealed in his thoughts, words, and actions. For anyone who is on the road to true Christian asceticism, true Christian perfection, when exposure of the passions is joined with even a little bit of enjoyment, it is called and considered a fall into sin.[13] Such falls are treated by immediate repentance.

Such falls are an inalienable part of the fallenness of the Old Adam, that is, human nature corrupted and infected by sin. Especially, the new ascetic should not stop to enjoy sinful thoughts, fantasy, and feelings. He is not yet able to avoid sinning in mind, in imagination, and in his emotions; he is not yet able to avoid sinning in word and in deed. These sins are treated by immediate repentance.

I am not speaking here of falls into mortal sins or about the willfully sinful life, which is complete fallenness. Here, I am speaking of small sins that one falls into as a result of human weakness. These are called forgivable sins; even the righteous ones were not completely free of them.

The Scriptures witness that a righteous man will fall seven times, and yet seven times will he rise up again through repentance.[14] The more we are purified, the less frequent our sinful desires torment us, but at the same time, they become more subtle, less obvious, and sometimes they seduce and fool even men filled with the grace of God.[15] Such falls into sin actually protect one from becoming arrogant; they become a reason for humility by keeping the ascetic constantly on the salvific path of repentance.[16]

If we have such a sober knowledge of our own selves, we will be able to preserve peace in our souls, never becoming upset or depressed or shocked when we uncover the effects of passions in ourselves. Sometimes these passions are light, but sometimes they are quite serious. We must courageously battle the passions.

The passions will not stop appearing in us and attacking us until the grave! Let us prepare ourselves for a lifelong battle against them, firmly convinced that we cannot always achieve victory against them, but that because of the frailty of our nature we will sometimes be defeated. Nevertheless these defeats themselves can serve to help our spiritual progress by supporting and strengthening repentance and its consequent humility in us.

Let us not trust our victories over passions, let us not be proud of such victories. The passions, like the demons that wield them as weapons, are cunning. They sometimes pretend to be defeated in order to give us a chance to become proud, because then their victory over us will be the more convenient and definite.

Let us prepare ourselves to look at our victories and defeats in the same way—courageously, dispassionately, unemotionally.

If you have fallen to sinful fantasy, felt pleasure from sinful thoughts, uttered a vain or foolish word, eaten too much, or done any other wrong such as this, do not be distressed and do not lose heart. If you do, you will only add more evil to already committed evil.[17] Repent immediately before the God who sees all hearts, try to improve and perfect yourself, become assured in the necessity of the strictest vigilance over yourself, and, maintaining calmness in your soul, firmly and with determination continue your spiritual journey.

God is our salvation, not our deeds. By the deeds of faith, by fulfilling the commandments of the Gospels, we prove the truth of our faith and our faithfulness to God.

Do not pay attention to the thoughts of false humility, which after every sinful fall tell you that you have angered your God irrevocably, that God has turned His face from you, that He has left you and forgotten you. You must recognize the source of these thoughts by their fruits. Their fruits are depression, weakness in spiritual struggles, and sometimes even the abandonment of ascetic labors for a long time or forever.

If we know that every ascetic must face both victories and defeats on the long and difficult path of spiritual life and that our limited, weak, sinful nature must occasionally assert itself, then how much more does God, our Creator and the Establisher of our ascetic labors, know it as well. With compassion, He looks at the falls of his ascetic, and for courageous constancy and loyalty, he prepares for him a crown of truth, victory, and glory.

How desirable is the purity of the heart and body! Through it we can see God.[18] This purity is gained by constant and ascetical labors against impurity. In order to enter this labor against impurity, it is necessary for it to become obvious before the eyes of our mind. It is opened in thoughts, in fantasies, in carnal desires. Whoever has never fought against impurity, who does not know it, considering himself pure, is in the worst kind of self-deception and is in danger of suddenly falling into the pit of mortal sins. Impurity is a telltale sign of the fallen nature, while purity is a gift of the grace of God that comes to purify a person when he labors correctly.

There is a great difference between sinning intentionally because of an inclination toward a particular sin, and sinning unintentionally because of human weakness while still maintaining a disposition to please God. There is a great difference between leading a sinful life and satiating all sinful desires and passions, and being tripped up by sins because of weakness, human deficiencies, and sinful disease, all the while still walking along the path of God.

Premature dispassion is very dangerous! Premature spiritual joy given by divine grace is dangerous. Supernatural gifts can destroy an ascetic who has not learned from his own falls into sin, who is inexperienced in life, who has not become skilled in the warfare with sinful thoughts, who does not have detailed knowledge of the cunning and hatred of the demons, and who is still under the influence of fickle human nature. A person is free to choose good or evil. Even if a person is a vessel of divine grace, he can end up misusing the very grace he was given. Because of its gifts, he may become arrogant and consider himself far above his neighbors; because of grace, he can begin to trust in himself. A consequence of trusting oneself is usually laziness, gradual lessening of ascetic labors, and even abandonment of the spiritual life. Following on the footsteps of this laziness is a sudden arousal of carnal desires in the soul and body of these holy men, which can carry them away like a strong current and can cast them out into the abyss of carnal lust, even into spiritual death.

Our God Who loves mankind, "Who desires all men to be saved and to come to the knowledge of the truth,"[19] allowed His servants, His beloved to be attacked during the whole course of their existence by external and inner sorrows. The war with passions and the sorrows that arise as a result of the passions are incomparably heavier than all external temptations. The heaviness and labor into which a Christian is led by this invisible, inner warfare raises its significance to that of the martyr's suffering. I repeat the words of the Fathers who were experienced in this warfare: "Give your blood, and accept the Spirit." Only the true servants of Christ, who assiduously fulfill the commandments of His Gospel, can carry the burden of such a difficult spiritual labor. "Keeping the commandments teaches a person his weaknesses," said St Simeon the New Theologian.[20] The entire structure of our salvation is built on the acknowledgment and understanding of our own sinfulness.

What a strange way of life it may seem to those who look only skin-deep. "Keeping the commandments teaches a person his weaknesses!" But these are the words of experience. Only when a person diligently fulfills the commandments of Christ can he see the multitude of his passions. Only when a person diligently fulfills the commandments of Christ can he become convinced of the utter powerlessness of the Old Adam when faced with the life of the New Adam. Only then can he see the truth of the fact that the spiritual law can only be followed with the mercies of Christ.[21]

In the all-powerful right hand of God's providence, even sin that makes its home in a man, which encompasses his entire essence, which covers all the members of his body and soul, actually helps that man's spiritual progress! But only if that person is a true Christian.

Poverty of spirit, a humble acknowledgment of one's own sinfulness, the knowledge of the necessity of a Redeemer, the striving of one's entire being to confess to our Redeemer, the Son of God, and God our Lord Jesus Christ—these are the fruits of the struggle with the passions. These fruits are the pledge of eternal blessedness.

These spiritual fruits are unknown to the son of this age. He serves the passions, considers himself full of spiritual worth, and sees his many virtues. Either he expects nothing in heaven since he never thinks of heaven, or he expects ample rewards there, as though it were a debt owed to him. Due to his profound ignorance of the only true virtue, he expects rewards in heaven. But this virtue that he lacks is Christianity itself!

The servant of God who fulfills the commandments of the Gospel reveals passions within himself in ever-increasing numbers. Even as the grace of the Holy Spirit within him creates blessed spiritual states such as poverty of spirit, tears, meekness, chastity, and spiritual wisdom, he considers himself the worst of all sinners, a man who has never done anything good, a man guilty of countless sins, worthy of eternal suffering in fiery Gehenna for constantly breaking God's Law.

The Holy Fathers, seeing in themselves the blossoming of spiritual fruits due to their struggle with passions, did not want the warfare to end. They wanted to continue the struggle courageously until the end.[22] What blessed men! They sought no other perfection except perfect humility. They never sought to find hope in salvation in themselves; instead, they trusted wholly in Christ. Where there is no humility, there is no Christian virtue, and where there is true humility, there are all the virtues in their fullness; Christ Himself is there. All the passions and the enemy who wields them "shall be able to do nothing against" the servant of Christ, and "the son of iniquity," sin, "shall not be able to hurt him."[23]

Let us follow in the footsteps of the Fathers, and we will reach the far shore of eternal blessedness. Amen.

CHAPTER 13

On Habits

Habits are as strong as the essential characteristics that make up our character. Thus, the follower of the Lord Jesus Christ must acquire good habits and turn away from bad ones.

Young man! Be wise and careful—in the years of youth, pay especial attention to the acquisition of good habits because in the years of your maturity, you will rejoice in the riches that you gathered without much toil during your youth.

Do not think it is a small matter to give in to your sinful desires, even if they seem insignificant. Every time you give in to such a desire, you will leave an indelible stamp on your soul. This impression can sometimes be very strong, leading to the formation of a sinful habit.

Did the gambler know, when he touched his cards for the first time, that the game would become his passion? Did the alcoholic know, when he drank his first shot, that he was starting on the path to suicide? For suicide is exactly what this terrible habit is, since it destroys both the body and the soul.

One careless glance can often wound the heart; several repeated glances can so damage the wound that it barely heals, even with numerous prayers and long years of ascetic labor, and tears.

Those of you who raise and guide our youth! Give the young people an opportunity to form good habits, and turn them away from bad habits as these are a terrible calamity.

Sinful habits are like chains weighing a person down—they take away his moral freedom and forcefully keep him in the foul-smelling bog of the passions.

Only one sinful habit is enough to destroy a person because it will constantly open the door of the soul to all other sins and all passions.

Train yourself in modesty—do not allow yourself any forwardness toward others, do not even touch another person without need; and the habit of modesty will make the great virtue of chastity easy for you to obtain. Your near ones, feeling the pledge of modesty that lives in you, will always be respectful in your presence, feeling the same kind of reverence they feel before a holy object.

Nothing destroys chastity as completely as habitual forward and brazen behavior and free interaction with members of the other sex, which contradict the rule of modesty.

Learn to be moderate in eating—by your moderation, you will give health and strength to your body and wakefulness to your mind, which is so necessary in the work of salvation and is extremely useful in earthly work.

Gluttony is nothing less than an evil habit, a foolish, insatiable fulfillment of a natural desire that has been corrupted by ill-use.

Train yourself to eat only the simplest food. For those who have acquired this habit, the simplest food becomes more flavorful than the most refined gourmet dishes; and we do not even begin to speak about how much healthier such food is.

What freedom and moral strength is gained by a person who has acquired the habit of eating simple food, even if this habit may seem insignificant and immaterial! But with it, a person requires only the smallest amount of food and little attention and work in its preparation. Even if the one who has acquired this habit is poor, he hardly notices his poverty.

But leaving a table that is laden with rich and fine foods for a simple table is very difficult! Circumstances have forced many to this sudden change, and many have lost their health and even their moral center as a result. Avoid this problem by slowly developing a wise and temperate habit of eating simple food.

Especially for those who desire to dedicate themselves to the service of Christ, such a habit of eating simple food is priceless due to its consequences—it allows one to choose the most remote place to live, and it makes frequent interaction with other people unnecessary. In this way, by removing all reasons for potential earthly distractions, one can be completely dedicated to contemplation of God and prayer.

All the saints took great care, not only to acquire the habit of moderate eating but also the habit of simple eating. The apostle Peter's daily food cost no more than a few copper coins.

What a terrible passion is drunkenness! This is a passion—a sickness—that enters the body through desire and very easily becomes as powerful as an essential characteristic of the person.

The servant of Christ must guard himself not only from drunkenness but also from the habit of frequent drinking of wine, which inflames the flesh and arouses animalistic desires. "And do not be drunk with wine, in which is dissipation," said St Paul.[1] It is permissible to drink wine in very small doses, but whoever cannot limit himself to moderate consumption would do better to abstain from it completely.

St Pimen the Great said, "The ascetic needs a sober mind above all other things."[2] Wine deprives a person of the ability to keep his mind sober. When an ascetic gives way to the influence of wine, then all his passions attack his weakened and darkened mind and he is no longer in any state to battle them. Tied down by the effect of the wine, he falls into the pit of sin! In one second, all the spiritual fruits he had gathered over a long time are destroyed because the Holy Spirit will not stay in those who are defiled by sin. This is why St Isaiah the Egyptian Hermit said that the lovers of wine will never be found worthy of spiritual gifts.[3] These gifts require constant purity if they are to remain in a person, and such purity is only possible with constant sobriety and vigilance.

Love of money, irritability, pride, and rudeness—these evil habits of the soul are formed when we listen to the corrupted desires of our fallen nature. They become stronger and weigh a person down more and more with habit.

The same rule applies to carnal lust, despite the fact that it is natural to the fallen man. Blessed is the youth who understands that such desires should be resisted from the first time they appear in him, that they should be bridled by the Law of God and wisdom. If such desires are limited from their first appearance, they will easily submit to the mind, and their demands will become weaker with time, acting like a slave who is chained. A desire fulfilled is a desire that will return with twice the demands. Carnal lust, which takes complete control of our reason once we become accustomed to it, becomes a lord over the body and the soul, slowly mortifying both.

In general, all passions develop within a person when he allows them access; the more one allows them in, the greater the habit; and eventually, a sinful habit gives passions lordship over a person.

"Fear evil habits," said St Isaac the Syrian, "even more than demons."[4]

When sinful desires begin to act in us, we must reject them. If we do, their next attack will be weaker, and finally they will cease completely. But if we sin, every time the desire returns it will be stronger because the sin gains increasingly more power over us the more we sin, and finally it becomes habitual.

The sins that we have a habit of committing seem light to us, no matter how devastating they may be to our spiritual reality. But a new sin is horrifying to the soul, and it will be slow to fall prey to it.

Passions are evil habits; virtues are good habits. Here, we speak of passions and virtues that are acquired and assimilated by a person as a result of his actions and his lifestyle. Sometimes, the Fathers call passions various qualities of the sickness that arose in us as a result of the Fall, or various forms of sinfulness that are common to all mankind; we are born with these passions. Conversely, the virtues in this case are the essential, natural, good qualities of a person. Such passions and such virtues do not leave a serious impression on a person; an impression is left only by inclinations that are developed willfully through constant or frequent fulfillment of the demands of sinful desire.

The servant of Christ must be as free as possible from sinful habits, so that they do not hinder his way to Christ. He must separate himself from his habits—not only the obviously sinful ones but also any that may lead to sin, such as habitual luxury and ease or a state of perpetual distraction.

Sometimes the most insignificant habit binds our feet and leaves us chained to earth, while we should be already in heaven.

Young man! I repeat this salvific counsel—while you are still in your moral freedom, avoid evil habits as you would avoid prison and its chains. Gather good habits, through which your moral freedom is preserved, confirmed, and impressed into your being.

If anyone in his mature years decides to become a servant of Christ and has unfortunately gathered many evil habits or has become used to living in luxury and ease, which usually keep the soul in a state of paralysis, he must not become despondent or duplicitous about the difficulties of his path. He must bravely enter the fray against his evil habits. Victory over them is not impossible with God's help.

Willful determination, blessed and bulwarked by the grace of Christ, can defeat even the most rooted habits.

At first, the habit will cruelly fight back against the one who desires to throw off his yoke, and at first this will seem impossible. But after some time, after constant warfare, after every single refusal to cooperate with it, the habit becomes weaker and weaker.

If during the battle you are defeated because of some unforeseen circumstances, do not be distressed and fall into despair. Just begin the battle anew.

Forceful warfare against sinful habits is considered by God to be akin to martyrdom, and he who defeats his habit is crowned with the crown of the confessors who labor for the Law of God.

The merciful and all-powerful God accepts all who come to Him. He stretches out His right hand to help our weakness. And so, even if you are full of evil habits that weigh you down like chains, do not despair of receiving your freedom. Begin the unseen warfare, fight bravely and constantly, and admit your defeats bravely. Sometimes God lets us see ourselves as we really are so that we can know through our own experiences how weak we are in our abandonment. With this knowledge, we will always hold on to God, Who alone can defeat sin in those who truly see themselves as defeated by sin. Amen.

CHAPTER 14

Conscience

The conscience is a sense of the human spirit, a subtle, bright voice that distinguishes good from evil.

This sense is better than the mind at distinguishing the one from the other.

It is harder to fool the conscience than the mind.

The conscience is capable of fighting long and hard against the mind deluded by its love of sin.

The conscience is Natural Law.[1]

The conscience guided mankind before the Law was written down. Fallen mankind slowly assimilated an incorrect manner of thinking about God, good, and evil; and this false reasoning passed on its deception to the conscience. The Written Law became indispensable as a guide to true knowledge of God and a God-pleasing way of life.

Christ's teaching, confirmed by holy baptism, heals the soul from the evil infection of sin.[2] The correct activity of the conscience, renewed in us by baptism, is strengthened and raised up by following the teaching of Christ.

For the conscience to be in a healthy condition and functioning correctly, it must be oriented according to the teachings of the Orthodox Church because every incorrect thought accepted by a person has an influence on the conscience—it begins to shift the conscience away from the correct path.

Willful sin darkens, dulls, and deafens the conscience, and puts it to sleep.

Any sin that is not purified by repentance leaves its negative influence on the conscience. A life of repeated willful sin can almost kill the conscience.

However, to kill the conscience is not possible; it will accompany a person all the way to the Final Judgment of Christ, and there it will accuse the person.

According to the explanation of the Holy Fathers, the *adversary* of a person, mentioned in the Gospels, is the conscience.[3]

This is true! It is an adversary because it fights against any act of ours that is contrary to God's Law.

Preserve peace with this adversary on your earthly path to heaven, so that it will not become your accuser in that moment when your eternal fate will be decided.

The Scriptures write: "A true witness delivers souls."[4] A true witness is a clear conscience—it will deliver the soul that hearkens to its counsels from sins before death, and from eternal suffering after death.

Just as the edge of a knife is sharpened by a whetstone, the conscience is sharpened by Christ. It becomes illumined by the study of the Gospels. It becomes honed by the fulfillment of the Gospel commandments.

A conscience illumined and honed by the Gospels clearly and exactly shows the person his sins, even the smallest ones.

Do not fight against your adversary, the conscience! Otherwise, you will be bereft of spiritual freedom—sin will imprison and bind you.

The sharpness of the conscience is very fragile—it must be constantly whetted. This is done when the person fulfills all the demands of the conscience and washes away any sin (committed either in weakness or by the fallen desires of the flesh) with tears of repentance.

From laziness and apparently insignificant sins, we slowly progress to more serious lapses into sin.

What does it matter? Is this a big sin? What kind of sin is it? This is not a sin!—these are the thoughts of the one who cares nothing for his salvation, when he decides to taste of the fruit of sin forbidden by God's Law. Based on such absurd reasoning, he constantly battles his conscience.

The conscience's sharp edge becomes dulled and its light dims; the darkness and cold of ignorance and lack of feeling grow in the soul.

This lack of sensitivity eventually becomes the normal state of the soul. Often it is content in this state; often it even considers it to be a state pleasing to God (i.e., a clean conscience). But such a state is nothing more than the loss of the sense of one's own sinfulness, the loss of a sense of grace and the spiritual life, a sleepiness and blindness of the conscience.[5]

In this state of terrible darkness and coldness, various sins freely enter the soul and find a comfortable home there. Such sins that settle in the soul eventually become habits as well-rooted as aspects of our nature, and sometimes even more so. These sinful habits are called passions. A person does not notice this, and yet he becomes bound on all sides by sin, in complete slavery and captivity to it.

Whoever has allowed himself to fall prey to sin by constantly ignoring the helpful reminders of the conscience can only break the bonds of his slavery and defeat the passions that have become natural to him with great difficulty, and only with the special assistance of God.

Beloved brother! Guard your conscience with all possible attention and care.

Guard your conscience before God. Fulfill all the commandments of God, both those visible to all and those that no one sees, which are visible only to your conscience and God Himself.

Guard your conscience before your brother. Do not be content with the mere appearance of goodness to your neighbor! Make sure that your very conscience is satisfied with your actions. It will only be satisfied when not only your deeds but also your heart itself is correctly inclined toward loving your neighbor, as the Gospel commands.

Guard your conscience with regard to the things of this world. Avoid all excess, decadence, and irreverence, remembering that all things utilized by us are the creation of God, the gifts of God to us men.

Guard your conscience. Do not forget that you are the image and likeness of God, that you are obliged to present this image in purity and holiness to God Himself.

Woe to you if God will not recognize His image, will not find in it any similarity with Himself! He will utter the dreadful words: "I do not know you."[6] The unworthy image will be cast out into the undying fires of Gehenna.

Endless joy will embrace that soul in which the Lord will see similarity with Himself, in which He will find not only that beauty that He gave it when He created it according to His eternal goodness, but a beauty restored and increased by His redemption, and preserved in undefiled wholeness by rejection of all sins and the fulfillment of all the Gospel commandments.

The conscience—never silent, always just—guards us and reminds us of what we must preserve, and what we must reject. Amen.

CHAPTER 15

The Eight Chief Passions with Their Subdivisions and Offshoots

1. Gluttony

Overeating, drunkenness, breaking or lessening the fast, secret eating, indulgence in eating, and intemperance in food in general. An incorrect or excessive attention to the body and the stomach and its needs, from which we develop self-love and from which come unfaithfulness to God, the Church, the virtues, and other people.

2. Fornication

Carnal lust, impure desires and feelings in the body, impure feelings and desires in the soul and heart, and acceptance of impure thoughts—conversation with them, pleasure in them, cooperation with them, persistence in them, lustful imaginings and bondage to them. Not keeping watch over the senses, especially sight, in which is found brazenness that destroys all virtues. Using foul language and reading sensual books. Natural carnal sins: fornication and adultery. Sins of the flesh contrary to nature: self-stimulation, homosexuality, bestiality, and others like them.

3. Avarice (Greed)

Love of money, or a general love for property and riches. The desire to become rich, thinking of ways to get rich, and imagining future riches. Fear of old age, sudden poverty, sickness, or exile. Miserliness. Avarice. Unfaithfulness to God and lack of trust in His providence. Passionate attachment or sickly, excessive love for various perishable things that destroy peace of soul. Preoccupation with earthly matters. Love of presents. Stealing things belonging to others. Usury. Cruelty to the poor and to all who are in need. Thievery and brigandage.

4. Anger

Irascibility, acceptance of angry thoughts; harboring evil thoughts about others and thoughts of revenge, disturbing the heart with anger, and the darkening of the mind through anger. Inappropriate yelling, arguments, fighting, cruel and hurtful words, striking others, pushing others, murder. Remembrance of evils, hatred, fighting, revenge, slander, judging others, and disturbing or offending your neighbor.

5. Sorrow

Causing sorrow to others, sadness, lack of hope in God, doubt in the promises of God, lack of gratitude to God for everything He has given, lack of faith, lack of patience, not blaming oneself, being offended at others, complaining, and rejecting one's cross.

6. Despair

Lack of enthusiasm for any good deed, especially prayer. Not performing the daily rule of prayer (both in church and at home), not praying constantly, ceasing the reading of spiritual books, and lack of attention or hurrying in prayer. Lack of care for the spiritual life. Laziness, too much sleep, and lying around or lazing about. Constant moving about from place to place. Frequently leaving one's cell for walks and visits with friends. Idle talk, jokes, blasphemy. Ceasing prostrations or other physical labors. Forgetting your sins. Forgetting the commandments of Christ. Lack of reverence for holy things. Lack of the fear of God. Hardness of heart. Lack of feeling for others. Hopelessness.

7. Vanity

Seeking the praise of men. Boasting. The desire for and seeking of earthly glories. Love for beautiful clothes, carriages, servants, or decorations in your cell. Paying attention to your physical appearance, the way you speak, or other qualities of your body. Inclination to the learning and sciences of this fallen age and seeking to succeed in them solely for earthly gain and glory. Being afraid to confess your sins; hiding your sins before people and your spiritual Father. Cunning. Self-justification.

Contradiction. Trusting in your own reason. Hypocrisy. Lies. Duplicity. People-pleasing. Envy. Demeaning others. Pretending to act unnaturally for the benefit of others. Lack of conscience. Demonic habits.

8. Pride

Disdain of our neighbors. Preferring ourselves first before all others. Brazenness. Darkening of the mind and heart; nailing them to the earth. Blasphemy. Lack of faith. Delusion. False opinions of oneself. Lack of submission to the Law of God and the Church; following your own fallen will. Reading heretical, impure, or vain books. Lack of submission to the ruling authority. Rude mockery of others. Abandoning the humble emulation of Christ and the path of humility and silence. Loss of simplicity. Loss of love for God and your neighbor. False teachings. Heresy. Godlessness. Ignorance. The death of the soul.

These are the sicknesses, the open sores that together constitute the great wound, the decrepitude of the Old Adam that befell him when he fell. The holy Prophet Isaiah speaks thus about this great wound: "From the sole of the foot even to the head, There is no soundness in it, But wounds and bruises and putrefying sores; They have not been closed or bound up, Or soothed with ointment."[1] According to Abba Dorotheos (Sermon 1), this means that the wound, sin, is not just partial, not just on one part of the body, but on the whole body—it covers the body, the soul, and has taken control of all the qualities and powers of the person. God named this great wound death, when He forbade Adam and Eve to eat the fruit from the tree of the knowledge of good and evil, saying: "for in the day that you eat of it you shall surely die."[2] Immediately after they ate the forbidden fruit, our forefathers felt eternal death. In their eyes appeared carnal feelings; they saw that they were naked. In the knowledge of the nakedness of their bodies was reflected the nakedness of the soul that had lost the beauty of innocence, the soul that used to house the Holy Spirit. The eyes were awakened to sensuality, the soul felt shame, in which all the sinful desires are united—pride, impurity, sorrow, despair, and hopelessness! Spiritual death is a horrible wound; its consequent decrepitude is incurable since it came about as a result of the loss of the likeness of God! The Apostle calls this great wound "the law of sin which is in my members, this body of death,"[3] because the deadened mind and heart have completely inclined to the earth. They are slaves of the perishable desires of the flesh, they are darkened and made heavy, they have themselves become flesh. This flesh is already incapable of interaction with God![4] This flesh is incapable of inheriting the eternal, heavenly blessedness![5] The great wound has spread itself over the entire human race, becoming an unfortunate inheritance of every person.

Looking at my own great wound, seeing the lifelessness in me, I am filled with terrible sorrow! I do not know what I must do. Will I follow the footsteps of the Old Adam, who, seeing his nakedness, hurried to hide himself from God? Will I, like he, justify myself, blaming the sin that is within me? It is useless to try to hide from the all-knowing God! It is useless to justify yourself before Him, Who always prevails when He is judged.[6]

Instead of putting on fig leaves, I will dress myself in the tears of repentance. Instead of self-justification, I will bring Him sincere confession. Robed in repentance and tears, I will stand before my God. But where will I find my God? In Eden? I am exiled from there! And a cherubim standing before the gate will not let me enter! Through the heaviness of my flesh I am nailed to the earth, my prison!

O thou, sinful descendant of Adam, rise up! The light has illumined your prison—God has Himself come to the country of your exile in order to bring you back to the heavenly homeland that you have lost. You wanted to know good and evil? He leaves you that knowledge. You wanted to become *as gods* and through this became like unto the demons, in your body like chattel and beasts. But God, uniting Himself with you, makes you god according to grace. He forgives you your sins. Even this is little! He uproots the very source of evil from your soul, the very infection of sin, the poison that the devil hurled into your soul, and He gives you medicine for the entire path of your earthly life, for healing from sins, no matter how many times you become infected with it again because of your weakness. This medicine is the confession of sins. Do you want to take off the Old Adam, you who through holy baptism are already robed in the New Adam, but through your own lawlessness hastened to reawaken decrepitude and death in yourself, to throttle life, to make it half dead? Do you, a slave of sin who inclines to it repeatedly through force of habit, wish to return to freedom and righteousness? Immerse yourself in humility! Defeat that vain shame that teaches you to be a hypocrite and cunningly pretends to be righteous, thereby keeping and strengthening spiritual death in yourself. Cast out sin; enter the fray with your sins through sincere confession. This healing must precede all other medicine; without it, the medicines of prayer, tears, fasting, and all others will be insufficient, ineffective, inadequate. Go, you proud man, go to your spiritual Father; seek the mercy of your heavenly Father at his feet! Only sincere and frequent confession can free you from sinful habits, can make your confession fruitful, a complete and true healing.

In the short, rare moment of compunction, during which the eyes of one's mind are opened for self-knowledge, I wrote this to denounce myself and to instruct, remind, and teach all of you. And you, who with faith and love in Christ read these words and may find in these something useful, bring a heartfelt sigh and prayer for my soul, which has suffered a great deal from the waves of sin, which has often seen before itself the inevitability of inundation by sins and death, which only finds comfort in one harbor—the confession of sins.

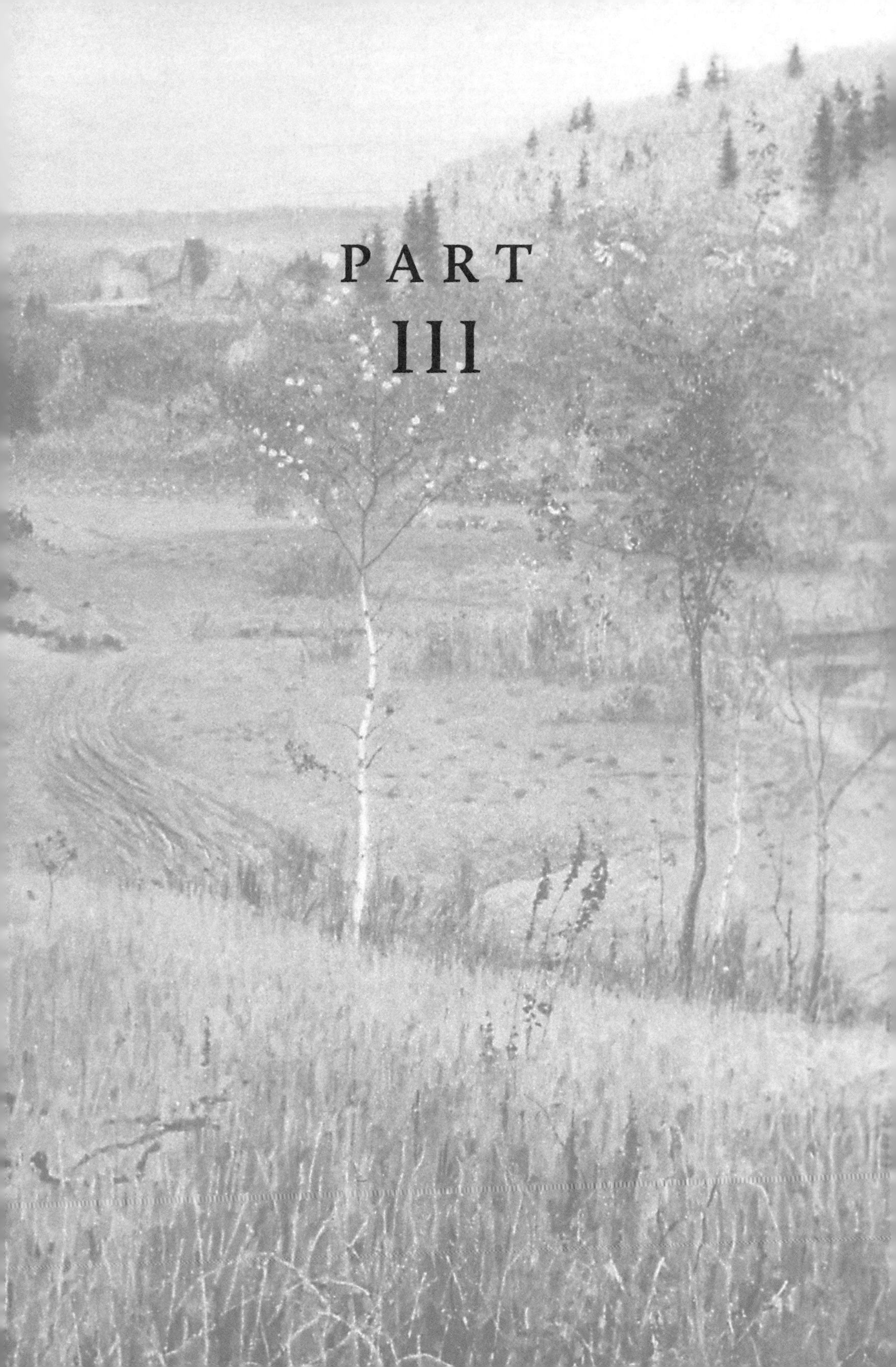

PART III

REFLECTION

Thoughts on the Shores of the Sea

To whom shall I liken a Christian who bears the sorrows of the earthly life with truly spiritual wisdom? He can be compared to a wanderer who stands on the shore of a stormy sea. Angry gray waves come crashing at his feet and, having struck the sand, dissipate at his feet into fine spray. The sea, fighting with the wind, screams, raises waves like mountains, seethes, and boils. The waves are born from and consume each other; their heads are crowned with snow-white foam, and the sea that is covered by them looks like a single immeasurable beastly maw, ringed with teeth. The mysterious wanderer looks on this frightening sight with a calm soul. Only his eyes are intent on the sea, but where are his thoughts, where is his heart? His thought is intent on the gates of death; his heart—on the judgment of Christ. He sees what lies ahead with his mind and his senses: here are his worries; here is his fear. From this, the fear of earthly temptations flees. The winds calm down; the sea becomes peaceful. Where the angry waves once rose, now the surface of the sea is untroubled by waves. After the boiling fury, they rest in death-like silence. In a transparent mirror, they reflect the evening sun when its stands above Kronstadt and spreads its rays along the Bay of Finland toward the waters of the Neva, toward Petersburg. What a beautiful view, so familiar to the residents of the Sergiev Hermitage! This sky, this shore, these buildings—how many proud, angry waves have they seen, crowned with foam? And all of them have passed; all have lain down in the silence of the grave and coffin. And those that will come in the future will lie down likewise! What is so unsteady, so fleeting, as a crown made of wet foam?

Looking from the quiet monastic haven on the sea of the world, boiling with the storm of the passions, I thank You, O my King and my God! You brought me into the safety of the holy monastery! You hid me "in the secret place of Thy presence from the provoking of all men." You covered me in a pavilion "from the strife of tongues."[1] Of this only is my soul sorrowful, only of this ignorance am I worried: will I ever leave this place? Will I ever leave this shore of the whirling, unsettled sea of the world to go to the "house of God, with a voice of rejoicing and thanksgiving, the noise of such as keep holy-day,"[2] will I come to live there for the ages of ages? Why should I worry about earthly sorrows—"in God have I put my trust; I will not fear what man can do unto me."[3]

Sergiev Hermitage, 1843.

CHAPTER 16

On the Virtues That Act Against the Eight Chief Sinful Passions

1. Abstinence

Abstinence from excessive consumption of food and drink, especially wine. Accurate keeping of the fasts established by the Church. Reining in the flesh through temperate and unvarying foods from which all passions in general begin to weaken, especially self-love, which consists of excess love of the flesh, the stomach, and its pleasure.

2. Chastity

Avoidance of all manner of carnal sins. Avoidance of sensual conversations and reading; avoidance of speaking impure, sensual, duplicitous words. Preservation of the senses, including sight and sound, but especially touch. Modesty. Rejection of impure thoughts and imaginings. Silence. Stillness. Serving the sick and crippled. Remembrance of death and hell. The beginning of chastity is the mind that is not disturbed by carnal thoughts and imaginings; the perfection of chastity is purity that sees God directly.

3. Non-acquisitiveness

Being content with only necessities. Hatred of luxuries and comfort. Giving alms to the poor. Following Christ's commandments. Love of evangelical poverty. Hope in the providence of God. Calmness and freedom of the spirit. Not being beholden to anyone in the financial sense. Gentleness of heart.

4. Meekness

Avoidance of angry thoughts and disturbance of the heart through anger. Patient bearing of ills. Emulation of Christ, who called his disciple to take up His cross. Peace in the heart. Quietness of mind. Christian strength and courage. Ignoring offenses. Lack of hatred.

5. Blessed Sorrow

Feeling the universal fall of mankind and one's own spiritual poverty, and grieving for them. The sorrow of the mind and compunction of heart—from them, the beginning of the lightness of the conscience, a grace-filled comfort and joy. Hope in God's mercy. Gratitude to God for sorrows, and calm bearing of these sorrows due to the multitude of our sins. The readiness to bear anything. Purification of the mind. Lessening of the burden of the passions. Death to the world. The desire to pray, to be in seclusion, humility, confession of sins.

6. Temperance

Enthusiasm for every good deed. Untiring completion of the prayer rule in church and at home. Attention during prayer. Careful watchfulness of every deed, word, and thought. Extreme lack of faith in oneself. Constant prayer and reading of the Holy Scriptures. Reverence. Constant battle with laziness. Not sleeping too much, avoiding excess comfort, idle talk, idle jokes, and sharp words. Love of nightly vigils, prostrations, and other physical labors that give strength to the soul. Rarely leaving the cell, and then only by necessity. Remembrance of eternal blessedness, and the desire and expectation of heavenly goods.

7. Humility

Fear of God. A palpable sense of it during prayer. Fear of disappearing and becoming nothing, fear that comes from especially pure prayer, during which the presence and greatness of God are especially vivid. A deep acknowledgment of one's own worthlessness. A sincere and unforced acknowledgment of everyone else's moral superiority. The appearance of simplicity of soul that comes from living faith. Hatred for all praises of the world. Constant self-condemnation. Truth and firmness. Lack of passionate attachment. Being dead to all things. Compunction. Realization of the mystery, hidden in the cross of Christ. Desire to crucify yourself to the world and to the passions; seeking this crucifixion. Rejecting and forgetting false habits and falsely meek words; or the desire or thought to pretend to be meek. Acceptance of the unseen warfare. Rejection of the wisdom of this world as incompatible with heavenly wisdom. Despising everything that is considered great in the world, but abhorrent to God.[1] Rejection of self-justification. Silence before those who offend you, as taught by the Gospels. Setting aside all personal intellectualizing and accepting the wisdom of the Gospels. Cutting off any thought that dares to imagine to be Christlike. Humble-mindedness, or spiritual discernment. Conscientious obedience to the Church in all things.

8. Love

The development of fear of God into love for God during prayer. Faithfulness to the Lord, proved by constant rejection of any sinful thought and emotion. Unutterable, sweet inclination of the whole person in love toward the Lord Jesus Christ and the Holy Trinity Whom we worship. Seeing in others the image of God and Christ; preferring all others to yourself and reverently honoring them in Christ's name. Brotherly love for your neighbor that is pure and equally expressed to all, without passionate attachment, equally fiery toward friends and enemies. Prayerful ecstasy of the mind, heart, and body with the love of God. Unutterable consolation of spiritual joy. Spiritual satisfaction. Relaxation of the body as a result of spiritual consolation.[2] The dormancy of bodily senses during prayer. The loosening of the dumbness of the heart. The cessation of prayer due to spiritual sweetness. Silence of the mind. Illumination of the mind and heart. Prayerful power, capable of defeating sin. The peace of Christ. Retreat of all the passions. The inundation of all reasoning by the superior reason of Christ. Theology. Acknowledgment of the existence of spiritual beings. The weakness of sinful thoughts, their inability to be drawn by the mind. Sweetness and great comfort during sorrows. Understanding of human fates. Depth of humility and the lowest opinion of oneself

The end is eternal!

CHAPTER 17

On Loving One's Neighbor

What can be lovelier, more wonderful than love for one's neighbor? To love is blessedness. To hate is torture.

All of the Law and prophets are concentrated in love for God and one's neighbor.[1]

Love for one's neighbor is the road by which we are led to love for God, since Christ deigned to mysteriously put on every one of our brothers, and through Christ, God Himself.[2]

Do not think, beloved brother, that the commandment to love your neighbor is already near to our fallen hearts. No, this commandment is spiritual, but our hearts are lorded over by flesh and blood. This commandment is new, but our heart is old.

Our natural love is corrupted by the fall; it must first be put to rest (this is commanded by Christ) and only then can holy love, love in Christ, be acquired from the Gospels.

The qualities of the new man must be all new; not one of the old qualities is appropriate for him.

Love, inspired by the movement of blood and the feelings of the body, has no value in light of the Gospel. And what value can it have, when one who swears to give his life for the Lord when his blood is hot, swears that he does not know Him only a few hours later, when his blood has cooled?[3]

The Gospel rejects love dependent on hot-bloodedness, on the feelings of the carnal heart. It says, "Do not think that I came to bring peace on earth. I did not come to bring peace but a sword. For I have come to 'set a man against his father, a daughter against her mother, and a daughter-in-law against her mother-in-law'; and 'a man's enemies will be those of his own household.'"[4]

The fall of mankind subordinated the heart to the lordship of the blood, and through the blood, to the lordship of the prince of this world.

The Gospels release the heart from this bondage, from this slavery, and bring it under the guidance of the Holy Spirit.

The Holy Spirit teaches how to love one's neighbor.

True love that is sustained by the Holy Spirit is fire. This fire puts out the fire of earthly, carnal, fallen love. [5]

"He who claims that he can have the one kind of love together with the other is deluding himself," said St John of the Ladder.[6]

How far has our nature fallen? He who is by nature capable of fiery love for his neighbor must exert a tremendous amount of willpower over himself in order to love him in the way the Gospels command.

Fiery, natural love easily turns to disgust, to irreconcilable hatred.[7]

Natural love has even been expressed with a dagger.

Our natural love is covered in open wounds! What a terrible wound is passionate attachment! The heart possessed by passionate attachment is capable of any injustice, of any crime, if only to satisfy the cravings of its diseased, so-called love. "Dishonest scales are an abomination to the Lord, but a just weight is His delight."[8]

Natural love gives only earthly goods to the beloved; it does not even think of the heavenly.

It battles against heaven and the Holy Spirit because the Spirit requires the crucifixion of the flesh.

It battles against heaven and the Holy Spirit because it is under the dominion of the spirit of evil, the fallen and impure spirit.

Let us approach the Gospels, dear beloved brother; let us look into this mirror! Looking at it, let us take off our old clothes into which we have been clothed by our fall, and let us decorate ourselves with a new robe, which is prepared for us by God.

The new robe is Christ Himself. "For as many of you as were baptized into Christ have put on Christ."[9]

The new robe is the Holy Spirit. "You are endued with power from on high," said the Lord.[10]

Christians are clothed with the qualities of Christ through the action of the all-good Spirit.

Such a robe is possible for every Christian. The Apostle says: "But put on the Lord Jesus Christ, and make no provision for the flesh, to *fulfill* its lusts."[11]

First, guided by the Gospels, throw off all enmity, remembrance of evil, anger, judgment, and everything else that acts against love.

The Gospels require that we pray for our enemies, bless those who curse us, do good to those who hate us, and forgive our neighbor anything that he may have done against us.

Whoever strives to emulate Christ, let him fulfill all these commandments through actions.

It is not enough only to read the commandments of the Gospel with pleasure and to be amazed at the level of morality they contain. Unfortunately, many are content only with this.

When you begin to fulfill the commandments of the Gospel through deeds, the lords of your heart will stubbornly battle against you. These lords are your own carnal state, which subjects your flesh and blood, and the fallen angels who dominate the carnal state of mankind.

The carnal mind, its truth and the truth of the fallen spirits, will require that you do not dishonor yourself and your worldly situation, but protect it at all cost. But you must bravely withstand this invisible war, guided by the Gospels, guided by the Lord Himself.

Sacrifice everything for the fulfillment of the commandments of the Gospel. Without such a sacrifice, you will never be able to follow them. The Lord said to His disciples, "If anyone desires to come after Me, let him deny himself."[12]

When the Lord is with you, you can hope for victory—the Lord cannot be defeated.

Ask the Lord to grant you this victory; ask it with constant prayer and tears. And unexpected grace will be given your heart; you will immediately feel a sweet satisfaction of spiritual love for your enemies.

But the battle still awaits you! You must still be courageous! Look at the objects of your affection; are they still pleasing to you? Is your heart still attached to them? You must reject them.

The Lord, the Giver of the Law of love, demands such a rejection from you not in order to deprive you of love and the ones you love. Rather, by rejecting carnal love tainted by sin, you will become capable of spiritual, pure, holy love, which is the highest blessedness.

He who has felt spiritual love will only despise carnal love, seeing it for the unsightly parody of love that it is.

How can one reject the objects of one's attachment, which seem to have become physically bonded to the very heart of man? Turn to God with the words: "All these things, Lord, are Yours. Who am I? I am an inconsequential creature who has no value. Today I wander through the world, today I might be useful to my beloved in some way, but tomorrow I may die, and become as nothing to them! Whether I desire it or not, death will come, other situations may arise that separate me from those whom I consider my own, and they will no longer be mine. They were never in actual fact mine. There was some sort of relation between us, and being fooled by this relation I called and considered them my own. But if they were truly mine, they would forever remain in my possession. The creature belongs only to the Creator. He is their God and Lord. My Lord, to You I give Your own. I have attached them to myself unlawfully and uselessly."

It is better for them to be God's. God is eternal, omnipresent, all-powerful, eternally good. To His own He is the most loyal, most dependable Helper and Defender.

God gives all that belongs to Him to His people, and when God gives such a gift to man, man's beloved becomes His own, at first in body, and eternally in spirit.

True love for one's neighbor is established on faith in God; it is in God Himself. "That they all may be one," said the Saviour of the world to His Father, "as You, Father, are in Me, and I in You; that they also may be one in Us."[13]

Humility and loyalty to God destroy carnal love. That means that it lives through lack of faith and arrogance.

Do whatever good you can—whatever the commandments declare—to your beloved ones; but always commit their care to God, and your blind, carnal, careless love will transform little by little into a spiritual, wise, holy love.

But if your love is passionate, contrary to God's Law, then reject it as foulness.

When your heart is not free, this is a sign of passionate attachment.

When your heart is enslaved, this is a sign of insane, sinful passion.

Holy love is pure, free, entirely in God.

It is the action of the Holy Spirit in the heart, depending on the extent of its purification.

Having cast aside any enmity, any passionate attachment, and having rejected carnal love, strive to acquire spiritual love: "shun evil, and do good."[14]

Give honor to your neighbor as the image of God, honor him in your heart secretly, so that only your conscience may see it. Then your deeds will mysteriously act in concert with your spiritual disposition.

While honoring your neighbor, make no distinction of age, gender, or social status, and slowly, holy love will begin to illuminate your heart.

The reason for this holy love is not flesh and blood or the vagaries of emotion, but God Himself.

Even those who are deprived of the glory of Christianity are not deprived of the glory that is given at their creation. They are still the image of God.

If the image of God is cast out into the horrible flames of hell, even there I must honor Him.

What do I care for the flames, for hell? The image of God has been cast there by the judgment of God. I must preserve my honor for the image of God, thereby preserving myself from hell.

Even the blind, the leper, the mentally insane, the child at the mother's breast, the convicted criminal—all these you must honor as the image of God. What business do you have with their diseases and their deficiencies? Watch over yourself, so that you might not be deficient in love.

In each Christian, you give honor to Christ Himself, Who said for our instruction, and will again say when our eternal fate is decided: "Inasmuch as you did *it* to one of the least of these My brethren, you did it to Me."[15]

In your interaction with your neighbor, remember these words of the Gospel, and you will become a confidant of love for your neighbor.

Thus, by being this confidant of love for your neighbor, you enter into the love of God.

If you think that you love God, but in your heart lives an unpleasant disposition toward even one person, you are grievously self-deluded.

St John the Theologian says, "*If someone says, 'I love God,' and hates his brother, he is a liar*. And this commandment we have from Him: That he who loves God must love his brother also."[16]

The appearance of spiritual love for one's neighbor is a sign of the renewal of the soul by the Holy Spirit. The Theologian says again: "We know that we have passed from death to life, because we love the brethren. He who does not love his brother abides in death."[17] The perfection of Christianity is contained in the perfect love for one's neighbor. Perfect love for one's neighbor is contained in love for God, which has no limit of perfection, which is eternal. Growth in God's love is eternal, because love is eternal God.[18] Love for one's neighbor is the foundation of all other love.

Beloved brother! Seek to reveal in yourself true spiritual love for your neighbor; having acquired it, you will acquire love for God, and you will enter the gates of resurrection, the gates of the heavenly kingdom. Amen.

CHAPTER 18

On Loving God

Love God in the way that He commanded us to love Him, not in the way that the deluded dreamers think to love Him.

Do not invent ecstasies for yourself, do not agitate your nerves, do not inflame yourself with a sensual fire, a fire of your blood. The sacrifice that pleases God is humility of heart, compunction of soul. God angrily turns away from a sacrifice brought with self-assurance and proud arrogance, even if it were a whole-burnt offering.

Pride agitates the nerves, inflames the blood, awakens the imagination, and stimulates a fallen life. Humility calms the nerves, cools the blood, destroys imagination, eradicates the fallen life, and awakens life in Jesus Christ.

"To obey *is* better than sacrifice, *and* to heed than the fat of rams"[1] said the prophet to the king of Israel, who dared to offer God an unlawful sacrifice. If you desire to bring God a sacrifice of love, do not bring it willfully, without preparing it thoughtfully. Bring it with humility, in the time and place that God Himself commanded.

The spiritual place where God commanded us to bring spiritual sacrifices is humility.[2]

The Lord gave exact and accurate signs by which one can distinguish the one who loves from the one who hates. He said, "If anyone loves Me, he will keep My word. He who does not love Me does not keep My words."[3]

Do you want to learn to love God? Separate yourself from any word, deed, thought, and feeling forbidden by the Gospels. Through your battle with sin, which is so loathed by God, show and prove your love for God. If you should fall into sin because of your spiritual sickness, immediately find healing in repentance. But it is even better to try not to fall into sin in the first place by strict watchfulness over yourself.

Do you want to learn to love God? Carefully study the commandments of the Lord in the Gospels and try to fulfill them in deed, trying to make the virtues of the Gospel into habitual characteristics of your nature. It is typical of the lover to completely fulfill the will of the beloved.

"Therefore have I loved Thy commandments more than gold and topaz. Therefore have I held straight to all Thy commandments; I have hated every wrong way," said the Prophet.[4] Such behavior is necessary to remain faithful to God. Faithfulness is inevitably linked to love. Without this faithfulness, love falls apart.

We attain the love of God through constantly turning away from evil and fulfilling the virtues of the Gospel (which contain the entirety of the Gospel's moral teaching). Through this process, we remain in love for God: "If you keep My commandments, you will abide in my love," said the Saviour.[5]

Perfection in love is found in union with God; success in love is connected with incomprehensible spiritual comfort, joy, and illumination. But in the beginning of our efforts, the disciple of love must withstand a terrible war with himself, with his deeply damaged nature. Evil, which has become natural through sin, has become a law for him, which fights and rebels against the Law of God, against the Law of holy love.

Love for God is built on love for one's neighbor. When remembrance of evil is removed from your heart, then you are near to love. When your heart is illumined with a holy, grace-filled peace toward all mankind, then you are at the very gates of love.

But these gates are opened only by the Holy Spirit. Love for God is the gift of God to a person who has prepared himself to accept this gift through purity of heart, mind, and body. The richness of the gift accords to his level of preparation because the Lord is just in His mercy.

Love for God is completely spiritual: "that which is born of the Spirit is spirit"[6] Carnal love, the product of flesh and blood, has sensual, impermanent qualities. It is inconstant, fickle; its love depends completely on worldly things.

When you hear in the Scriptures that our God is fire,[7] that love is fire, and when you feel in yourself the fire of carnal love, do not think that this fire is one and the same. No! These fires are at war with each other, and each puts out the other.[8] Whereby "we may serve God acceptably with reverence and godly fear. For our God is a consuming fire."[9]

Natural, fallen love inflames human blood, agitates the nerves, and awakens fantasy; holy love cools the blood, calms both the soul and the body, inspires prayerful silence inside a person, and submerges him into the fullness of humility and spiritual joy.

Many righteous individuals, having assumed natural love to be divine, inflamed their blood and their fantasy as well. This condition of inner warmth very easily transforms into a trancelike state. Those who are in such an inflamed trance state often consider themselves full of grace and holiness, while they are only the unfortunate victims of self-delusion.

There were many zealots in the Western Church—especially from the time it fell into papism—who blasphemously ascribed to themselves qualities proper only to God, and venerated man in a way only appropriate to God Himself. Many of these zealots wrote books in their deluded state, in which they imagined their insane self-deception to be divine love, in which their shattered imagination created many visions that only added to their self-love and pride.

Son of the Eastern Orthodox Church! Turn away from reading such books, turn away from following the teachings of the deceived. Be guided by the Gospels and the Holy Fathers of the true Church, and ascend with humility to the spiritual height of divine love through the keeping of Christ's commandments.

Be assured that love for God is the highest gift of the Holy Spirit, and a person can prepare himself to accept this great gift that changes mind and heart and body only through purity and humility.

Useless, fruitless, and dangerous is any effort that tries prematurely to uncover inner spiritual gifts. God gives them mercifully in His own time, and only to the constant, patient, humble doers of the commandments of the Gospel. Amen.

CHAPTER 19

On Fasting

The greatest of virtues is prayer; the foundation of prayer is fasting. Fasting is the constant moderation in eating, along with wise discernment.

Proud man! You imagine so much, you think so highly of your own mind, but it is in constant and complete dependence on your stomach.

The law of fasting, which is externally a law for the stomach, is in essence a law for the mind.

If the mind, the crown of man, wishes to enter and preserve its proper dominion, it must first submit itself to the law of fasting. Only then will it be constantly awake and illumined; only then can the mind rule over the desires of the heart and body. Only through constant temperance can it learn the commandments of the Gospel and follow them. The foundation of virtues is fasting.

The newly created man, when he was given Eden, was also given one single commandment, the commandment to fast. Of course, only one was given because it was enough to preserve the first man in his sinlessness.

The commandment did not speak about the quantity of food, but only forbade a quality, a type of food. May those who believe that fasting refers only to the quantity, not quality, be silent! If they were to fully immerse themselves in the study of fasting, they would see the importance of the quality of the food they eat.

The commandment to fast, pronounced by God to man in Eden, was so important that it was accompanied with a warning that man would be punished if he broke the commandment. The punishment was eternal death.

And even today, sinful death continues to strike down those who break the holy commandment to fast. Those who do not preserve moderation and the necessary discernment in food can preserve neither virginity nor chastity. They cannot rein in anger; they fall prey to laziness, depression, and sadness; and they become the slaves of vanity, the home of pride, all of which lead the person into a carnal state that is most obviously revealed in his luxurious and overflowing table.

The commandment to fast is renewed, or even confirmed, by the Gospels. "But take heed to yourselves, lest your hearts be weighed down with carousing, drunkenness, and cares of this life, and that Day come on you unexpectedly," said the Lord.[1] Overeating and drunkenness not only make the body weak but also the mind and heart. In other words, they lead the person both in his soul and body into a carnal state.

Fasting, on the contrary, leads a Christian into a spiritual state. He who is cleansed by fasting is contrite in his spirit; chaste, humble, silent, and refined in the emotions of the heart and thoughts; light in his body; capable of spiritual labors and contemplation; and capable of accepting the grace of God.

The carnal man is completely submerged in sinful pleasures. He is sensual in his body, in his heart, and in his mind. He is incapable not only of spiritual joy and accepting God's grace, but he cannot even repent. He is incapable of any spiritual work; he is nailed to the earth, he has drowned in a sea of possessions that have no life. While still alive, he is dead in his soul.

"Woe to you who are full, for you shall hunger."[2] Such is the word of God to those who disregard the holy commandment to fast. What will satisfy you in eternity, when here on earth you have learned only to be sated by perishable food and worldly enjoyments, none of which exist in heaven? What will you eat in eternity, when you have never even tasted a single heavenly food? How can you eat and enjoy heavenly food when you have never appreciated it, even despised it on earth?

The daily bread of a Christian is Christ Himself. Insatiable satiety from this bread is salvific satisfaction and joy, to which every Christian is called.

We are called to insatiably fill ourselves with the word of God, to insatiably fill ourselves with the commandments of Christ, to insatiably fill ourselves with the food of the Lord: "Thou hast prepared a table before me against them that trouble me; Thou hast anointed my head with oil, and Thy cup that inebriateth me, how strong it is!"[3]

"Where shall we begin," says St Macarius the Great,[4] "we who have never studied our own hearts? Standing without, let us knock on the door through prayer and fasting," as the Lord Himself commanded us: "Knock, and it will be opened to you."[5]

This labor, which is offered to us by one of the greatest teachers of the monastic life, was the labor of the holy apostles. Through it, they were granted to hear the words of the Spirit. "As they ministered to the Lord and fasted, the Holy Spirit said, 'Now separate to Me Barnabas and Saul for the work to which I have called them.' Then, having fasted and prayed, and laid hands on them, they sent them away."[6] From this labor, in which they combined prayer and fasting, they heard the command of the Spirit to include the Gentiles in their missionary endeavors.

What a marvelous union is achieved by fasting and prayer! Prayer is without effect if not established on fasting, and fasting is fruitless if prayer is not created from it.[7]

Fasting releases a person from passions of the flesh while prayer battles against spiritual passions, and having defeated them enters the very fabric of the person, cleanses him from within, and leads God into this cleansed, rational temple.

Whoever begins to sow the land without first clearing it destroys the seeds before they can even sprout, and instead of wheat he reaps thorns. If we sow the seeds of prayer in a similar manner, we will reap nothing, but we will harvest sins instead of truth. Prayer will be destroyed and dissipated by various vain and sinful thoughts and imaginings; our feelings will be defiled by sensuality. Our flesh has come from the earth, and if we do not clear it as we would a field, we will never be able to grow the fruit of truth.[8]

However, if someone works the land with great effort and labor, but leaves it unsown, then it will be completely covered in weeds. Thus, when the body is mortified by fasting but the soul is not cultivated by prayer, reading, and humble-mindedness, then fasting becomes the source of many spiritual passions—vanity, arrogance, contempt.

What is the passion of overeating and drunkenness? It is the natural desire for food and drink that has lost its proper orientation, which demands a great deal more in quantity and variety than is necessary for the support of life and physical strength. Ironically, this excess acts in the opposite way on physical strength, becoming harmful, weakening, and even destroying the body and its strength.

Desire for food is sated by simple food, and from overeating and excessively enjoying food by abstinence. At first, one must reject satiety and gluttony—through this, the desire for food is reoriented according to its natural purpose. When this hunger becomes properly directed, then a person becomes satisfied with simple food.

On the contrary, the desire for food that is satisfied with overeating and gluttony becomes blunted. In order to reawaken it, we invent various delicious foods and drinks. At first, our hunger seems to be satisfied, but it gets more and more picky, and finally it becomes a sickening passion that constantly seeks satiety and satisfaction yet always remains unsatisfied.

If we have decided to dedicate ourselves to the service of God, let us put fasting as the foundation of our labors. The essential quality of any foundation must be unbreakable firmness; otherwise, a building will never remain standing, even if it is built properly. And we must not under any circumstances allow ourselves to break a fast through satiety, especially through drinking too much.

The Holy Fathers generally consider the best fast to be eating once a day, but not to complete satiety. Such a fast does not weaken the body because of long abstinence yet does not burden it with excessive food, and still makes it capable of soul-saving activity. Such a fast is not particularly difficult, and so the one fasting has no reason to think highly of himself, something he would be inclined to do if his fasting was out of the ordinary.

Whoever does physical work or is so weak bodily that he cannot be satisfied with only one meal a day can eat twice daily. The fast is for the person, not the person for the fast.

But in any case, whether you eat often or rarely, eating until you are full is strictly forbidden. This only makes a person incapable of spiritual labors and opens the door to other carnal passions.

But immoderate fasting—that is, prolonged, excessive abstinence from food—is not recommended by the Holy Fathers. A person also becomes incapable of spiritual labor when his body is weakened through excessive abstinence, and often his fasting is soon followed by gluttony or he falls into the passions of vanity and pride.

The quality of food is extremely important. The forbidden fruit in Eden was pleasing to the eye and taste, but it acted poisonously on the soul by giving the premature knowledge of good and evil, thereby destroying the purity in which our forefathers were created.

And today, food continues to act strongly on our soul, which is especially evident when one drinks wine. Thus, all alcoholic drinks, especially those made from wheat, are forbidden to the ascetic laborer since they rob his mind of temperance and make him incapable of the invisible war with the thoughts. The defeated mind, especially the victim of sensual thoughts, is deprived of spiritual grace. That which has been carefully acquired through many long labors is lost over the course of a few hours, even a few minutes.

A monk should not drink wine, said St Pimen the Great in the *Saying of the Desert Fathers*. Every pious Christian who desires to preserve his virginity and chastity should also follow this rule. The Holy Fathers followed it, and even if they did drink wine, it was very rare and in great moderation.

Spicy food should be removed from the table of the ascetic since it awakens carnal passions. Such foods include pepper, ginger, and other sweets.

The most natural food is the one that was allotted to man immediately after his creation—food from the plant kingdom. God said to our forefather: And God said, "See, I have given you every herb that yields seed which is on the face of all the earth, and every tree whose fruit yields seed; to you it shall be for food."[9] Only after the flood was meat allowed for food.[10]

A vegetarian diet is best for the ascetic. It warms the blood the least, fattens the body the least, and its constituent parts affect the brain the least. Finally, it is the healthiest kind of food. For these reasons, one who follows it most easily preserves his purity and watchfulness of mind and its ability to rule over the body of the person. The passions have less hold over the body and the person is more able to dedicate himself to ascetic labors.

Fish dishes, especially those prepared from large sea fish, have a completely different quality. They have a palpable effect on the mind, they fatten the body, they inflame the blood, and they fill the stomach to satiety, especially when eaten often and in large quantities.

These effects are greatly magnified when eating meat. Meat fattens the body excessively, giving it an especial laziness, and inflames the blood. It has a deadening effect on the brain. For this reason, monks must never eat meat. It belongs to people who live in the world, who are constantly burdened by heavy physical work. But even for them, constant eating of meat is harmful.

So! I can hear the so-called know-it-alls saying: meat is allowed by God, and you dare forbid it?! To this I answer with the words of the Apostle: "All things are lawful for me, but not all things are helpful; all things are lawful for me, but not all things edify."[11] We refuse to eat meat not because we consider it to be unclean, but because it has a deadening effect on our entire body and mind, which hinders our spiritual development.

The Holy Church in its wisdom has established that Christians living in the world can partake of meat, but not constantly. Periods of meat eating are separated by times of abstinence from meat, times during which the Christian cleanses himself from the meat in his system. Such a beneficial effect of fasting is evident to anyone who keeps the fast.

It is absolutely forbidden for monks to eat meat; they are only allowed to eat dairy and eggs during the nonfasting periods. On certain days and time periods they are also allowed to eat fish. But the majority of the time they are allowed only plant foods.

Such a diet is almost exclusively used by the most zealous ascetics, especially those who already feel the grace of the Spirit of God,[12] for reasons of its beneficial effect on the body and its low cost. They limit themselves to drinking water, not only avoiding alcoholic drinks but also rich ones such as kvass[13] and all other wheat-based drinks.[14]

The rules of fasting are established by the Church with the purpose of helping its children, as a guide for the entire Christian society. In addition to this, it is recommended that every Christian seek the advice of an experienced and discerning spiritual father, and not decide by himself to fast beyond his abilities. Again, I repeat that the fast is for the person, not the person for the fast. The food that is given for the support of the person must not become the source of his destruction.

"If you curb your stomach," said St Basil the Great, "you will enter heaven. If you will not, you will be the victim of death."[15] By heaven, he means a grace-filled prayerful state; by death, he means a passionate state. A grace-filled state while still on earth is a promise of eternal blessedness in the heavenly Eden. Falling into sin's grasp and the soul's death is a promise of eternal suffering in the depths of hell. Amen.

CHAPTER 20

On Prayer

Article 1

It is natural for a poor man to beg; it is also natural for a man grown poor through sin to pray.

Prayer is the conversation of a fallen and repentant person with God. Prayer is the crying out of the fallen and repentant man to God. Prayer is the pouring out of the heart's desires and requests. It is the sighs of the fallen man, killed by sin, before God.

The first inkling, the first movement of repentance is the sorrow of the heart. This is the prayerful voice of the heart that comes before the prayer of the mind. And soon the mind, enraptured with the prayer of the heart, begins to give birth to prayerful thoughts.

God is the only source of all true, good things. Prayer is the mother and the head of all virtues,[1] as a path toward, and a state of communion with God. It takes good deeds directly from the source of goodness, God Himself, and makes them natural in that person who tries to attain communion with God through prayer.

The path to God is prayer. The measures of this path are the various states of prayer into which the one who prays enters slowly, correctly, and through constant perseverance.

You must learn how to pray to God properly. When you learn how to pray properly, pray constantly, and you will easily inherit salvation. Salvation comes from God in its appointed time to the one who prays properly and constantly, and it announces itself undeniably in the heart.

In order to attain proper prayer, it must be uttered from a heart filled with spiritual poverty, from a heart full of compunction and humility. All other spiritual states of the heart, before it is renewed by the Holy Spirit, are surely unnatural for a repenting sinner who is begging God for the forgiveness of his sins and for freedom from the bondage of passions.

The law of Moses commanded that the Israelites bring their sacrifices only to one holy place determined by God. And spiritual law requires that every Christian bring his sacrifices to one spiritual place, especially the sacrifice of sacrifices—prayer. This spiritual place is humility.[2]

God does not need our prayers! He knows what we need even before we ask it. He, the All-Merciful, gives bountiful gifts even to those who do not ask for them. We need prayer—it unites us with God. Without it, a person is unknown by God, while the more he becomes adept at prayer, the closer he comes to God.

Prayer is communion of life itself. Leaving it brings unseen death to the soul.

What air is for the life of the body, the Holy Spirit is for the life of the soul. The soul breathes this holy, mystical air through prayer.

When you rise from sleep, let your first thought be of God. Bring to God the very beginning of your thoughts before they have been spoiled by any worldly impressions. When you lie down to sleep, when you ready yourself to descend into this image of death, let your last thoughts be of eternity and God who rules over eternity.

An angel once revealed to a holy monk the following proper progression of thoughts in God-pleasing prayer: "The beginning of prayer should consist of praise for God coming out of gratitude for his countless gifts; then we must bring to God a sincere confession of our sins, with pain of heart, and only in conclusion can we bring, and only with the greatest humility, our petitions to the Lord for the needs of our soul and body, leaving the fulfillment of these petitions completely to His will."[3]

The first reason for prayer is faith: "I believed, so I spake"[4] with my prayer to the merciful God, who in His goodness commanded me to pray and gave His promise to hear my prayer.

"Whatever things you ask when you pray, believe that you receive them, and you will have them," said the Lord.[5] And thus, having rejected all doubts and duplicity of heart, let us constantly immerse ourselves in prayer before God, who commanded "always . . . to pray, and not lose heart;"[6] that is, never to fall into despair because of the difficulty of our prayer, as at first it is heavy and unwieldy for the mind, which has become accustomed to freely wander wherever it wills.

Blessed is the soul that through prayer constantly knocks at the doors of God's mercy, and through complaints against the "adversary,"[7] that is, sin, constantly tires the Tireless One.[8] Such a soul will rejoice in the appointed time because of its purity and dispassion.

Sometimes our petitions are heard immediately; sometimes, according to the words of our Saviour, "Shall God not avenge His own elect which cry out day and night to Him, though He bears long with them?"[9] In other words, He fulfills our petitions after some delay. He sees that we need some time to be confirmed in our humility, that we need to become tired and to see our sickness, which always reveals itself very unexpectedly when we are faced with ourselves.

Prayer, like conversation with God, is by its very nature a great good, which is in itself often much greater than those things that we ask of God; and the all-merciful God, when He does not fulfill our petitions, leaves the petitioner with his prayer so that he may not lose it or leave this great benefit as soon as he receives the lesser good he requested.

God does not grant petitions whose accomplishment would be accompanied by negative consequences. He does not grant those requests that are against His holy will or contrary to his all-wise, unaccountable purposes.

The great Moses asked to be allowed to enter the promised land contrary to God's will and his prayer was not answered.[10] The holy David prayed for the preservation of his son, strengthening his prayer with fasting, ashes, and tears, and his prayer was not answered.[11] And you, whenever your request is not acceptable to God, submit yourself humbly to the will of the all-holy God, Who, for unknown reasons, left your petition unanswered.

The holy Apostle James says the following to those sons of the world who ask God for earthly goods for the satisfaction of their worldly desires: "You ask and do not receive, because you ask amiss, that you may spend it on your pleasures."[12]

When we desire to gain an audience before an earthly king, we prepare for this with special care. We try to conform our heart's emotions to the proper tone of the conversation, so that we, bursting with excitement, might not offend the king by a word or gesture. In advance, we think of what we will say to him, so that we might only say the appropriate things, thereby inclining him to think well of us. We even take care that our external appearance might attract his attention. How much more should be properly prepared when we desire to stand before the King of kings, and to begin a prayerful conversation with Him!

"For man looks at the outward appearance, but the Lord looks at the heart."[13] However, the condition of a man's heart is most often reflected in his face and his general appearance. Thus, when you pray, you must position your body in the most appropriate way for prayer. Stand like a convicted criminal, with head bowed low, not daring to look up at heaven, with hands either lying at your side or folded behind your back as if bound with ropes, as criminals caught in the very act are also bound. The sound of your voice should be the woeful sound of sorrow, the groan of someone with a life-threatening wound or horrifying disease.

God looks into the heart. He sees our most hidden, subtlest thoughts and feelings. He sees our entire past and our entire future. God is all-knowing. And thus, stand during your prayer as if you stood before God Himself. Indeed, you do stand before Him! You stand before your Judge and all-powerful Lord, on Whom your temporal and eternal fate depends. Use this time before Him to ensure your future blessedness; do not let this audience with the King become a reason for your temporal and eternal suffering.

Having determined to bring your prayer before God, reject all thoughts and worries of this life. Do not pay any attention to thoughts that come to you during prayer, no matter how important, brilliant, or necessary they may seem to be. Give to God the things that are God's, while the things necessary for the temporal life can be done in their own time. It is impossible to simultaneously work for God in prayer and clutter the mind with wayward thoughts and cares.

Before prayer, cense your heart with the fragrance of the fear of God and holy reverence. Remember that you have angered God with countless sins, which are to Him more evident than even to your conscience. Try to win the compassion of the Judge through your humility. Be careful! Do not incite His anger with your carelessness and impudence. It is with His good blessing that even those closest to Him, the purest of the angelic hosts, tremble before Him with complete reverence and most-holy fear.[14]

The garments of your soul must shine with the whiteness of simplicity. There should be nothing complicated! There should be no evil thoughts or feelings of vanity, hypocrisy, falsity, people pleasing, arrogance, or sensuality—these dark and foul spots that soil the spiritual robes of these praying Pharisees.

Instead of pearls and emeralds, instead of gold and silver, decorate yourself with chastity, humble-mindedness, tears of meekness, and spiritual wisdom. And before you receive these tears, adorn yourself with tears of repentance, with childlike, angelic gentleness—here is a most precious treasure! When the King of kings sees these decorations on your soul, His merciful gaze will incline to your soul.

The fundamental condition of successful prayer is forgiveness of all offenses, even the most grievous, without any exception. The Saviour commanded: "And whenever you stand praying, if you have anything against anyone, forgive him, that your Father in heaven may also forgive you your trespasses. But if you do not forgive, neither will your Father in heaven forgive your trespasses"[15] "The prayer of those who recall evils done to them, are seeds sown among the stones," said St Isaac the Syrian.[16]

Temperate, wise, constant abstinence from food and drink makes the body light, clears the mind, gives it strength, and thus also serves as a preparation for prayer. Lack of abstinence in terms of food makes the body heavy, stupid, coarsens the heart, and darkens the mind. No sooner does the one satisfied with food stand up for prayer than somnolence and laziness attack him, his imagination paints many impure thoughts, and his heart is incapable of feeling compunction.

As harmful as intemperance is, even more so is excessive fasting.[17] The weakness of body that invariably accompanies it does not allow for prayer in the necessary amount or with the necessary concentration and power.

The proper amount of prayer is determined for each person depending on the manner of his life and the amount of his spiritual and physical strength. The two mites of the widow, which were brought by her to the temple and made up the entirety of her earthly holdings, were counted greater on the scales of the just God than the large donations brought by the rich from their excess money. You may judge similarly with prayer: assign yourself an amount that accords to your strength, and remember the wise advice of the great ascetic guide: "If you force your weak body to work beyond its strength, you will darken your soul and bring it only confusion, not benefit."[18]

But from him who is healthy and full of strength is expected a correspondingly powerful prayer. "Any prayer," said the same great Father, "during which your body is not forced to submit, and your heart is not brought to compunction, will not be accepted as fruitful, since such prayer is soulless."

If you are busy with various responsibilities, or if you are a monk burdened with many obediences that do not allow you to dedicate as much time to prayer as you would like, do not be downcast. If your work is done properly and with a good conscience, it will prepare you for deep prayer and will replace quantity of prayer with quality. Nothing prepares a person for successful prayer as much as a clean conscience satisfied with God-pleasing work.

The fulfillment of the commandments of the Gospel also concentrates the mind and heart in pure prayer, full of compunction; and in its turn, true prayer helps the person think, feel, and act according to the commandments of the Gospel.

Compassion for your neighbors and humility before them, expressed through external deeds, fostered in the heart and together with purity of heart, especially from carnal thoughts and feelings—these are the foundation and power of prayer.[19] They are like prayer's wings, with which it flies to heaven. Without them, prayer cannot lift off from the earth, that is, free itself from the carnal mind-set—it is tied down as if in a snare, it becomes agitated, impure, and is finally destroyed.

The soul of prayer is attention.[20] Just as the body is dead without the soul, prayer is dead without attention. Without attention, the prayer uttered by the lips is no more than empty words, and he who prays thus is included among those who take the Lord's name in vain.

Pronounce the words of prayer slowly; do not allow your mind to wander aimlessly, but firmly keep it fixed on the words of the prayer.[21] This path is narrow and full of sorrows for the mind long accustomed to wander freely all over the universe, but this path leads to attentive prayer. Whoever tastes of the great good of such attentive prayer will come to love forcing his mind to this narrow path that leads to blessed attentiveness.

Attentiveness is the first gift of divine grace sent to the one who patiently labors in prayerful ascesis.

Grace-filled attention must be preceded by forcible attentiveness during prayer, which must be an active witness of the sincere desire to receive the gift of attentive prayer. The effort of forced attentiveness is burdened with thoughts and imaginings and is weakened by them; grace-given attentiveness is firmly established.

Forbid your mind to be scattered during prayer, come to hate reverie, reject earthly cares through the power of faith, strike your heart with the fear of God, and you will train yourself in attentiveness.

The praying mind must be in a state of complete sincerity. Any kind of fantasy, no matter how attractive or seemingly beneficial, is a self-created, willful invention of the mind that leads the mind out of the state of divine truth and into a state of self-deception and delusion, and thus must be rejected in prayer.

During prayer, the mind must be diligently kept free of all images that draw themselves in the imagination because the mind in prayer is standing before the invisible God, Whom it is impossible to imagine in any visible form. If images are accepted by the mind during prayer, they will become an opaque veil, a wall between the mind and God. "Those who see nothing during their prayer, see God," said St Meletios the Confessor in his work *On Prayer.*

During your prayer, if the appearance of Christ, an angel, or some other saint seems to arise palpably or draws itself in your imagination or appears in any way, under no circumstances must you accept this vision as truth. Do not pay any attention to it; do not begin to speak to it.[22] Otherwise, you will become invariably fooled and be seriously spiritually damaged, which has happened to many. A person is incapable of conversing with holy spirits before the Holy Spirit renews him. As one still under the influence of the fallen spirits and in bondage to them, he is capable of seeing only them, and they often appear to such a person in the form of bright angels or as Christ Himself; they see his high opinion of himself and try to use this deception to destroy his soul.

Holy icons are accepted by the Holy Church for the inspiration of pious remembrances and feelings, but never for the inflaming of the imagination during prayer. As you stand before the icon of Christ, stand is if you are before the Lord Jesus Christ Himself, who is everywhere present in His divinity and physically present before you in His icon. When you stand before the icon of the Mother of God, stand as though before the very all-holy Virgin, but keep your mind without images. There is a great difference between being in the Lord's presence and imagining Him directly. The experience of the Lord's presence brings the soul into a salvific sense of awe and feeling of reverence, while imagining the form of Christ and His saints burdens the mind with a kind of carnality and brings it into a false, proud high opinion of itself. The soul is led into a false state of delusion.[23]

The experience of God's presence is a very high state! In it, the mind is kept from conversation with thoughts that distract from prayer; in it, the person feels only his great sinfulness; in it, the person becomes especially vigilant over his own soul and watchful to keep himself from any sin, even the smallest ones. This state is only gained by attentive prayer. It is also much aided by praying reverently before the holy icons.

The words of attentive prayer enter deeply into the soul, pierce the heart, and inspire compunction. The words of prayer uttered by a scattered mind barely scratch the surface of the soul without making any deep impression on it.

Attentiveness and compunction are the gift of the Holy Spirit. Only the Spirit can stem the tides of the mind, which flow every which way, said St John of the Ladder.[24] Another venerable Father said, "When compunction is with us, then God is with us."[25]

He who has acquired constant attentiveness and compunction in his prayers has reached the state of blessedness that the Gospels call "poverty of spirit and mourning." He has already torn the chains of many of his passions asunder, already smelled the sweet fragrance of spiritual freedom, and already bears within himself the promise of salvation. Do not leave the narrowness of this true path of prayer, and you will attain the blessed peace of the mystical Sabbath—for on the Sabbath, no earthly work is done and all labors and battles cease. In this blessed dispassion, away from all distraction, the soul stands before God in pure prayer and receives His calm through faith in His endless goodness, through faithfulness to His all-holy will.

In the zealot, flourishing prayer begins at first to reveal itself through a special active attentiveness—from time to time, the mind is unexpectedly taken by it and bound to the words of the prayer. Later, this state becomes more constant and longer lasting: the mind somehow attaches itself to the words of prayer, and through them is united to the heart. Finally, attentiveness is unnoticeably linked with compunction, and the person becomes a temple of prayer, a temple of God.

Bring to God quiet and humble prayers, not fiery and passionate ones. When you will become a mystical priest serving at the altar of prayer, then you will be able to enter God's sanctuary, and from there you will fill the censer of your prayer with divine fire. Impure fire—the blind, fleshly warmth of the blood—is forbidden as an offering to the all-holy God.

The divine fire of prayer taken from God's sanctuary is holy love that is poured on true Christians by the Holy Spirit.[26] He who tries to offer his prayer through the fire of his blood believes in his self-deception and delusion that he is serving God while, in actual fact, he is angering Him.

Do not search for exalted experiences in prayer—they are not proper to a sinner. Even the desire of a sinner to feel exalted is already delusion. Seek instead the resurrection of your dead, petrified heart, that it may become open to the knowledge of its own sinfulness and the depth of its fall and its insignificance, to see it and to admit it with self-denial. Then you will find within yourself the true fruit of prayer—sincere repentance. You will stand before God and will cry out to Him with prayer from this suddenly revealed state of spiritual helplessness. You will cry out as if from a prison, from the grave, from hell itself.

Repentance gives birth to prayer with its many spiritual fruits. Sweetness in prayer is the exclusive gift of the holy chosen ones of God who have been renewed by the Holy Spirit. Whoever invents a false sweetness for himself through the warmth of his blood, through vain imaginings and sensuality, is in the most grievous self-delusion. The soul darkened by a worldly, carnal life is very capable of such invention. Such a soul is fooled continually by its own pride.

The feelings that arise from prayer and repentance consist of a clean conscience, a calm soul, peace with all your near ones and contentment with the circumstances of life, mercy and cosuffering toward all men, abstinence from all passions, coldness toward the world, submission to God, and strength during the fight with sinful thoughts and inclinations. With such feelings, in which one can foretaste salvation, you should be content. Do not seek exalted spiritual states or prayerful ecstasy before their time. They are not as you imagine them to be—the activity of the Holy Spirit, who gives high states of prayer, is not comprehensible to a worldly mind.[27]

Learn to pray with your whole mind, with your entire soul, with all your strength. You may ask—what does that mean? It is impossible to know exactly without actually experiencing it. Try to constantly exercise yourself in attentive prayer. Attentive prayer will answer this question for you through blessed experience.

The labor of prayer seems heavy, boring, and dry to the mind that is used to entertaining itself with only perishable things. Prayer becomes habitual only with great effort, but when one attains such a habit, it then becomes a source of endless spiritual consolation.

I have already said that prayer is the mother of all virtues. Acquire it! With it, all of its children will come into the house of your soul and will make it a house of God.

Before you begin any work, pray to God. Through this prayer, you will gain the blessing of God for your work, and through it judge your works—in other words, prayerful thoughts prevent any work that is contrary to the commandments of God.

Whoever turns to God with prayer for discernment, help, and blessing before any deed or word lives under the gaze of God, under His direct guidance. It is easy to cultivate such a habit. The Great Barsanuphius said that there is nothing faster than the mind, and there is nothing more proper than raising one's mind to God at every need.[28]

During life's difficult times, make your prayers to God more frequent. Prayer is more dependable than the empty reasoning of man's weak mind that leads to nothing. It is better to lean on the almighty God with faith and prayer than to trust your own sick reason with its feeble ideas and solutions.

Do not be foolish in your petitions, so as not to anger God through your stupidity. Whoever asks something pitiful from the King of kings demeans Him. The Israelites, ignoring the miracles of God done on their behalf in the desert, asked only for the satisfaction of their stomachs: But while "the food was still in their mouths, the heavy wrath of God came upon them."[29]

Bring to God petitions that are appropriate to His greatness. Solomon asked for wisdom; he received it, and with it many other benefits because his request was wise. Elisha asked for the grace of the Holy Spirit, greater even than his teacher's, and his request was granted.

Whoever seeks through prayer to receive perishable earthly goods only angers the heavenly King. Angels and archangels, the leaders of God's hosts, look upon you and your petitions during prayer. They are amazed with joy when they see an earthy creature leave his earth behind him to seek heavenly goods. However, they mourn the one who leaves the heavenly unnoticed, asking only for his own dust and ashes.

We are commanded to be children in our gentleness, not in our minds.[30] During prayer, the babbling and fickle reason of this world is rejected. This does not mean that prayer requires stupidity. Prayer instead requires absolute reason, reason filled with humility and simplicity, which in prayer is often revealed not in words but in something much higher than words—silence. Prayerful silence only then visits the mind, when suddenly a new, spiritual understanding appears, indescribable in the words of this world and age, when the living presence of God is palpably sensed. Before God, who is inconceivable in His greatness, His feeble creature—man—falls silent.

The long prayers of the pagans that the Lord rejected consisted of oft-repeated, long-winded petitions about temporary goods,[31] as if rhetorical flourishes, pleasing delivery, or the power of the spoken word could act in the same way on God as on the hearing and emotions of carnal man! Rejecting such inane babbling, the Lord in no way rejected long prayers per se, as some heretics imagine. He Himself sanctified long prayer when He remained in prayer for long periods of time.[32]

The long prayers of the Lord's righteous were not long because of excessive words but because of the many spiritual experiences that were revealed to them during prayer. Through the power of these experiences time is conquered, becoming a foretaste of eternity for the saints of God.

The practitioner of prayer achieves success in his blessed labor when the variety of thoughts expressed in psalms and other prayers no longer correspond to his spiritual needs. The prayer of the publican and other short prayers more succinctly express the unutterable, magnificent desires of the purified heart, and often the saints of God spend many hours in such prayer, never feeling the need for diversity of thoughts for their powerful, concentrated prayer.[33]

The prayers invented by heretics are, in fact, quite similar to the prayers of the ancient pagans—they are long-winded, beautifully phrased, passionately expressed, and lack repentance. In them is a desire for the Bridegroom that is taken straight from the brothel of the passions. They are full of self-deception. They are not of the Holy Spirit; rather, they stink of the death-bearing infection of the spirit of darkness, the spirit of evil, the spirit of lies and perdition.

Prayer is a great work! The holy apostles even refused to serve their brothers in their daily needs, preferring instead to serve the Word in prayer. "It is not desirable that we should leave the word of God and serve tables. But we will give ourselves continually to prayer and to the ministry of the word"[34]—that is, in conversation with God in prayer and conversation about God with their neighbors, teaching them about the tri-hypostatic God and the incarnation of God the Word.

The work of prayer is the highest work for the human mind; the state of purity, needing no pleasant distractions, given by prayer to the mind, is the highest natural state of the mind. The ascent of the mind to God, which only begins with pure prayer, is a state beyond the natural.[35]

This supernatural state is reserved for the holy ones of God, renewed by the Holy Spirit, those who have cast off the old Adam and put on the New, capable of "with unveiled face, beholding as in a mirror the glory of the Lord, are being transformed into the same image from glory to glory,"[36] through the action of the Spirit of the Lord. They receive the greater part of divine revelation during the work of prayer because during this time the soul is especially prepared, especially purified, and directed to communion with God.[37] Thus did the Apostle Peter see the amazing shroud descend from heaven during prayer.[38] Thus did Cornelius the centurion see an angel during prayer.[39] Thus, when the Apostle Paul prayed in the temple of Jerusalem, the Lord appeared to him and commanded him to leave Jerusalem immediately: "Depart: for I will send you far from here to the Gentiles."[40]

Prayer is commanded by the Lord, as is repentance. The end of prayer as well as repentance is the same—entry into the kingdom of heaven, into the kingdom of God, which is within us. "Repent, for the kingdom of heaven is at hand,"[41] "the kingdom of God is within you,"[42] "ask, and it will be given to you; seek, and you will find; knock, and it will be opened to you. For everyone who asks receives, and he who seeks finds, and to him who knocks it will be opened. Your heavenly Father give[s] the Holy Spirit to those who ask Him."[43] "And shall God not avenge His own elect who cry out day and night to Him? I tell you that He will avenge them speedily."[44] Entry into the kingdom of heaven, which is planted into the heart of every Christian by holy baptism, is the development of that kingdom through the action of the Holy Spirit.

Hurry to pray, o soul that thirsts for salvation, hurry to follow the Saviour who is accompanied by His countless disciples. Cry out to Him as He passes with your prayer, as did the woman of Canaan; do not be offended by His long inattention to your prayers; patiently and humbly bear the sorrows and offenses, which He will allow to come your way. For success in prayer, you fundamentally need help from temptations. According to your faith, for your humility, for the constancy of your prayer, He will comfort you with the healing of your daughter who is possessed by the passions. He will heal your thoughts and feelings, transforming them from passionate to dispassionate, from sinful to holy, from earthly to spiritual. Amen.

Article 2

The labor of prayer is holy, great, soul saving. It is the first and most important of the monk's labors. All other ascetic labors are servants of this one; they exist solely for the success of the labor of prayer. St. Macarius the Great said, "The crown of every pious life and the height of all good deeds is the constant work of prayer."[45]

What human condition can be more wonderful, what can be compared with the situation of the person who is allowed to speak in prayer to the King of kings, to the God of gods, to the Creator and the all-powerful Lord of all things visible and invisible, the visible and invisible worlds?

As important as this work is, it requires a great deal of preliminary preparation.[46]

The King of kings requires that those who desire to approach Him have the proper mind-set and state of heart, through which all of the righteous ones of the Old and New Testament came closer to Him and pleased Him.[47] Without this proper mind-set and state of heart, access to God is impossible, and all attempts and efforts are futile.

You, who desire to approach God and become united with Him through constant work in prayer—be careful! Carefully study the manner of your thoughts—are they infected with even the slightest false teaching? Do you exactly follow the teaching of the only true, holy, apostolic Orthodox Church, without any exceptions?[48] Christ said to his disciple: If anyone "refuses even to hear the church, let him be to you like a heathen and a tax collector,"[49] who are separated from God, who are the enemies of God. What sort of significance can the prayer of an enemy of God have? How effective will be the prayer of one who is far away from God?

Admitting your sinfulness, acknowledging your sickness, your worthlessness—this is absolutely necessary for your prayer to be acceptable and heard by God. All the saints put the knowledge and confession of their sinfulness and the sinfulness of all mankind as the foundation of their prayer. The holiness of a person depends on the acknowledgment and confession of this sinfulness. He who gives humanity sanctity for their repentance, said, "I did not come to call the righteous, but sinners, to repentance."[50]

You, who desire to begin the work of prayer! Before you begin this labor, try to forgive everyone who may have offended you, slandered you, or belittled you, anyone who may have done you any kind of evil. He, before Whom you have decided to stand with prayer, commands you: "If you bring your gift [of prayer] to the [heavenly] altar" of the King of kings, "and there remember that your brother has something against you, leave your gift there before the altar, and go your way. First be reconciled to your brother, and then come and offer your gift."[51]

Prepare yourself for prayer through lack of passionate attachment and lack of cares for the things of this world. From passionate attachments come all manner of worries. Your thoughts, tied down by passions and distracted by worries, cannot strive directly to God through prayer. "You cannot serve God and mammon. For where your treasure is, there your heart will be also. Therefore, do not worry, saying, 'What shall we eat?' or 'What shall we drink?' or 'What shall we wear?' But seek first the kingdom of God and His righteousness, and all these things shall be added to you."[52] Lift up your mind and heart from the earth and from everything earthly, and it will be easy for you to begin the invisible movement toward heaven in prayer.

If you are stricken by poverty, or if you are suffering from sorrowful events in your life, or if you are slandered and your enemy is persecuting you—pay no attention to any of it so that your attention during prayer is not distracted by any diversions or any worries. Pay no attention to your remembrances or the circumstances of your poverty, your everyday worries, or your enemies. He who rules over your circumstances, yourself, and your enemies, said to His beloved ones: "Let not your heart be troubled, you believe in God, believe also in Me."[53]

"When you pray, go into your room, and when you have shut your door, pray to your Father who is in the secret place"[54] Whether you are in company or are alone, try to constantly descend into your inner spiritual cell, closing the doors of your feelings and tongue, in order to pray secretly with your mind and heart.

Having fallen in love with the labor of prayer, come to love also the solitude of your physical cell. Close its door for yourself and others. Bear the loneliness of solitude with patience—it will very soon be replaced with more pleasant feelings. "Remain in your cell," says the Holy Father, "it will teach you everything you need to know,"[55] that is, the monastic life, which is completely focused on prayer.

Having fallen in love with the labor of prayer, come to love silence also. It preserves the powers of your soul undivided, capable of constant prayer in the inner cell. The habit of solitude gives the possibility of silent prayer of the heart, even amid the noise of the crowded world.[56]

Bring sensual enjoyment, the pleasures of fantasy, curiosity, and inquisitiveness as a sacrifice to your love of prayer. Keep your soul free from all external impressions so that, through the help of prayer, God himself can be impressed upon it. His all-holy, invisible, spiritual image cannot bear to be in a soul that is befouled with images of the vain, sensual, transient world.

Do not delight in visible nature; do not contemplate its beauty; do not waste precious time and your inner strength acquiring the knowledge given by human sciences.[57] Use your strength and time to acquire prayer, serving God in the depths of your inner cell. There, inside yourself, prayer will reveal such a vista that will absorb all of your attention; prayer will give you knowledge into which the world itself will not be able to fit, the existence of which it does not even have the slightest idea.

There, in the depths of the heart, you will see the fall of mankind; you will see your soul, destroyed by sin; you will see the grave; you will see hell; you will see the demons; you will see chains and shackles; you will see the fiery sword of the cherubim who protects the way to the tree of life, preventing mankind from entering heaven; you will see many other mysteries, hidden from the world and from the sons of the world.[58] When this vista will open before your eyes, your attention will be completely enthralled. You will cool toward everything temporal and perishable that you previously adored.

"Today, or tomorrow, we will die," said St Andrew to one of his monks,[59] distracting him from his attachment to earthly things and explaining the foolishness of such attachment. What truth is in these words! It is a very accurate portrayal of the unknown length of our life! If not today, tomorrow we will die. There is nothing so easy as to die. When even the longest life comes to its end, it seems no longer than a fleeting second. What is the purpose of concerning oneself with something that, of necessity, you will have to leave behind you forever, and that very soon? How much better it is to study yourself through prayer, to study the coming life and world, in which we will remain forever.

The solitude of the cell and the desert—these are the abodes of prayer. "He who has tasted of prayer," said St John of the Ladder, "will flee from crowds of people. What, if not prayer, makes his beloved, like the wild ass of the desert, free from the necessities of social life?"[60] If you want to dedicate your life to the work of prayer, separate yourself from the sight of the world and reject the society of people, separate yourself from conversations and from the usual friendly visits to your cell, even if they come because of love for you. Separate yourself from everything that hinders or disturbs your mystical communication with God.[61] Live on earth and in the society of men as if you were a stranger. You are a wanderer. The earth is your hostel. The hour in which you will be called is unknown to you. The call is inevitable and inexorable; it is impossible to turn away from it or to fight against it. Prepare yourself for the joyful departure from the hostel through holy prayer.

Prayer joins a person to God. The fallen angels look upon its labor with unutterable envy and anger since, from their fall, they have gone from union with God to a frightful, insane war against Him. They try to frighten the one who is praying with various temptations, seeking to drive him away from his salvific ascesis, to wrest from him that success and blessedness that he will indubitably receive from his labors. And so the one who desires to dedicate himself to the exercise of prayer must prepare himself in advance for sorrows, so that he is not shocked and disturbed when they attack him, so that he courageously withstands them with the power of faith and endurance.[62]

The demons attack the monk who exercises in prayer by physical diseases, by poverty, and by the lack of attention and help from others, in the same way that they attacked and oppressed John, with God's permission. But we, like this righteous man, must bless and thank God for everything He allows the demons to do to us.[63] With praise and gratitude, let us do the all-holy will of God that is revealed to us by the Holy Spirit: "in everything give thanks; for this is the will of God in Christ Jesus for you."[64]

The demons teach people to rise up against the practitioners of prayer, to judge them for their strange behavior and for their lack of useful work, denouncing them as lazy, hypocritical babblers. They ascribe to them evil and malicious intentions and sinful actions, they destroy and disturb their silence, they force them to various activities that are contrary to their way of life, activities that are united with diversions, scattered thoughts, and the destruction of the peace of the heart. Knowing the source of these temptations, let us pray for our neighbors as the Gospel commands and as the Holy Fathers instruct, for they sin in ignorance, being led to it by others. These traps of the devil will be destroyed by God.

Tempting us from without, the demons also attack us within. When we go into seclusion, we begin to exercise prayer. They immediately inspire in us various sinful desires that we never experienced before. They worry our heart with countless sinful thoughts and imaginings, which until this moment never even occurred to us. They do this with a definite purpose—to bring us into confusion and despair when we do not see any purpose in our labor of prayer and solitude, and to convince us to stop our ascesis.[65] To the inexperienced ascetics, these actions of the demons seem to be the natural inclinations of the soul itself. Our invisible and cunning enemies do us evil and simultaneously try to hide themselves so that their victim will lose all hope of becoming untangled from their snares, so that his despair and perdition will become inevitable.[66]

Just as the demons find it very important to hide themselves from their victim, it is equally important for the ascetic to understand that they are the original sinners, the source of all temptation. When we live our lives in service to God, the sources of temptation are not our friends, not ourselves, not isolated events in our lives. Having seen our enemies, we will slowly learn, under the guidance of the word of God, to vigilantly watch them and ourselves, to firmly withstand them. The great Apostle Peter instructs us: "Humble yourselves under the mighty hand of God, that He may exalt you in due time, casting all your care upon Him, for He cares for you. Be sober, be vigilant; because your adversary the devil walks about like a roaring lion, seeking whom he may devour. Resist him, steadfast in the faith."[67]

These battles, these attacks of the demons on those who wish to be saved through prayer, are allowed by God Himself. They are the result of our fall, in which we submitted ourselves to the authority of the demons. Let us submit to God's just will for us, and let us bow our heads under all the blows of sorrows and sicknesses with which God's good will desires to chasten our sinfulness and our sins in this temporary life, so that He may deliver us from the eternal sorrows and sicknesses that we deserve. Allowing us to be tempted and giving us over to the devil, God never ceases to think of us. Chastening us, He does not stop doing good for us. The Apostle says: "God is faithful, who will not allow you to be tempted beyond what you are able, but with the temptation will also make the way of escape, that you may be able to bear it."[68] And the devil, being the slave and creation of God, attacks us not as much as he desires, but only as much as God will allow him. He tempts us not whenever he wishes, but when he is given permission.[69] According to the counsel of the Apostle, let us give unto God all care for our own selves, all our sorrows, and all our hopes, and in order to do this, let us make our prayer to Him more frequent and more powerful.

The permission given to the demons to tempt us is necessary for our success. When they hinder our prayer, they force us to learn how to become especially proficient in the use of this weapon. The weapon of prayer destroys the fiery sword of the cherubim who guards the way to the tree of life, and the victor becomes a communicant of eternal life.[70] According to the unutterable wisdom of God, "evil helps the good, even though the intention be evil."[71] In our solitude and during our exercise in prayer, when we suddenly feel the roiling of sensual passions, when impure thoughts attack us, and when sinful images inscribe themselves on our minds with vivid, enticing clarity—these are the signs of the demonic attack. That is not the time for despair; that is not the time for lassitude; that is the time for labor. Let us rebuff the enemies through the redoubling of our prayer to God, and He will scatter and expel our enemies.[72]

Victories in the unseen warfare do not always occur or happen quickly. Victory is a gift from God, given to the ascetic by God in its own time, known only to God and determined exclusively by God Himself. In fact, defeats are necessary for us. Here we have in mind defeats that arise out of our own weakness and sinfulness, not from a change in our desires. Defeats are allowed for our humility so that we might see and learn the fallenness of our nature and that we might admit the necessity of the Redeemer, believe in Him, and confess Him.[73]

When we are defeated, our invisible enemies inspire guilt in us for our failure, which leads to lassitude in our labor of prayer, doubt in its efficacy, and the desire to stop praying and go instead and do good work before the eyes of all men. Let us not fall prey to this lie! Let us open our wound with self-denial and lack of shame before our all-good and all-powerful Physician, who commanded this salvific lack of shame and promised to crown it with defeat for our enemies.[74] Let us lay down this promise in our soul—until our last breath never to leave the labor of prayer, and from it to pass into eternity.

The shame we feel after defeat is senseless; worse—it is the evil mocking of our enemies. Is this fig leaf (shame and other feelings like it) capable of covering the sins of man from the all-knowing God? God sees our sins even without our confession! He seeks our confession only in order to heal us. If He instructed His apostle to forgive his repentant brother "seven times in a day," then how much more will He Himself forgive us, if we constantly come to Him with prayer and confession![75]

Let us pay diligent attention to the following: is our own duplicity strengthening our enemies in the unseen war? Is it perhaps the reason for their frequent victories? Are we not ourselves perhaps making their authority and influence over us stronger by doing their will through the fulfillment of our carnal desires, inclinations, and passions? Do we not anger God by these actions; do we not send Him far away from ourselves? Is not the love of the world active in us, which leaves us only with the veneer of being God's servant, but makes us in essence the enemies of God?[76]

"A double-minded man, unstable in all his ways [of virtue],"[77] so much more does he waver on the higher path that precedes virtues—the path of prayer. He rejects God, as does the one who is neither hot nor cold.[78] He is incapable of becoming a true disciple of prayer, which brings its students before the very face of God for supernatural instruction, leading them in the footsteps of Christ if they do not reject all that they have,[79] that is, the sickly deviation of mankind's fallen nature toward the world. "And those who are Christ's have crucified the flesh with its passions and desires."[80] Only those who belong completely to Christ can acquire true prayer.

Our apparently insignificant passions, our apparently innocent love for something or someone can bring down the mind and heart from heaven and cast them down to the earth among the innumerable snakes and reptiles of the vast sea of life.[81] The Holy Fathers liken the ascetic who succeeds in prayer to an eagle but pitiful passions to the threads of a net; if even one talon of the eagle's majestic foot becomes caught in this snare, then the eagle becomes incapable of his flight upward, and he becomes an easy and inevitable prey of the fowler.[82] Useless, then, are the strength and courage of the kingly bird.

Taking their cues from the holy Gospels, the Holy Fathers instruct us to "go, sell what you have [of the world], and give to the poor," and taking up your cross, reject yourself by resisting your passions and your fallen will,[83] so that you may be able to pray without frustration and distraction.[84] While your passionate attachment to the world lives within you, it will fight your prayer through frustration and distraction.

It is necessary, at first, to reject all that you have of the earth, to separate yourself from the world, to disown the world; only after such a rejection can a Christian see his inner bondage, prison, chains, wounds, deadness of soul.[85] The battle with the lifelessness of our heart, which is waged with the help of prayer, with the guidance of the word of God, is crucifixion—death of the soul for the salvation of the soul.[86]

Unite your prayer with wise fasting. Such a union of two spiritual weapons is commanded by the Lord Himself for expelling the demons out of ourselves.[87] "When you fast, anoint your head and wash your face," the Lord Himself commanded.[88] According to the explanation of the Holy Fathers, the oil with which the head was customarily anointed indicates mercy that must always accompany our spiritual judgment, as the Apostle said, "Therefore, as the elect of God, holy and beloved, put on tender mercies, kindness, humility, meekness, longsuffering; bearing with one another, and forgiving one another, if anyone has a complaint against another; even as Christ forgave you, so you also must do."[89] You must wash the face of your body and soul with tears—they will only appear on the face of the one who prays and fasts, and only when his heart will be overfilled with mercy for his neighbor and compassionate cosuffering with all mankind, without any exception.

Do you want to be united with God through prayer? First, unite your heart with mercy, through which we are called to become like our heavenly Father,[90] and to become perfect in grace.[91] Force your heart to become merciful and good, and submerge and robe your entire spirit in these qualities until you feel within yourself true love for your neighbor, such love that its rays shine equally "on the evil and on the good."[92]

When from your heart you forgive all your neighbors their sins, then you will see your own sins. You will see how much you need God's mercy, how much all of mankind needs it. You will cry aloud before God for yourself and for all mankind.

The Holy Fathers include all of the deeds of the monk, all his life, in one word—*tears*. What are the tears of a monk? They are his prayer.[93]

When the Holy Spirit enters into a man, "the Spirit Himself makes intercession for us with groanings which cannot be uttered."[94] The divine and heavenly Spirit, making Himself like unto the soul of a person, prays and weeps for him; He intercedes for the saints according to the will of God,[95] because to Him alone is the will of God revealed. "No one knows the things of God except the Spirit of God."[96] Promising His disciples a great gift, the gift of the Holy Spirit, the Lord said, "the Helper, the Holy Spirit, whom the Father will send in My name, He will teach you all things,"[97] if all things, then tears and prayer as well. He will cry aloud for us, He will pray for us, "for we do not know what we should pray for as we ought."[98] So weak, limited, darkened, and damaged are we by sin.

If, upon entering us, the Holy Spirit cries out for us, how much more should we cry for ourselves before receiving this all-holy traveler inside ourselves? After renewal by the Holy Spirit, if our state is worthy of tears (and it is worthy of tears according to the witness of the very Holy Spirit), how much more is it worthy of tears in its decrepitude, in its fallenness, to which we have led ourselves? Tears must be an inalienable quality of our prayer, its constant, ever-present fellow traveler and pilgrim, its very soul.

Whoever unites his prayer with tears labors according to the instruction of God Himself; he labors properly, lawfully. At the appropriate time, he can expect to reap a great harvest—joy that promises salvation. Whoever removed tears from his prayer labors contrary to God's instruction, and he will bear no fruits at all. Not only that, but he will instead reap the thorns of vanity, self-deception, and perdition.

Brothers! Let us not allow ourselves to be fooled by the false, ridiculous, foolish, pernicious thought—let us not strive to feel delight in our prayer! It is not appropriate for a sinner to feel the joy of grace; a sinner deserves only tears. Let us seek them diligently; let us find this treasure, the key to all other spiritual treasures.

He who has no tears is in a false position—he is fooled by his own pride.

The Holy Fathers call such tears guides in spiritual labors. They must come before all our good thoughts; they must lead them to their proper goal. Thoughts that are not infused with sorrow or are not guided by it are wayward thoughts.[99]

St Pimen the Great said, "The life of a monk must be full of tears. This is the path of repentance, given us by the Scriptures and the Fathers, who said: weep! There is no other path, other than the path of tears."[100]

Another great Father said, "If you want to please God, leave the world, separate yourself from the earth, leave creation, approach the Creator and unite with God through prayer and tears."[101]

Monks who live in large monasteries and want to acquire prayerful tears must pay special attention to the rejection of their own will. If they will cut it off and pay no attention to the sins and the actions of others around them in general, then they will acquire both prayer and tears. When thoughts descend into the heart, they inspire the heart to pray and sorrow for God, and this sorrow leads to tears.[102]

Since, in our time, there is a frightful lack of true instructors of prayer, let us choose tears for our guide and instructor. They will teach us to pray and keep us from self-deception. All who have rejected tears and removed it from their prayer have fallen into self-deception. This is maintained by the Holy Fathers.[103]

He who has acquired pure prayer with the help of tears remembers only God and his own sinfulness during prayer. Death and the judgment that will follow immediately after death seem to him already present. He stands with his heart before the inexorable Judge Who is no respecter of persons, before the Judge Who can still be mollified and can receive the petition of the sorrowing one at the judgment that is established by prayer. He develops in the appropriate time a proper fear, sorrow, and groaning, in order to escape the futile horror, trembling, shock, tears, and despair that the rejected sinners feel upon receiving their condemnation from God, Who is angered at them for eternity. He condemns himself, so that he might not be condemned. He admits himself a criminal worthy of every punishment so that he might divert punishment from himself. He confesses himself a sinner in order to receive righteousness from the right hand of God, Who gives this righteousness in excess to all sinners who admit and confess their sinfulness.

The Lord commands: "Ask, and it will be given to you; seek, and you will find; knock, and it will be opened to you." Here is indicated not an action once performed, but a constant work; the commandment applies to the entire earthly life of a person. "For everyone who asks receives, and he who seeks finds, and to him who knocks it will be opened. Your heavenly Father [will] give the Holy Spirit to those who ask Him."[104]

According to the very promise, it is absolutely necessary to vigilantly, constantly work: "for you do not know when the master of the house is coming—in the evening, at midnight, at the crowing of the rooster, or in the morning—lest, coming suddenly, he find you sleeping."[105]

It is impossible, says St John of the Ladder, to teach prayer only with words to those who desire it.[106] The true teacher is experience and tears. In compunction and humility of heart let us begin the labor of prayer, let us submit to the guidance of tears. God Himself, who gives prayer to the one who prays, will become our instructor in prayer.

"Come to Me" (with such words prayer, the holy mother of all virtues, invites us), "all you who labor" under the yoke of passions in bondage to the fallen spirits "and are heavy laden" by various sins, "and I will give you rest. Take My yoke upon you, and you will find rest for your souls," through the healing of your sores. "For My yoke is easy,"[107] capable of healing all sins, even the most grievous.[108]

"Come, ye children" (with such words prayer, the holy mother of all virtues, invites us) "and hearken unto me; I will teach you the fear of the Lord."[109] I will teach you the fear of the Lord through experience, I will bring it palpably into your hearts. I will teach you also the beginner's fear, through which every man turns away from evil, and the pure fear of the Lord, who endures for ever and ever, the fear with which all the Lord's children reverence Him.[110] For the Lord is fearful even to the fiery cherubim and the glorious, six-winged seraphim.

Leave behind your fruitless and pointless attachment to all that fades, all that you will be forced to leave behind whether you wish it or not! Leave behind all attractions and enjoyments of temptations! Leave behind idle chatter, inappropriate laughter, and excess talk, which leave the soul empty! Remember, analyze, and convince yourselves that you are here on earth only as temporary wanderers, that your homeland, your eternal home, is heaven. You need a strong and faithful guide there. I, prayer, am this guide—no one else! All the saints who have ascended from earth to heaven traveled on no other path than the one offered by me. I reveal the fall and sinfulness of man to those who unite themselves with me, and I pull them out as from a deep pit. I show them the princes of the air, their traps and snares; I tear apart these snares; I defeat and expel these princes.

I reveal the Creator to the created and the Redeemer to the redeemed; I reconcile man with God. I reveal to my students and my beloved the inconceivable greatness of God, and lead them into that state of reverence and submission to Him, which is appropriate for the creation before its Creator. I sow humility in the heart, and give the heart a great harvest of tears. My communicants become communicants of divine grace. I will never leave those whom I guide, until I lead them before the very face of God, until they are united with God. God is the limitless fulfillment of all desires, both in this world and in the eternal life. Amen.

CHAPTER 21

On Faith

I pour out the words of my heart, which is quietly moved by unfading and unutterable joy. Brothers! Enter with a pure mind into my words, and find joy in this spiritual feast! Faith in Christ is life. He who nourishes himself with faith has a foretaste of the eternal life appointed for the righteous while still in this earthly life of wandering. The Lord said: "He who believes in Me has everlasting life."[1] Through faith, the righteous ones of God patiently bore cruel temptations; since they kept riches and the joy of the eternal life in their hearts, they considered this earthly life with its enticements less than nothing. Through faith, they accepted sorrows and suffering as gifts from God through which God allowed them to emulate and take part in His earthly life, when He willed that one of His persons[2] take up our human nature and effect our redemption. The endless joy given by faith overcame the pain of sorrows so much that during suffering they felt only pleasure. The Great Martyr Eustratius witnessed this in his last prayer before death, uttered as he bowed his head under the sword. "The suffering of the body," he said to God, "is joy to your slaves!"[3] Through faith, the saints immersed themselves in the depths of humility; they saw through the pure eyes of faith that the things people bring in sacrifice to God—the gifts of God in man, the debts of man—are not necessary to God. They are necessary and salvific for man when man tries to bring them to God, increase them, and return them to God. God said: "Hear, O my people, and I will speak unto you, and I will testify against thee, O Israel; I am God, even thy God. I will not reprove thee because of thy sacrifices, for thy whole-burnt offerings are always before Me, for the whole world is Mine, and the fullness thereof."[4] "And what do you have that you did not receive? Now if you did indeed receive it, why do you boast as if you had not received it?"[5] "For everyone to whom much is given, from him much will be required; and to whom much has been committed, of him they will ask the more."[6]

God's holy ones performed miracles, raised the dead, foretold the future, were filled with spiritual sweetness, and at the same time humbled themselves and stood in awe before God, seeing with fear and wonder that God allowed mere dust and mud to accept His Holy Spirit. O wonder! The mind is thrust into silence upon seeing these mysteries; the heart is filled with unutterable joy; the tongue is incapable of describing it. Through faith, the saints began to love their enemies. The eye of the mind, enlightened by faith, looks without turning away directly at God in His providence, and it ascribes all external events to this divine providence. Thus, when David saw before himself God revealed, in order to remain undaunted in the face of all sorrows and disasters that could terrify and disturb his heart,[7] he said of Shimei, when Shimei cursed him and threw stones at him: "The Lord has said to him, 'Curse David.' What have I to do with you, you sons of Zeruiah," ye thoughts full of anger and vengeance! "Let him alone, and let him curse; for so the Lord has ordered him. It may be that the Lord will look on my affliction."[8] The soul accepts temptations as medicine for its diseases and thanks the Physician—God—and sings: "Examine me, O Lord, and prove me; try out my reins and my heart."[9] When a person sees his temptations in this light, people and other tools of temptations remain on the side, as tools. There can be no anger directed at them, no enmity! The soul that praises the Creator, that thanks the heavenly Physician in ecstasy of unutterable heavenly joy, begins to bless the tools of its own healing.[10] And behold! Suddenly, the soul is enflamed with love for enemies; the person becomes ready to lay down his life for his enemy and sees in this not a sacrifice but a duty, the inevitable duty of a slave. From this moment, heaven itself is opened to us and we enter into love for our neighbor; through it, we enter into love for God, we unite ourselves with God, and God resides in us. What a treasure is contained in this faith, this mediator and giver of hope and love! Amen. (1840, Sergiev Hermitage)

PART IV

REFLECTION

Dew

Along the azure, cloudless sky, one gorgeous summer day, the glorious sun was traveling its usual path. The golden crosses of the five-domed church named for the all-holy Trinity sparkled; the silvery domes reflected the blinding light of the sun's rays. The shadows bespoke the beginning of the ninth hour, when the Divine Liturgy usually begins. A great multitude of people hurried from the highway to the peaceful monastery—it was a Sunday, or a great feast, I do not remember exactly.

Beyond the walls of the monastery, on the eastern side, lies a large meadow. During that time, it was covered by dense, soft grass and various sweet-smelling wildflowers that grew without a care in the world under the open sky. That day, the grass was covered in dew. The myriad drops glistened on every petal, every stem, and the tiniest leaf, and in every drop, the sun was painted. Every drop shone with rays like the rays of the sun. The meadow looked like a huge velvet carpet on which some brilliant hand had scattered an infinite multitude of different-colored precious stones, faceted perfectly to catch the rays of the sun.

At that moment, a monk-priest who was preparing to serve the Divine Liturgy came out of the side doors of the monastery wall, deep in thought.

Taking a few steps forward, he stopped before the wide meadow. It was calm and quiet in his heart; the silence of his heart was answered by the inspired calm of the surrounding nature, the kind of calm that happens only on a magnificent June morning, when it is so easy to contemplate and pray. Before his eyes was the sun in its pure, azure sky, and the countless reflections of the sun in the drops of dew covering the meadow. His thoughts lost themselves is some kind of infinity—his mind was without thoughts; as though prepared on purpose, it was specially tuned to accept spiritual impressions. The monk-priest looked at the sky, the sun, the meadow, the glistening drops of dew, and suddenly, before the eyes of his heart, the greatest of Christianity's mysteries revealed itself—an explanation that could actually make clear the undecipherable and inconceivable, an explanation through a living image, a natural painting that now lay before his eyes.

It was as if someone had said to him: "Look! The sun is completely reflected in every humble, pure drop of dew. Every drop of dew, taking on itself the rays of the sun, begins to shine like the rays of the sun. In the same way, Christ is fully present and offered in the Eucharist in every Orthodox Christian church. He gives light and life to his communicants, who themselves become life and light upon communing of the divine light and life. If the physical and mortal sun, created by the Creator with a mere movement of His will, can at the same time be imprinted in the myriad drops of water, why then cannot the Creator Himself, omnipotent and omnipresent, be present completely and at the same time with His all-holy Body and Blood, united with them in His divinity, in the many churches where according to His command the all-fulfilling, all-holy Spirit is summoned to overshadow the bread and wine, for the fulfillment of the great, salvific, inconceivable mystery?"

Carrying within himself this profound and powerful spiritual impression, the servant of the mystery returned to his cell. The impression remained alive in his soul. Months passed, years passed, but it remained as alive as it had on the first day. Hoping to give my neighbor benefit and instruction, I now share his story with my words and my pen. But mine is a poor description! The word and the pen are too weak to exactly and completely describe spiritual mysteries.

O holy mystery! O holy vision of the mind! With what unexpected immediacy you appear in vivid pictures in the mind that is prepared to see such visions through repentance and attentive, solitary prayer! How clear, powerful, alive is the knowledge given by You! How full of indubitable, unattainable certainty! You are independent of people—You come to the one that You choose, or to the one to whom You are sent. Useless is the desire to plumb the depths of Your mysteries with one's own will, with one's own strength! Such a person will be no more than a weak daydreamer who wanders in the darkness of his self-deception with only his outstretched hands as guides. He can neither feel nor impart light or life. Just as chains rattle on the hands and feet of a criminal, so in the thoughts and works of this daydreamer, you will always hear the faint sound of hollow falseness, of sinful slavery and foulness. The path to spiritual vision is constant repentance, weeping and sorrow for one's own sinfulness. Tears and sorrow are the only medicine to heal the eyes of the spirit.

CHAPTER 22

On Repentance

"Repent, and believe in the gospel! Repent, for the kingdom of heaven is at hand."[1] These were the first words of the God-Man's preaching. These same words today He pronounces to us through the Gospels.

When the world's sin became most virulent, then the all-powerful Physician came down to the world. He descended to a country of exile, to a world of our longing and suffering, which was only the beginning of our eternal suffering in hell. He brought the good news of redemption, joy, and healing for all people, without anything in return. "Repent!"

The power of repentance is founded on the power of God—the Physician is all-powerful, and the medicine given by Him is also all-powerful.

At that time, during His preaching on earth, the Lord called all diseased with sin to be healed, calling no sin incurable. And now He continues to call everyone; He promises and gives forgiveness of any sin, healing of any sinful ailment.

O, pilgrims on earth! You who rush or are dragged along the wide path, through the never-silent noise of earthly cares, pleasures, and enjoyments, along the path of flowers that hide stems covered in thorns, who hurry along this road to the end that everyone realizes and yet forgets—the dark coffin, and an even darker and more frightening eternity, stop! Throw away the enchantment of the world that is constantly keeping you in chains! Listen to what our Saviour has to say, pay due attention to His words! "Repent, and believe in the gospel," He says to you, "Repent, for the kingdom of heaven is at hand."

It is absolutely necessary for you, earthly wanderers, to pay full attention to this essentially useful, salvific admonition. Or else you will gain nothing but the coffin and the gateway of eternity without acquiring any true understanding either of eternity or of the responsibilities of those who enter it, thereby only gaining eternal and just torments for your sins. The heaviest of sins is disregard of the words of the Saviour, disdain of the Saviour. "Repent!"

The earthly path is full of flattery and deception. For him who first steps on this path, it appears as an unending field full of authentic realities. For him who is at the end of the road, it seems extremely short and full of empty dreams.

Glory and riches, and all other perishable acquisitions and benefits that the blinded sinner wastes his entire earthly life seeking, all his spiritual and bodily strength, all this he must leave in that moment, when the soul is forcibly stripped of its clothing, his body, at that moment when the soul is led by inexorable angels to the judgment of the righteous God, a God whom he knows not, whom he disregards. "Repent!"

People work and hurry to enrich themselves with knowledge, but only trifling knowledge, useful only for a time, necessary only for the gratification of the needs, comforts, and desires of an earthly life. That knowledge and action that is so essential, and for which we have only a short earthly life, we completely despise—that knowledge of God and reconciliation with Him through the mediation of the Redeemer. "Repent!"

Brothers! Let us look objectively, through the light of the Gospel, into our earthly life. It is useless! All its goods are taken away by death, and often before this, by various unexpected circumstances. These goods—so perishable, so fleeting—do not even deserve to be called goods! More likely they are lies, traps. Those who are caught in these snares are deprived of the true, eternal, heavenly, spiritual goods, which are given by faith in Christ and emulation of Him along the mysterious path of the Gospel life. "Repent!"

We are in such a frightening blindness! How obvious this blindness becomes through our falls! We see the death of our brother, we know that it will definitely come for us, and maybe soon, because no one has ever remained indefinitely on earth. We see that many, even before their deaths, are betrayed by this so-called earthly happiness that often turns into earthly misery, similar to a daily taste of death. Despite this vivid experiential proof, we rush after only earthly goods, as if they were permanent, eternal. All of our attention is absorbed only in them! God is forgotten! Majestic and awful eternity is also forgotten! "Repent!"

Brothers, these perishable goods will most definitely betray us. Rich men will be betrayed by their riches; the powerful will be betrayed by their glory, the young by their youth, and the wise by their wisdom. There is only one eternal, essential good that a person may acquire during his earthly sojourn—true knowledge of God, reconciliation and union with God, given by Christ. But to receive these highest of goods, one must leave the life of sin, one must hate it. "Repent!"

"Repent!" What does it mean to repent? A certain great Holy Father answers this question (St Pimen the Great). It means to admit and feel remorse for one's sins, to abandon one's sins, and to never return to them. In this way, many sinners became saints; many wicked men became righteous.

"Repent!" Reject not only the obvious sins—murder, theft, fornication, slander, lying—but also sinful entertainments, pleasures of the flesh, sinful fantasy, and unlawful thoughts, everything forbidden by the Gospels. Wash away your previous sinful life with tears of sincere repentance.

Do not say to yourself in your despair and spiritual paralysis: "I fell into heavy sins, I acquired sinful habits through a long sinful life; with time they have become like congenital defects, they have made repentance impossible for me." These dark thoughts are inspired by your enemy, whom you still do not notice or understand.[2] He knows the power of repentance, and he fears that it will tear you from his grasp, so he tries to distract you from repentance, ascribing weakness to God's all-powerful treatment.

The establisher of repentance is your Creator, Who created you out of nothing. It is so easy for Him to re-create you, to transform your heart, to make a God-loving heart out of a sin-loving heart, to make a pure, spiritual, holy heart out of a sensual, carnal, evil-intentioned, earthly heart.

Brothers! Let us come to know the unutterable love God shows to our fallen human race. The Lord became incarnate so that through the incarnation He would take upon Himself the punishments deserved by mankind, and through the punishment of the all-holy, He would redeem the guilty from punishment. What attracted Him to us here, on earth, to the country of our exile? Our righteousness? No! He was called down by the fallen state to which we had descended because of our sinfulness.

Sinners! Let us be bold. For us, truly for us, did the Lord accomplish the great work of His incarnation; He looked upon our sicknesses with unimaginable compassion. Let us stop vacillating! Let us stop falling into despair and doubt! Let us approach repentance full of faith, zeal, and gratitude, and through its mediation let us be reconciled with God. "But if a wicked man turns from all his sins which he has committed, keeps all My statutes, and does what is lawful and right, he shall surely live; he shall not die. None of the transgressions which he has committed shall be remembered against him; because of the righteousness which he has done, he shall live."[3] Such a promise is given by God to the sinner, through the words of His great prophet.

Let us reciprocate, as much as our feeble strength allows, the Lord's great love for us, but only in accordance with our situation as fallen creatures of a loving Creator. Let us repent! Let us repent not only with our lips. Let us prove our repentance not with a few, fleeting tears, not with a superficial participation in the Church's services and rites, with which the Pharisees were content. Together with tears, with external piety, let us reap a harvest worthy of repentance. Let us change our sinful life to a Gospel life.

"Why should you die, O house of Israel?"[4] Why do you perish eternally with your sins, O Christians? Why is hell filled with you, as if the Church of Christ never established all-powerful repentance? This eternal gift is given to the house of Israel, to Christians, and it has the same efficacy no matter what time of life, no matter how heavy the sin. It cleanses every sin; it saves every person who runs to God, even if only in the last moments before death.

"Why should you die, O house of Israel?" Christians die an eternal death because they dedicate their entire lives to breaking their baptismal oaths, to dedication to sin. They perish, since they pay not the slightest attention to the word of God, which tells them of repentance. And in the very last moments of their lives, they cannot take advantage of all-powerful repentance! They cannot because they have no understanding of Christianity, or they have only the most insufficient and confused understanding of it, something closer to complete lack of knowledge.

"'As I live,' says the Lord God"—as if He is forced to increase faith amid faithlessness, and to awake those still asleep— "'As I live,' says the Lord God, 'I have no pleasure in the death of the wicked, but that the wicked turn from his way and live. Turn, turn from your evil ways! For why should you die, O house of Israel?'"[5]

God knew the weakness of man, knew that even after baptism people would fall into sin. For that reason, He established His mystery of repentance in His Church, through which sins committed after baptism are cleansed. Repentance must go hand in hand with faith in Christ; it must exist even before baptism; and after baptism, it reestablishes those who have rejected Christ as those who have been baptized into Him.

When many from Jerusalem and all Judaea came to the Jordan to be baptized by John, the prophet of repentance, they confessed their sins. According to St John of the Ladder, they confessed not because the Baptist needed to hear their sins, but because their repentance would only be true if their confession was united with a feeling of remorse for falling into sin.

The same Father continues, saying that the soul knows it must confess its sins. This same thought, like a bridle, helps prevent repetition of the same sins. On the other hand, unconfessed sins are committed as if in darkness, and they are quickly repeated.

Our friendship with sin is broken by confession of sins. Hatred for sin is a sign of true repentance, as is a firm resolve to lead a virtuous life.

If you have become a habitual sinner, then confess more often, and soon you will be released from bondage to sin, and quickly and joyfully will you follow the Lord Jesus Christ.

He who constantly betrays his friends soon becomes their enemy, and they abandon him as a traitor. He who confesses his sins is soon abandoned by these sins, which were established and strengthened through the pride of fallen nature since they cannot abide exposure and shame.

He who sins willfully and intentionally, hoping to repent later, insidiously schemes against God. He will be struck down by unexpected death, without the time he counted on to begin a life of virtue.

All sins, whether done in word, deed, or thought, are completely washed away by confession. But in order to erase sinful, deeply rooted habits from our hearts, we need time; we need to repent constantly. Constant repentance is constant contrition, constant battle with thoughts and feelings that were long hidden in the depths of the heart by sinful passions, constant bridling of our flesh, constant humble prayer, and frequent confession.

Brothers! Through our own willful sin, we have lost our holy innocence, which was untouched not only by sinful deed but even knowledge of evil; the innocence into which we were created by the hands of the Maker. We lost even that innocence that was restored to us in baptism. All along life's path we have stained our robes, made white by the Redeemer, with our various sins. Now we have only one kind of water left for washing—the water of repentance. What will happen to us when we scorn even this laver? We will have to stand before God with souls defiled by sins, and He will look with loathing on our foul soul and will condemn it to the fires of Gehenna.

"Wash yourselves," says God to us sinners, "make yourselves clean; put away the evil of your doings from before My eyes. Cease to do evil. Come now, and let us reason together." How will this judgment of God end, this judgment of repentance to which God incessantly calls the sinner during his earthly life? When a person recognizes his sinfulness, sincerely repents, and determines to improve, then God judges the person according to these words: "Though your sins are like scarlet, they shall be as white as snow; though they are red like crimson, they shall be as wool."[6]

However, if the Christian despises this most compassionate call of God, God will condemn him to perish eternally. The Apostle says, "the goodness of God leads you to repentance."[7] God sees your sins; He patiently bears the sins you commit under His very gaze, this chain of sins that constitute your life. He awaits your repentance, and at the same time offers salvation or perdition to your free will and choice. And this is the goodness and long suffering of God that you abuse! You do not improve! Your laziness only becomes stronger! Your disregard of God and your own eternal fate becomes only stronger! You only care for increasing your sins; you only add more and more sins to your previous ones!

> But in accordance with your hardness and your impenitent heart you are treasuring up for yourself wrath in the day of wrath and revelation of the righteous judgment of God, who "will render to each one according to his deeds": eternal life to those who by patient continuance in doing good seek for glory, honor, and immortality; but to those who are self-seeking and do not obey the truth, but obey unrighteousness—indignation and wrath, tribulation and anguish, on every soul of man who does evil.[8]

Amen.

CHAPTER 23

On Humility: A Conversation Between an Elder and His Disciple

Disciple: What is humility?

Elder: Humility is a Gospel virtue that unites the strength of a person with the peace of Christ, which is greater than human understanding.

Disciple: If it is greater than human understanding, how can we know of its existence? How can we acquire such a virtue if we cannot even understand it?

Elder: We know of its existence with the help of faith, from the Gospels, and we come to understand it the more we experientially acquire it. But even after acquiring it, it remains unattainable.

Disciple: And why is that?

Elder: Because it is divine. Humility is the teaching of Christ, it is a quality of Christ, it is the action of Christ. The words of the Saviour! "Learn from Me, for I am gentle and lowly in heart."[1] St John of the Ladder interprets these words thus: "You must learn not from an angel, not from a man, not from a book, but from 'Me,' that is, from my assumption of your nature and will, 'for I am gentle and lowly in heart,' thought, and manner of thinking."[2]

The peace of God is the beginning and the immediate consequence of humility; it is the action of humility and simultaneously its source. It acts on the mind and heart through omnipotent divine power. Both its power and action are essentially unknowable.

Disciple: How can one attain humility?

Elder: Through the fulfilling of the commandments of the Gospel, and especially through prayer. The grace-filled action of humility works together with the grace-filled power of prayer, or it is even better to say that they have one and the same action.

Disciple: Please do not hesitate to describe in detail both ways of acquiring humility.

Elder: They are both described in the teachings of the Holy Fathers. St John of the Ladder says that only those who are led by the Spirit of God can properly speak of humility,[3] while St Isaac the Syrian says that the Holy Spirit mystically teaches a person humility, if he has prepared himself for such instruction.[4] We, who have gathered the crumbs that fall off the spiritual feast table of our lords the Holy Fathers, received only a poor understanding of humility. We try to strive toward it ourselves, while at the same time passing along the priceless tradition of the Fathers to those who ask. It is entirely fair to call our understanding, received from them, crumbs—the actual feast, in its fullness, is only given to the one who has acquired Christ in himself.

Abba Dorotheos said,

> Humility naturally forms itself in the soul as a result of living according to the Commandments of the Gospel . . . Here you have the same process as learning the sciences or the art of medicine. When someone learns them well and begins to exercise his knowledge, then little by little, with practice, the physician or scientist will acquire skill, while they will not be able to say exactly how they acquired it, because the soul acquired it little by little with practice. The same happens in the acquisition of humility. The soul acquires certain skill in humility from living by the Commandments of the Gospel, a process that can't be described in words.[5]

From this teaching of Abba Dorotheos, it becomes obvious that he who desires to acquire humility must first carefully study the Gospels, and with equal assiduity must fulfill all the commandments of our Lord Jesus Christ. He who fulfills the commandments of the Gospel can come to an understanding of his own sinfulness and the sinfulness of all mankind, and eventually to a knowledge and conviction that he is the most sinful and worst of all people.

Disciple: It seems incongruous to me that the one who fulfills the commandments of the Gospel completely can come to an understanding of his own great sinfulness. It seems to me the opposite should be true. He who constantly acts virtuously, and does so with especial eagerness, cannot help but see himself as virtuous.

Elder: The person you imagine does only apparent good from himself,[6] from his own fallen nature. He who does such good according to his own understanding, according to the prompting of his own heart, cannot help but be impressed by his own virtue; he becomes proud of his virtue and cherishes the sweetness of human praise, beginning to seek after it and demand it, even growing angry and antagonistic toward those who do not offer it to him. He counts his good deeds, and depending on their number, he builds a correspondingly high opinion of himself, and naturally judges others by his own lofty standard, as did the Pharisee mentioned in the Gospel parable.[7]

This type of virtuous activity only encourages a delusional attitude toward one's own righteousness; it forms the kind of righteous men whom the Lord rejects and who reject the Lord, or they only superficially and coldly confess Him with a moribund confession.[8]

The opposite occurs from true fulfillment of the commandments of the Gospel. The ascetic only begins to live according to them, and already he sees that he fulfills them very inadequately and impurely, and that he is distracted every hour by the pleasure of his passions, that is, he is damaged by his will to commit those actions forbidden by the commandments. Then he will clearly realize that the fallen nature is antagonistic to the Gospel. Further fulfillment of the commandments of the Gospel reveals ever more clearly the inadequacy of his own good deeds, the multitude of his falls into sin and defeats, and the miserable state of the fallen nature that has separated itself from God and has even developed an antagonistic relationship with God. When he examines his past life, he sees that it has been an unending chain of sins, falls, and actions that anger God, and from the sincerity of his heart he admits himself the greatest of sinners, who is worthy of temporal and eternal suffering, and who is totally in need of a Redeemer, in Whom all his hopes for salvation rest.

Such an opinion of oneself is formed naturally from the fulfilling of the commandments. One can truly insist that he who is led by the commandments of the Gospel will not stop to admit even that he knows of no single good deed he has ever done![9] Even this fulfillment of the commandments he calls a perversion and defilement of the commandments, as St Peter of Damascus wrote.[10] "Teach me to do Thy will," the prophet cried out to God, that will that You commanded me to do, that I try to do but cannot, because my fallen nature does not understand it and refuses to submit to it. All my efforts have been useless and will continue to be if You do not extend a helping hand to me. "Thy good Spirit," and only He alone, "shall lead me into the land of righteousness."[11] "Virtue cannot be accomplished, cannot even be imagined outside of Christ Jesus and the Holy Spirit."[12]

Disciple: Will not such a self-assessment lead to despair and hopelessness?

Elder: No, it will lead one to Christianity. For such a sinner did the Lord come down to earth, as He Himself said: "I did not come to call the righteous, but sinners, to repentance."[13] Such sinners can accept and confess the Redeemer with their whole soul.

Disciple: Let us assume that living by the commandments of the Gospel leads one to the knowledge and conviction of one's own sinfulness; but how can one truly reach the level of admitting oneself to be more sinful than all other people, among whom are terrible criminals and villains?

Elder: This is the natural consequence of asceticism. If we have two objects before our eyes, and one of them we scrutinize with all possible and constant attention, while not paying any attention to the other, then we will have a very accurate, vivid, concrete understanding of the first object, but will have only the most cursory knowledge of the second. He who lives by the commandments of the Gospel constantly looks at his own sinfulness; through confession to God and tears, he tries to open within himself more wounds and disorders. Even as he reveals them with God's help, he strives for more and more such revelations, driven by a desire to attain God-pleasing purity. He does not look at the sins of others. If, at every opportunity, he would look at the sins of his neighbor, even so his glance would be superficial and cursory, as is usual with people who are intent on some specific task. From his own life, he naturally and logically admits himself the worst sinner of all sinners. The Fathers ever require such a disposition of us.[14]

Without such a self-assessment, the Holy Fathers declare even prayer to be useless. A certain monk said to St Sisoes the Great: "I see that I have attained constant remembrance of God."

The holy man answered: "It is not good that your thoughts are always with God. It is good to see yourself lower than all of creation."[15]

The foundation of prayer is the most profound humility. Prayer is essentially the cry and weeping of humility. Where there is a deficiency of humility, prayer makes one susceptible to self-deception and even demonic delusion.

Disciple: With my question about how one goes about using good deeds to attain humility, I forced you to deviate from the order of conduct.

Elder: I return to it now. In the already mentioned teaching of Abba Dorotheos, we see the words of a certain holy elder: "the path of humility is reasonable physical ascesis." This teaching is especially important for monks who work various monastic obediences, some of which are physical labors, while some are spiritual. What does "reasonable ascesis" mean? It means to labor at your monastic obediences as if they were a punishment for your sinfulness, and in the hope of receiving forgiveness from God. What does it mean to "work recklessly"? When working, you are physically flushed with arrogance, with boasting, by demeaning other brothers who are not capable of such labors due to weakness, lack of ability, or even laziness. In such a case, physical labors, no matter how heavy, tiresome, or useful for the monastery, are not only not beneficial for the soul but are actually harmful because they fill the monk with a high opinion of himself, in which state there is no room left for any virtue.

A good example of reasonable ascesis that led to the peak of Christian perfection through the depths of humility is seen in the life of blessed Isidore of Alexandria. He was one of the leading citizens of Alexandria. Called by the mercy of God to a monastic life, Isidore entered a cenobitic monastery not far from Alexandria and gave himself in total obedience to the abbot of the monastery, a man who was filled with the Holy Spirit. The abbot, seeing that Isidore's status in the world had given him a harsh and proud character, decided to act against this spiritual disease through an obedience that was not so much harsh on the body as it was for a diseased heart. Upon entering the monastery, Isidore announced to the abbot that he gave himself to him as a piece of iron to the smith. The abbot ordered him to stand constantly at the gates of the monastery and bow to every person walking in or out of the monastery with the words: "Pray for me, I am possessed by a demon."

Isidore showed obedience to his abbot like an angel to God. Having labored for seven years in this obedience and having foreknown the time of his death from a divine vision, Isidore died with joy. He described the state of his soul during his ascesis to St John of the Ladder in the following words:

> At first, I thought that I had sold myself for the redemption of my sins, and so I bowed to the ground with great sorrow, forcing myself as though I was shedding my own blood. After a year, my heart stopped feeling sorrow, because it was expecting a reward for its patience from

> God Himself. But after yet another year, I understood in my heart that I was unworthy even to remain in the monastery, to be seen by the fathers, to speak to them, to meet with them, even to commune of the Holy Mysteries. Only lowering my eyes to the ground, and my thoughts even lower, could I sincerely beg every person entering or departing the monastery to pray for me.[16]

Here is true physical labor and obedience that are done in wisdom! This is their fruit! One humble thought led to the next, as if training him, until he entered into the most complete, mystical feeling of humility. Through this holy sensation, heaven was opened for St Isidore, since he was the living temple of God. "Humility makes man the dwelling-place of God," said St. Barsanuphius the Great.[17]

In the beginning of his teaching on humility, St Dorotheos of Gaza said that the cornerstone of his teaching is this saying of one of the holy elders: "First of all, we need humble-mindedness, and we must be ready to say 'forgive me' at any moment, because humble-mindedness destroys all the arrows of the enemy and adversary."[18]

The great power of humility is made evident by rejecting justification, and by blaming oneself and forgiving others in all those situations that in the world are usually characterized by justifications in ever-increasing quantity. All the Holy Fathers kept to it and all of them bequeath it to us. This is only strange if one looks at it superficially. But actual experience proves that it is filled with spiritual benefit and flows directly from Truth Himself, Christ. Our Lord rejected justifications, and never used them before people, even if He could reveal himself to them in the whole power of His divine Truth. Instead, to the Pharisees He said: "You are those who justify yourselves before men, but God knows your hearts. For what is highly esteemed among men is an abomination in the sight of God."[19]

The Prophet Isaiah had this to say about the Lord: "Behold! My Servant whom I uphold, My Elect One in whom My soul delights! I have put My Spirit upon Him; He will bring forth justice to the Gentiles. He will not cry out, nor raise His voice, Nor cause His voice to be heard in the street."[20]

The Apostle Peter has this to witness about the exact fulfillment of the prophecy: "Christ also suffered for us, leaving us an example, that you should follow His steps, who, when He was reviled, did not revile in return; when He suffered, He did not threaten, but committed Himself to Him who judges righteously."[21]

And so if we, who are guilty in countless sins, came to the monastery to suffer crucifixion on account of our sins at the right hand of our Saviour, then we must accept as timely every sorrow, no matter what it is, accept it as righteous reward for sins and a fair punishment for them. When we have such a disposition, the request for forgiveness in any possible situation will indeed be a correct and logical action. "Justification in words does not belong in a Christian life," said St Isaac the Syrian.[22] St Pimen the Great said: "We fall into many temptations because we do not preserve the rank that is appropriate to our name. Do we not see that the Canaanite woman accepted the name given her, and the Lord consoled her?" Abigail said to David, "upon me let this iniquity be,"[23] and David loved her for this saying. Abigail is the image of the soul, and David is the image of God—if the soul blames itself before the Lord, the Lord will love the soul. The saint was asked what "highly esteemed"[24] meant. He answered: "Justifications. Do not justify yourself, and you will find peace."[25]

He who does not justify himself is guided by humble-mindedness, but he who justifies himself is guided by high-mindedness (i.e., arrogance). The Alexandrian patriarch Theophilus once visited Nitria. That mountain was the dwelling place of a large monastic community, all whom lived the hesychastic lifestyle. The Abba of the mountain monastery was a man of great holiness. The patriarch asked him what he thought was the most important aspect of the monastic path. The Abba answered: "Constantly blaming and judging oneself." The patriarch answered him: "That is so! There is no other way, except that one."[26]

I will conclude my meager teaching on humility with the wonderful teaching of St John the Prophet on this virtue:

> Humility means never to consider yourself as anything important, to cut off your own will in everything, to submit oneself to everyone, to bear everything that happens to us without becoming upset. This is true humility, in which there is no place for vanity. The humble-minded must not show his humility through "humble-wordedness." It is enough for him to say "I am sorry," or "pray for me." He must not also strive to do anything demeaning—this is the same as the first, and it leads to vanity, it hinders spiritual progress, and is more

harmful than good; but when someone orders us to do something demeaning, we must not disagree, and we must do it with obedience. This leads to progress.[27]

Disciple: Can it really be true that speaking humbly, which you call "humble-wordedness," is harmful? It seems to me very appropriate for the monk and is very instructive to laypeople, who are often moved by such humble speech of monastics.

Elder: The Lord said: "For what profit is it to a man if he gains the whole world, and loses his own soul?"[28] Evil can never be the reason for good. Hypocrisy and flattering people can never be the source of good instruction—they can be pleasing to the world because they are always pleasing to the world; they can attract the love and trust of the world because they have always done so. The world loves its own; it raises up those in whom it recognizes its own spirit.[29] The fact that the world approves "humble-wordedness" is enough reason to condemn it. The Lord Himself commanded that virtues be done in secret,[30] but "humble-wordedness" is the evisceration of humility for everyone to see. It is a sham, a lie first of all to itself, then to others, because hiding one's virtues is one of the qualities of humility, but "humble-wordedness" and acting humbly destroys that essential hiddenness.

"When you are among the brethren," said St John of the Ladder, "keep a strict watch over yourself, lest you in any way appear to be more righteous than they. If you do not, you will commit a double evil—you will wound the brethren with your hypocrisy and falsity, and in yourself you will inevitably develop arrogance. Be humble in your soul, never show it in your body, neither with your look or word or even a hint."[31]

As beneficial as it is for you to upbraid yourself and condemn yourself of sinfulness before God, it is very harmful to do so before people. If we do so, we will begin to think very highly of ourselves, we will believe ourselves to be humble, and we will announce this fact to the blind world. A certain monk told me that in the early days of his monastic path, he began to practice "humble-wordedness," thinking (according to his own ignorance) that it was something very significant. One time, he did this so effectively that instead of his listeners accepting his words as lies and him as humble (which is the whole point of "humble-wordedness"), they agreed that he was speaking the truth about himself (i.e., agreed with the low opinion of himself that he professed aloud without believing in his heart). Then he became offended and grew angry.

Among people, a monk must always carry himself carefully and reverently, but simply, answering complements with silence and answering insults in the same way, except in those cases when asking forgiveness or offering gentle explanations could calm and pacify the one who is antagonizing us. Those who have achieved success in the monastic life acquire a special freedom and simplicity of heart, which cannot help but be obvious in their interactions with other people. They are not pleasant to the world! The world calls them proud, as St Simeon the New Theologian very accurately notes.[32] The world seeks flattery, but in simplicity, it finds an unpleasant sincerity because it contains a hidden denunciation that it hates.

When I was younger, a certain elder visited a large city on monastery business together with his young disciple. He was very experienced in the spiritual life. A few pious laypeople wanted to visit him. They found him distasteful. However, they really liked his disciple, who was amazed by the riches in the stately homes he visited and made low bows to everyone. "How humble he is!" the laypeople said with special pleasure at his low bows. The elder lived in constant sorrow over his own sinfulness; he considered it the greatest happiness to see one's own sins, and with sincere love and compassion for fallen mankind—equally for the poor and the rich, in simplicity of heart, with incredible discernment, and given with equally incredible purity of mind—he desired to share his spiritual treasures with his brothers, but by doing so only inspired the enmity of the world.

Disciple: What is the difference between humble-mindedness and humility?

Elder: Humble-mindedness is a frame of mind that is taken wholly from the Gospels, from Christ. Humility is a feeling of the heart; it is a pledge in the heart of humble-mindedness. At first, one must learn humble-mindedness; the more one exercises humble-mindedness, the more the soul acquires humility because the state of the heart always depends on the thoughts that the mind assimilates. When the actions of a person become illumined by God's grace, then humble-mindedness and humility will begin to give birth and supplement each other, with the help of the establisher of prayer—tears.

Disciple: Please explain how, in your experience, humble-mindedness gives birth to humility and vice versa.

Elder: I knew a certain monk for a short time, who constantly underwent various sorrows, through which, as he himself said, God was pleased to instruct him instead of through a spiritual father. In spite of the constant sorrows, I saw him almost always calm and often joyful. He studied the Scriptures and practiced the Jesus Prayer. I asked him to reveal to me the way he acquired such consolation for himself. He answered: my consolation comes from God's mercy and the teachings of the Holy Fathers, whom I have loved from my childhood. When sorrows come upon me, I sometimes repeat the words of the thief, who from the cross, confessed the righteousness of God's judgment within the judgment of men, and through this confession came to the knowledge of the Saviour. I say, I received the due reward of my deeds: "Lord, remember me when you come into Your kingdom."[33] With these words, calm and peace pour out into my heart. At other times, I countered my thoughts of sorrow and confusion with the words of the Saviour: "He who does not take his cross and follow after Me is not worthy of Me."[34] Then confusion and sorrow are replaced with peace and joy. All other such words of the Holy Scriptures and the Holy Fathers have the same effect. Repeating the words "Glory to God for all things" or "The Lord's will be done" effectively acts against even the heaviest sorrow. What a strange thing! Sometimes from the heaviness of sorrow I lose all strength to live; the soul somehow becomes deaf, unable to feel anything. At such a time, I begin to say aloud, forcefully and perfunctorily, with my tongue alone, the words "Glory to God!" And my soul, having heard the praise of God, begins to slowly awake to the doxology, then becomes stronger, and then calms down and finds consolation. Those who are allowed to undergo suffering would not be able to remain strong in them if the help and grace of God did not secretly support them. Again: without sorrows, a person is incapable of attaining that mystical and at the same time essential consolation, which is given to him in accordance with his sorrow. As the psalmist said, "According to the multitude of sorrows in my heart have Thy comforts refreshed my soul."[35]

One time, a dangerous trial was prepared for me. Having found out about it, and having no means to prevent it, I felt sorrow even unto total helplessness. I came to my cell, and, having barely pronounced the words of the Saviour: "Let not your heart be troubled: you believe in God, believe also in Me,"[36] my sorrows disappeared. Instead, an indescribable joy filled me, and I had to lie down on my bed, and all day I was as a drunk man, while in my mind the words repeated and continued to pour down consolation on me: "you believe in God, believe also in Me." The reason for the confusion of the heart is lack of faith; the reason for calmness of heart, for grace-filled peace of heart is faith. Through the powerful effect of faith, the entire being of man is filled with spiritual consoling joy through the holy peace of Christ, as if he is soaked and overfilled with this feeling. This euphoria makes a person impervious to the arrows of confusion. The Fathers spoke truly when they said that faith is humility,[37] that "to believe means to be in humility and goodness."[38] Such an understanding of faith and humility is given by holy experience in true monastic life.

At other times, sorrows are allowed to buffet the soul for long periods of time. Once, from sudden sorrow, I felt a nervous shock in my heart, and for three months I remained bedridden in my cell in a state of shock. "The Lord always doeth with us things great and inscrutable, glorious and awesome" (the sixth morning prayer). We must understand that we are His creation, that we are completely under His authority, and so in complete submission, "let us commit ourselves, and one another, and our whole life unto Christ our God."[39]

I will also tell you the following wonderful story, which somewhat explains the action of humility directly from the heart, without a prior thought of humble-mindedness. One time, I was submitted to a punishment and shamefully used. When this occurred, I unexpectedly felt a fire in my entire body and some kind of indescribable deadness, after which my heart was inflamed with the desire to receive universal condemnation and public punishment at the hands of an executioner for my sins. At the same time, my cheeks became rosy, unutterable joy and sweetness overtook my whole self, and for two weeks I was in ecstasy, as if outside myself. Then I clearly and exactly understood that the holy humility in the martyrs, together with God's love, could not be destroyed by any tortures. The martyrs accepted horrible tortures as though they were gifts, as though it were a cooling drink, satisfying their thirsty humility.[40] Humility is this indescribable grace of God that is unutterably reached only through the spiritual feelings of the soul.

Disciple: You promised to explain to me how humility is developed through prayer.

Elder: The union of humility and prayer is very clearly described by St Abba Dorotheos:

> Constant practice in prayer counteracts pride. It is evident that a humble and pious person, knowing that it is impossible for him to do any good deed without the help and protection of God, never ceases to pray to God, that He may have mercy on him. He who constantly prays to God, if he is able to do anything good, knows that he did it only through the mediation of God, and he cannot ascribe the good deed to his own strength, but ascribes to God all his improvement. He thanks God constantly and prays to Him without ceasing, fearing lest he should lose the help from Above and realize his complete powerlessness. He prays from humility.[41]

If anyone begins to feel compunction that comes about as a result of attentive prayer, then he will know from experience that in those treasured moments of compunction his mind will be filled with humble-minded thoughts, which give rise to humility. This is especially evident when compunction is accompanied by tears. The more often such compunction appears, the more often the practitioner of prayer is a listener to the mystical teaching of humility, the deeper this teaching roots into his heart. Constant compunction keeps the soul in constant humility and makes one capable of constant prayer and mindfulness of the presence of God.

The Holy Fathers have noted that, contrary to vanity, which tends to scatter a person's thoughts all over the universe, humility concentrates the thoughts in the soul. A person stops contemplating the world in a useless and scatterbrained fashion, but begins to contemplate himself deeply, becomes capable of mental silence; a state that is at the same time an absolute prerequisite for attentive prayer and a product of attentive prayer.[42]

In conclusion, the grace-filled action of humility and the grace-filled action of prayer is one and the same, as already mentioned. This action appears in two forms—in Christ-emulating humility and in divine love, which is the highest effect of prayer. This action within our hearts belongs exclusively to our Lord Jesus Christ, who lives and acts in his chosen vessels, through the unutterable and inconceivable mediation of the Holy Spirit. Amen.

CHAPTER 24

On True and False Humble-Mindedness

"Let no one cheat you of your reward, taking delight in false humility."[1]

True humility is found in obedience and emulation of Christ.[2]

True humble-mindedness is spiritual wisdom. It is a gift of God; it is the activity of divine grace in the mind and heart of a person.

But there can also be a voluntary humble-mindedness—it is created for itself by the vain soul, the soul deceived and flattered by false teachings, the soul that flatters itself, the soul that seeks flattery from the world, the soul that totally strives for earthly success and earthly pleasures, the soul that has forgotten eternity and God.

Voluntary, self-invented humble-mindedness consists of a countless variety of tricks through which a person's pride tries to snatch the honor due to true humble-mindedness, seeking it from the blind world, form the world that loves its own, from the world that praises sins masquerading as virtue, from the world that hates virtue when virtue appears in its holy simplicity, in the holy and firm obedience to the Gospels.

Nothing is as antagonistic to Christian humility as willful humble-mindedness that rejects the yoke of obedience to Christ, and under the hypocritical mask of service to God instead blasphemously serves Satan.

If we will constantly look at our own sins, if we will try to study them in detail, then we will find in ourselves not a single virtue, certainly not humble-mindedness.

True humility hides true, holy virtue, in the same way that a chaste virgin conceals her beauty, in the same way the holy of holies is hidden from the eyes of the people by a curtain.

True humble-mindedness is an evangelical character, a way of life according to the Gospel, an evangelical manner of thinking.

True humility is a divine mystery. It is unattainable by human efforts. Being the highest wisdom, it is considered madness by the carnal mind-set.

The divine mystery of humility is revealed by the Lord Jesus to his faithful disciple who constantly sits at His feet and hears His life-giving words. Even when revealed, it remains secret, for it is impossible to express with the words and tongues of the world. It is inconceivable for the carnal mind-set; it is ineffably revealed to the spiritual mind-set, and when it is revealed, still remains inconceivable.

Humility is the heavenly life on earth.

A grace-filled, miraculous vision of the greatness of God and his countless benefits to man, the grace-filled experience of the Redeemer, the emulation of Christ with self-denial, seeing the abyss into which the fall has cast humanity—these are the invisible signs of humility, these are the first chambers of the spiritual palace created by the God-Man.

Humility does not consider itself to be humble. On the contrary, it sees all manner of pride in itself. It tries to find all its possible roots, and when it finds them it continues to search for more, knowing how much there is still left to be found.

St Macarius of Egypt, a true Spirit-bearing Father called Great by the Church for the perfection of his virtues, especially for his profound humility, said in his exalted, holy, mystical writings that even the purest and most perfect human being has in himself a grain of pride.[3]

This holy man reached the highest level of Christian perfection. He lived in a time replete with saints, even seeing the greatest of monks, St Anthony the Great. Still, he said he did not see a single person who could be called completely perfect.[4]

Only false humility considers itself humble, and it pitifully finds solace in this delusional, soul-killing security.

Satan sometimes appears as an angel of light, and his followers sometimes appear as the apostles of Christ.[5] His teaching pretends to be the teaching of Christ. The states that are produced by his delusion often appear to be superficially similar to exalted, grace-filled spiritual states. His pride and vanity and their attendant self-deception and delusion take the form of the humility of Christ.

Oh! How is it that the words of the Saviour hide from these pitiful dreamers, so terribly satisfied with themselves and their state of self-deception, who imagine that they are enjoying true blessedness. Can they not hear His words? "Blessed are you who hunger now. Blessed are you who weep now. Woe to you who are full! Woe to you who laugh now!"[6]

Beloved brother! Look intently and without prejudice at your own soul. Is not repentance more fitting for it than pleasure? Is it not better for you to weep on this earth, in this vale of tears where sorrow is appropriate instead of inventing for yourself premature, delusional, foolish, damaging pleasures?

Repentance and tears over your sins gives eternal blessedness. This is well-known, this is true, this was said by the Lord Himself. Why do you not submerge yourself into these holy states, why do you not remain in them, instead inventing for yourself false exaltation? Why do you find enjoyment in it, why are you filled by it, why are you content with it, and why do you destroy in yourself the blessed hunger and thirst after the righteousness of God, the blessed and salvific sorrow over your sins and your sinfulness?

Hunger and thirst after God's righteousness are proof of poverty of spirit. Tears are an expression of humility, its very voice. The lack of tears, self-satisfaction, and contentment in yourself and in your falsely spiritual state prove the pride of your heart.

Be afraid, lest your empty, delusional ecstasy does not lead to eternal sorrow, which is promised by God for those who are satisfied with themselves, in contradiction to the will of God.

Vanity and its children—false spiritual states that appear in the heart which have not been pierced by repentance—create the apparition of humility. This appearance becomes a substitute for true humility in the soul. The apparition of truth, having taken the temple of the soul by force, blocks all entry into the soul of Truth Himself.

Alas, my soul, you temple of truth created by God! When you accept within yourself the mere appearance of truth, when you bow to it instead of the real Truth, you become a pagan temple!

Inside this pagan temple is an idol—delusional humility. Delusional humility is the worst kind of pride. With great difficulty is pride rooted out, when the person admits its presence. But how can a person root out pride when he believes it to be humility?

This pagan temple contains an abomination of desolation! In this temple, incense is burned constantly before the idol and hymns are sung to it that make hell rejoice. There the thoughts and feeling of the soul taste of the forbidden food offered to idols, and they get drunk on wine mixed with deadly poison. The temple, the house of idols and all impurity, is closed off not only for divine grace and gifts of the

Spirit but it is also shut to any true virtue, for any commandment of the Gospel.

False humility so weakens a person that it forces him not just to think to himself or gently hint to others that he is humble, but he openly announces this and loudly proclaims it.[7]

Falsehood cruelly ridicules us when we, deluded by it, believe it to be the Truth.

Grace-filled humility is invisible, just as the Giver of grace, God, is also invisible. It is hidden by silence, simplicity, sincerity, genuineness, freedom.

False humility is always connected with external manifestations—it wants to make itself seen in public.

False humility loves to make a scene, through such means it fools itself and others. The humility of Christ is clothed in the raiment and vesture of the Crucified One, into the most common homespun. In such clothing, it is not noticed or recognized by people.[8]

The effect of humility can be compared to the effect of the passion of avarice. The more a person who is infected with love for earthly treasures gathers for himself, the more he hungers and the less he is satisfied. The richer he becomes, the more he appears to himself to be destitute. In the same way, the more a humble man enriches himself with virutes and spiritual gifts, the poorer and weaker he appears before his own eyes.

This is natural! When a person has not yet tasted of the highest goods, then his own virtue, though it is defiled by sin, seems to him worth something. When he comes into contact with divine, spiritual good, then his own virtue appears useless to him, since it is united with and befouled by sin.

For the poor man, even a bag of pennies gathered with difficulty over a long period of time is precious. But then a rich man unexpectedly pours a countless multitude of gold coins into the poor man's lap, and he throws aside the little bag of copper pennies with disdain because now it is a useless burden to him.

The righteous, long-suffering Job, after his many torments, was found worthy of the vision of God. Then he said to God in an inspired prayer: "I have heard of You by the hearing of the ear, But now my eye sees You." And what is the fruit of this divine vision for the righteous man? "Therefore I abhor myself, And repent in dust and ashes."[9]

Do you wish to acquire humility? Follow the commandments of the Gospel. Through them, your heart will acquire and assimilate holy humility, the qualities of our Lord Jesus Christ Himself.

The beginning of humility is poverty of spirit. The middle of the path toward humility is the peace of Christ, which surpasses all wisdom and understanding. The end and perfection of humility is the love of Christ.

Humility is never angry, never tries to please men, never gives way to sorrow, never fears. Can the person who has at the beginning determined himself to be worthy of all sorrows ever feel any sorrow?

Can the one who has condemned himself to suffering as the only way to salvation ever fear calamities?

The saints of God came to love the words of the good thief who was crucified near the Lord. During their sorrows, they would usually say: "we receive the due reward of our deeds. Lord, remember me when You come into Your kingdom."[10] They greet every sorrow with the admission that they have deserved it.

Holy peace descends into their hearts merely for words of humility! It brings holy consolation to the bedside of the sick man, to the prison of the one behind bars, to the one persecuted by men and demons.

The cup of consolation is brought by the hand of humility even to the one crucified on the cross. The world can only bring him vinegar mixed with gall.[11]

The humble man is not capable of anger or hatred because he has no enemies. If any person hurts him in any way, he sees that person as a tool of God's justice or His providence.

The humble man gives himself completely to the will of God.

The humble man lives not his own life, but the life of God.

The humble man trusts not in himself, and so he constantly seeks the help of God, and constantly remains in his prayer.

A branch heavy laden with fruit stoops to the ground. But a branch with no fruit continues to grow up without any purpose or use.

The soul that is enriched with evangelical virtues plunges deeper and deeper into humility, and in the depths of this sea it finds precious pearls—the gifts of the Holy Spirit.

Pride is a sure indication of a hollow man, a slave to the passions. It is a sign of a soul that has blocked all access to the teaching of Christ.

Do not judge a person by his appearance, and do not decide that a person is proud or humble by how he looks. "Judge not according to appearance, [but] you will know them by their fruits."[12] The Lord told us to recognize people by their action, their deeds, and from the consequences of these deeds.

"I know your pride and the anger of your heart,"[13] it was said of David, but God witnessed to David's righteousness: "I have found David My servant; with My holy oil have I anointed him."[14] "The Lord does not see as man sees; for man looks at the outward appearance, but the Lord looks at the heart."[15]

Blind judges often consider the hypocrite and lowly people pleaser to be humble, while he is rather an abyss of vanity.

In contrast, these ignorant judges consider the one who does not seek human praise and glory to be proud, because he does not constantly appear before their faces. But he is the true servant of God. He has experienced the glory of God that reveals itself only to the humble. He sensed the stench of human glory, and turned away the eyes and senses of his soul.

What does it mean to believe? A certain great ascetic was once asked this question. He answered: "To believe means to remain in humility and compassion."[16]

Humility hopes in God, not on itself or on other people, and so a humble person is simple, direct, firm, and noble in his behavior. The blind world calls such behavior proud.

Humility considers earthly goods to be useless. In the eyes of the humble man, only God and the Gospels are great. He strives toward them, giving neither attention nor glance to the perishable things of this world. His holy indifference to the vanity of the world is considered to be pride by the sons of the world, who serve vanity.

There is a holy prostration that comes from humility, from respect for your neighbor, from respect for the image of God, from respect for Christ in your neighbor. And there is a sinful prostration, an avaricious prostration, a people-pleasing prostration that is simultaneously people-despising, a prostration hateful to God. This is the prostration that Satan demanded of the God-Man, when he offered him all the kingdoms of the world and their glory.[17]

How many people nowadays prostrate themselves only to receive earthly benefits! Those people to whom they do obeisance praise them as humble.

Be attentive and pay attention! Is the one who bows before you bowing out of respect for you as a person, from feelings of love and humility? Or is his prostration only flattering your pride, hoping to gain from it some personal benefit?

You who are considered great in the world! Pay attention! Before you are slithering vanity, flattery, and depravity! When they have achieved their goals, they will laugh at you and betray you at the first opportunity. Never waste your generosity on a vain man. Although he prostrates himself before the great, he lords it over and torments those who are below him.[18] You will recognize the vain man by his special talent for flattery, for servility, for lying, for everything that is base and depraved.

Pilate was offended by Christ's silence, which seemed to him proud. He said, "You don't want to answer *me?* Don't you know that I have the power to release and the power to crucify you?"[19] The Lord explained that His silence was through the revelation of God's will, whose blind tool Pilate was, though Pilate imagined himself capable of acting independently of it. Pilate, because of his own pride, could not understand that he was faced with the most exalted humility—the incarnate God.

The exalted soul, the soul with spiritual hope, the soul that despises the goods of the world, is beyond all pitiful people pleasing and servility. It is incorrect to call such a soul proud only because it refuses to act according to the requirements of your passions.

Humility is the Gospel teaching, an evangelical virtue, the mystical vesture of Christ, the mystical power of Christ. He who is clothed in humility, God Himself, appeared to man, and whoever clothes himself in humility becomes like God.[20]

"If any man wishes to follow me," said Holy Humility "Let him deny himself and take up his cross and follow me." Otherwise it is not possible to be a disciple and follower of the One who humbled himself even to the death of the cross. He sat at the right hand of the Father. He is the New Adam, the Father of a new holy, chosen nation. Faith in Him makes one a member of this chosen nation. The new member is accepted by Holy Humility, and confirmed by Holy Love. Amen.

CHAPTER 25

On Patience

"The house of the soul is patience, because the soul abides in it. The food of the soul is humility, because the soul is fed by it."[1]

Exactly! Being fed by the holy food of humility, one can remain in the holy habitation of patience. When such food is in short supply, the soul leaves the habitation of patience. Like a fierce wind, confusion takes the soul away and spins it out of control. Like waves, various passionate thoughts and feelings arise in it, drowning it in the depths of foolish and sinful thoughts, fantasies, words, and deeds. The soul becomes paralyzed, depressed, and often comes close to the abysses of deadly despair and total catastrophe.

Do you want to remain constantly in the holy habitation of patience? You must stock up on the food necessary for such a long stay—you must acquire and multiply within yourself thoughts and feelings of humility. The kind of humility that prepares one for the patient bearing of sorrows even before their coming, and helps one patiently withstand the attack of sufferings is called *self-accusation* by the Holy Fathers.

Self-accusation is simply blaming oneself for one's sinfulness, which is common to all men and to you in particular. At the same time, it is useful to remember and list all one's sins against God's law, except those of a carnal nature because remembrance of such sins is expressly forbidden by the Fathers since such memories can renew the feeling and enjoyment of the sin in the person.[2]

Self-accusation is true monastic work, it is the prayer of the heart, which counteracts and stands against the sickly state of our fallen nature due to which all people, even the most obvious sinners, try to make themselves out to be righteous and to prove their righteousness through all possible scheming. Self-accusation is violence against the fallen nature, as are prayer and other ascetic labors, through which "the kingdom of heaven suffers violence," and through which "the violent take it by force."[3]

In the beginning, self-accusation is done mechanically; that is, it is pronounced by the tongue without any accompanying feeling in the heart, and sometimes in direct opposition to the heart's disposition. Later, little by little, the heart begins to be attracted by the words of self-accusation. Finally, self-accusation will be pronounced with the whole soul, with a strong sense of sorrow. It will hide others' deficiencies and sins from our eyes, it will reconcile us with all people and all circumstances, it will unite all our scattered thoughts to the doing of repentance, it will give attentive prayer, full of compunction, and it will inspire and arm us with the insurmountable strength of patience.

All the prayers of the Orthodox Church are filled with the humble thoughts of self-accusation. But monks further allot special time every day for practice in self-accusation. They try, with its help, to convince themselves that they are sinners. The fallen nature does not want to believe this, does not want such knowledge to become assumed. In general, self-accusation is useful for all monks—both for beginners and for the experienced, both for those who live in a community and those who live in solitude. For a hesychast, the worst passion that can destroy all the fruits of their labors is arrogance, and so the most effective virtue for them, on which all their other virtues hang, is self-accusation.[4]

When self-accusation has reached its fullness, it completely extirpates anger from the heart, along with all the evil and hypocrisy that constantly reside in the heart as long as any form of self-justification finds refuge there. St Pimen the Great said that hatred of evil consists of justification of everyone else, accompanied by self-condemnation in all cases.[5] These words are based on the words of the Saviour Himself, who called everyone who judges his neighbor a hypocrite.[6] When a hesychast accuses himself, he will see all people as saints and angels but himself as the chief of all sinners. He will plunge himself into the deep abyss of constant compunction.

A superlative example of self-accusation is seen in the Lamentations of St Isaiah the Recluse in Homily 20 of St Isaac the Syrian. St Isaac, whose book is exclusively intended for hesychasts, wrote the following epigraph to the homily: "This homily contains necessary and helpful daily reminders to hesychasts in their cells and anyone who wishes to become attentive only to himself."

The homily continues:

A certain monk wrote the following, and he kept it constantly before himself as a reminder: In madness have you lived your life, O dishonored man who is worthy of all evils! At the very least, keep yourself pure this one day that is left to you; among all the other days you have brought as a sacrifice to vanity, the days bereft of any good deeds, the days that have become rich in evil doings. Don't ask about this world, about its state, don't inquire about other monks or their doings, don't wonder about the quality and quantity of their ascetic labors. Don't give yourself to useless thoughts of any kind. You left the world mysteriously, you have become dead for the sake of Christ. Do not live for the world any more, neither for anything that belongs to the world, and then you will be visited by peace, and you will live in Christ. Be ready to accept any accusation, any sadness, any denunciation, any angry words from anyone. Accept all this with joy, since you surely deserve it all! With gratitude and patience bear any sickness, any sorrow or tribulation from the demons, since you have done their will. Courageously bear any deprivation and trial that happen naturally. With hope in God, overcome self-imposed bodily limitations, since it will soon turn to rot. Accept all this with a good disposition, with hope in God, neither expecting deliverance, nor consolation from anyone. Lift up to God all your hope, and in all temptations judge yourself as the reason for their existence. Do not be tempted by anything, and contradict none who insult you, because you have tasted the forbidden fruit and you have acquired various passions. With joy accept all these sorrows, let them shake you up at least a little, so that you can taste of heavenly joy afterwards. Woe to you and to your foul-smelling glory! Your soul, filled with all manner of sin, you have left without any attention, as though uncondemned, while others you have condemned in word and thought. Leave behind this pig fodder which, until now, you have fed yourself. What business have you with other people, you, who are so foul? Are you not ashamed to appear in their presence, you who have lived your whole life in madness? If you pay attention to this, and will remember all this, then maybe you will be saved thanks to the mediation of God. If not, then you will go into the dark country, into the habitations of the demons, whose will you have shamelessly done. Pay attention! I have witnessed all this for you. If God will righteously send people to punish you for all the sorrows and trials that you have imagined and done against them,

> then the entire world must constantly rise up against you. And so, from this moment, cease acting as you have been up to this point, and accept the sorrows sent to you.
>
> All this the brother reminded himself every day, in order to remain in the proper state to patiently accept any temptation or sorrow, whenever they may come, with gratitude to God and for the benefit of his soul. May we also patiently bear our burdens with gratitude, and receive benefits through the grace of our man-loving God.

Self-accusation has a special, beneficial, mystical quality that encourages us to remember even those sins that we have long forgotten, or to which we have never paid any attention.

Practicing self-accusation gives one skill in doing so. When he who has acquired this skill is attacked by any kind of sorrow, immediately it begins to act in him, and the sorrow is accepted as deserved. Abba Dorotheos says the following:

> The main reason for any disquiet, if we carefully analyze it, is the fact that we do not accuse ourselves. Every kind of calamity comes from this; for this reason we never find any peace. And so it is not strange that we hear the following from all the saints: "there is no other path except for this one." We do not see that any of the saints, walking along a different path, ever found peace! And yet we want to have this peace and to keep to the right path, but never to accuse ourselves. Truly, if a person performs a thousand virtues, but does not hold to the path of self-accusation, he will never cease to be upset and to upset others, destroying all his hard work. On the contrary, he who accuses himself is always joyful and always peaceful. He who accuses himself, according to Abba Pimen, no matter where he goes, no matter what happens to him, either harm or shame or some sort of sorrow, he already considers himself worthy of every unpleasant thing, and so never becomes upset. Can there be anything more peaceful than such a state?
>
> But perhaps someone will say, if a brother insults me, and I find that I have given him no reason for this, then how can I accuse myself? Truly, if someone examines himself with the fear of God, he will find that he gave all kinds of reasons, whether they be in action or word or any other way. If he sees, as he says, that this particular insult was given without reason, then he must have previously offended him or

another brother, and must then suffer either that sin or some other sin, which happens often. Thus, if someone examines himself, as I said, with the fear of God and scrutinizes his conscience, he will always find himself at fault.[7]

What a strange thing this is! When we begin to accuse ourselves perfunctorily and forcefully, we eventually reach such a convincing and active state of self-accusation that with its help, we can bear not only the usual sorrows but even great deprivation. Temptations no longer have such power over those who used to be enslaved to them, and the more a person acquires such skill, the lighter the temptations seem, even if they are objectively much heavier. According to the skill gained, the soul becomes stronger, and it receives the strength to patiently bear any event. This firmness is given like an energy-rich food to those who have descended into their hearts with humility. This firmness is patience.

Unshakable faith in the providence of God confirms one in patience and makes self-accusation possible. The Lord said to his disciples: "Are not two sparrows sold for a copper coin? And not one of them falls to the ground apart from your Father's will. But the very hairs of your head are all numbered."[8]

With these words, the Saviour of the world illustrated the indefatigable care that God has and that only the omnipotent and omnipresent God can have for His slaves and servants. Thanks to such divine watchfulness, we are released from any fainthearted fear or worry about ourselves. "Therefore humble yourselves under the mighty hand of God, that He may exalt you in due time, casting all your care upon Him, for He cares for you."[9] When we are subjected to sorrows, God sees it. It happens not only because of His permission but also because of His all-holy forethought for each of us. He allows us to suffer for our sins in time, to deliver us from suffering for them in eternity. It often happens that a secret and heavy sin remains unknown to the surrounding world and remains unpunished, being covered by the mercy of God. At the same time, or after some time has passed, we are obliged to suffer a little bit as a result of slander or personal attack that seems to be undeserved. But our conscience tells us that we are suffering for our secret sin! The mercy of God, which covered the sin, gives us the means to be crowned with the crown of the innocents who suffer from unjust slander and at the same time to be purified of our secret sin through suffering. When we see this, let us praise the all-holy providence of God, and let us humble ourselves before it.

An instructive example of self-judgment and self-accusation, combined with the praise of the righteous and greatly merciful judgment of God, is given by the three Hebrew youths in the captivity and furnace of the Babylonians:

> Blessed are you, O Lord, God of our ancestors, and worthy of praise; and glorious is your name forever! For you are just in all you have done; all your works are true and your ways right, and all your judgments are true. You have executed true judgments in all you have brought upon us and upon Jerusalem, the holy city of our ancestors; by a true judgment you have brought all this upon us because of our sins. For we have sinned and broken your law in turning away from you.[10]

The holy youths, cast into the fiery furnace for their loyalty to the true God, did not burn, but remained in it as if it were a cool room. They admitted and confessed themselves to having sinned along with their people, who had truly rejected God. Because of their love for their neighbors, they laid upon themselves the sins of their near ones. Because of their humility, being holy and righteous young men, they did not want to be separated from their brothers, who were in bondage to sin. From this state of self-accusation, humility, and love for humanity, and from the justification of God's judgments, they already brought to God a prayer for their salvation. Thus, also let us praise the providence of God and confess our sinfulness whenever we are met by misfortune, either personal or general, and thanks to these praises and confessions let us pray God for mercy. The Holy Scriptures witness that the slaves of God, who walk the way of God's commandments, are given special sorrows to help their work. As the Saviour of the world Himself said, "Every branch in Me that does not bear fruit He takes away; and every branch that bears fruit He prunes, that it may bear more fruit"[11] These purifying sorrows are called the judgments of God. David the Psalmist sings of them thus: "The judgments of the Lord are true, and righteous altogether"[12] "Teach me Thy judgments!" May I know and understand that everything bitter that happens to me is due to the providence of God, the will of my God! Then I will know that "Thy judgments shall help me"[13] in the sickly and insufficient attempts I make to please my God.

As an example of how the judgments of God help His servants who desire to please Him, and how they lead them up to holiness that they would never have reached without the help of the judgments of God, we will mention the life of the Constantinopolitan noble Xenophontos, with his wife and two sons. The rich and famous Xenophontos led as pious a life as was possible for a Christian living in the world, a life that now is only possible in separation from the world. He desired that his two sons be heirs of both his riches and his position in the imperial court, as well as heirs of his piety. During that time, the Syrian city of Beirut was known as a center of learning. Xenophontos sent his sons there to learn the wisdom of that age. The best way to travel from Constantinople to Syria at that time was by boat. One time the sons, having visited their father because of his serious illness, returned to Beirut by sea. Unexpectedly, they were caught by a terrible Mediterranean storm, the ship was ripped apart and sank, and the youths were thrown out by the waves to different parts of the Palestinian coastline. In this calamitous situation, the sons of Xenophontos (named John and Arcadius), who were fed from childhood by pious thoughts and interests, understood their calamity to be a call from God to the monastic life, and, as if by mutual consent, each of them entered a Palestinian monastery.

After the passage of a considerable amount of time, they met each other; later, Xenophontos found out that the ship that carried his children was lost at sea, and that all who were on the ship were lost without any news. The deeply distressed father turned to prayer. After praying all night in his room, he received a divine revelation that his sons were protected by a special mercy and grace of God. Understanding this to mean that they entered the monastic life, and knowing that Palestine (the shoreline nearest where the storm struck their ship) had a great multitude of monasteries, Xenophontos and his wife went to Jerusalem. There they saw their sons, and they decided not to return to Constantinople. From Jerusalem, they made arrangements for the sale of their estates, and the money was given to various monasteries, churches, and to the poor. Xenophontos and his wife, Maria, soon followed their sons' examples and entered monasteries. Both the parents and the children attained great spiritual heights.[14]

None of them would have reached such heights if they had remained in the world, even though they lived a life of piety. God, foreseeing their sanctity, led them to it through His inconceivable judgments. The way of the judgments of God is bitter, as the Apostle Paul witnessed, "For whom the Lord loves He chastens, And scourges every son whom He receives."[15] The consequences of these bitter judgments, however, are desirable and priceless. We see in many other saints' lives that God sends sorrows to help the good work of his servants; through them He purifies and accomplishes this good work. The good works of men alone are insufficient, as St Simeon the New Theologian mentions:

> Gold that has been covered with rust cannot be cleaned and cannot reclaim its lost splendor until it has been thrown into the smith's fire and reforged with care. In the same way, the soul that has become defiled with the rust of sin and become completely useless, can only be purified and recover its previous beauty if it will first undergo many temptations and the forge of sorrows. This is explained by the words of our Savior Himself: "Go and sell what thou hast, and take up thy cross, and follow me."[16] Here the cross represents temptations and sorrows. To give away all that you have, while at the same time not courageously bearing all the temptations and sorrows that come your way, seems to me a sign of a lazy soul that doesn't recognize what it needs, because those who only give away their riches will receive nothing, unless they patiently bear temptations and sorrows until the very end for the sake of God. Christ didn't say that in rejection of earthly goods, but in *patience* is the soul saved. It is clear that giving away one's riches and rejecting the world are exemplary and beneficial; but they alone, without patient bearing of sorrows, cannot make a man perfect in the sight of God . . .
>
> He who has given away his riches to the poor and left the world boasts with great pleasure in his own conscience, expecting a great reward, and sometimes vanity steals away all his reward. Whoever bears distress with gratitude and lives among sorrows after giving everything away to the poor, receives his reward in whole; he can expect great rewards in this and the future age, as an emulator of Christ's sufferings, as one who has suffered with Him in the days of His temptations and sorrows. And so I implore you, brothers in Christ, let us try to strive to follow the words of our Lord, God, and Savior Jesus Christ. Just as we have renounced the world and everything that belongs to the world, so let us also enter in through the narrow gates, which consists of the severing of our carnal mind and

> will and fleeing from them, because without the mortification of the flesh, its desires and wills, it will be impossible to receive the joy and deliverance from passions and the freedom that comes from the consolation given by the Holy Spirit.[17]

Why do we not desire to be subjected to sorrows that the providence of God allows for the salvation of our souls, to which God Himself calls us? Because we are governed by sensuality and vanity; the first vice prevents us from constraining the body, the second makes us treasure the opinions of others. Both of these passions are destroyed by living faith since they exist as a result of lack of faith. When Abba Dorotheos asked St John the Prophet, "What should I do? I am afraid of worldly shame," St John answered in the following words:

> Not to bear shame is the doing of faithlessness. Brother! Jesus became man and bore the worst shame, and are you greater than Jesus? This is faithlessness and demonic delusion. Whoever desires humility with his tongue, and yet cannot bear to be shamed before men, such a man cannot acquire humility. Here, you have now heard the true teaching—do not ignore it. Otherwise, you yourself will be neglected by grace. On shame: If you remember the universal shame before the Lord that will be the lot of sinners, you will consider this temporary shame to be nothing.[18]

In general, the remembrance of God's omnipresence and omnipotence restrains the heart from the kind of vacillation that lack of faith creates in the thoughts when the mind leans only on vanity and the incorrect love for one's own body. The holy Prophet David said, "I foresaw the Lord always before me, for He is on my right hand, that I should not be moved. Therefore did my heart rejoice, and my tongue was glad; moreover, my flesh also shall rest in hope!"[19]

My heart is glad from the effect of faith and humility! The words of doxology and self-accusation give joy to my mouth and tongue! My whole body feels the strength of incorruption that enters and overflows in it from a heart that is broken and humbled, a heart that is consoled by God!

If no temptation can even touch a person without God's will, then complaints, grumbling, chagrin, self-justification, and blaming others and circumstances are the actions of a soul that are contrary to God's will. They are attempts to oppose and resist God.[20] Let us fear such a calamity! When we think of whatever sorrows we may be facing, let us not lose time in analyzing them, lest they distract us from humble-mindedness and lead us to evident or subtle self-justification, a state contrary to God's vision for us. Not trusting in our own weakness, let us rush quickly to the trusty armor of self-accusation!

Near the Saviour, on two crosses, two thieves were crucified. One of them insulted and blasphemed against the Lord; the other admitted that he was worthy of suffering for his evil deeds, while he recognized the Lord's innocent suffering. Immediately, self-accusation opened the eyes of his heart, and in the innocent victim, he recognized the all-holy God, suffering for mankind. Neither the educated, nor the priests, nor the high priests of the Jews recognized Him, despite the fact that they scrupulously studied the letter of the Law of God. The thief is made a theologian, and before the eyes of all the people who considered themselves wise and powerful, who laughed at Christ, he confessed to Him, trampling on the lies of the world-wise and powerful with his holy faith. The other thief was hurled to hell by the weight of his sin of blasphemy, the heaviest of all sins. The thief who came to true knowledge of God through his sincere self-accusation was led to heaven by his confession of the Redeemer, something only possible for those who are humble. The two thieves were condemned to the same cross, but they thought, felt, and spoke in opposite ways, leading to two opposite fates.

It is entirely accurate to see the two thieves as images of mankind in general.[21] Every person who has wasted his life opposed to God's purpose for him, harming his own salvation and blessedness in eternity, is a thief and a murderer of himself. Such a criminal is given a cross as the last possible means for salvation, so that he, having confessed his crimes and admitted himself worthy of death, would hold on to salvation given to him by God. In order to lessen the sufferings and give consolation during crucifixion, incarnate God Himself is crucified and hung on the cross near the crucified sinner! He who complains, murmurs, and hates his sorrows ultimately rejects his own salvation because by not recognizing and confessing his Saviour, he is cast into hell, into eternal and pointless agonies, since he is the one who has completely rejected and turned away from God.

On the contrary, the one who reveals his own sinfulness through self-accusation, who admits himself worthy of temporary and eternal tortures, enters little by little into an active and living knowledge of the

Redeemer, who is Life Eternal.[22] He who is crucified by the will of God and praises God from his cross is given knowledge of the mysteries of the cross and of the redemption of man by the God-Man. This is the fruit of self-accusation. With reference to the all-powerful and all-holy will of God, there can be no other feelings in a person except boundless reverence and equally boundless humility. When these feelings become part of the person, then he gains *patience*.

Our Lord Jesus Christ, the King of heaven and earth, Who came to save mankind with indisputable proof of His divinity, Who has limitless power of all things visible and invisible, not only was not accepted by people with the glory and honor that are due to Him but rather was met with anger, suspicion, and murderous plots. During the entire length of His earthly life, He was persecuted by slander, calumny, captiousness, and hypocrisy. Finally, He was seized like a common criminal during His nightly prayer; He was tied up and forcibly brought to a court that had already decided on His death sentence. He was ridiculed, buffeted, spit upon, variously tortured and beaten, and killed on a cross, a shameful death reserved for the worst criminals. And yet the Lord stood silent and still as a lamb before His shearers—the godless judges and inhuman killers—answering their brazen accusations, slanders, and insults with divine silence. Self-judgment and self-accusation are contrary to Him Who has no sins—through silence He hid His divine Truth so that we, with the help of self-condemnation and self-accusation would reject our false, so-called truth and so become partakers of His all-holy and all-encompassing Truth. Neither the truth of the fallen nature nor the truth of Moses's law could lead us to our lost eternal bliss. Only the truth of the Gospel and the cross leads us there.

There is no one among us humans who has attained Christian perfection. Christian perfection is reached by the cross of Christ; it is only ever etched in a person through the Holy Spirit. Humility raised up the Lord to the cross, the apostles to the cross, which is holy *patience*, inconceivable for the carnal mind. Herod, Pontius Pilate, and the chief priests of the Jews could not understand the silence of Jesus.

Let us pray to the Lord that He would reveal to us this mystery, give us love for His cross, and grant that we correctly bear all the sorrows that are allowed by God's all-good providence in this temporal world for our salvation and blessedness in eternity. The Lord promised us: "But he who endures to the end shall be saved."[23] Amen.

CHAPTER 26

On Purity

Fornication was a sin when the Old Testament was in force. It was a sin, a dishonoring of nature, a misuse of an important quality of human nature, and a transgression against natural laws. It was considered such a serious sin that those who were guilty of it were condemned to the death penalty. In the New Testament, this sin became even heavier because the human body was newly honored, becoming a part of the Body of Christ, and so the destroyer of purity brings dishonor directly on Christ and divides himself from communion with Him, making "the members of Christ . . . members of a harlot."[1] The fornicator is condemned to spiritual death. He who falls into the sins of the flesh is left by the Holy Spirit; the sinner is considered to have committed a mortal sin, a sin that takes salvation away from him, a sin that is the pledge of imminent perdition and eternal suffering in hell, if this sin is not healed by repentance in time.

What is purity? It is a virtue that is opposed to carnal passion. It is the keeping of the body from active falling into sin and from all action that could lead to sin. It is the preservation of the mind from carnal thoughts and fantasy, and the heart from feelings and desires of the flesh, which help prevent the body from feeling desires of the flesh.

Some maintain that sins of the flesh committed by the body are as equally serious and heavy as sins committed by the mind and heart. They base this opinion on the words of the Saviour: "Whoever looks at a woman to lust for her has already committed adultery with her in his heart." This is not good reasoning! These words were spoken to add to the Old Testament commandment, and it was spoken to those who considered only bodily fornication to be sinful, not understanding that "evil thoughts," to which we can include carnal thoughts, proceed "out of the heart. . . . These are the things which defile a man,"[2] separate him from God and take away his purity, which is the only means to see God.

Enjoyment of carnal thoughts and emotions is fornication of the heart and defilement of the person, making him incapable of communion with God, while fornication of the body is a fundamental change of the entire person's nature due to his mixing with another body.[3] Fornication of the body is complete isolation from God, death, and perdition. In order to come out of the first state, one must become restrained, but in order to leave the second state, one must be resurrected; one must be born again through repentance.

Some maintain that a person cannot be freed from desires of the flesh, much less from impure thoughts and emotions—that such a state is unnatural. God gives the commandment, God knows what is possible and impossible for us better than we do ourselves, and therefore the attainment of purity, both in body and in heart, is possible for a person. God, the Creator of nature, gives the commandment, and therefore purity of heart is not contrary to human nature. It is unnatural to the fallen nature; it was natural to the newly created nature of man, and it can become natural again upon our renewal. It can be cultivated and acquired—wheat, vegetables, fruit-bearing trees do not grow on the earth of themselves; only when the land is prepared in the proper way can these plants flower in abundance for the feeding and enjoyment of the gardeners. Land that is not harrowed in advance only gives rise to tares or merely grass; food for swine, not people. Labor is needed—the object of our labor is worth a long and difficult labor. Purity is called holiness in the Scriptures: "For this is the will of God, your sanctification: that you should abstain from sexual immorality; that each of you should know how to possess his own vessel in sanctification and honor, not in passion of lust."[4]

In married life, purity consists of the faithfulness of the spouses to each other. Purity of maids and widows who have become brides of Christ consists of faithfulness to Christ. And to them I now speak my meager, encouraging words of truth, words taken from the teaching of the Truth, from the all-holy word of God, described by the holy words and experience of the Holy Fathers.

When the Lord forbade willful divorce (which was allowed by the law of Moses) and declared that those who have been joined together by God cannot be divided by men, except in cases when the separation has already been effected by the unfaithfulness of one of the spouses, the disciples asked him about the virtue of unmarried life. The Lord answered them: "All cannot accept this saying, but only those to whom it has been given . . . He who is able to accept it, let him accept it."[5] Who is this one "who is able to accept it"? What signs in each of us can help us determine our own ability or lack of ability to live a life of celibacy? The answer is taken from the writings of the Holy Fathers:

"The ability is given to those who ask God for it with a sincere heart," says St Theophilact the Bulgarian. "The Lord said, 'ask, and it shall be given you; every one that asketh, receiveth.'"[6]

The sincerity of the petition is proven by one's way of life and the constancy of the petition, even if the fulfillment of the petition is delayed by a long or short amount of time; even if our sincere desire becomes less sharp due to various temptations. The labors with which a monk tries to defeat and transform his fallen nature are only the proofs of our sincere desire, while victory and the renewal of our nature belong only to God.

"Where nature is defeated," said St John of the Ladder, "there we recognize the coming of the One who is above nature."[7]

God transforms the desires of nature only in those who used all the means at their disposal to prove the sincerity of their desire to transform their fallen nature; then the Spirit of God touches the spirit of man, who, when he feels the touch of the Spirit of God, completely directs his thoughts and feelings to God, having lost all interest in carnal desires.[8] Then the words of the Apostle come true: "But he who is joined to the Lord is one spirit with Him."[9] Then, even the body itself aspires to follow the spirit toward God.

Because of their own willpower, experientially proven and witnessed by others, many men who did not know women remained until the end of their lives in this blessed state, preserving their virginity. Others have preserved their widowhood unsullied after the death of a spouse, while others have begun living a chaste and holy life after a life of fornication, and finally some, who have wavered in their will to remain chaste, again return to chastity, and regain their lost chastity through repentance. All of these not only abstained from falling into bodily sin but entered the battle against passionate thoughts and fantasy, eventually defeated them, and received from God the freedom of purity, which is completely foreign to any association with sin, even if sin never ceases its onslaught.

Thus, the difficulties of bad weather finally leave the traveler when he enters a well-built house. Even if the bad weather continues or becomes even more violent, the traveler remains unharmed.

My dear brother monks! Let us not waver in our fortitude, nor let us despair! Let us not pay the least attention to the demons that constantly inspire doubt in our chosen path; let us not pay the least attention to the opinions and advice of people, which are uttered either from ignorance or carnality or ill will. Let us believe the Lord our God, Who promised to hear us and help us if we remain faithful to Him. Let us prove our faithfulness through constant striving toward Him and constant repentance of our inconstant efforts. It is impossible not to occasionally waver in our determination more or less, either because of our weakness or our limitations, because of the damage inflicted on our nature by sin, because of the cunning of our invisible enemies, or because of infinitely multiplying temptations. We only have a short time in which to labor! We have only a short battle with ourselves! Soon the hour of death will come, snatching us from the exhausting battle and the danger of falling into sin. Oh! May we in that hour, before the gates of eternity, see the outstretched arms of the Heavenly Father, and hear His consoling voice: "Well done, good and faithful servant; you have been faithful over a few things, I will make you ruler over many things. Enter into the joy of your lord."[10]

Until that hour, let us continue to fight bravely, never trusting our flesh, never trusting our apparent lack of passions, even if it be actual. Whoever has put trust in himself and in the mortification of his flesh, his own dispassion and state of grace—the same has been subjected to horrific temptations.

St Isaac the Syrian said: "He who doesn't remove himself from the causes of sin forcefully is unwillingly led to sin."[11] This rule, which refers generally to the monastic life, is especially important for those who have begun to battle with natural urges that appeared in them after they fell into sins of the flesh. It is better for us never to even see this fruit, which we have sworn never to taste. For this reason, the Holy Fathers forbid women to even enter men's monasteries, a tradition that is still followed in Holy Mount Athos.

In the life of St John of the Ladder, it is said that he completely quashed the flame of carnal lust through living in the desert alone and keeping himself far away from all people. All the Holy Fathers tried to avoid the society of women as much as possible, and they encouraged all other monks to the same kind of behavior in their soul-saving, God inspired writings. The Fathers, knowing how easily man can be wounded, never trusted in their own holiness or even their old age and its natural lessening of carnal desires. Until the last moment of their lives, they never ceased to run from all causes of sin—such behavior is the surest means toward victory against sin. When St Sisoes the Great became very old, his student Abba Abraham offered to move him to a place closer to the nearest town. The ninety-year-old elder answered him: "Let us live in a place where there are no women." The disciple countered: "Where is there a place without women, except the desert?" The elder answered: "Put me in the desert then, my child."[12]

The good intentions of a man are strengthened far away from temptations, where they develop incredible firmness and power, whereas proximity to temptations leads little by little to weakening resolve, leading eventually to total moral collapse. Just as ice on a river becomes thicker and thicker the colder the winter gets, if there is the faintest hint of warmth, it begins to melt and disappear. Brothers! We must remove ourselves from the company of women, especially close acquaintances, from frequent conversations and meetings with them. Oh you, who have desired to defeat your own nature! Remember that such a victory is impossible if we subject ourselves constantly to the influence and activity of the fallen nature within us.

St Pimen the Great said to a certain monk who was embattled by carnal passions: "If a monk reins in his stomach and his tongue, and keeps to a life of wandering, he will never die" the death of the soul that snatches everyone who falls into the sin of fornication.[13] By a life of wandering, the elder means separation from a scattered life, free conversation, and numerous friendships, all of which inflame the desires of the flesh.

St Isaiah the Hermit said that the battle with concupiscence becomes more intense as a result of these five factors: idle talk, vanity, excessive sleep, lavish dress, and overeating. Two factors are especially responsible for inciting powerful and dangerous carnal desires—rejection of a wandering life (as defined by St Pimen) and overeating. It is difficult to decide which one of these is worse! One and the other lead to perdition. Whoever submits either to one or the other of these will not be able to withstand the war against his nature. To acquire purity, one must reject both of these.

As we pay especial attention to preserving ourselves from these main sources that inflame carnal desires, let us not also forget about the lesser reasons and let us keep ourselves from them as well. Even the lesser factors become powerful from habit and lack of attention. For example, some fast, live in solitude and in poverty, and pray to God for release from their fallen desires. But at the same time, they allow themselves to slander, malign, judge, and laugh at their neighbor, and the help of God flees from them; they are left to themselves, and they find no strength to battle against the sinful desires of their fallen nature.

In a certain monastery lived a recluse named Timothy. One of the other monks of this monastery became subjected to a serious temptation. The abbot, having found out about this, asked Timothy how to best deal with the fallen brother. The recluse recommended throwing the brother out of the monastery. After this was done, the same temptation attacked Timothy and brought him to a very dangerous spiritual state. Timothy began to beg God with tears to help him and have mercy on him. And he heard a voice, saying, "Timothy! Know this! I have sent you this temptation only because you despised your brother during his temptation."[14]

One must be very careful and wise in how one treats the members of the body of Christ—Christians. One must try to enter into their suffering during their spiritual sicknesses and to cast off only those who have no desire to become healed and will infect others with their illness.

It is extremely important to protect your body from falling into fornication, but this alone is not enough for God-beloved purity, through which one can see God. We have an unavoidable responsibility to purify our very soul from impure thoughts, images, and feelings, as the Saviour Himself commanded.

"Just as the body," said St Macarius the Great, "becomes infected with defilement when it is joined with another body, so the soul sickens when it enjoys and unites itself with evil and foul thoughts. If anyone infects both his soul and his mind, entering into communion with evil, he is worthy of punishment. One must preserve not only the body from obvious sin, but the soul from improper thoughts, for the soul is the bride of Christ."[15]

Once we have rejected the external sources of carnal sin, including frequent conversation and friendship with women, a scattered way of life, overeating and excessive enjoyment of food and drink, lavishness and decadence in clothing and other physical belongings, judging others, slander, laughing at others, and idle and excessive talk, let us also reject the sweetness of sensual thoughts, feelings, and fantasy. Let us not inflame such thoughts in ourselves, and let us courageously reject them when they appear in us, thanks to our fallen nature, or if they are cunningly offered to us by the enemies of our salvation, the demons. St Hesychius of Jerusalem says the following: "'Not everyone who says to Me, "Lord, Lord," shall enter the kingdom of heaven, but he who does the will of My Father in heaven.'[16] The will of His Father is the following: 'O ye that love the Lord, hate the thing which is evil.'[17] Thus, let us exercise the Jesus Prayer, and let us hate evil thoughts. In this way we will do the will of God."[18]

"Let us cleanse ourselves from all filthiness of the flesh and spirit," Apostle Paul tells us.[19]

The Holy Fathers command us to bruise the head of the serpent,[20] that is, to watch out for the very beginning of a sinful thought and to reject it. This refers to all sinful thoughts, but especially to carnal thoughts, because these are encouraged by our fallen nature, and for this reason they have more influence over us. St John Cassian tells beginner monks to confess a sinful thought to his elder as soon as it appears.[21] This method is superlative, especially for the beginner, but also for the experienced monk because it definitively breaks the inner friendship with sin to which the corrupted nature tends. Blessed is the one who can use this method in actual fact! Blessed is the beginning monk who has found an elder to whom he can open his inner thoughts! To those monks who do not have the opportunity to constantly run to an elder, the Fathers recommend immediately cutting off a sinful thought, never beginning to converse with it or fight with it (because that way leads to inevitable falls into sin), and instead to strive to pray intensely. This was the method used with great success and fruitfulness by the venerable Mary of Egypt, which is evident in her life.

"If anyone immediately cries out with tears for help to the goodness of God when attacked by a thought from the enemy," said St Nilus of Sora, "he will soon feel peace in his heart, if he prays wisely."[22]

"Just as it is natural for fire to destroy straw, it is natural for pure tears to destroy all defilement of flesh and spirit," said St John of the Ladder.[23]

When we find ourselves alone and under attack by carnal thoughts, and we feel our body become aroused by the thoughts, it is good to fall on our knees and face before the holy icons, following the examples of St Moses the Black and St Mary of Egypt, and with tears to beg God for mercy. Experience will never fail to show God's nearness to us and His power over our fallen nature. This will give us living faith, and living faith will inspire us with tremendous strength, through which we will constantly be victorious. We should not wonder, however, if after a long battle and its ensuing long period of spiritual calm (during which we naturally think that the poison of impure thoughts has finally left our hearts), once again a terrible battle descends on us and the same impure desires and movements once again appear in our bodies.[24]

Our enemy has no shame; he will never stop aiming his arrows against the greatest of God's saints, because experience has shown him that sometimes his doggedness pays dividends, and even the vessels of the Spirit are sometimes brought to great sins, as was David when he took an evening walk on his roof and saw Bathsheba bathing.[25] Our flesh is a false friend, because it craves another body not only by its own inclination but also because of the attacks of the fallen spirits, who feel pleasure in the defilement of bodies not their own. Often unexpected is the awakening of the impure, insistent, unrelenting desire! For this reason, St Pimen the Great said, "The bodyguard of the king is always next to him, prepared. Exactly in the same way must the soul be constantly on guard against the demon of fornication."[26]

In many ways, we can only marvel at the lives and deeds of the ancient monks, and not in any way can we emulate their greatness. We can only contemplate them as a miracle of God, and praise God working through them, Who gave sinful man such unattainable power and holiness. Some of these deeds, which are now impossible, included specific methods of battling against carnal thoughts and fantasy. They would not immediately fight against the carnal thought, allowing it slight entry into their mind, and then they would attack it.

Before he achieved Christian perfection, St Pimen the Great tried to find instruction and guidance from contemporary elders. He turned to a certain Abba Joseph, a hesychast in Panethos, for advice. Pimen once asked the elder: "How should I act when carnal desires begin to bother me? Should I fight them off, or should I let them enter?"

The elder answered: "Let them enter and then begin to fight them." Having received such an answer, Pimen returned to Skete, where he was leading a life of hesychasm. After this, a certain monk came to Skete from the Thebaid. He told the brothers that when asked, Abba Joseph told him *not* to allow the carnal thoughts in, but to cut them off immediately. When St Pimen heard that Abba Joseph gave the monk such advice, he returned to him and said, "Abba! I hid not a single thought from you, but you said one thing to me, and the complete opposite to the monk from the Thebaid."

The elder answered him, "Don't you know that I love you?"

"Yes, I do."

The elder continued, "Was it not you who told me that I should tell you the same things that I would tell myself? When carnal thoughts begin to attack you, and you let them in, only then beginning to fight them off, you will later become a more experienced fighter. I said this to you, because it is what I would have said to myself. But when carnal thoughts begin to attack beginners, then it is dangerous for them to let them in. They must immediately cut them off."[27]

When St Pimen himself became a guide for other monks, he similarly forbade certain monks to allow carnal thoughts to enter their mind since they would inevitably allow themselves to enjoy the impure thoughts. Only those already living the life of the angels were allowed to employ such a dangerous battle tactic.

The existence of such a method of battling temptations can be explained by the superhuman spiritual heights reached by the monks of that time. It is obvious that for such an ascetic labor one must have already reached a state of dispassion. Later Fathers forbade such methods for all monks, since it is extremely dangerous and most likely there were several instances of unfortunate failures in this battle. St Isaac the Syrian, for example, said the following: "Do not allow your mind to be tempted by carnal thoughts or images that have influence over you, thinking that you will not be defeated by them. Even the wisest were thus darkened and made a laughing stock."[28] We must follow this advice.

From the lives of God's saints we see that some of them withstood terrible and continuous battles with carnal thoughts and feelings while they passed from a passionate state to one of dispassion. This happened not only to those who led a dissolute life before monasticism (such as St Moses and Mary of Egypt) but also to virgins such as St Simeon the Fool for Christ, St John the Long-Suffering of the Kiev Caves, and others. The fierceness of the battle raised them to incredibly advanced, even superhuman ascetic labors. And since the gifts of divine grace always multiply with increased sorrows and labors, the aforementioned saints were deemed worthy of incredible gifts of grace, thanks to their unbelievable labors and the ferocity of the battle they waged. Both the battle and their labors were exceptional events in asceticism—they cannot be the guide for all ascetics. It is good and even necessary to emulate as much as possible the strength of their willpower, determination, faith, and self-limitation, but their actual ascetic labors remain impossible to emulate.

In general, it is said by the wise Fathers that when one fights carnal passions, abstinence from food and other purely physical ascetic labors should be practiced wisely and in moderation because carnal passions can only be reined in by such labors. Defeating them requires humility and tearful prayer, which attracts divine grace. In fact, excessive physical labors can be more damaging than beneficial when they weaken the body, making it difficult to concentrate on prayer, tears, and the works of humility. I once read the following story:

A certain pious man in Egypt left his wife and children, rejected the world, and departed into the desert. He was immediately attacked by the demon of fornication, who constantly reminded him of the wife he left behind. He confessed this to the Fathers. Seeing that he was an ascetic who did everything that they told him to do, the Fathers laid on him an especially heavy labor, taken from various lives of the Holy Fathers. He became so weak from this ascetic labor that he was brought low by disease. By God's providence, a certain elder from Scetis came to that monastery (Scetis was renown for its monks, who had special gifts of the Spirit, including the gift of spiritual discernment). The elder asked the sick man: "Abba! Why are you ill?

The man answered, "I am a married man, and I only recently came into this desert, and the enemy made war on me because of my wife. I told this to the Fathers, and they prescribed various labors taken from the lives of the Holy Fathers. I have become weak from these labors, but the carnal passions only become more pronounced in my body."

Having heard this, the Scetis elder grew sad, and said to him, "The Fathers are strong, and were right to command you to act thus. But, if you wish, listen to my humble advice and leave the ascetic labors for a time. Instead, eat a moderate amount of food in its proper time, fulfill your moderate prayer rule, and lay your sorrow at the feet of the Lord. He will defeat the enemy that battles against you. By your own efforts you will not be able to win this war."

The embattled brother began to do as the Scetis elder instructed. After a few days, his sickness left him, as did the impure thoughts.

St Agathon, a monk of Scetis famous for his gift of spiritual discernment, was once asked about carnal passions. He answered thus, "Go and admit your strength as nothing but dust before God, and you will find peace."[29] Other Fathers answered this question similarly. And what a proper answer it is! If the transformation of our nature can only be effected by God, then admitting that original sin has corrupted our nature and humbly praying for healing and the renewal of our nature by its Creator is the strongest, most effective weapon in the battle against our nature. This weapon weakens the trust we have in ourselves, which is often a result of excessive and immoderate physical ascesis.

St Cassian of Rome noticed that "the carnal passion of necessity battles the soul until that moment when the soul recognizes that the victory is beyond its power, when the soul understands that victory cannot be achieved through its own willpower and labors if the Lord will not send His protection and help."[30] This Holy Father spent a considerable amount of time among the Scetis Fathers, and he was filled with the treasure of their teaching. As we speak about purity, we find it essentially necessary to speak to the ignorance of our time, so full of false knowledge, and to stretch out a helping hand to those who are drowning and suffering in confusion, despair, and sorrow as a result of their ignorance. A very great many people who desire to live a pious life are completely shocked when carnal thoughts and desires suddenly arise in them. They look at this as something strange, something that should not be, and they fall into hopelessness, often preferring to leave the God-pleasing life, thinking themselves incapable of leading it. This is a most mistaken self-assessment! Our nature is in a state of corruption. In the state of corruption, carnal desires are natural; in fact, it is impossible for them *not* to appear. And so you should not be shocked and distressed at the appearance of these thoughts, fantasies, and feelings of lust—these are essentially unavoidable. Every person is subject to them, even the saints were subject to them.

But one cannot stop there. For success in the spiritual life, it is necessary that our passions reveal themselves.[31] When the passions reveal themselves in the ascetic, then he can begin to battle with them. When he begins this war and courageously fights it, he can find victory and be crowned by the spoils of war—the Holy Spirit. We implore our beloved brothers to carefully read the lives and writing of the Holy Fathers—we will see that all the saints of God were subjected to the tortures and difficulty of this particular battle, they all went through the fire of passions and the water of tears.

After Abba Dorotheos entered the monastery, he was attacked by particularly strong carnal passions, and in the heat of the battle, he sought the advice and instruction of St Barsanuphius the Great. The answers of the great saint contain a wonderful instruction on how to courageously stand firm in the midst of the mad and impure demands of our fallen nature. In one of these answers, St Barsanuphius mentions that he himself was embattled with this particular temptation for the entirety of five years: "The war that is waged by the flesh is calmed by prayer with tears."[32]

St Anthony the Great (as mentioned in his life) was also attacked by passionate thoughts and fantasies. Many other saints, even after they were renewed by the Holy Spirit and had attained the blessed shore of dispassion, were suddenly plunged again into impure thoughts and desires of corrupted nature, as happened to St Macarius of Alexandria, St Ioannicius the Great, and others. For this reason, the Fathers said that the flesh can only be trusted when it lies down in the coffin.[33]

For this reason, we enter the monastery in the first place, so that we may reveal within ourselves the hidden passions and secret cooperation of our nature with the spirits of hatred, to whom it willingly submits. For this, we cut all ties with the world; we leave the society of men, relatives, our lands, and our riches in order to see our inner bonds and to break them apart through the right hand of the Lord.[34] Only then can we approach humility of spirit, when we see within ourselves the fall of man, his bondage, and the cruel lordship of the demons and eternal death over our very nature. Only then will we cry out to God with prayer and weeping from the depths of our heart, with our whole soul; and with such weeping, such an admission of our own perdition and helpless weakness, we will attract the help of divine grace. For this reason, the rising tide of war in our hearts actually helps our spiritual growth, if we battle courageously and do not faintheartedly give up the fight.

Abba Dorotheos mentions that a disciple of a certain great elder was subjected to passions of the flesh. The elder, seeing how bravely his disciple battled, said to him: "Do you wish for me to pray God, that He lessen your suffering?"

The disciple answered, "My Father! Even though I labor, I see in myself the fruit of this suffering. It would be better if you prayed God to grant me patience in this fight."

As a conclusion to his tale, Abba Dorotheos cried out, "This is a monk who truly wishes to be saved!"[35]

St Pimen the Great used an example from the life of St John Kolovos to instruct and console his monks. St John prayed to God and was released from the demon of lust, and because of this he remained in constant peace. Then he went to a certain extremely experienced elder and told him what had happened to him. The elder told him: "Go and implore God to return the passions to you, and with them the compunction and humility you had as a result of the battle with them. This battle brings the soul to spiritual heights."[36]

Therefore, let us not become disturbed, depressed, fainthearted, and lazy when the ferocious waves of carnal lust inundate us! We must fight back against the sin, and through this war, we will develop in ourselves a living faith in God and a living knowledge of God.

Often, we harm ourselves when we demand of ourselves more than we are able to do. Thus, we have hardly entered the fray, filled to the brim with carnal desires, and we expect that we will be able to prevent ourselves from agreeing to the sin, from accepting the thoughts, fantasies, and feelings of lust. But they exist; they are natural to our fallen nature; they cannot just stop existing. It is foolish to seek that which is impossible. Impure desires have to arise in infected nature, but as soon as they have appeared in whatever form, we must immediately, forcing ourselves, fight them off with all the methods mentioned already. We must tear ourselves from our bondage, from the strong will of corrupted nature, from the reign of our old man, through the weak will of our mind,[37] led by the word of God. "The Kingdom of heaven suffers violence," said the Lord, and only those who force themselves to fight against their own sinful will can "take it by force."[38]

When the grace of God begins to openly help us, the first sign of this assistance is the so-called "conflicting thought."[39] In other words, little by little, the mind begins to feel aversion to passionate thoughts and fantasies, instead of feeling that previous sympathy and fascination with sin at every turn, when the mind did not strain very hard to fight off the approach of the carnal thoughts.

O you virgins, you who have never tasted of spiritual death through actual bodily sins of fornication! Preserve your virginity as the most precious of treasures. If you live a proper monastic life, you will not fail to notice what is called by the Holy Fathers "spiritual activity," or the direct influence of the Holy Spirit on your souls, activity that is passed from the soul to the body, and gives us indisputable proof that our bodies were created for spiritual joys, that they only began to feel attraction to animalistic pleasures as a result of the fall, that they can return to the natural attraction to spiritual pleasures with the help of sincere repentance.

Alas! Even this knowledge of the body's natural inclination toward spiritual joys is lost by mankind, who trumpet their vast store of so-called wisdom. They scoff at this higher calling of the body, as though it were some kind of strange and new teaching. It is not new, and it is not strange! Read the writings of the Holy Fathers! You will find this teaching there. If you do not wish to search there, you will also find it in the Holy Scriptures. The redemption given to man by God is filled with unutterable, essential benefits, but we, contenting ourselves with purely superficial knowledge, choose not to strive toward the deeper knowledge of experience, which requires crucifixion, and so we deprive ourselves of the knowledge that gives life.[40] The emotions of the heart transform when it enters into communion with spiritual pleasures. Such a heart begins to feel revulsion for sensuality, eagerly fighting off its desires and suggestions, crying out with tears to God for deliverance from this foul bondage.

All you who were widowed by the providence of God, who from desire or necessity carry the burdens of this state! Do not cease to fall down before God with warm and humble prayer, and He will give you victory over your nature and over your evil habits, which have strengthened and encouraged your corrupted nature. Do not abandon your fortitude in these short-lived sorrows of the carnal war; this sorrow means nothing when compared to the consolation that you will receive after your victory. This sorrow means nothing compared to the freedom that appears in the soul after victory.

All you who are in the pit of adultery and fornication! Listen to the voice that calls you to repentance, and accept the all-powerful medicine of repentance offered you by the all-powerful Physician. This medicine is already proven effective. It made adulterers into paragons of chastity; it made the dissolute saints and righteous men. It transformed the vessels of the devil into vessels of the Holy Spirit, and many repentant sinners have risen to spiritual heights greater than those who have never sinned in the flesh. The Redeemer determines the worth of every Christian, and the Christian who achieves the greatest worth is he who has united himself essentially to the Redeemer.

Many Holy Fathers who lived a life of virginity called themselves foul sinners and adulterers. Even this is nothing! Some of them, having been slandered and condemned unjustly in carnal sin, said nothing to justify themselves, instead subjecting themselves to punishments and sorrows, as though they were truly guilty. Such behavior, if judged superficially, can seem very strange; but such labors are very effective in developing holy purity. They serve as a reminder to the ascetic that if he had not been rescued from corrupted human nature by the right hand of God, he would be helpless before its demands. He has no other choice but to consider himself an adulterer. His purity is the work of God within him, not a quality of his own nature and not a result of his own labors. The length of this labor has a significant effect on the assimilation of such a correct opinion of oneself. Truly, one can say that the saints admitted themselves defiled by fornication much more than those who, having lived a carnal life, constantly drowned in fornication. Thus, St Basil the Great, Archbishop of Caesaria in Cappadocia, uttered the following words about himself: "I have never known a women, yet I am no virgin!"[41] What profound sorrow is in these words!

May the limitless mercy of God grant us to approach the holy purity of the saints of God and their holy humility. Amen.

CHAPTER 27

A Short Rule of Vigilance for Those Who Live in the World

The essence of any striving toward the Lord is *attentiveness*. Without attentiveness, all our labors become fruitless, dead. He who desires to be saved must strive to maintain attentiveness to himself, not only in solitude but in the midst of distraction, into which circumstances sometimes hurl him against his will. May the fear of God outweigh all other feelings in the scales of his heart—then it will be easy to preserve attentiveness to oneself, both in the silence of the cell and in the midst of the surrounding noise of the world.

Temperance in eating, which lessens the fire in the blood, greatly aids watchfulness over oneself; while the warming of the blood that occurs either from overeating, from excessive physical movement, from the inflammation of anger, from intoxicating vanity, or from other reasons, gives birth to a multitude of thoughts and images, in other words—scattered thoughts. The Holy Fathers recommend that he who desires to be watchful over himself must first control his appetite temperately, steadily, and constantly to abstain from excessive eating.[1]

When you awake, it is an image of the universal awakening of all people from the dead. Direct your thoughts to God, bring to God a sacrifice of the first thoughts of your mind before it has had an opportunity to accept any worldly impressions. In silence, with extreme care, fulfill any of your bodily needs after rising, then read the usual prayer rule, paying attention not so much to the number of prayers as to the quality of the prayer; that is, take care that your payer is done attentively, and as a result of this attentiveness, may your heart be blessed and enlivened by prayerful compunction and consolation. After your prayer rule, once again taking great pains to remain attentive, read the New Testament, especially the Gospels. During this reading, carefully notice all the commandments of Christ, so that you can direct your actions (both inner and external) according to them. The amount of reading can depend on the strength of the person as well as external circumstances. In the same way as excessive eating disrupts and weakens the digestion, the intemperate consumption of spiritual food weakens the mind and makes it look on the ascetic life with disgust, leading it to despair.[2]

The Holy Fathers recommend beginners to pray often, but not for long periods of time. When the mind becomes more spiritually mature and becomes stronger and firmer, then it will be capable of praying unceasingly. The following words of the Apostle Paul refer to those Christians who have already grown in Christ: "I desire therefore that the men pray everywhere, lifting up holy hands, without wrath and doubting."[3]

Such prayer is without passion or distraction or false exultation, and is appropriate for the grown man, but not yet for the child.

Having been enlightened through prayer and reading by the Sun of Truth, our Lord Jesus Christ, you may begin your daily work, keeping watch over yourself, that in all deeds and words, in your entire being, may the all-holy will of God (as revealed and explained to man in the commandments of the Gospel) rule and act in you.

If you have any free minutes during the course of the day, use them to read some chosen prayers with attentiveness, or read selected passages from the Scriptures, and through them once again strengthen your spirit, which has become tired through constant activity in the busy world. If you cannot wrest even a few such moments for yourself, you should mourn for these free moments, as though you have lost a precious treasure. What you have lost today, you must not waste on the next because our heart easily gives in to lassitude and forgetfulness from which we can fall to dark inactivity, which is so disastrous to God's work, to the work of the salvation of mankind.

If you happen to do or say anything contrary to God's commandments, immediately treat the sin with repentance, and through genuine confession return to the path of God from which you have veered through the breaking of God's will. Do not waver from the path of God! Battle every sinful thought, imagination, or emotion with faith and the humility of the Gospel commands, saying together with the Patriarch Joseph: "How then can I do this great wickedness, and sin against God?"[4]

He who is watchful over himself must reject all flights of fancy in general, no matter how attractive or seemingly good they may seem. Any flight of fancy is a scattering of the mind outside truth, into the land of insubstantial shadows that flatter the mind and lie to it. Consequences of such distraction are the loss of attentiveness, the scattering of the mind, and hardness of the heart during prayer—that is, spiritual disorder.

In the evening, as you prepare for sleep, which is the death of the day that has passed, examine your actions during the day. For him who leads a watchful, attentive life, such examination of the self is not difficult because as a result of his watchfulness, his forgetfulness (so usual for a scatterbrained person) is destroyed. Thus, having remembered all the sins of the day done in deed, thought, word, or emotion, bring them to God with repentance and a firm intention to correct yourself. Then, after reading the prayer rule before sleep, finish the day that began with thoughts of God in the same way.

Where do the thoughts and emotions of a sleeping person go? What a mysterious state is sleep, during which the soul and body are alive, and yet not alive; outside the knowledge of their own life, as though they were already dead! Sleep is as unknowable as death. During sleep, the soul rests, forgetting all the worst sorrows and pains of the world, in an image of the eternal rest. But the body! If it rises from sleep every day, then it will doubtlessly rise up from the dead as well!

As the great Agathon said: "It is impossible to progress in the virtues without intense watchfulness over yourself."[5]

Amen.

PART V

REFLECTION

A Tree in Front of My Cell's Window During Winter

The winter of 1828 I spent in the monastery of St Alexander of Svir. Before my window stood a tree, exposed by the cold like a skeleton is revealed by death. Solitude is conducive to thoughts and emotions; their activity is allowed more space. In the meantime, the sea that St John of the Ladder mentioned in the fourth step of *The Ladder* as inevitably tempestuous began to storm inside me. The naked tree was a consolation to me—it consoled me with the hope of the renewal of my soul.

"With my voice," with the voice of my mind, the voice of my heart, the voice of my sickly body, the voice of my weakness, the voice of my fall, "I cried unto the Lord, hear my prayer, consider my petition,"[1] which I raise up to You from the midst of the battles that are raging in my mind and heart, from the midst of sicknesses that burden and weaken my body, from the midst of many weaknesses that have overcome my entire life. You, who heard Jonah praying in the belly of the whale, hear me who crys out to You from the belly of my sins, from the midst of hell.

Out of the depths, out of the abyss of sins, out of the abyss of my falls and temptations have "I cried unto Thee, O Lord!" Lord, hear my voice! "Bring my soul out of [the] prison" of passions, illumine it with the light of grace! When You will pour this light on my soul, a bright, joyful, life-giving life, then it will "give thanks unto Thy name."[2] Such confession, inspired by grace, acts in the soul to fill the mind with unutterable sweetness. The mind, having descended into the heart, closes itself up inside it through lack of attention to everything that belongs to the perishable world, utters Your name, bows down before it, is nourished by it, carries Your name, and is carried it in. Your name, word of God, and God makes all other words superfluous for the mind. "Deliver me from my" demonic thoughts and intentions that persecute me, "for they have become too strong for me,"[3] against the desires of my soul, against the thoughts of my mind! "And my spirit is despondent within me, and my heart within me is vexed,"[4] "the pains of death compassed me round about, and the perils of hell gat hold upon me."[5] Lord! I do not have any trust in my own strength; my falls teach me to know my own weakness. You, O Lord, are my hope! Only then will I be "in the land of the living,"[6] in the land of Your holy Truth, when You, O Lord, will send into my heart Your grace, when, having entered into my heart, You will be "the portion of mine inheritance,"[7] my only property and treasure! Your holy angels, the choirs of people who have pleased You will rejoice, seeing my salvation. "The righteous await me, until Thou shalt requite me"[8] Your mercy, not according to the multitude of my sins but according to the greatness of Your love for mankind. Amen.

CHAPTER 28

The Cemetery

After many years of absence, I visited that beautiful village where I was born. It has belonged to my family for a long, long time. In that village is a majestic cemetery, surrounded by age-old trees. Under the luxurious branches of those trees lie the bodies of those who planted them. I came to that cemetery. The sorrowful, plaintive songs, the comforting hymns of the holy panikhida began. The wind played with the tips of the trees; their leaves rustled, and that rustle mingled with the voices of the singing clergy.

I heard the names of the deceased—those who are still alive to my heart. Their names were read in order—my mother, my brothers and sisters, my grandfathers and great-grandfathers. What solitude is in this cemetery! What a miraculous, holy silence! How many remembrances! What a strange, long life! I contemplated the inspired, divine hymns of the service. At first I only felt sadness; later, it began to lessen slowly. By the end of the service, a quiet consolation replaced my deep sorrow—the prayers of the Church dissolved the vivid remembrances of the deceased with spiritual joy. They announced the resurrection that awaits the dead! These prayers declared their life; they attracted blessedness to this life.

The graves of my ancestors are surrounded by age-old trees. Their wide branches cast a shadow over the grave sites. Under the shadow, my large family sleeps. Many generations lie here. O earth, earth! On your surface, generations of people replace each other, like leaves on a tree. They calmly grow green, they innocently rustle, brought into movement by the quiet breath of the spring wind. But autumn will soon come—they will become yellow; they will fall off the trees onto the graves, they will shrivel up on them. When spring returns, new leaves will beautify the branches, and they also will last only a short time, then will fade and disappear.

What is our life? Almost the same thing as the life of a leaf on a tree!

May 20, 1844, Village of Pokrovskoe, Vologda Region.

CHAPTER 29

A Voice from Eternity: Thoughts on the Grave

During the twilight hour of a quiet summer evening, I stood thoughtful and alone at the grave site of my friend. This was the day of his funeral; this day, his family remained a long time at his grave. There were almost no words spoken among those present; only sobs were heard. Weeping was interrupted by deep silence; silence was interrupted by weeping. For a long time, weeping was replaced by silence and silence by sobs.

I stood thoughtful and alone at the grave; I stood surrounded by impressions of the day. Suddenly, I was seized by an unexpected, wonderful inspiration. It was as if I heard the voice of the deceased—his words from beyond the grave, a mysterious conversation, a miraculous sermon. I will hurry to write what I heard in my soul, with shaking fingers:

"My father! My mother! My wife! My sisters! You who are dressed in black, enrobed in deep sadness both in body and soul, you came here to my lonely grave and surrounded it with bowed heads. Silently, with only your thoughts and emotions, you converse with the silent inhabitant of the coffin. Your hearts are phials of incurable sorrow. A stream of tears pours from your eyes; after these streams exhaust themselves, new streams are born—your sorrow has no limit, your tears have no end.

"My children, my little ones! Even you are here at the tombstone that covers my grave. Even your eyes are covered with tears, though your hearts don't know what it is that you cry about, only emulating the tears of my father, the tears of my mother. You find the tombstone beautiful, brilliant, the granite like a mirror; you like the sign written in gold; but they—this granite and this sign—they are the harbingers of the early loss of your parent.

"My father, my mother! My wife, my dear friends and relatives! Why do you stand so long over my grave, over the cold stone standing like a sentinel of death? My breathless body has long become cold; according to the will of the all-powerful Creator, it returns to its own earth, it dissipates into dust. What heavy thoughts are weighing you down, keeping you here at my grave? The servers of the altar have brought their prayer for my eternal rest, they sang for my eternal memory with the God who saves me and gives me rest. They left the silent grave—you must go as well. You need rest after your labors in body and soul, you who have been tortured, torn apart by grief.

"But you do not leave! You are still here! You are rooted to the place of my burial! In your silence, that speaks louder than even the most eloquent oratory, with your heart, in which the amount of emotion drowns out their particularity, you do not walk away from the grave that is to be untouched for many ages, from the stone, the unfeeling monument. What do you need? Do you expect to hear my voice from under the stone, from the depths of the dark grave?

"There is no such voice! I only speak to you with my silence. Wordlessness, silence that cannot be broken—this is the fortune of the cemetery until the very trumpet of the resurrection. The dust of the dead speaks without the sound that the word of the living requires; even in their corruption they speak a loud sermon, the most convincing speech for the stormy, loud searchers for worldly corruption.

"And yet I still have a voice! I am speaking to you, I am answering your unanswerable thoughts, your unuttered and unresolved questions. Listen to me! Hear my voice in the general voice of eternity speaking to time! The voice of eternity is one—unchanging, inviolable. It has no inconstancy, fickleness; it has but one day, one heart, one thought. The one who united them all into one is Christ Himself. From Him comes the single voice of eternity.

"In this voice, with which eternity speaks, in this soundless and yet thundering voice; hear my voice! Can you really not recognize my voice, my dear ones? My voice in this one great voice of eternity has its own distinct sound, like the sound of a note in a chord played on the piano.

"This voice of eternity has spoken to us, has spoken since our appearance into this world. It spoke to us when we were still unable to understand it; it spoke to us in our advanced age, when we could and should have been listening to it, understanding it. The voice of eternity! Alas! There are so few people in the noisy hostel of the world that listen to you! At first, our childhood hinders us; then our everyday worries hinder us, our worldly enjoyments. But you still don't fall silent. You speak, you speak, and finally, through the terrible messenger—death—you require attention from both the attentive and inattentive listener to hearken to the great words of eternity.

"In order for the voice of eternity to have an especial resonance, to especially penetrate into our hearts, to yoke our minds to the word of salvation, God added me to those who speak from eternity. My voice has united in perfect harmony with the universal voice of the great invisible world. For those wandering in the world, I am a dead man without a voice, like all dead men. But for you I am alive, and though dead, I speak the word of salvation openly, powerfully, much more so than I would have had I remained among you and, rushing about with you after the shadows of alleged benefits this world falsely offers and through which it destroys the exiles from Eden, who have been placed for a short rest in the hostel of the world for reconciliation with the God whom they have offended.

"God is merciful, and His mercy knows no bounds. If it would be useful and necessary, I would speak to you loudly, even from the dark of the grave, from under the heavy stone! But heaven has acknowledged the personal voice from eternity to be superfluous . . . And what voice from eternity is not already superfluous, when God has allowed that not only people equal to the angels, but His only begotten Son declare His will to the universe, announce holy and strict rules of eternity—joy for the obedient, terror for the disobedient? 'They have Moses and the prophets; let them hear them,'[1] this was the answer of heaven to the request of the dead rich man to warn those living a carnal life on earth, those already dead with the eternal death of the soul. 'If they do not hear Moses and the prophets, neither will they be persuaded though one rose from the dead.'[2]

"My friend is a dead man, yet he still speaks with the living word! Receive from me his instruction and fulfill it!

"Here is my father! Here is my mother! Here is my wife! Here are my dear ones! I can speak with them only with the universal voice of eternity. In this voice, they also hear the sound of my voice! But I don't have a separate, personal word . . . My friend! Be my word; from our common treasure, from holy eternity, tell them a short, needed word on my behalf. Tell them that the earthly life is a momentary, illusory dream. Eternity is inevitable. And there is such a thing as a painful eternity! Acquire blessed eternity through vigilance, obedience to the all-holy Law of the all-holy God, and come join me in the unshakable, unending joy, each in his own time, determined only by God alone!"

1848, Sergiev Hermitage. These thoughts were written down after the death of K. F. O—n, who was, from his youth, a close friend of Archimandrite Ignatius Brianchaninov.

CHAPTER 30

Thoughts on Death

Death is the inevitable fate of every human being on this earth. We fear it as the cruelest of enemies, we bitterly mourn those whom it seized, but we live our life as though death does not even exist, as though we were immortals on this earth.

Oh my coffin! Why do I forget you? You wait for me, you wait, and I will definitely be your inhabitant, so why do I forget you and act as though the coffin were the fate only of other people, not my fate?

Sin has taken and continues to take away any knowledge or sense of truth that I had. It takes away from me the remembrance of death, of this event that is so important for me.

To remember death, one must lead a life according to the commandments of Christ. The commandments of Christ purify the mind and heart, making them dead to the world and alive in Christ. The mind that has rejected earthly passions begins to turn often to the mysterious passing into eternity—to death. The purified heart begins to foresee death.

The mind and heart that have rejected the world strive to eternity. Having loved Christ, they tirelessly hunger to appear before Him, even though they fear the hour of death, understanding the greatness of God and their own worthlessness and sinfulness. To them, death seems at the same time a terrible labor and the awaited deliverance from the prison of the world.

If we are not capable of desiring death because of our coldness to Christ and our love for the fading world, then at the very least, let us try to recall death as a bitter medicine against our sinfulness because once the "remembrance of death" (as the Father called it), has taken root in the soul, it cuts off the soul's friendship with death, with all sinful pleasures.

"Only he who has become closely linked with the thought of his own death can put an end to his sins."[1] "Remember your end, and you will never sin."[2]

Rise up from your bed as one who is resurrected from the dead; lie down in your bed every evening as though it were your coffin. Sleep is an image of death, and the darkness of the night is a foreshadowing of the darkness of the tomb, after which the light of the resurrection will shine forth; so joyful for the slaves of Christ, so fearful for His enemies.

Even though clouds are nothing more than gases, they can prevent the light of the sun. Similarly, insignificant bodily pleasure, distraction, and cares of the world occlude majestic eternity from the eyes of our soul.

The sun in its pure sky shines in vain for the blind man, and so eternity seems to not exist for the heart that is passionately attached to the world, to all its glories and honors and sweetness.

"The death of sinners is evil."[3] It comes to them in that time when they expect it least; it comes to them, but they have not prepared for it in the least, nor have prepared for eternity. They have not even gained any real understanding of what death or eternity are. And death snatches unprepared sinners from the face of the earth, upon which they only angered God, and it hands them over to the eternal prisons of hell.

Do you wish to acquire remembrance of death? Keep to a strict moderation in food, clothing, and all personal belongings. Make sure that useful things never become indispensible, and study the Law of God day and night, or at least as often as you can. Then, remembrance of death will come to you. This remembrance will unite with torrents of tears, with repentance of sins, with a firm desire to change, and with many fervent prayers.

What human being has ever remained to live forever on the earth? No one. I also will follow my fathers, ancestors, brothers, and all my near ones. My body will go down into a dark tomb, and the fate of my soul will become an impenetrable mystery for those inhabitants of earth who remain.

My friends and relatives will weep for me, perhaps even bitterly, but then they will forget me. Thus, innumerable thousands of people are mourned and forgotten. They are only counted and remembered by the all-perfect God.

Hardly was I born, hardly was I conceived, and already death stamped me. "He is mine!" said death, and immediately prepared a scythe especially for me. From the very beginning of my existence, it began to swing the scythe. Any minute I can become the victim of death! There were many misses of the scythe, but a true swing and strike is inevitable.

Death looks on the earthly works of man with a cold smile of derision. The builder erects huge buildings, the painter did not finish his beautiful painting, the genius makes great plans for himself and begins to put them into practice; but unexpected and incorrigible death comes and makes impossible all of the great man's lofty plans.

Cruel death only respects the slave of Christ. Since it was trampled down by Christ, it respects only the life in Christ. Often, a heavenly messenger comes to tell the servants of Truth of their imminent passage into blessed eternity. Those who were prepared for death by their life, who were consoled both by their clear conscience and a message from above, quietly, with a smile on their faces, fall asleep into the long sleep of death.

Has anyone ever seen the body of a righteous man after the soul has departed? It does not smell. One does not fear to approach it, and during the funeral all sorrows dissolve into an unexpected joy. The expression of the face, the same as it was in the last minutes of life, sometimes shows the deepest calmness, sometimes the joy of a long-expected meeting—of course, they saw the angels and the saints sent from heaven to accompany the souls of the righteous.

Oh my death! Help me to remember you! Come to me, you bitter but beneficial remembrance! Frighten away my sin! Direct me to the path of Christ! Let this remembrance weaken my hands to the doing of any empty, vain, sinful deed.

Oh my death! Help me to remember you! My bitter masters, vanity and sensuality, will flee from me. I will remove all fine foods from my table; I will take off my opulent clothing and I will put on the clothes of mourning; I will mourn myself as though I were already dead, since I have been a condemned dead man from the moment of my birth!

"So! Commemorate yourself; mourn yourself as already dead," says the remembrance of death. "I have brought you grief for your own benefit, and I have brought with me a host of most beneficial thoughts. Sell your excessive things, and give the profits to the poor, thereby sending your treasures directly to heaven, as the Saviour commanded. They will await their master there, having been increased a hundredfold. Shed bitter tears for yourself, pray fervently for yourself. Who will commemorate you after death with such eagerness and assiduity as you can commemorate yourself before your death? Do not trust your salvation to others, when you can yourself accomplish this most important of all works! Why must you rush about after perishable things, when death will take all of them away from you? Death is the accomplisher of the commands of the all-holy God. No sooner does it hear the summons then it rushes faster than lightning to the one who is called. Death is not ashamed of the rich man or the lord, nor does it fear the hero or the genius. It does not spare youth or beauty or any earthly happiness. And the servant of God is led by death to an eternity of joy, but the enemy of God is led into eternal suffering."

"Remembrance of death is a gift of God," said the Fathers.[4] It is given to those who fulfill the commandments of Christ in order to accomplish the holy labors of repentance and salvation.

Blessed remembrance of death is preceded by one's own forceful attempts to remember death. And so, force yourself to remember it often, convincing yourself of the definite fact of your own unknown death, and soon it will begin to come on its own, as a profound and powerful reminder. It will strike down all your sinful desires.

The lover of sin is far from this spiritual gift. Even at the grave site, he does not stop to satiate his sinful desire, never thinking of death, even though it is grinning before his face. Conversely, the servant of Christ remembers the coffin that awaits him, and even in magnificent palaces he will pour out saving tears on behalf of his soul. Amen.

CHAPTER 31

Proof of the Resurrection of the Body, Taken from the Effect of the Jesus Prayer

In an isolated, little-known, and insignificant monastery that stands between woods and bogs, there lived a certain monk. With fear, with lack of trust in himself, and with careful study of the writings of the Fathers, he delved into the prayer of the mind in the depth and mystery of the heart's cell.

One time this monk stood in church, submerging his mind in his heart. His heart effortlessly moved in prayer toward the mind, and of its own accord led the monk's entire body into a holy, spiritual state, impossible to describe with words, only attainable through experience. When the monk saw this incredible new state of his body, his mind was illumined with mystical knowledge. He understood the heretofore cryptic and strange words of St John of the Ladder, who said: "I have called out with my whole heart, that is, with my body, soul, and mind."[1]

Here is the proof for the resurrection from the dead that I have within my own body! If the body is capable of spiritual feelings, if it can feel the consolation of grace together with the soul, if from now on it can be a communicant of grace, then how can it not resurrect for the future life according to the Scriptures?

The bodies of God's saints were salted with grace, and corruption could not touch them! Through this victory over corruption they already foretold their resurrection; by pouring forth healing, they prove that grace abides in them and that eternal life inhabits them, which must in its own time blossom into the all-blessed resurrection, intended for and given to mankind by our Redeemer, the Lord Jesus Christ. Amen!

PART VI

REFLECTION

The Garden During Winter

In 1829, I spent the winter in the Ploshchanskii Hermitage.[1] And until this day, there stands a lonely wooden cell in the middle of the garden. My friend and I lived there. When the weather was calm during the bright, sunny days, I would walk out to the porch, sit on the bench, and contemplate the large garden. Its nakedness was covered by a recent snowfall; everything all around was quiet, a kind of frozen and majestic calm. This vista began to appeal to me, and I began to read in it a kind of mystery.

One day, I sat thus and watched the garden. Suddenly, it was as if a veil fell from the eyes of my soul, and the book of nature was opened to them. This book was given as reading for the first-created Adam, a book that contained in itself the words of the Spirit, like the Holy Scriptures. What was this teaching that I read in the garden? It was the teaching of the resurrection from the dead, a powerful teaching, a teaching illustrated by natural processes that resemble resurrection. If we were not already accustomed to seeing the reawakening of nature during spring, it would appear to us incredible, completely miraculous. We do not wonder because of habit; seeing a miracle, we already somehow do not see it! I look at the exposed branches of the trees, and they speak to me in their mysterious language: "We will come alive, we will be once again covered with leaves, we will become fragrant, and we will be decorated with flowers and fruits. Can you not see that the dry bones of mankind will also come alive in their allotted time?"

Indeed, they will come alive, they will be covered in skin; they will enter a new life and a new world in a new form. Just as trees that cannot stand the cruelty of winter, lose all their vital juices, and in the spring are chopped down and used as fuel, sinners who have lost the source of their life—God—will be collected in the last day of this age, in the beginning of that future eternal day, and will be cast into the fire that never stops burning.

If it would be possible to find a person who did not know about the natural transformations made by the changing seasons, if such a stranger could be brought into the garden that majestically sleeps during winter in a slumber of death, could be shown the naked trees, and then could be told of the luxurious robes that they will put on in spring, he would look at you instead of answering and would only smile at the absurdness of your fairy tale! Just in such a way, the resurrection of the dead seems improbable to the wise men who wander in the darkness of earthly wisdom, who do not know that God is all-powerful, that His multifaceted wisdom can be seen but cannot be understood by the minds of His creatures. For God, all things are possible—there are no miracles for Him. The mind of man is weak—that which we are not used to seeing, we imagine to be an impossible thing, an incredible miracle. The works of God that we constantly and indifferently see are incredible works, great miracles that are unattainable by the mind.

And before our eyes every year, nature replays this teaching on the resurrection of the dead, drawing it vividly through transformational, mysterious action.

1843, Sergiev Hermitage

CHAPTER 32

My Cross and the Cross of Christ

The Lord said to his disciples: "If anyone desires to come after Me, let him deny himself, and take up his cross, and follow Me."[1]

What does the cross signify? Why is it that "his cross," that is a separate one for each person, is also called "the Cross of Christ"?

My cross is the sorrows and sufferings of this earthly life, unique for each individual person.

My cross is fasting, keeping vigil, and other pious ascetic labors through which the body is humbled and submits to the spirit. These labors must be appropriate to the strength of each individual person, and so each person has his own cross.

My cross is my disease of sin, or passions, which also differ in each individual person. Some of them are already present at birth; others infect us during our earthly life.

The cross of Christ is the teaching of Christ.[2]

Filled with worry and futility is my cross, no matter how heavy it may be, if it does not become the Cross of Christ through our following in His footsteps.

My cross becomes the Cross of Christ if I am a disciple of Christ, because a disciple of Christ is firmly convinced that Christ watches over him at all times; that Christ allows his sorrows as the inescapable and inevitable condition of Christianity; and that no sorrow would ever approach him if it were not allowed by Christ; and that through sorrows, the Christian becomes one with Christ, becomes a partaker of His lot on earth, and later in heaven.

My cross will become the cross of Christ, because a true disciple of Christ considers the fulfillment of Christ's commandments as the only purpose of his life. These all-holy commandments become for him a cross on which he constantly crucifies his old man with his passions and lusts.[3]

Thus, it is clear that before taking up the cross, one must first deny oneself even unto the mortification of one's own soul.

In order to lift the cross to one's shoulder, one must first deny the body its carnal desires and give it only what it needs to survive; one must consider one's own truth to be the worst falsehood before God, one's own reason to be complete madness; and finally having given oneself over to God, with all the power of faith, dedicate oneself to the constant studying of the Gospels, and rejecting one's own will.

He who has accomplished such denial of the self is capable to take up his cross. With obedience to God and trust in God's help to make his weakness strong, he looks at all the imminent sorrows and disturbances without fear. Courageously, he prepares to overcome them, hoping that with their help he will become a participant in the sufferings of Christ, and that he will attain the mystical confession of Christ not only with his mind and heart, but in actual fact, with his very life.

The cross is heavy only as long as it remains "my cross." When it becomes the Cross of Christ, it suddenly becomes very light—"for My yoke is easy, and My burden is light," said the Lord.[4]

The cross is lifted to the shoulders by the disciple of Christ when he acknowledges himself worthy of the sorrows allowed by God's providence.

The disciple of Christ carries his cross correctly when he admits that exactly those sorrows which were sent to him, and not any others, are necessary for his formation in Christ and his salvation.

Patient bearing of "my cross" is true recognition of one's sins. In this knowledge, there is no self-deception. However, he who admits himself to be a sinner but at the same time complains and groans from his cross, only proves that he is lying to himself with his superficial admission of sinfulness.

Patiently bearing the cross is true repentance.

Oh, you who are crucified on the Cross! Confess to the Lord, Who is righteous and just. By your self-accusation, justify the judgment of God, and you will receive forgiveness of your sins.

You, who are crucified on the Cross! Come to know Christ, and the gates of Eden will be opened to you.

Praise God from your cross, cutting off all thoughts of self-pity and murmuring, since they are no less than blasphemy.

Thank God from the cross, thank Him for the priceless treasure of your own cross, for the precious gift to be able to emulate Christ's sufferings.

Praise God from your cross, because the cross is the only true instructor, guardian, and throne of theology. Outside the cross, there can be no living knowledge of God.

Do not search for Christian perfection in human virtues. There you will not find it, because it is hidden in the Cross of Christ.[5]

My cross becomes the Cross of Christ when I, a disciple of Christ, carry it with an active knowledge of my own sinfulness, admitting I am worthy of death; and when I carry it with gratitude to Christ, with praise for Christ. From praise and thanksgiving, spiritual consolation appears in the sufferer; praise and thanksgiving become an endless source of unutterable, undying joy that fills the heart, overflows into the soul, and even onto the body itself.

The Cross of Christ is a cruel sight only to those who see things with the eyes of the body. The disciple and follower of Christ sees it as the source of spiritual joy. So great is this joy that sorrows are completely muted by it, and the follower of Christ feels only joy, even amid the most horrifying pain.

The young wife Mavra said the following to her young husband Timothy when he was suffering terrible tortures and invited her to join him in dying for Christ: "I am afraid, my brother, that I will not be able to stand firm when I see the horrors of the angered torturer; I will not be able to bear them because of my youth."

Her husband answered her: "Put your trust in our Lord Jesus Christ, and these tortures will feel like healing oil pouring over your body, giving you relief from your diseases."[6]

The cross is power and glory of all the saints that ever lived.

The cross is a healer of passions, a destroyer of demons.

The cross is a death dealer to those who have not transformed their own cross into the Cross of Christ, who complain about God's providence from their cross, who blaspheme Him, and who give themselves up to hopelessness and despair. Sinners who remain unrepentant and ignorant on their cross will die an eternal death, bereft of the true life in God because of their lack of patience. They come down from their cross only to go down with their souls into the eternal tomb—the prisons of hell.

The Cross of Christ raises the crucified disciple of Christ from the earth. The disciple of Christ who is crucified on his cross thinks only of the heights, with his mind and heart he lives only in heaven, already seeing the mysteries of the Spirit in Christ Jesus, our Lord.

"If anyone desires to come after Me, let him deny himself, and take up his cross, and follow Me." Amen.

CHAPTER 33

The Cup of Christ

Two of the Lord's beloved disciples asked him for thrones of glory. Instead, he gave them His cup.[1]

The cup of Christ is suffering.

The cup of Christ gives its communicants participation in Christ's kingdom of grace, and it prepares heavenly thrones of eternal glory for them.

We all have nothing to say before the cup of Christ; no one can complain about it or refuse it, because He Who has commanded us to drink it, Christ Himself, drank it before everyone else. Oh, you tree of the knowledge of good and evil, you killed our forefathers in paradise by deceiving them with the pleasures of sensuality and the deceitful promise of knowledge. Christ, the Redeemer of the lost, brought His saving cup to earth, to us who are fallen and exiled. Through the bitterness of this cup, the sinful, deadly pleasure of sin is eradicated from the heart. Humility, which flows from the cup abundantly, destroys the proud, carnal mind-set. He who drinks the cup with faith and patience regains eternal life, which was taken and continues to be taken from us through our continual tasting of the forbidden fruit.

I will take the cup of salvation, the cup of Christ![2]

A disciple of Christ takes his cup when he bears earthly troubles with humility inspired by the Gospel. Saint Peter rushed to the defense of the God-Man, sword in hand, when He was surrounded by evildoers. But the most meek Lord Jesus said to Peter: "Put your sword into the sheath. Shall I not drink the cup which My Father has given Me?"[3]

When you are surrounded with difficulties, comfort and strengthen your soul by saying to it: "Shall I not drink the cup which My Father has given Me?"

The chalice is bitter. One has merely to glance at it, and all human reasoning vanishes. Replace your reasoning with faith, and bravely drink the bitter cup. The all-good and all-wise Father gives it to you.

It is not the Pharisees, or Caiaphas, or Judas who prepared it. It is not Pilate and his soldiers who give it. "Shall I not drink the cup which My Father has given Me?"

The Pharisees conspire, Judas betrays, Pilate orders the lawless murder, and the governor's soldiers perform it. Through their crimes, they all prepared for themselves inevitable perdition. Do not condemn yourself to the same fate through your remembrance of evil, through your desire for revenge, through hatred for your enemies.

Our heavenly Father is all-seeing, all-powerful. He sees your troubles and afflictions, and if He should find it necessary and profitable to remove the cup from you, He would certainly do so. The Lord, according to Scripture and Church history, allowed His beloved servants to suffer, while in other cases He prevented suffering, according to His incomprehensible judgments.

When the cup appears before you, do not look at the men who give it to you, but raise your gaze to heaven and say: "Shall I not drink the cup which My Father has given Me?"

I will take the cup of salvation. I cannot reject the cup, which is a pledge of heavenly, eternal blessings. Christ's apostle teaches me patience: "We must through many tribulations enter the kingdom of God."[4] Shall I refuse the cup, which is a means of acquiring and developing the kingdom within me? I will take the cup, for it is God's gift.

The cup of Christ is the gift of God. "For to you it has been granted on behalf of Christ, not only to believe in Him, but also to suffer for His sake."[5]

You accept the cup, so it would seem, from the hands of men. What business is it of yours whether those men are acting rightly or wrongly? Your duty is to act virtuously, as a follower of Christ. With gratitude to God, with living faith approach, and bravely drink every drop.

Accepting the cup from human hands, remember that it is not only the cup of the innocent one but also of the all-holy One. Having remembered that, repeat for yourself and for fellow sufferers, sinners like yourself, the words of the blessed and wise thief, which he uttered while crucified at the right hand of the God-Man: "We receive the due reward of our deeds . . . Lord, remember me when You come into Your kingdom."[6]

Then, turn to the people and say to them (if they are not able to understand and accept your words, do not cast the precious pearls of humility under the feet of those who cannot appreciate them, but say it with your mind and heart): "Blessed are you, instruments of the justice and mercy of God, now and forever!"

In this way, only you will be carrying out the commandment of the Gospel, which says, "Love your enemies, bless those who curse you."[7]

Pray to the Lord for them, that they be given temporal and eternal rewards for the insults and offenses they heaped on you, so that what was done to you may be imputed to them for righteousness in the judgment of Christ.

Though your heart may not want to do this, force it; for only those who compel their heart to carry out the commandments of the Gospel can inherit heaven.[8]

If you do not wish to act in this manner, you do not wish to be a follower of the Lord Jesus Christ. Carefully examine yourself to see whether you have not preferred another teacher or even submitted to him. The teacher of hatred is the devil.

To offend, to wrong, to persecute one's neighbor is a terrible crime. A still more terrible crime is murder. But he who hates his persecutor, slanderer, betrayer, or murderer, and who harbors resentment against them or seeks to avenge himself is very near to the same crime. Such a man pointlessly pretends to be righteous. "Whoever hates his brother is a murderer."[9]

A living faith in Christ teaches us to accept the cup of Christ, and it fills the hearts of its communicants with hope in Christ. Hope in Christ gives the heart strength and consolation.

What suffering, what hellish torture it is to complain and murmur against the cup predestined for us in heaven!

Complaints, lacks of patience, faintheartedness, and especially despair are sins, the foul progeny of lack of faith.

It is sinful to complain about our neighbors when they are the instruments of our sufferings, and how much more sinful is it to complain when the cup comes down to us directly from heaven, from the right hand of God!

Whoever drinks the cup with gratitude to God, while blessing his neighbor, has attained holy rest and the peace of Christ, and already he enjoys the spiritual paradise of God.

Temporal sufferings in themselves have no meaning; we only ascribe importance to them because of our attachment to earth and to perishable things, through our coldness to Christ and eternity.

You can bear the bitter and disgusting taste of medicines. You can bear painful surgeries to your body. You can withstand long periods of hunger, or being shut in a room for a long time. You bear all that in order to restore lost health to your body, which, when healed, will inevitably become sick again, and will eventually die and decay. Why can you not bear the bitterness of the cup of Christ, which gives healing and eternal blessedness to your immortal soul?

If the cup seems to you unbearable and poisonous, you are fittingly condemned by it. Though you call yourself Christ's follower, you are not!

To true followers of Christ, this cup is a cup of joys. Thus, the holy apostles, after being publicly flogged before a gathering of the Jewish elders, left the presence of the Sanhedrin, rejoicing that they were considered worthy to suffer dishonor for the name of the Lord Jesus.[10]

Righteous Job heard terrible news. One calamitous report followed another to attack his brave heart. The last news was the hardest to bear—the loss of all his sons and daughters by a sudden, cruel, and violent death. In bitter anguish, righteous Job tore his robes and sprinkled ashes on his head; through his obedient faith, he fell on the ground and worshipped the Lord, saying: "Naked I came from my mother's womb, and naked shall I return there. The Lord gave, and the Lord has taken away. Blessed be the name of the Lord!"[11]

Entrust yourself in simplicity of heart to Him Who has counted even the hairs on your head. He knows in what measure the healing cup must be given you.

Look often at Jesus. Before His murderers, He was like a lamb that in the hands of its shearers is dumb. He was delivered to death like a silent sheep to the slaughter. Do not take your eyes off Him, and your sufferings will dissolve into heavenly, spiritual sweetness. Through the wounds of Jesus the wounds of your heart will be healed.

"Stop!" cried the Lord to those who wanted to defend Him in the Garden of Gethsemane, and he healed the mutilated ear of the one who had come to seize Him.

To the man who tried to take the cup from Him by means of arms, He said: "Do you think that I cannot now pray to My Father, and He will provide Me with more than twelve legions of angels?"[12]

When you are suffering, do not seek human help. Do not waste precious time; do not squander your spiritual strength on searching for that powerless help. Await help from God. According to His will, people will come and help you at the proper time.

The Lord was silent before Pilate and Herod; He did not utter a single word in His own defense. Imitate His wise and holy silence when your enemies judge you with the intention of finding you guilty, only using the appearance of justice to satisfy their own hypocrisy.

Whether the cup of Christ is preceded and announced by gathering clouds, or whether it appears suddenly, as if carried by a fierce wind, always say to God: "Thy will be done."

You are a disciple, follower, and servant of Jesus. He said, "If anyone serves Me, let him follow Me; and where I am, there My servant will be also."[13] Jesus spent His earthly life in suffering; He was persecuted from the cradle to the grave; from His very infancy, hatred prepared for Him a violent death. Having achieved its aim, it was not satisfied; it did its utmost to wipe the very memory of Him from the face of the earth.

All of the Lord's chosen have followed Him into eternal blessedness along the path of temporal suffering. It is impossible for us, still chained to the pleasures of the flesh, to attain a spiritual state. Therefore, the Lord constantly offers His beloved His cup, through which He makes them indifferent to the world and capable of living the life of the Spirit. St Isaac the Syrian said: "A person for whom God especially cares is known by the constant sorrows sent to him."[14]

Pray that God will spare you from every suffering, every temptation. One must not eagerly jump into the midst of sufferings because that would be proud self-assurance. But when troubles come by themselves, do not fear them, and do not think that they have come accidentally or at random. No, they are permitted by the unknowable providence of God. Full of faith and its resulting courage and strength, sail fearlessly through the darkness and raging storm to the quiet harbor of eternity. Jesus Himself is invisibly guiding you.

Through reverent, deep contemplation, study the prayer that the Lord offered to the Father in the Garden of Gethsemane at the hour of His agony preceding His passion and death on the cross. With this prayer you will face and conquer every affliction: "O My Father, if it is possible, let this cup pass from Me; nevertheless, not as I will, but as You will."[15]

Pray that God averts your sufferings, but at the same time, renounce your own will as a sinful and blind will. Surrender yourself, your soul and body, your present and future circumstances, and those dearest to your heart, to the all-holy and wise will of God.

"Watch and pray, lest you enter into temptation. The spirit indeed is willing, but the flesh is weak."[16] When troubles surround you, pray more frequently to attract the special grace of God. Only with the help of this special grace can we defeat all temporal troubles.

Having received from on high the gift of patience, keep attentive and watch over yourself to preserve in you the grace of God. Otherwise, sin will be sure to steal into your soul or body and drive out the grace of God.

If you allow sin to enter because you are inattentive or distracted (especially those sins to which our weak flesh is most vulnerable, the kind that defile both soul and body), then grace will abandon you and leave you alone and exposed. Then afflictions sent especially for your salvation and perfection will attack you savagely and will crush you with sorrow, despondency, and despair for having held the gift of God without due reverence. Hasten with sincere and determined repentance to restore purity to your heart, and through purity—the gift of patience. For since patience is a gift of the Holy Spirit; it resides only in the pure.

The holy martyrs sang joyfully in fiery furnaces, walking on nails, cut by sharp swords, or sitting in cauldrons of boiling water or oil. Likewise, when your heart attracts grace-filled consolation through prayer, preserving it by watchfulness over yourself, it will also sing songs of joyful praise and thanksgiving to God within miseries and cruel misfortunes.

The mind purified by the cup of Christ becomes worthy of spiritual vision. It begins to see the all-embracing providence of God, which is invisible to carnal minds; to see the law of corruption in everything corruptible; to see limitless eternity; and to see God in His great acts—the creation and re-creation of the world. Earthly life seems to it a short-lived wandering, its events no more than dreams and its benefits no more than a mirage, a temporary delusion of the mind and heart.

What is the fruit of temporal suffering in eternity? When the holy Apostle John saw heaven, one of the inhabitants of heaven pointed to the countless multitude of radiant saints, robed in white, celebrating their salvation and blessedness before the throne of God, and asked:

> "Who are these arrayed in white robes, and where did they come from?" And I said to him, "Sir, you know." So he said to me, "These are the ones who come out of the great tribulation, and washed their robes and made them white in the blood of the Lamb. Therefore they are before the throne of God, and serve Him day and night in His temple. And He who sits on the throne will dwell among them. They shall neither hunger anymore nor thirst anymore; the sun shall not strike them, nor any heat; for the Lamb who is in the midst of the throne will shepherd them and lead them to living fountains of waters. And God will wipe away every tear from their eyes."[17]

Estrangement from God, eternal torment in hell, eternal life with the devil and demonic people, fire, coldness, the darkness of Gehenna—that is what deserves to be called suffering! It is truly great, terrible, unendurable agony.

Earthly pleasures lead to this great, eternal suffering.

The cup of Christ preserves and saves from this suffering those who drink it with thanksgiving and praise to God, Who gives mankind His limitless, eternal mercy in the bitter cup of temporal sorrows.

CHAPTER 34

On Monasticism: A Conversation Between Two Orthodox Christians: a Layman and a Monk

Layman: My father! I consider myself blessed that I found in you a person before whom I can reveal my heart, and from whom I hear a true, sincere word. I desire with my whole heart to be a member of the Orthodox Church, to follow its dogmatic and moral traditions. With this purpose in mind, I have tried to formulate a proper understanding of all these aspects of tradition. I know that erroneous ideas lead to incorrect actions, and that these in turn are the source of personal and social ills. In our conversation today, please explain to me the meaning of monasticism in the Church of Christ.

Monk: May God bless your intentions! You are correct; every good thing comes from a proper understanding, and all evils come from false and erroneous ideas. This is an opinion found in the Gospel itself. It offers us the Truth as the first reason for our salvation, and indicates that lies are the source of all perdition.[1] Why do you wish today to speak in particular about monasticism?

Layman: In high society, monasticism is often discussed, and people have the most divergent opinions on it. My acquaintances often turn to me, since I am in close contact with many spiritual authorities, expressing a desire that I give them my own opinion. I want my opinion to be as correct as possible, and so I ask you to tell me more about monasticism.

Monk: I do not know how capable I am of fulfilling your desire, but I do want to be sincere with you, and so I will tell you everything that I have learned from the Holy Scriptures and the Holy Fathers, also from conversations with venerable and experienced monks, and even from my own discoveries and experiences. I will state this as the, so to speak, cornerstone of our conversation. Monasticism is a divine institution, not a human one.

Layman: Imagine! I have never heard even the inkling of such a thought in society.

Monk: I am aware of this. This is because all conversations about monasticism in the world go something like this. One person says, "I think this!" Another says, "But I think that!" Yet a third says, "Well, I would act this way," while another says, "I would act in the opposite way!" One hears a thousand contradictory opinions and ideas from people who have no idea at all what monasticism is, and all of them consider themselves experts on the matter without ever bothering to check the facts. Some of them even repeat blasphemies invented by Protestants or atheists. The heart is filled with sorrow and even fear from such ideas and opinions, in which their ignorance is like a swine that tramples underfoot the precious pearls of divine traditions and dogma.

Layman: Exactly so! The reason for this is truly ignorance, just as you say!

Monk: Do not think that ignorance is an insignificant evil. The Holy Fathers call ignorance a great, even foundational evil, from which evil grows to its full potential. St Mark the Ascetic says that ignorance is the first, most important reason for anger.[2] Ignorance does not recognize its own lack of knowledge; it is content with its own apparent knowledge, said St Peter of Damascus.[3] It is capable of much evil, without even realizing it. I say this because I feel sorry for such people who do not understand what the true dignity of man is, especially for Christians who do not know what Christianity is, and end up acting in their ignorance against their own interests. Do not think that I have any intention of hiding human weakness and sin in divine institutions. No! Revealing abuses and sins of men within divine institutions is a sign of reverence for this institution; it is a way to preserve those things given by God to the care of men in their proper state of holiness.

Layman: This thought is also new to me. I never looked at monasticism from this perspective before. Nor have I ever heard anyone express such an opinion.

Monk: What I said does not apply merely to monasticism, but to the whole Church, both in the Old Testament and the New. That the Old Testament Church was established by God and given to human practitioners, that is, the Hebrew people, is shown by the Lord in His parable about the vineyard, in the twenty-first chapter of the Gospel according to St Matthew. That the New Testament Church was established by the God-Man, that it was given to a different nation made up of all nations, the Christians, is made clear in the Gospels and the entire Holy Scriptures, especially in St Paul's letter to the Ephesians. The Jews needed to account to God for their preservation and use of God's gift. Since their behavior was found to be criminal, they were rejected. In fact, they were already separated from God, of their own volition by their spirit, and they were punished terribly. In the same way, Christians will have to answer to their care and use of God's institution—the New Testament Church, including monasticism.

Layman: Can one not learn from the Holy Scriptures exactly what the fate of the New Testament Church will be?

Monk: The Holy Scriptures witness to the fact that Christians, like the Jews, will slowly begin to cool to the revealed teaching of God. They will begin to forget about Christ's renewal of human nature, they will forget eternity; instead, lowering their gaze only to their earthly life. In such a frame of mind, they will spend all their time advancing their position on earth, as though it were eternal, and they will grow in their fallen nature only for the fulfillment of every damaged and perverted human desire of both body and soul. Of course, such a life is completely foreign to the life intended for us by the Redeemer, Who saved us for eternal blessedness. This is the life of rejection of Christianity. This falling away will happen, as witnessed by the Scriptures.[4] Even monasticism will not preserve itself from this general falling away, because no member of the body can escape a disease that has infected the whole body. Holy monks, inspired by the Holy Spirit dwelling in them, have foretold this same truth.[5] When Christianity will diminish to its absolute minimum on earth, then the life of the world will end.[6]

Layman: What is the significance of monasticism in the Christian Church?

Monk: Monks are those Christians who leave (as much as possible) all earthly activities for the sake of practicing prayer, which is the virtue above all virtues. They pray in order that they may be united by God through their prayer, as the Apostle Paul said in his letter to the Corinthians: "But he who is joined to the Lord is one spirit with Him."[7] And since prayer takes its strength from all other virtues and the whole teaching of Christ, monks take special care to fulfill all the Gospel commandments, which is something all Christians should do. But monks add two additional recommendations of Christ: nonacquisitiveness (i.e., poverty) and virginity.[8] Monks try to emulate the life of the God-Man; for this reason, holy monks are called "venerable ones."

Layman: Where did monastics receive their name?

Monk: The words *monk, monastery,* and *monasticism* come from the Greek word μόνος, meaning "one." The word monk indicates a person living in solitude or in seclusion; the monastery is a solitary or faraway living space, and monasticism is solitary life. This life is different from the normal life common to all people, and so in Russian, it has also acquired the name *inochestvo* (a different life). In Russian, a monk is also an *inok* (other). The words *cenobium, skete, hesychasm, hermit, reclusion,* and *desert dweller* indicate various forms of the monastic life. The monastic cenobium is a community of a large or a small number of monks who have a common church life, refectory, and manner of dressing, and they all submit to the authority of one abbot. Hesychasm often refers to two or three monks living in a separate cell, either living by mutual consent or under the guidance of the elder. They have a common refectory and dress code, and remain in their cell for five days out of seven. On Saturdays and Sundays, they join the wider community in church. A hermit is a monk who lives alone. When a hermit lives in his cell and never leaves, he is called a recluse, and his life is a life of reclusion or seclusion. When he lives in a desert, he is called a desert dweller.

Layman: When was monasticism founded?

Monk: According to St John Cassian, monasticism existed from the time of the apostles.[9] St John, a writer and monk of the fourth century, was a witness of the flourishing of monasticism in the deserts of Egypt. He spent a considerable amount of time among the monks of Egyptian Sketis, and he left behind him a considerable amount of writing, including the rules and teachings of the Egyptian monks. He said that in the first century of the Church's existence, a group of the Apostle Mark's followers in Alexandria were first called monks. They left the city to settle in the most desolate places outlying Alexandria, where they lived an exalted life according to a rule given them by the evangelist himself.[10] In the life of the martyr nun Eugenia, it is written that during the rule of Emperor Commodus (who became emperor in A.D. 180), a certain Roman nobleman named Philip was made the governor of Egypt. During that time, the Alexandrian countryside already had a monastery, and the bishop of Alexandria, St Eli, is mentioned as having entered a monastery in his youth. The Jewish historian Philo, who was a contemporary of the apostles and a citizen of Alexandria, in his *History of Christianity*, writes of a group of hermits who departed to the desert outskirts of the city in the exact same way that St John Cassian described the life of the first Alexandrian monks. Philo also calls their dwelling places monasteries. Philo does not mention whether or not these hermits were Christians, but he was a secular writer, and many at that time had not yet learned to distinguish Christianity from Judaism, considering it a mere sect of the latter.

The life of St Anthony the Great, written by his contemporary St Athanasius the Great, archbishop of Alexandria, mentions that during the time when St Anthony began a monastic life, Egyptian monks already lived a solitary life in the outskirts of various cities and towns. St Anthony the Great died in A.D. 356 at the age of 105.

There is also evidence proving that monasticism existed in Syria from apostolic times. The holy nun martyr Evdokia, who lived in the Syrian town of Heliopolis during the reign of Trajan, was converted by St Germanos, an abbot of a male monastery consisting of seventy monks. After being baptized, Evdokia entered a woman's monastery in which there were thirty nuns. Trajan began to rule in A.D. 96.

In the last years of the third century, St Anthony established desert monasticism; at the end of the first half of the fourth century, St Pachomius the Great established a monastic community in Tabenissi in the deserted Thebaid, while St Macarius the Great established a community of hesychasts in the wild desert of Sketis near Alexandria, which is why this kind of monasticism is called "skete" monasticism and monasteries under his rule were called "sketes." St Basil the Great, archbishop of Caesaria in Cappadocia, who lived in the second half of the fourth century, studied monastic life among the Egyptian monks. When he returned to Cappadocia, he lived a monastic life in the desert until he began to serve the Church, and he wrote a rule for monastics, which was later partially accepted as canonical, partially as useful for instruction, by the entire Eastern Church. Eventually, monasticism moved farther away from the outskirts of cities and into the deep, inhospitable desert, where it developed and flourished, finding fertile ground for itself. At the same time, some monasteries remained in the outskirts and within cities, and more would later be built.

St John Cassian wrote a much more detailed account of the establishment of early monasticism in Alexandria in a *History of the Church,* which did not survive the Moslem attacks of the seventh century. In general, most of the written acts of Egyptian monasticism were destroyed, both in Egypt and in other countries under the Moslem yoke.

Layman: For what reason did monasticism move away from the cities and towns and into more remote areas?

Monk: This move happened at the same time as the end of the age of martyrdom, when Christianity was accepted not only by the elect, a small, exclusive group of people who were ready to suffer and die for their faith. It became the faith of the Empire, at first tolerated and then adopted by the emperors. Christianity soon became universal, but it did not preserve its previous character of extreme self-denial. Christians in the cities and towns began to spend more time in worldly pursuits, allowing themselves luxuries, physical pleasures, participation in civil holidays, and other weaknesses that would have horrified the first confessors, since they would have seen such things as rejection in essence, of Christ. The desert became a natural refuge far away from the temptations of the world for Christians who wished to preserve and develop Christianity to its fullest degree.

St Isaac the Syrian said the following: "The desert is useful both for the weak and the strong—for the former it helps avoiding physical objects and the lusts that are inflamed as a result of attachment to them, the latter, when they achieve a state beyond that of the world, will be able to battle demons."[11]

St Basil the Great and St Dimitry of Rostov describe the seclusion of St Gordius in the desert thus: "Gordius fled from the noise of the city, the clamor of the marketplaces, the honor of the nobility, the games and pleasures, the empty laughter and temptations of the city; for his own hearing was pure, his own eyes were pure, and first of all he had a pure heart, which could see God and His Divine Revelations. Great mysteries were revealed to him, not by any people or any great philosopher, but by the Spirit Himself."[12]

As monasticism left for the desert, it developed a special code of dress to stress the monk's complete seclusion from the world. During times of persecution, however, monks and priests would wear more usual clothing to hide from the persecutors.

Layman: The exalted level that St Gordius reached is unattainable for the majority of people. In our own time, the Christian faith is competently taught in seminaries, and higher education in the faith is available in the academies.

Monk: The teaching that is (or should be) learned in monasteries differs significantly from what is taught in the seminaries, even if their subject is the same—Christianity. The Saviour of the world, when He sent His holy apostles to preach to the whole world, taught them to preach all nations the *faith* in the true God and the *life* according to His commandments. He said, "Go therefore and make disciples of all the nations, baptizing them in the name of the Father and of the Son and of the Holy Spirit, teaching them to observe all things that I have commanded you."[13] The preaching of faith must come before baptism; teaching them to live according to the commandments must come after baptism. The first teaching is theoretical, the second practical. The first is thus described by the Apostle Paul: "How I kept back nothing that was helpful, but proclaimed it to you, and taught you publicly and from house to house, testifying to Jews, and also to Greeks, repentance toward God and faith toward our Lord Jesus Christ.[14] The second teaching is described thus: "Christ in you, the hope of glory. Him we preach, warning every man and teaching every man in all wisdom, that we may present every man perfect in Christ Jesus."[15]

God gave two instructions about coming to know Him—the learning of the Word and acceptance by faith; and the study of His life that is accompanied by a life lived according to the commandments of the Gospel. The first can be likened to the foundation of a building, the second is the building itself. It is obviously impossible to build a house without a foundation. In the same way, the foundation itself is useless unless a building is put over it. "Faith without works is dead."[16]

The holy Apostle Paul describes the necessity of the first kind of learning in the following words: "So then faith comes by hearing, and hearing by the word of God. How then shall they call on Him in whom they have not believed? And how shall they believe in Him of whom they have not heard? And how shall they hear without a preacher?"[17] This is the beginning of catechetical teaching. The apostles and their followers taught new converts and expounded on the basics of Christianity, about God and the God-Man; on man, on his place within time and his place in eternity; on the mysteries, on the heavenly blessedness, on the horrors of hell,[18] and other foundational dogmas of the Christian Church, including the theoretical teaching of a life according to the Gospel commandments.[19] This exalted and holy teaching is the beginning of dogmatic and moral theology.

Even from the apostolic times, heretical teaching began to appear, teaching regarding the revelation of God founded on false human reasoning. In the revelation of God's teaching, there is no room for false human reasoning. From alpha to omega—everything is God's. The Holy Catholic Church tried to carefully preserve the priceless spiritual treasure that it received—the revelation of God's teaching. It openly accused its enemies—the idol worshippers, the philosophers of both pagan and Jewish stamp—and it repelled their attacks. It also uncovered its internal enemies—the heretics—rejecting their teachings, casting them out of the Church, and warning faithful members of their danger. For this reason, after the passage of time, theology began to widen its formulations more and more. Soon, the necessity of specialized theological schools arose. The oldest of these schools was in Alexandria, flourishing from the second to the third centuries. Teachings contrary to divine Truth constantly appeared in ever greater and more varied numbers, and the need for a systematic organization of theological schools became apparent.

The West, which separated from the East by falling into heresy, accepted the education and life of the pagans. From that time, teachings antagonistic to the Orthodox Church—the most cunning, brazen, ugly, blasphemous heresies—increased ad infinitum. Theological school became an essential need for the Orthodox Church, like breathing is for a man. You yourself be the judge: a future priest needs to know in all possible detail not only the true teaching of the Orthodox Church, but all its triumphant battles with secret and open enemies that have been continual for eighteen centuries, becoming ever more fiery and dangerous. One has to study the false teachings of Arius, Macedonius, Nestorius, Eutyches, the iconoclasts, papists, and Protestants with their countless offshoots, the crown of which are atheism and the new philosophies. One must know how to competently discredit all of these teachings.

In the early church, theology took a short time to learn, when sermons pronounced in church were enough, but now it requires a systematic curriculum taking several years. This is the purpose of our seminaries and academies—to learn this teaching in its fullness. They teach the foundations of Christianity, knowledge that St Mark the Ascetic calls "preliminary" in his fourth homily. They teach this to youths who have not yet begun their life in the world; young men who have only theoretical knowledge, who have not learned from life experience. This theoretical knowledge must be supplemented with experiential knowledge, which is alive and fed by the grace of the Spirit. Our life on earth is given to man precisely for the acquisition of this kind of knowledge.

The Christian who lives in the world according to the Gospel commandments will inevitably be enriched, not only with experiential knowledge but also with knowledge given him directly by divine grace, in even greater amounts. Of course, he who has left behind the world and its cares will be enriched incomparably more if he uses all his time and his energy to please God. This is the monk. He is the one who, according to the Gospel, has the commandments of the Lord, because these commandments are his entire inheritance. "He who has My commandments and keeps them, it is he who loves Me. And he who loves Me will be loved by My Father, and I will love him and manifest Myself to him."[20] For this reason, zealous Christians in all eras, having completed their studies in schools, entered the monastic life for the acquiring of that knowledge given by monasticism. Who were the great teachers of the Church in all eras? Monks. Who described Christianity's teaching in detail, preserved its traditions for posterity, and accused and fought the heresies? Monks. Who articulated the Orthodox creed by the price of their blood? Monks. This is natural. Christians who live in the world and are caught in its snares, who are busy with various willing or unwilling cares, have no time to dedicate themselves and their love completely to God.

"He who is unmarried cares for the things of the Lord—how he may please the Lord. But he who is married cares about the things of the world—how he may please his wife."[21] The married man cannot continually and intensely attach himself to the Lord through prayer that is removed from all earthly things and become "one spirit" with the Lord,[22] as is appropriate for the monk.

For his personal spiritual progress, the Christian does not need the kind of education that is necessary for the pastors of the Church—many illiterate Christians (one of whom, by the way, was St Anthony the Great), having become monks, reached Christian perfection and poured out the light of the Spirit on their contemporaries through their example, their oral teaching, and their spiritual gifts. "Who among the laypeople has ever been a wonderworker? Who resurrected the dead? Who cast out demons? No one! All this is the honor of the monk, whom the world cannot contain."[23]

Layman: But not all monks reach such an exalted state, not all of them fulfill their calling. Only a few reach such heights.

Monk: Those monks who live according to the monastic rule always acquire grace according to the promise of God. The promise of God must be fulfilled, thanks to the quality of the word of God and the commandments of the Gospels that gives its doers the Spirit of God. Conversely, monks who are lax in the fulfillment of the God-given rule, who live a willful, scattered, sensual, world-loving life, are denied spiritual progress. The same is true of all Christians. Those Christians who live a Christian life are saved, but those who are called Christians but lead a pagan life, perish. Before, there were many more saints among the monks and saved among the Christians than there are now. The reason for this is a universal weakening in faith and morality. But even today there are true monks and true Christians. I repeat—there are monks who are not worthy of their name and calling, but this is a crime against the decrees of God. The institution of God does not stop being the institution of God if man begins to mistreat it. In the same way, Christianity does not lose its great worth if some or even a great many of its members live a way of life contrary to the teaching of Christ. One must judge both monasticism and Christianity by its true members. This is not easy—piety and virtue, like chaste virgins, always remain in seclusion, in monastic cells, in anonymity, as though under the cover of a sheet; in contrast, loose women try to appear half naked to the public eye. Often the exalted life of a monk is revealed only after his death or just before it. Often a monk who is a communicant of the grace of God is reviled by the world because of its hatred for the Spirit of God.[24] Even progress itself has many levels because, as we already said, monastic seclusion, while being useful for strong Christians in some ways, is useful in other ways for the weak. Of course, it is obvious that there was always a greater number of the latter.

Layman: After everything you have said, I think it is necessary for you to explain and prove that monasticism is a divine institution. What you have said already leads one to this conclusion in large part.

Monk: The Saviour of the world indicated two paths, two ways of life for those who believe in Him—the path or the life that leads to salvation, and the path or life that leads to perfection. The second way of life the Lord called "following Me," since it is the most exact expression of the

Lord's teaching and a forcible emulation of the way of life that Christ led during His earthly life. Those who wish to follow the first path need the following: faith in Christ,[25] life according to God's commandments,[26] and the healing, through repentance, of a deficiency in the fulfillment of the commandments.[27] Consequently, salvation is attainable and given to all, as long as a person works and lives in a way not contrary to the Law of God.

As for the second path, the emulation of Christ, some were called to it directly by the Lord, such as the apostles, but in general, the Lord leaves the choice of this path to each person,[28] which is clear in every Gospel passage where the Lord speaks of this path.[29] The choice of this path remains with the person, but God Himself dictates the conditions of such a life; without keeping to these instructions, a life in emulation of Christ is not possible. Christ describes the path of perfection in the following words:

> If anyone desires to come after Me, let him deny himself, and take up his cross, and follow Me. If you want to be perfect, go, sell what you have and give to the poor, and you will have treasure in heaven; and come, take up the cross, and follow Me. If anyone comes to Me and does not hate his father and mother, wife and children, brothers and sisters, yes, and his own life also, he cannot be My disciple. And whoever does not bear his cross and come after Me cannot be My disciple. So likewise, whoever of you does not forsake all that he has cannot be My disciple.[30]

These are exactly those conditions that make up the vows of monasticism. Monasticism, as I already mentioned, in its beginning was basically solitude, a life of Christians who strove for Christian perfection away from the world.

The Christians of populous and rich Alexandria fled to the outskirts of the city with the guidance of the holy Apostle and Evangelist Mark; this is the same instruction given by the Apostle Paul to all Christians who wish to enter close communion with God. He says the following:

> You are the temple of the living God. As God has said: "I will dwell in them And walk among them. I will be their God, And they shall be My people." Therefore, "Come out from among them And be separate," says the Lord. "Do not touch what is unclean, And I will receive you.

I will be a Father to you, And you shall be My sons and daughters,"
Says the Lord Almighty.[31]

St John of the Ladder interprets this passage as referring to the monastic calling.[32] The aforementioned words of the Lord were also understood in this way by the early Church. St Athanasius the Great states, in the life of St Anthony the Great, that Anthony, while he was still a youth, walked into church to pray. That day, the reading was from the Gospel according to Matthew (ch. 19), about the rich man who asked the Lord about salvation and perfection. When he heard the words: "If you want to be perfect, go, sell what you have," St Anthony, who at that moment was questioning the course his life should take, felt a special affinity with those words, and accepted that the Lord Himself spoke to him. So he immediately sold all he had and entered a monastery. This same reading is also read at the tonsure of a monastic.

As for the establishment of monasteries far away from the cities, in the deep desert, this was also done according to the revelation and command of God. St Anthony the Great was called by God to live in the deep desert; St Macarius the Great saw an angel who ordered him to settle in the desert of Sketis; and St Pachomius the Great was also given the rule for cenobitic monasticism by an angel, which he then wrote down. These saints were men filled with the grace of the Holy Spirit, who remained constantly in communication with God, and so they are for monastics the visible form of the command of God, just as Moses was for the Israelites. The Holy Spirit has always, in all the eras of Christianity, illumined monasticism. Holy monks with all clarity and fullness in their God-inspired writings write down the teaching of the Holy Spirit, the teaching of Christ, the teaching of God on monasticism, on this science of sciences, as St John Cassian called it. All of them witness that the establishment of monasticism, this supernatural way of life, is not a human invention. It is the work of God. Since it is superhuman, it cannot be a human institution, but only a divine one.

Layman: Some believe that the first reason for monasticism was the persecutions during the early centuries of Christianity.

Monk: The carnal mind-set always errs when it makes assumptions about spiritual men. Spiritual men, such as the monks of the first centuries, thirsted for martyrdom, and many of them were crowned with the martyr's crown, such as Saints Nikon, Julian, Evdokia, Eugenia, Fevronia, and others. When persecutions arose in Caesaria of Cappadocia, the aforementioned St Gordius openly came into the city during a pagan festival and began to accuse the people of idolatry, confessed Christ, and witnessed to his faith by dying for Christ. When Emperor Diocletian began a ferocious persecution of Christians, St Anthony the Great was already a monk in the desert. When he heard that Christians were subjected to tortures and death for confessing Christ, St Anthony left his desert and ran to Alexandria, joined himself to the crowd of martyrs, and confessed Christ before all the people, in every action proving his desire to be martyred. His life said that the saint became a martyr by his love and his intentions, but though he desired to suffer for the name of the Lord, the Lord did not grant him a martyr's crown. By that point in history, the Lord had already collected the bountiful harvest of the holiness of the martyrs, and had sown a new harvest of sanctity, a different kind of martyrdom belonging to the monastics. The persecutions had hardly ended, the blood of Christians had hardly stopped flowing in the city squares and arenas, when thousands of Christians moved to the wild desert in order to crucify their flesh with its passions and lusts,[33] to confess Christ before the face of the very prince of the world, with his powers and principalities of hatred.[34]

The reason St Paul of Thebes went into the deep desert was a desire to flee the persecutions of Emperor Decius. Maybe some others also came to the desert for that reason. Others left the world for completely different reasons. But these are only exceptions that do not prove the rule for monasticism. The actual initial reason for monasticism is not the weakness of men, but the power of the teaching of Christ. St John the Dwarf, the writer of St Paisius the Great's life, says the following in his introduction to the saint's life:

> Those who wish to acquire endless heavenly blessings, and have a limitless thirst for them, are filled in their hearts with a certain insatiable Divine sweetness that forces them always to remember the blessedness of the future life. They labor in asceticism, remembering the joyful triumph of ascetics, and force themselves to always have this limitless thirst, so that they not only despise all that is temporary and vain, but don't even spare their own lives, desiring, according to the words of the Gospel, to lay down their beloved life for the sake of Christ. They love death for Christ far more than all pleasures and

attractions. But since in our time there are no persecutors, and this desired death is not found quickly, they try to find it in other ways, laying on themselves a long and forceful mortification of their own selves. Every day, they suffer thousands of afflictions as they fast and labor in various ways, battle with the invisible demons, constantly forcing their nature clothed in flesh to fight against the bodiless enemies.

Layman: You compare the labor of monasticism with martyrdom?

Monk: Yes, it is in fact the same ascetic labor, but in different forms. Both martyrdom and monasticism are established on the same words of the Gospels; both are not the institutions of men but gifts of the Lord to mankind; both cannot be accomplished without the all-powerful help of God and the action of divine grace. You will be sure of this if you read the lives of St Anthony the Great, Macarius the Great, Theodore the Studite, Mary of Egypt, John the Long-Suffering, Nikon the Withered, and other monks whose labors and sufferings were supernatural. St Simeon the New Theologian said of his teacher, the Pious Simeon of the Studite monastery, that through the labors and suffering of his body he was likened to the martyrs.[35]

Layman: My Father, please explain the significance of virginity and nonacquisitiveness (i.e., poverty) in the monastic life. This is difficult to understand for worldly people who work for the good of society, who give large sums of money to charities, and who do a great number of good deeds that are indicated and sanctioned by the Gospels. To such people, because of their lack of knowledge about monasticism, the monastic life seems a lazy life, bereft of usefulness and activity.

Monk: You have mentioned those laypeople whose actions, meaning the fulfillment of the Gospel commandments through the actions of their bodies, are necessary for *salvation*, but these are not sufficient for *perfection*. Nothing hinders one from doing such good deeds, even among the cares and responsibilities of a worldly life. Success in social terms even helps one do more good deeds—thus, a rich man can do a great deal to help his poor brothers with alms, and the nobleman can help protect them from injustice in the courts. But even in this kind of life, it is important not to act from one's own pride, as did the Pharisee in the parable, who also did many good deeds, but with an incorrect assessment of his own virtue. Because of this, he developed an incorrect opinion about himself in relation to others; his virtue became unpleasing to God.

The Apostle Peter said that those who do good deeds should do them "as good stewards of the manifold grace of God."[36] It is good for the rich man to give alms from his estate, not as if they come from him, but from the benefits given him by God. Let the nobleman intercede in the affairs of the poor, but only as a warden of God's blessings. Then, any judgment of the neighbor's insufficient virtue will cease, and the conscience will begin to ask whether his own virtue is sufficient in the eyes of God, as happened to the righteous Job.[37] He will begin to ask himself, "Does my virtue have small or large deficiencies?" Then, little by little, he will begin to have a more complete understanding of the proper ways of life.

You will agree that the monastic life seems most useless especially to those people who consider their own life (erroneously) to be very virtuous. The inevitable sign of proper Christian virtue is always humility. Any sign of pride or conceit is a true indication of false virtue, according to the words of the Lord Himself. The opinion that you expressed shows ignorance and a perverted understanding of Christianity. Christian perfection was offered by the very God-Man to His chosen disciples. This perfection only begins at the point where the virtue of laypeople has reached its absolute height. Study Christianity and learn what it means to reach Christian perfection, and you will understand the significance of monasticism, you will understand how foolish it is to accuse of laziness those people who strive to fulfill the most exalted commandments of the Gospel, which are completely unattainable by those in the world. Those who slander and blaspheme monasticism by necessity blaspheme the entire idea of Christian perfection, which was instituted by the Lord Himself!

Layman: I agree, I agree! But, please do explain the meaning of virginity and poverty in this way that leads to Christian perfection.

Monk: They are incredibly important! I will try to explain it to you adequately. He who gave away his money to the poor in order to fulfill literally the command of the Saviour and then followed him completely, who himself became a poor man in order to subject himself to physical privations for the sake of acquiring humility, he puts aside all hope in the world and lays all his hope on God. His heart is lifted from the earth to the heavens.[38] He begins to sail above the waves of the sea of life, kept afloat by his faith. His trust is fully in the Lord, Who, commanding His nearest disciples to give away all they had,[39] and lay aside all worries about physical needs, promised that he who seeks the kingdom of God and its truth will receive all that he needs from the Heavenly Father.[40]

The followers of God are given various sorrows during which the providence of God seems to hide from them and the influence of the world seems impossibly strong, but this is necessary to teach them living faith in God, which only increases and becomes stronger with such experience. This experience uncovers lack of faith, which is natural to the fallen nature; it exposes rejection and renunciation of God; because as soon as vigilance ceases even for a moment, the heart begins to blindly seek to put trust in itself, in the world, in created matter, and to stop trusting in God.[41]

I think it should be apparent from my short explanation that leaving behind the cares of everyday life lifts the ascetic of Christ to an exalted spiritual state that separates him from his brothers who live in the world and cannot be made known to them by experience. However, this exalted state is also a state of suffering for the body and the entire corrupted nature—this is what the Lord calls the cross.

In a spiritual sense, the effect of virginity is similar to the effect of nonacquisitiveness. The striving to defeat the qualities of the fallen nature inspires the monk to such asceticism that those who have never attempted it cannot even imagine. This labor, which is a rejection of one's very nature, supplements the crucifixion and cross of poverty, which is only a rejection of money. This labor leads one to the very depths of humility, it brings one to living faith, it raises one to a state of grace. During this labor, as we see in the lives of St Anthony the Great, St John the Long-Suffering, and others, the fallen angels come to the aid of fallen nature and try to keep the ascetic under the influence of the fall. The fruits of victory are often as great as the difficulty of the battle, according to St John of the Ladder.[42] After this victory comes the renewal of human nature, thanks to the spiritual senses that appear in the heart.[43] The nature remains the same human nature, but its senses (or "tastes") change.[44] In the same way, paper that has been dipped in oil will no longer absorb water, not because the nature of the paper has changed, but because it has been filled with a different substance that has no affinity with water.

Layman: In our days, many insist that virginity is unnatural for people and even impossible for them. They say that closing this lawful door forces human nature to open other, forbidden doors.

Monk: Of course, every person can only judge by his own experiences. All that is outside of his knowledge and experience seems impossible to him, but that which he knows and experiences must be the same for everyone else. When the Holy Fathers write about virginity, they agree that it is unnatural for fallen human nature, but it was natural for man before the fall.[45] After the renewal of human nature, man is once again capable of virginity, and for this reason, virginity and an unmarried life are honored higher than marriage, even though Christianity raises married life to a much higher level than it was before the advent of Christianity.[46] The God-Man lived a life of chastity; the all-holy Theotokos was and remained a virgin; the holy Apostles John the Theologian, Paul, Barnabas, and doubtless many others were also unmarried. With the appearance of Christianity, entire armies of virgins appeared. This labor was very rare before the renewal of human nature by the Redeemer. Through the deliverance of the Redeemer, God's blessings poured out on mankind, as the angels announced in Bethlehem,[47] and mankind was sanctified with the numerous gifts of grace. The grace-filled gifts of Christianity are vividly described in the instruction that, according to church practice, should be read by the priest to the newly married after the mystery of their marriage:

> The great field of the Church of the great Master, God, is sowed in three ways, is decorated by three kinds of harvest. The first kind of fruit is cultivated by those who have loved virginity and kept it untainted until the end of their lives, and their virtuous harvest is reaped a hundred-fold. The second fruit is planted by those who remain widows; their harvest is reaped sixty-fold. The third part of the field is worked by those who live in lawful marriage, and if they lead a righteous life in the fear of God, their harvest is reaped thirty-fold. This one field has different parts for different seeds, but they are all blessed and worthy of praise, according to their own calling. The wise Ambrose said that we praise virgins in such high prose in order not to reject the widows; and we respect the widows in such a way so that marriage also be considered worthy of its honor.[48]

Layman: How can a Christian know if he is capable or incapable of the unmarried life? In my opinion, this question should be very difficult to answer for anyone who desires to enter monasticism.

Monk: He who desires it, is capable of it.[49] In the pristine state, man had the choice to remain innocent or to leave his state, and in the same way after the renewal of human nature, man has the choice to raise his renewed nature to perfection or to develop it to the level necessary for salvation, or to remain in a fallen state and instead develop the fallen nature to its dark fullness. The renewal of human nature is a gift of the Redeemer. For this reason, every evangelical virtue is chosen by good intention. It is given by Christ as a gift for the one who desires it. Forcing oneself in virtue proves intention, and virtue is asked of God by constant and patient prayer. All evangelical virtues are unnatural to fallen nature; the ascetic must coerce himself; and for all this, he must ask God with a humble, sorrowful prayer of the heart.[50] Like other Gospel virtues, forcing oneself chooses virginity; through battle with the desires of the fallen nature and by reining in the body with ascetic labors, one proves the sincerity of this intention. The request for purity from God is accompanied by "a burning prayer full of compunction" with the knowledge that our fallen nature is incapable of "purity."[51] "The gifts of divine grace that change" and renew our nature are given from above.[52] Blessed Theophilact the Bulgarian, explaining man's ability to live an unmarried life, concludes his explanation with the words of Christ: "For everyone who asks receives, and he who seeks finds."[53]

Study the lives of those saints in which this particular ascetic labor is described. You will see that all the saints passed from their usual state (in which a person is incapable of the virginal life) to a state in which virginity is natural, but only after a fierce battle against the desires and inclinations of their fallen nature. You will see that the main weapon they used was prayer and tears. You will see that not only virgins avoided marriage, not only widows avoided second marriage, but even the worst fornicators, who were filled with all kinds of passions and were completely emptied and tied up by their sinful habits, raised themselves up to the heights of purity and holiness. I repeat: in the New Testament Church, thousands of virgins, widows, adulterers, and prostitutes who became the vessels of chastity and grace prove without a doubt that the labor of chastity is not only possible but also not as hard as it is imagined to be by those people who make theories about it without experiential knowledge, without knowledge given by the moral traditions of the Church. Such people think and make conclusions—I will be honest with you—out of their own fornication, out of their blind and stubborn prejudice, out of hatred for monasticism and for Orthodox Christianity in general. St Isidore of Pelusium was correct when he wrote to St Cyril of Alexandria: "Prejudice cannot see straight; and hatred is completely blind."[54]

Layman: But you must admit that examples of bad monks are common and visible to the public eye. They also serve as a reason for prejudice against monasteries and monks.

Monk: I agree with this. Do not think that I want to hide immorality, which is harmful for everyone. On the contrary, I sincerely desire all evil to be uprooted from the field of Christ, so that only pure and healthy wheat can grow there. I repeat: it is necessary to determine with all exactness the rules instituted by God, and then separate them from the misuse of men so that we can successfully root out these misdeeds. It is necessary to have the right attitude toward evil in order to take up the proper weapons against it; otherwise, we may just replace one evil with another, one mistake with another, one sin with another. If we are not careful, we may end up rejecting or perverting God's institution, as the Protestants did with respect to the Catholic Church. It is necessary to know the very methods and arts of healing in order to choose the correct medicines for a given disease, or else we may give the sick man a medicine that could end up killing him.

In general, people's view of monasticism is very erroneous because they separate themselves excessively from monastics in a spiritual and moral sense. In actual fact, there is a close moral union between Christians who live in monasteries and Christians who live in the world. The inhabitants of monasteries did not appear from the moon or from some other planet; they entered the monastery from the midst of our sinful, earthly world. The lack of morality in monasteries comes from the world and is fed and supported by interaction with the world. Thus, the fall in morality among monastics is connected with the general fall of morality among laypeople; in fact, the fall of monastic morality is a direct result of the fall of morality and piety among laypeople. Monasticism is founded on Christianity, it is built and kept strong on its foundation, and it succeeds or weakens in direct proportion to the success or weakness of Christianity. The source of everything is Christianity itself. Monasticism is a form of it, a special revelation. But the disease is universal! Let us weep for it together, and together let us work on healing it! Let us suffer together with our brother, let us show him our love! Let us leave behind our cruel, mutual judgment, our pharisaical hatred that strives to heal diseases in the sick by beating them with logs!

Layman: Your understanding of the moral connection between monks and laypeople is another new idea for me. I know that you have found this out through your own experience. If not, your ideas could not possibly be so profound, could not be so at odds with theoretical knowledge, which is always superficial. Please explain it in more detail.

Monk: You are correct. These ideas that I have expressed are partially the fruit of my own experience, partially the experiences of others who are worthy of complete trust. Metropolitan Seraphim of St Petersburg, during a conversation about the increased number of divorces in his diocese, told me that when he was a vicar bishop in Moscow, there were a maximum two divorces brought before the church court. His elder bishops told him that in their youth, there were no divorces brought before the church court. This fact vividly illustrates the mores of the times before ours, and the general degeneration of morality in our own time that is progressing without abating. The words of other elders only confirm the observations of Metropolitan Seraphim. In the beginning of this nineteenth century, many virgins entered monasteries, people who never tasted wine, who never took part in any worldly gatherings, who never read secular books, who were educated only by reading the Holy Scriptures and the writings of the Fathers, who developed a habit of constant attendance of church services, and who were filled with other pious habits. They brought to the monastery a complete, already-formed morality, untainted by bad habits. They brought to the monastery their complete health, undamaged by any ill-use, which made them capable of bearing ascetic labors, hardships, and privations. The strict piety of the world itself educated and trained strict and strong monks, both in body and in spirit.

Today's weakened Christianity prepares and delivers correspondingly weakened representatives for monasticism. In our time, people who enter monasteries are rarely virgins. Nowadays, a postulant who has not gathered scores of bad habits is a rarity! A prospective monk who has kept his body in full health, undamaged by drinking or other bad habits, capable of true monastic asceticism, is a rarity! Most often, new postulants are weak, damaged in body and soul. They enter the walls of the monastery with a memory and imagination full of novels and other such books. They enter the monastery having become sated with pleasures of the senses, having acquired a taste for all manner of temptations, with which the world is now filled. They enter the monastery with bad habits already completely assimilated to their nature, with a conscience dulled and mortified by their previous manner of living, when they allowed themselves every possible sin and all possible lies to cover their sins. For such people, the battle with the self is very difficult. It is difficult because of their deeply rooted bad habits, because of their lost innocence, because of their inability to be sincere. For this reason, it is also very difficult to guide them.

They enter a monastery, take off their worldly clothes, and put on the black robes of the monastic life, but their habits and their worldview remain with them, and since they are no longer continually satiated, they begin to reveal themselves in all their vehemence. These sinful habits and worldview can only be weakened when the one who is controlled by them begins to act against them by confessing them and battling them according to the direction of the Holy Scriptures. Otherwise, even just allowing an old habit the opportunity of reasserting itself will result in repeated falls into sin with all the old enthusiasm and madness. Many monasteries that used to be safe harbors for those suffering from spiritual diseases have lost their effectiveness with the passage of time. Many monasteries that were founded in the deep desert, have ended up in the middle of the world and all its temptations, thanks to the growth of population. It used to be that the spiritually ill man, unable to stand up to temptation face to face, could avoid it except for occasional necessity; but now temptation itself storms the walls of the monastery and has its way with the sick man.

The modern hatred for monasticism considers it a triumph when temptations enter the monastery walls; it laughs loudly at monasticism's dishonor, clapping its hands like it would after a notable military victory, while sin remains a universal calamity. Because of the world's lack of morality and its continuing downward trajectory, nowadays more than ever before, it would be good for monasteries to remain far from the world. When the life of the world was united with the life of the Church, when the world lived the life of the Church, when pious laypeople were no different from monks in virtue, except for marriage and property, then it was natural for monasteries to be inside cities, and city monasteries proved this by producing many holy monks. But in our time, we must pay special attention to what Apostle Paul said, and take extra care to fulfill his command:

> You are the temple of the living God. As God has said: "I will dwell in them And walk among them. I will be their God, And they shall be My people." Therefore, "Come out from among them And be separate," says the Lord. "Do not touch what is unclean, And I will receive you. I will be a Father to you, And you shall be My sons and daughters," Says the Lord Almighty.

Layman: Many people believe that there should be a law that makes it illegal for young people to enter monasteries. This would reduce the number of temptations because it is clear that young people are especially susceptible to them since they are full of boiling passions. This law would limit the monastic life only to people of more mature years.

Monk: This measure, which externally seems so beneficial (according to a carnal mind-set) and is intended to protect and raise up monasticism, is in essence nothing more than a very effective way of destroying monasticism completely. Monasticism is the science of sciences. In it, theory and practice go hand in hand. Throughout history, the Gospel has sanctified this whole extensive path; on this path, one can progress from external labors to self-contemplation, with the help of the heavenly light. The correctness of this self-contemplation given by the Gospel is indubitably proven by internal experiences. It is proven by and convincingly proves the truth of the Gospel. Let us express ourselves in the language of the learned of this world: the science of sciences gives the most exact, complete, profound, and exalted knowledge in the field of experimental psychology and theology, or in other words, it gives a useful, living understanding of man and God, as much as this is possible for man.

Any secular science needs to be approached with fresh abilities, with complete impressionability, with the energy of youth; how much more is this true for the proper study of the science of sciences—monasticism! The monk is faced with a battle against his very nature. The best time of life to begin this battle is during youth. The youth is still not in bondage to his bad habits; his desires are still free! Experience shows that the best monks are those who entered the monastic life in tender youth. The majority of monks in our time are those who entered the monastery early in life. Those of more mature years rarely enter monasteries, and those in old age even less so. Those who enter a monastery after their prime of life often cannot bear the monastic life and return into the world, not even having gained an understanding of what monastic life is. Among those who remain monks, one usually notices purely external reverence and a very exact fulfillment of the entirely superficial parts of the monastic rule, those that so appeal to laypeople, who are content with them alone. One very rarely finds a true monastic among such late bloomers.

Let us listen to the instruction given to us by the Holy Church. The wise Sirach, inspired by the wisdom of God, says the following:

> My son, from your youth up, choose instruction, and you will find wisdom also into old age. Come to her as one who plows and sows, And wait expectantly for her good fruits.[55] Rejoice, O young man, in your youth; and walk in the ways of your heart unsullied, and not in the sight of your eyes.[56] I loved her [i.e. Wisdom], and sought her from my youth, and desired to take her as a bride for myself, and I became a lover of her beauty. She glorifies her noble birth by living with God, and the Master of all loves her. For she is the initiate of the knowledge of God and one who chooses His works.[57]

These words of the Holy Scriptures are applied by the Holy Fathers to monastic life, but it should be obvious to anyone that they do not apply to the wisdom taught by the wise of this world and their evil prince. The Sixth Ecumenical Council said in its fortieth canon that it is extremely salvific to attach oneself to God by leaving the cares of this world, but it said that one should take care and not tonsure just anyone, and definitely not younger than *ten* years old, but only when the mental capabilities have reached a necessary development. We see in many saints' lives that they often entered monasteries at the tender age of twelve! The Holy Fathers agree that old age is not capable of the monastic life. I repeat: old age is not capable of monasticism! A person in mature years has many deeply rooted habits, a fully formed mind-set, and his ability to act freely has long been wasted. The ascetic labor is too difficult for him! St Anthony the Great at first refused to accept the sixty-year-old Paul the Simple to be a monk under his care, telling him that he was not capable of the monastic life because of his age. On the contrary, many Fathers became monks in childhood, and reached spiritual heights by reason of the wholeness of their intentions, purity, constant striving toward the good, and impressionability—all qualities of childhood.[58]

Layman: Firmness of will and a determination that is decisively directed toward the fulfillment of one's goal are indispensible in spiritual progress. And these qualities must be directed early in life for those who wish to become monks.

Monk: That is a very fair assessment! Care has always been used in the choice of a monastic life, and today it is even more evident, especially in the many legal hurdles for potential monks not of the clerical class that make the process quite long and often very difficult. But firmness of will and true determination are sometimes revealed only after a long time, and sometimes, initial firmness turns out to be ephemeral after prolonged difficulties. Upon entering the monastery, some at first feel reverence and self-denial, but later feel significant weakness. Conversely, others at first feel lack of focus and have scattered thoughts, but later begin to assimilate the monastic life more and more, and finally become strict and zealous monks.

St Isaac the Syrian said:

> It often happens that a person is useless, constantly damaged and beaten down because of his insufficient experience of and knowledge of the monastic life. He is in a state of constant spiritual paralysis, but after this, suddenly he manages to seize the banner from the warriors of the enemy's army, his name becomes proclaimed, and he is raised up much higher than the ascetics famous for their early victories. He takes the crown and precious gifts in abundance before all of his friends. For this reason let no one, no matter who he is, allow himself to despair. Only let us never become lazy in prayer and in constant supplication of the Lord for help.[59]

Often, great sinners were transformed to become great and righteous men. The monastery is a place of repentance. It is impossible to deny a person the right to repent—even if he has no control over himself, like a man possessed by a demon—when repentance is given by God Himself, and the refuge for repentance, the *monastery*, is not taken away, even by God. In listing the possible reasons for beginning a life of hesychasm, St John of the Ladder considers the desire to avoid sin and separate one's weakness from temptations to be a more common reason for such a lifestyle, rather than the desire for Christian perfection, which is attainable only by a few.[60]

Now, when there are so many temptations in the world and occasions to fall into sin; when man's strength is turned into weakness before the power of the all-encompassing sins of the world; and while people still have a sense of their sinfulness and the need to free themselves from it, many still enter monasteries precisely to take off this yoke of sin, to heal their illness, to rein themselves in. St John of the Ladder was one of the first to call the monastery a hospital,[61] and now that name is even more appropriate. Should we then deny mankind this essential help if mankind is everywhere suffering from moral sickness? If we take special care to build hospitals for the lame, the old, and the bodily ill, why do we not also build hospitals for sicknesses, wounds, and paralysis of the spirit? Those who judge monasteries based on their own false reasoning require that these hospitals be filled with people who are already healthy, that there be no trace of sickness in them! Do you expect such places to be effective places for convalescence?

I have seen the effectiveness of monastic treatment with my own eyes. In the diocese of Kaluga, near Kozelsk is the Optina Hermitage. In 1829, a famous and experienced monk named Father Leonid moved to this monastery, and later, his closest disciple Father Makary joined him. Both of them were elders, spiritually fed by reading the Holy Fathers on the monastic life, and they themselves were guided by these writings. Through these writings they guided others, who turned to them for instruction and advice. They learned this way of life from their spiritual fathers; in fact, it began with the very first monks and has been passed on until our own time, and contains the treasure and inheritance of monks who are worthy of that name and calling. Soon, the brotherhood of the Optina Hermitage began to increase significantly and became a paragon of Christian morality and perfection. The elders explained the proper and easy way of asceticism to eager brothers; they supported and emboldened those who wavered; they strengthened the weak; and they brought to repentance and healed those who fell into sins and sinful habits. Soon, many secular people of all classes began to flock to the meager huts of the elders, to reveal to them their secret pain, to seek restoration, consolation, encouragement, and healing. Thousands are beholden to them for their newfound pious intentions and spiritual peace.

These elders looked on the suffering mass of humanity with compassion; they lessened the heaviness of their sins, they explained how Christ's redemption has made it necessary for a Christian to leave the life of sin. They condescended to people's weakness, and at the same time, they gave strong medicine for the healing of this weakness! This is the spirit of the Orthodox Church; such were its saints in all ages.

A certain monk confessed to St Sisoes the Great that he constantly fell into the same sin. The saint encouraged him, recommending that he confess every fall into sin and continue his ascetic labors. Is this advice good for everyone? What do the new theorists recommend for the healing of this sinner? Most likely, something quite different!

I visited the Optina Hermitage for the first time in 1828, and the last time in 1856, when it was at the absolute peak of its flourishing—there were more than two hundred monks. Father Leonid was already commemorated among the number of those who had a blessed repose, and seventy-year-old Father Makary was in charge of the spiritual guidance of the brotherhood and the many visitors of the monastery. In spite of the spiritual success and the large number of monks, there turned out to be very few monks who were capable of becoming physicians and guides of others, something that requires both God-given talent and the spirit that is developed through true monastic asceticism. This is the general characteristic of any hospital—there are more ill people than doctors. In our own time, the number of physicians constantly decreases and the number of sick constantly increases. The reason for this is, again, the world.

Whom does the world allot for monasticism? Not the chosen few among the Christians, as it were in the beginning of monasticism; nowadays, monks are not members of the higher circles of society. Today, monasteries are filled almost exclusively by members of the lower classes, and what kind of people? The most incapable of serving in their class, these are the ones exiled to monasteries. Many of these lower-class people enter with already-established habits that are typical of their class, especially drunkenness, which Prince Vladimir admitted was a national vice. Those who are infected with this weakness go into a monastery with the intention of abstaining from alcohol, even if others force them to do it, but the habit claims its own, and occasionally, it shows its lordship over the one who has served it carelessly and foolishly. Many people of wonderful quality and piety are subject to this vice; they lament their lapses bitterly and try to fix them by repentance. But the tears shed in the secrecy of the cell and secret repentance are not as visible to people as are the lapses. These lapses serve as a source of great temptation for the upper classes, who are the ones most often offended by vices in monasteries. They have their own vices that they excuse very readily and would also excuse those same vices if they appeared in monasteries, but when they enter the monastery walls in all their finery and good manners and see the vices of the common folk, they are offended, forgetting that they have made monasteries the refuges for the poor. They consider monks to be creatures completely separate from laypeople—the former must be paragons of virtue, while the latter are allowed whatever vice they choose.

The members of the lower class see their weaknesses in a different light. In a certain monastery that was located far from the world, a certain elder spent his life writing helpful instructions to his neighbors. He left a great deal of material regarding the vice of drunkenness. The elder was a commoner, and with total compassion for his suffering brothers, he said that it is impossible for those who have lost control over themselves to be healed, or even to abstain from their passion, amid constant temptations. For this reason, he offered those ailing from it a place in his monastery, since it was completely removed from any possible temptations. This is a very kind and useful piece of advice. Monasteries that are far removed from cities can be true refuges and hospitals for the spiritually sick, and at the same time, they can hide the ugliness of the passion from those foolish people who cannot avoid being offended by it.

Layman: From what you have said, however, it becomes obvious that today's monasteries, or at least many of them, do not follow their calling, and that certain measures to improve them are helpful and even necessary.

Monk: Yes! In our time, when secular education advances rapidly, when civil life has separated itself from the life of the Church, when many teachings antagonistic to the Church invade us from the West, and when it is obvious that religion and morality is weakening in all classes, we need to bring our monasteries to proper order. There are two reasons for this. First, this is needed to preserve monasticism itself, since it is essential and useful for the Church. Second, we need to protect people from temptations. Whether people are right in judging the monasteries or not, they are still becoming weaker and weaker in faith. But to combat this, we do not need a superficial kind of knowledge of monasticism, but a proper one—we need a foundational, experienced knowledge of the institution of monasticism that can be taken only from the Holy Church and the Holy Fathers. We need to realize in the depths of our beings how important and holy this divine institution of monasticism is. Any attempts to reform monasticism undertaken with a superficial understanding of it, taken from the foul-smelling treasuries of the carnal mind-set, will always be extremely dangerous for monasticism. If the proud and darkened world uses such measures, carelessly destroying the holy rules given by the Church and the Fathers, which were inspired and given by the Holy Spirit, it can end up by destroying monasticism completely, and Christianity with it.

Layman: Can you give me an example of one Holy Father's instructions regarding monasticism, according to which it may become clearer what kinds of changes our monasteries need and what we can institute for their essential benefit?

Monk: I suggest you look at the *Rule of St Nilus of Sora*, our fellow countryman who lived in the fifteenth century, perhaps the last holy writer on the monastic life. This work, despite its brevity, is complete in itself. It is a profound and spiritual work. It was published in 1852, with the blessing of the Holy Synod in a print run of a thousand and sent to various monasteries. St Nilus entered the monastic life and remained in it with the purpose of learning and advancing in the spiritual monastic labor according to the traditions of the ancient Holy Fathers. In order to study the Fathers more thoroughly, he traveled to the East and spent a long time on Mount Athos in conversations with the disciples of the holy Gregory of Sinai and Palamas, and he also was in communication with monks who lived in the outskirts of Constantinople. When he returned to Russia, he settled in the deep forest on the Sora River and became the founder of *skete* monasticism in Russia. His *Rule*, or *Tradition*, as it is also called, was written for this skete. The work of St Nilus is precious to us because it is most appropriate for contemporary monasticism, which cannot allow its monks to follow the total obedience of ancient monastics due to the lack of Spirit-bearing elders. Instead of total submission to an elder, St Nilus offers the monk of the modern times to be instructed by the Holy Scriptures and the writings of the Holy Fathers, with occasional advice also given by experienced monks, but only after carefully checking their advice against the Scriptures.

Having learned true monastic asceticism, St Nilus offered his humble voice against various abuses within contemporary Russian monasticism that came about as a result of simplicity and ignorance. But this voice was given no heed. The problems of the time started out as habit, but became the general rule, which led to the political attack on monasteries in the eighteenth century. This habit was the acquisition of large amounts of land and property.

Layman: What is especially useful for the modern monk in the works of St Nilus?

Monk: First, his example is incredibly instructive. He learned the Holy Scriptures and the writings of the Holy Fathers on monasticism, not only by the letter but also through his own personal experiences. Not finding contentment in this, he wanted to see the life of holy monks in Athos and Byzantium, and to supplement his own knowledge and activity with their advice and way of life. Having reached a high level of spiritual progress, he refused to admit it to himself, and never sought to be the teacher of others. He was asked not to refuse even a word of advice; and after many requests, he submitted to the desires of the brotherhood and became their abbot, which he viewed as an obedience laid upon him.

From this behavior of St Nilus, it should be obvious that the maintenance, support, and improvement of monasteries requires worthy men to become abbots—monks who have studied the Holy Scriptures and the writings of the Fathers, who have educated themselves according to these writings, and who have acquired active, living knowledge that attracts divine grace. We must pray to God that He sends such people, because such men who essentially understand them from their own experience can only bring the holy monastic rules to action in the proper way. St John Cassian said that in the Egyptian monasteries, which were the best in the world, the position of abbot was only offered to such monks who themselves were in submission to others for a long time and who had thus learned the traditions of the Fathers.[62]

The most important of St Nilus's rules is this reliance on the Sacred Scriptures and the Holy Fathers for guidance. St John of the Ladder signifies a monk in the following words: "A monk is the one who holds fast only to God's rule and the Word of God in all time, in any place, in every action."[63]

St Nilus was guided by this rule, and he taught his disciples to do the same. He said:

> We have decided if this is the will of God, to accept those who come to us with the intention to follow the traditions of the Holy Fathers and to the keep the commandments of God, but not who justify themselves or offer explanations for their sins, saying that nowadays it is impossible to live according to the Scriptures and the instructions of the Holy Fathers. No! Even though we are weak, we must, according to our strength, become like the fathers and emulate them, even if we cannot achieve their high level.[64]

Whoever knows Russian monasticism in its current incarnation can witness that only those monasteries that encourage their monks to read holy books flourish in a moral and spiritual sense. Only those monks who are educated and fed by this holy reading are truly worthy of their name. St Nilus never gave instructions or advice from himself, but offered the petitioner either the teaching of the Scriptures or the teaching of the Fathers. In one of his letters, he mentions that when he could not remember any specific advice about a particular problem from the holy sources, he would not give any advice at all until he found that particular instruction in the Scriptures. This method is taken from the writings of St Peter of Damascus, St Gregory of Sinai, Saints Ignatius and Kallistos Xanthopoulos, and other Fathers, especially the most recent ones.

The monks of the Optina Hermitage followed the same advice. Their memories were decorated with thoughts of the saints. Never did they give any advice from themselves, always basing their guidance on the words of the Scriptures or the Fathers. This gave their advice special power, because those who would be ready to contradict the words of men were more willing to listen piously to the word of God and were more willing to subjugate their carnal mind-set to it.

Such a way of acting keeps the guide in strict humility, which is also seen in the rule of St Nilus, since the teacher does not give his own instruction, but God's. The giver of this advice becomes a witness and carrier of holy Truth, and the question appears in his own conscience—am I fulfilling my calling as well when I preach?

The divine Word and the words of the Holy Fathers are limitless, like sand in the ocean. By studying them without laziness, we can give instruction to those who come to us. Or it would be more proper to say that it is not we who give the advice (we are not worthy) but the Holy Fathers themselves inspired by the Holy Scriptures. All the holy ascetic writers of the last few centuries maintain that because of the general diminution of Spirit-inspired guides, the study of the Holy Scriptures (especially the New Testament) and the Fathers—as well as the assiduous and constant following of their advice in one's life and in the guiding of others—is the only path to spiritual progress, given by God to the monastics of the last days. St Nilus announced that he would reject any monk who did not want to live according to this rule.[65] It is that important; it is that essential!

The second moral rule that is offered by St Nilus is the daily confession to an elder. The elder is a monk advanced in the spiritual life to whom is given the guidance of the brothers. They confess their sins, even the most insignificant, even their thoughts and sinful emotions, so that he may see everything that ails them. This action is full of incredible spiritual benefit—not a single ascetic labor kills passions so effectively and powerfully as this. The passions retreat from the other who mercilessly confesses them. Carnal lust withers from this confession more than from fasting and vigils. Monks who have learned from the beginning of their monastic life to confess every day continue to run to this medicine even in old age, because they have tasted its fruits. They know what freedom it gives to the soul. Thanks to this labor, they are able to fully come to know the fall of man in themselves. Treating themselves with the confession of their sins, they gain knowledge and skill to help their brothers in their spiritual confusion.

The monks of the Optina Hermitage had many disciples who would reveal their consciences daily, after the evening rule. These disciples were drastically different from those who lived according to their own whims and desires. The thought of the coming confession acted as a constant watchdog over their behavior, slowly teaching them to be vigilant over themselves, while the confession itself made them focused inside themselves, submerged constantly in the Scriptures. Simply said, it made them proper monks.

Daily confession, or the daily revealing of one's conscience, is an ancient monastic tradition and practice. It used to be universal, which is seen clearly in the writings of St John Cassian, St John of the Ladder, St Barsanuphius the Great, Abba Isaiah, Abba Dorotheos, and basically in all the Holy Fathers who wrote on monasticism. Most likely, the apostles themselves established this practice.[66]

Monks who are trained in these two monastic rules can be compared with people who are able to see to live, while those monks who lack such spiritual upbringing are blind and moribund. The institution of these two rules into every monastery can significantly improve the moral and spiritual direction of the brotherhood without changing anything on the surface. This is only proven by experience. In order to institute the second rule, however, one needs a monk experienced in the spiritual life, who has himself already been raised according to this rule. Here, experiential knowledge is an absolute necessity.

St John Cassian said, "It is very helpful to reveal your thoughts to the father, but not just to anyone, but to spiritual elders who have discernment, elders by experience, not necessarily by their white hair. Many, distracted by the external appearance of so-called elders revealed their thoughts to them and instead of medicine received great harm from the lack of experience of those who listened to them."[67]

Layman: I see that you have indicated the most essential beginnings for the moral improvement of monasteries. Please do not refuse to tell me of other rules and traditions of the Holy Fathers that might be useful in further improving the state of monasticism.

Monk: The education of a person depends on the impressions of his surroundings; he is formed by them. It cannot be otherwise; this is how we were created. The Holy Fathers realized this truth with their pure minds, and used their holy traditions to surround the monk with impressions that would lead him to his goal, while keeping him away from all impressions that would distract him from his goal, even if they seem to be good. In order to explain this, let us once again turn to the precious books of St Nilus of Sora. The saint says that the church building in a monastery must be built very simply. He cites St Pachomius the Great, who did not want his cenobitic church to have any architectural flourishes. The saint said that he is avoiding architectural beauty so that the minds of his monks do not get distracted by complements of men about the church building.They are thereby becoming prey of the devil, whose cunning is multifaceted. St Nilus adds these words, as well: "If the Great Pachomius spoke and acted like this, how much must we be careful! We are weak and passionate and easily wounded in our minds."[68]

St Nilus said that the cells and other monastery buildings should be simple and inexpensive, without any decoration. The great saint of God, St John the Prophet, a recluse who lived a life of silence in a monastery in Gaza, before his death gave advice to the new abbot of the monastery, his spiritual son. He told him to build cells without excessive comfort, with only the basic necessities or even with some privations, keeping in mind the transitory nature of this life, since the buildings of this age, in comparison with eternity, are little more than tents.[69]

Based on the teachings and instructions of the ancient Church Fathers, St Nilus made it a rule that the monastery vestry and the church vessels be as simple, inexpensive, and rudimentary as possible. In the same way, he orders that all of the monastery's property be simple, not excessive, only enough to satisfy the needs of the brothers, so that the monks do not become proud and avaricious and can dedicate their full energies toward God.

St Nilus also forbade women entry into his skete. In ancient times, this was a general rule, and the monasteries of Mount Athos enforce it to this day. This is a rule that is absolutely essential for those who wish to defeat the desires of their fallen nature! They must completely avoid inciting these desires; when they remain in its sphere of influence, they cannot help but waver. And in our own time of diminishing morality, the usefulness and even essentialness of this rule becomes immediately obvious.

In Russia, there is an essential need to remove wine from all monasteries. Wise and pious abbots understood this, one of whom is the recently deceased righteous Theophan, the former abbot and rebuilder of the Kyrill-Novoezersk Monastery. He worked especially hard to eliminate drinking from his monastery, but ultimately for naught. And all other such efforts will be useless if the rules of the Holy Fathers concerning monasteries do not become fully reinstituted.

Having seen monastic life in the place of its birth (the East) and returned to Russia, St Nilus chose the deep desert for his monastic life. He was happy with the place he chose. The reason for this is indicated in one of his letters: "By the grace of God, I have found a place that is good for my mind, because it is difficult for the worldly to access it." Let us here use a syllogism of St Nilus: If, for such a holy man, the chosen place of his asceticism is appropriate because worldly people rarely visit it, how much more should we—who are weak in determination and wisdom and easily inclined to all sins—choose a place for our monastery that is far from the habitations of the worldly, and not attract to ourselves crowds of laypeople with their scores of sins and temptations?

St Nilus desires that the monks of his monastery would be supported by the work of their hands, and if there were any need in alms from laypeople, that they would only ask for moderate amounts.

Here are the foundational rules given by the Holy Fathers to monasticism, accepted by the Holy Church. All other rules that refer to specifics have the same character and the same goal.

Layman: Many monasteries have stopped following the rules you have listed, in greater or lesser degree. These lapses must be fixed at some point. As you know, the education and spirit of our times requires that this improvement happen soon. This is a common theme in social conversations. It would be preferable if among the numerous voices of the ignorant one would hear a voice of true knowledge. In your opinion, what measure can be taken to help bring monasteries to an advantageous position?

Monk: This is a very difficult question. I recall the words of the Saviour about the field, where the good grain was sown, but as it grew, many tares appeared. Not people, but the angels themselves offered the Master to pull out the tares from the field. But the Lord said to them: "No, lest while you gather up the tares you also uproot the wheat with them. Let both grow together until the harvest."[70] So of course this is not the best approach for monasteries. At the very least, this is a question that requires a great deal of attention. When a builder begins improving old buildings, he needs to be careful not to damage them. Wise physicians refuse to treat old sicknesses that have become assimilated to the organism, because removing them may result in the person's death. The Holy Spirit through his chosen vessels, the venerable Fathers, established monasticism and monasteries. The rebuilding of monasteries in their previous spiritual beauty, if this improvement is part of God's providence, can only be effected by a special grace of God, through the same kind of holy men. That is all I can say about the improvement of monasteries. But there is one important consequence from what I have said, and that is that the improvement and restoration of monasticism cannot be the work of secular people. Secular people will do the pious and right thing if they leave this work to those whom God has assigned to it, to those who will answer for it at the final judgment.

I consider it my sacred duty to give you this wise advice that I heard from experienced elders who are worthy of respect and honor. They told both monk and laypeople who sincerely desired to be saved, "In our time of ever-increasing temptations one must especially pay attention to the self, not to pay attention to the life and actions of one's neighbor, and not judge them, because the killing effect of judgment causes the temptation that we judge to turn around and attack us." These elders advised laypeople to be guided in their life by the Gospels and by those Holy Fathers who wrote for all Christians in general, such as St Tikhon of Zadonsk. They advised monks to also be guided by the Gospels and the Holy Fathers, especially those who wrote for monastics. A monk who is guided by these Fathers will be able to find salvation in any monastery, but this salvation will be wasted by the monk who lives according to his own will and reasoning, even if he lives in the deepest desert.

"Woe to the world because of offenses!"[71] "And because lawlessness will abound, the love of many will grow cold."[72] The increase of offenses or temptations is part of God's unattainable foreknowledge, since He Himself said, "offenses must come."[73] After his redemption, man is given the freedom to choose good or evil, as it was offered to him after his creation. Yet mankind continues to do as Adam did—most often, we choose evil. Even in the garden of Eden, evil appeared dressed up as good in order to make our falls into sin more likely. Today, evil appears in the very heart of the Holy Church, hidden and decorated, in an attractive multiplicity of temptations, calling itself "innocent pleasures," calling the progress in a carnal lifestyle and the humiliation of the Holy Spirit "spiritual progress and the progress of mankind." People will believe lies as a result of their reverence for falsity, "disapproved concerning the faith, having a form of godliness, but denying its power."[74] For those who have received this power and willfully rejected it, its return is very difficult,[75] since the proper determination has already been lost, which always follows after willful disdain of God's gift. *A form of godliness* can sometimes hide the cunning of men, but the renewal of the power of godliness belongs exclusively to the one who gives men power from on high. An aging, dying tree is often covered and thickened with a cover of green leaves, which suggest its trunk is still full of life. But its heart has already withered, and the first storm will break it.

CHAPTER 35

Words of Consolation for Sorrowing Monks

The Scriptures say,[1] "Child, if you begin to do the work of the Lord God, prepare your soul for temptations. Make strong your heart, and be patient. Everything that will be sent to you, accept, and bear it all in the transformation of your heart."[2]

From the beginning of time, sorrows were a sign of God's election. They were signs of God's pleasure for the patriarchs, the prophets, the apostles, the martyrs, and the monastics. All the saints had to pass through the narrow path of temptations and sorrows, and by bearing them, they brought themselves as a sweet-smelling sacrifice to God.

And in our own time, holy people are sometimes sent various difficulties so that their love for God will be revealed in all its vividness.

Nothing happens to a person without the permission and providence of God.

A Christian who wants to follow our Lord Jesus Christ and to become a son of God by grace, reborn of the Spirit, first must make it a rule to always patiently bear all sorrows—bodily pain, insults from people, attacks from the demons, and the arousal of one's own passions.

The Christian who desires to please God more than anything else needs patience and a firm reliance on God. He must constantly hold on to this weapon mentally, so to speak, "in his right hand," since our evil enemy, the devil, never ceases to use all possible means to plunge us into despair because of our sorrows, thereby stealing the treasure promised us by the Lord.

God never allows his true slaves to be subjected to temptations that are beyond their power. "God is faithful," said the Apostle Paul, "who will not allow you to be tempted beyond what you are able, but with the temptation will also make the way of escape, that you may be able to bear it."[3]

The devil, being the creation and slave of God, attacks the soul not as much as he desires, but only as much as God allows.

If a person can easily find out how much weight oxen or other chattel can bear, then how much more does the endless wisdom of God know about the limits of suffering of each individual soul?

A potter knows how long he has to keep his clay vessels in the fire. If he keeps them there too long, they burn up, but if he removes them early, they will be weak and useless for daily tasks. How much more, then, does God know how strong the fire of temptations should be for the spiritual vessel of God—the Christian—in order for him to become capable of inheriting the kingdom of heaven?

A child is not capable of working in society—he cannot run a household, he cannot farm the land, he is not ready for any earthly work. In the same way, souls that have already received divine grace but have not yet been refined and tested by sorrows sent by the evil spirits remain in a kind of spiritual childhood, and they are, so to speak, incapable of receiving the kingdom of heaven.

"If you are without chastening, of which all have become partakers, then you are illegitimate and not sons."[4]

Temptations and sorrows are sent to a person for his benefit. The soul that is refined by them is made strong, exalted before its Lord. If it patiently bears everything until the end, hoping in God, then it cannot fail to gain the benefits promised by the Holy Spirit and complete freedom from the passions.

Souls that are given over to various sorrows, either obvious (from other people) or secret (from the arousal of impure thoughts in the mind, or bodily illnesses), will be found worthy of the same crowns as the martyrs, if they bear everything until the end.

The martyrs suffered at the hands of other people. They willingly gave themselves up to various tortures, showing courageous patience until their very deaths. The more heavy and painful their suffering was, the more they were glorified, and the more they were given boldness before God. Monks suffer at the hands of evil spirits. The more the devil makes them suffer, the more glory God will give them in the age to come, and the more consolation they will receive from the Holy Spirit here, during their earthly wandering, even in the midst of their sufferings.

The road leading to eternal life is narrow and full of sorrows. There are few who walk it, but it is the only road for all who wish to be saved.

One should never walk away from it! Let us firmly and constantly bear any temptation that the devil hurls at us, looking with the eyes of faith at the treasures awaiting us in heaven.

No matter what sorrows we are subjected to in this earthly life, they can never be compared with the benefits that are promised us in eternity, with the consolation that the Holy Spirit gives even here on earth, with the freedom from the dominion of the passions, with the forgiveness of our many debts, or with any of the inevitable consequences of our patient suffering.

"For I consider that the sufferings of this present time are not worthy to be compared with the glory which shall be revealed in us" when we are renewed by the Holy Spirit.[5]

Let us bravely bear everything for the sake of the Lord, as brave warriors who are not afraid even to die for their king.

Why were we not subject to such insults and suffering when we served the world and its numerous cares? Why now, when we have begun to serve God, are we subjected to so many problems? Know this: for Christ's sake are these sorrows poured on us like arrows. Our enemy, the devil, fires them at us to take vengeance on us for the eternal blessings upon which we trust and which we try to attain. He wishes to weaken our souls with sadness, despair, and laziness; and, in this way, to deny us our desired blessedness.

Christ invisibly battles on our side. This powerful and matchless Mediator destroys all the tricks and traps of our enemy.

He Himself, our Lord and Saviour, during His entire earthly life, walked along the narrow and sorrowful path, and not on any other. He was constantly persecuted, He was beaten, laughed at, and finally He was killed by the most shameful death possible, on the cross between two thieves.

Let us follow Christ! Let us humble ourselves as He did! Like Him, let us be called liars and madmen, let us not spare our honor, let us not turn our face away from the spitting and our cheeks from blows, let us not seek honor or beauty or pleasures, let us complete our earthly travels as though we were wanderers with no place to lay our heads. Let us accept the insults, condescension, and hatred of others as an inevitable component of our chosen path. Let us openly and secretly fight against proud thoughts, let us with all our strength cast down the thoughts of our old man, who is eager to revive his ego under various apparently good guises.

Then the Son of God, who said "I will dwell in them and walk among them,"[6] will appear in our hearts and will give us authority and power to tie the strong one, to steal his treasures, to step on the basilisk and asp, to destroy them.[7]

Let us reject complaints, let us reject murmurs against our fate, let us reject the heaviness and sadness of the heart, from which weak souls suffer more than from actual sorrows. Let us reject any thought of vengeance and answering evil with evil. "Vengeance is Mine, I will repay," said the Lord.[8]

Do you wish to bear sorrows with ease and comfort? Then make death your heart's desire, for the sake of Christ. Let this death constantly remain before your eyes. Mortify yourself by the cutting off of your will and by rejecting self-justification, the products of false reasoning and the evil conscience of the old man. Mortify yourself by vividly imagining your imminent death. We are given a commandment to follow Christ, having taken up our cross. This means that we should always be ready to joyfully die for Christ. If this is our inner disposition, then we will easily bear any sorrow, both visible and invisible.

He who wishes to die for Christ can be disturbed by no attack, no insult!

Our sorrows seem heavy to us only because we do not wish to die for Christ, because we do not want to confine our desires, all our hopes, all our wisdom, all our riches, all our being in Him alone.

He who strives to emulate Christ and be an heir of His promise must eagerly emulate His suffering. Lovers and followers of Christ find and prove their sacred pledge by bearing any sorrow sent to them not only with greatheartedness, but with eagerness and diligence and joy and gratitude, laying all their hope on Christ.

Such patience is the gift of Christ.

This gift is given to the one who asks for it humbly through constant prayer to Christ, who proves the sincerity of his desire to receive this priceless spiritual gift by forcefully and painfully demanding the unwilling heart to patiently bear all the sorrows and temptations that it may meet.[9] Amen.

CHAPTER 36

On Tears

Tears are natural to the fallen human nature. Before the fall, we did not know tears, we only knew the purest joy in the blessedness of Eden. We have lost this blessedness, and we are left with tears as the best expression of our loss of blessedness, as a witness to our fall, as a witness of God's anger with our state, as hope to return someday to that blessedness. This hope is true because our need for this blessedness has not left our nature. This hope is true because our sorrow for the loss of our heavenly blessedness cannot be satisfied with any temporal pleasure. This sorrow, remaining disconsolate, waits for consolation and declares the existence of this one consolation. This consolation lives mysteriously in tears, and in tears abides joy.

No matter how successful a person is in his life, no matter how high he may stand, no matter how many riches he has, he encounters and suffers such minutes, hours, and days in which he needs the consolation given by tears— he finds no comfort in any other consolation. "Blessed is the man whose help is from Thee" commemorated at his prayer with tears! In this way, unseen and spiritual in "his heart he hath proposed ascents into the valley of tears," that earthly life that You have assigned for repentance. Cleansing ourselves with tears, we "go from strength to strength, the God of gods shall appear in Zion" in the spirit of man, prepared for the acceptance of God by true repentance.[1] "They that sow in tears shall reap in joy." Those who walk the earthly path, upon the narrow and sorrowful path, who "went on their way and wept, sowing their seed, shall return in joy, bearing their sheaves."[2]

Tears, as a quality of our fallen nature, are themselves infected with the sickness of our fall, like all our other natural qualities. Some people are naturally inclined to tears and weep copious tears at the drop of a hat—such tears are called natural tears. There are also sinful tears. Sinful tears are those that are shed for sinful reasons. Such tears are shed in large amounts and at the slightest provocation by people who are dedicated to sensuality, people who are in self-deception and delusion, and people who are vain, hypocrites, who cry from motives of people pleasing and falsity. Even anger helps such tears fall—when anger is denied the opportunity to commit a vile deed, to shed the blood of man, then it sheds tears. Nero had such tears, Nero who was so cruel and antagonistic to Christianity that the Christians who suffered under him believed him to be the antichrist.[3]

Natural tears include tears from offenses; when this offense has a sinful character, the tears coming from it also have a sinful character. Both natural and sinful tears, immediately after they appear (according to the Holy Father) must at once be turned into God-pleasing tears, that is, the reason for tears must be changed. We must force ourselves to remember our sins, our inevitable and unknowable death, and the judgment of God, and we must cry for those reasons.[4]

What an incredible truth! Those who pour out streams of easy, senseless, and fruitless tears by natural inclination, or those who cry from sinful reasons immediately feel an unaccountable dryness when they desire to pour out God-pleasing tears. They find it impossible to squeeze even one tear from their eyes. From this, we learn that God-fearing tears of repentance are a gift from God, and in order to receive them, we must work first on acquiring the proper reasons for tears.

The reason for such tears is the acknowledgment and admission of one's own sinfulness. The Prophet David says: "Mine eyes gushed out streams of water, because I kept not Thy Law."[5] The reason for tears is poverty of the spirit—since the soul is essentially full of blessedness, it gives birth to another kind of blessedness—tears.[6] It feeds, supports, and strengthens tears.

"Weeping comes not from tears, but tears from weeping," said holy John the Prophet. "If anyone living in a monastic brotherhood cuts off his own will and pays no attention to others' sins, he will acquire such holy sorrow. Through this, his thoughts gather, and gathering thus they give birth in the heart to weeping for God, and this weeping gives birth to tears."[7]

Tears, as a gift from God, are a sign of God's mercy. Said St Isaac the Syrian:

> Tears in prayer are a sign of God's mercy which the soul has deserved for its repentance and for its entry into the field of purity through

> tears. If thoughts are not cut off from fleeting objects, if they do not reject the useless hope in this world, if these thoughts don't develop disdain for this world and begin preparing for their journey away from it, if thoughts of eternal good things do not become active in the soul, then the eyes will not be able to shed tears.[8]

Those who have acquired true vision of their own sins, those who have acquired the fear of God must ask God to grant them the gift of tears through insistent prayer. Thus did Achsah, the daughter of Caleb, having been given in marriage and acquired a large tract of land as a dowry, when she sat on a donkey to begin the journey to her husband's house, with tears and groaning asked her father that he would grant her another tract of land that is covered with water. "Since you have given me land in the South, give me also springs of water."[9] Caleb granted his daughter's wish. The Holy Fathers interpret Achsah as the soul that sits, as if on a donkey, in the wordless desires of the flesh. The dry land is interpreted as spiritual work under the guidance of the fear of God, and the fact that Achsah with groaning asked for sources of water indicates that every ascetic has an extreme need of tears. Every spiritual laborer must beg God with sighing and pain of heart for the gift of tears.[10]

Along with prayers for the granting of tears, personal effort for their acquirement is absolutely necessary. Personal efforts and labors sometimes precede the flow of tears, whilst on other occasions they accompany them. The work preceding tears consists of a wise abstinence from food and drink, moderate vigils, nonacquisitiveness, and turning away our attention from everything surrounding us and concentrating our attention to our inner selves. St John of the Ladder said in his sermon on tears that "Repentance is the willing rejection of every consolation for the body."[11] The holy David describes the situation of the one who weeps thus: "I have been smitten down like grass, and withered, for I forgot to eat my bread. From the voice of my groaning hath my bone cleaved unto my flesh. I am become like a pelican in the wilderness, I was like an owl in the ruins. I have watched, and was even as it were a sparrow, that sitteth alone upon the house-top. For I have eaten ashes as it were bread, and mingled my drink with tears."[12] Without such death to the world, it is impossible to acquire tears and sorrow: we acquire them as much as we mortify the world in ourselves.

The work that accompanies sorrow and the shedding of tears consists of forcing oneself to sorrow, in a greathearted patience whenever one feels dryness or lack of tears, which is a state that sometimes tests a true laborer; after which the patient ascetic is always rewarded with a fervent outpouring of tears. Like soil that has long waited for the rain finally receives it in abundance and suddenly covers itself with gentle, bright greenery, so the heart long overcome with dryness, when it is enlivened by tears, bears much fruit of spiritual thoughts and emotions decorated with the color of humility. The work of sorrow, which is inextricable from prayer, requires the same conditions for success as prayer. Like prayer, it requires a patient, constant effort. Prayer requires the mortification of the body and results in bodily exhaustion, as do tears, which require the exhaustion and mortification of the flesh for their own outpouring. The great worker of sorrow, David, wrote: "I am worn out with my groaning; every night wash I my bed, and water my couch with my tears."[13]

Forcing oneself to such work must correspond to one's physical strength. St Nilus of Sora recommends and blesses sorrow and tears. "This is the path of repentance and its fruit," he said. "Whoever cries for help to the mercy of God, whether under attack from the passions or protecting himself from any sinful thought, he will soon find consolation if he prays with spiritual wisdom." But even this Father, himself guided in his work by those instructions that are found in the books of St John of the Ladder and St Simeon the New Theologian, gives a warning, taken from St Isaac the Syrian, not to bring the weak body to total collapse through excessive ascesis. "Then," he says, "it is not useful to push nature beyond its limits. When the weak body will be forced to do labors that exceed its strength, then the soul is darkened more and more, and it falls into total confusion.[14]

Of course, even those who have a weak body and poor health must to a certain degree, as much as possible, force themselves to ascetic labors. The appropriateness of the labor can be easily ascertained even with little spiritual experience. Those who are physically weak must bring themselves to sorrow and tears more than anything with attentive prayer and try to acquire sorrow in their spirit,[15] in which state, silent tears fall, accompanied by pain in the heart that is not as severe. Any spiritual work, since it is a free gift in us from God, absolutely requires us to force ourselves to acquire it because this self-coercion is an active revelation and witness of our good desire to labor. Self-coercion is especially needed when (either from our fallen nature or from the attacks of the demons) we incline toward or disturbed by some sin. Then it is necessary to speak the sorrowful words of prayer slightly aloud. Excessive, mechanical, loud, passionate, and forced weeping is not appropriate for the weak, since they affect the body strongly and can bring it to the brink of an emotional breakdown. The Fathers liken this emotional anguish to a woman giving birth;[16] some of its consequences can lead to significant physical weakness even in strong ascetic laborers. Monks who have significant physical strength can force themselves more insistently to acquire tears. This is beneficial for them, and especially in the beginning of their work, they must utter the words of the prayer in a sorrowful way before they can expect to acquire the tears of the spirit, so that the soul, having fallen into deathly sleep from enjoyment of sin, would awake at the sound of sorrow, and itself feel the emotion of tears. This is how the great David wept. "I roared for the very groaning of my heart,"[17] he said of himself. He roared as a lion who deafens the desert with his roars, fearsome both in their expression of power and sorrow.

For audible prayer and tears, one must at the very least retreat to the solitude of the cell—this work has no place among the brethren. From the lives of the Holy Fathers, we see that those who had the opportunity did practice audible tears that inadvertently were heard across the walls of their cells, even though they took every precaution that all of their labors remained secret, known only to God. Just as the overabundance of vapor causes thunder during heavy rainfall, thus does the overabundance of sorrow in the soul discharge itself in weeping aloud with plentiful tears. This happened with a monk whose labors are described by St Isaac the Syrian in his tenth sermon. After the thunder and rain, there is an especially fragrant atmosphere, and the soul, consoled of its sorrow and cooled down through tears, tastes of an especial quiet and peace from which, like fragrance from aromatic flowers, pure prayer begins and acts.

In general, it is very beneficial to learn the various types of monastic labor directly from the Holy Scriptures and the writings of the Holy Fathers, to try them out, to choose for oneself the work that will appear to be the most suitable. People are created with such variety, their abilities and qualities are so diverse, that one and the same labor or method, being practiced by several ascetics, will act on each one's soul in a completely different way. For this reason, experience is necessary, as the Apostle suggests: "Test all things; hold fast what is good."[18]

The gift of sorrow and tears is one of the greatest gifts of God. It is a gift that is fundamentally essential for our salvation. The gifts of prophecy, prescience, and miracle working are signs that a person has especially pleased God and God has rewarded him, but the gift of compunction and tears is the sign of accepted or acceptable repentance.

"Sorrow in thoughts is a true gift of God; he who has it and keeps it as he must, is like a person who keeps a holy object within himself. Physical ascetic labors without sorrow of the thoughts are like a body without a soul."[19]

Tears that are shed for one's sins at first seem bitter, being shed due to pain and suffering in the spirit, which are passed on from the spirit to the body. Little by little these tears are united with consolation, consisting of unusual calmness, of a palpable sense of meekness and humility; at the same time, these tears, in the appropriate number and manner for the new consolation, themselves begin to change, becoming much less bitter and flowing with less pain, or with none at all. At first these new tears are stingy, and come rarely; with time, little by little, they begin to appear more often and to flow more abundantly. When the gift of tears becomes strong in us through God's mercy, the unseen warfare becomes less violent, the thoughts begin to quiet down, and the prayer of the mind or the prayer of the heart begins to act in an especially developed way, enriching and giving joy to the inner man.

Then the veil of the passions is lifted from the mind, and the mystical teaching of Christ is revealed to it. Then bitter tears are transformed into tears of sweetness and joy. Then spiritual consolation appears in the heart, a joy that has no comparison with the joys of earth, and is known only to those who labor in prayerful sorrow and have the gift of tears.[20] Then the promise of God is made real: "Blessed are those who mourn, for they shall be comforted."[21] Then the ascetic greets you according to the inspiration and promise of the Holy Spirit: "The Lord preserveth the simple; I humbled myself, and He saved me. Turn again then into thy rest, O my soul, for the Lord hath prospered thee. For He hath delivered my soul from death, mine eyes from tears, and my feet from stumbling."[22] Then the ascetic, seeing the impotence of the sinful thoughts and feelings, begins more and more to subdue them to his influence, boldly saying to them: "Away from me, all ye that work iniquity, for the Lord hath heard the voice of my weeping. The Lord hath heard my petition; the Lord will receive my prayer."[23]

The spiritual state of a monk who has seen the fall of human nature, who is not deceived by lies of the passing world, but who completely directs his soul's gaze to this fall is vividly expressed in the lamentations of the Prophet Jeremiah, who gave himself up completely to deep mourning in total solitude.[24] All of Jerusalem's hope has been lost and all possible deliverance is vain—all that remains is to weep for Jerusalem. At one time, the Prophet instructed the city with his prophetic word that could not be silenced. Now there is not even anyone left to hear these prophetic words. Not only are there no people left, there are not even any buildings; only ruins are left, ruins that are only useful as stages for weeping. No one understands these tears, and there is no need to worry that they be comprehensible to people. Through them, the Prophet expresses his unspeakably heavy sorrow; they echo through the desert of Jerusalem's ruins, only God in heaven hears them. What a horrible state! He is the only one in the massive ruins of the city; he is the only living man among the abundant dead signs and witnesses of a past life; he is the only one living in the land of death. As one living, he gives voice to his sorrow for the loss of life; he calls this life to return to the houses it has left, to replace the horrifying, unfeeling death all around him.

"How lonely sits the city That was full of people! How like a widow is she, Who was great among the nations! The princess among the provinces Has become a slave!"[25] The Prophet represents the mind of the monk who is enlightened by the revelation of God's teaching; the great city is mankind, created by God; the inhabitants of the city are the qualities of the soul and body; the Babylonians are the demons who were far below mankind in his pristine state, and have become his masters after his fall. The monk himself is in a fallen state, as is all of mankind; therefore, he weeps for himself and for all mankind. But the monk weeps alone because he alone; in the light of the word of God, he sees the fall of mankind; all other men do not see this, do not take part in the monk's tears, do not understand his weeping, and consider him to be insane. The monk cries alone on behalf of himself and all mankind, unable to separate himself from mankind because of the love he has for them and because of the blood he shares with them. The monk weeps for himself and for all mankind; he weeps for our fallen nature, common to all. He alone weeps on the unfeeling ruins among the fallen rocks and boulders, which represent the image of mankind that is stricken with lack of feeling; humanity that does not feel or understand its own fall and eternal death, pays no attention to them at all. The monk weeps alone, and only God understands his tears.

"She weeps bitterly in the night," throughout our earthly life, and "her tears are on her cheeks; among all her lovers she has none to comfort her. All her friends have dealt treacherously with her; they have become her enemies"[26] In order to weep tears for God, one must leave behind the world and other people, to die for the world and for all people, to become solitary in heart and mind. "Leaving all cares behind will help you come closer to the city of wordlessness; if you will not listen to yourself, then you will enter it; if you will die for all men, then you will become the inheritor of the city and its treasures," said Barsanuphius the Great to a monk who he was preparing for silence and an eremitic life in a cell-tomb,that beloved home of prayerful sorrow.[27]

The Hebrews, finding themselves in bondage and slavery to the Babylonians, are an image of willing sorrows—that is, of privations and bodily labors to which the monk subjects himself in order to acquire repentance, as well as sorrows allowed by the providence of God for the purification of sins. The spiritual guide of ascetic laborers, tears, sends them a message from the ruins of Jerusalem, on which they silently work in solitude. The message tells the ones in bondage that their deliverance will come after a certain time. There is a time for bitter tears, and the cup of sorrows willing and unwilling has its limit. These limits and times are determined by God,[28] as the holy David said, "Thou feedest us with the bread of sorrow, and givest us tears to drink in full measure"[29] "Thou hast put my tears before Thee, even as in Thy promise"[30] of mercy and salvation. There were days in which my tears were my bread both night and day,[31] and they were followed by days in which, "According to the multitude of sorrows in my heart have Thy comforts refreshed my soul."[32] "When the Lord turned again the captivity of Zion, then were we like unto them that are comforted. Then was our mouth filled with joy, and our tongue with merry-making."[33] The inspired Jeremiah speaks as from the mouth of God Himself to the chosen nation, justly captured and exiled for their sins: "do not be dismayed, O Israel! For behold, I will save you from afar, And your offspring from the land of their captivity; Jacob shall return, have rest and be at ease."[34] The sorrows and pain of repentance contain within themselves the seed of consolation and healing. This mystery is revealed to the disciple of sorrow through tears.

All monks who have cleansed themselves from sins did so through tears, and all Christians who have gained perfection have acquired it through tears. This perfection was especially widespread among the numerous silent monks of lower Egypt, in the desert of Sketis, in Mount Nitria, in Kellia, and in other solitary places. It transformed the choirs and hosts of monks into choirs and hosts of angels. When St Macarius the Great—the founder of monastic life in the desert of Sketis and a man who even other desert dwellers considered the Father of all Fathers—reached advanced years, the monks of Mount Nitria, which is close to Sketis, asked him to visit them before he departed for the Lord. Macarius came to the mountains; many monks who practiced silence there met him. They asked him to teach them. Shedding tears, Macarius said, "Brothers! Let us weep. Let our eyes shed tears until we depart to the place where our tears will burn our bodies." All started to weep, fell on their faces and said, "Father! Pray for us."[35]

From his own gift of tears, the holy guide of the ancient holy monks uttered his short teaching about tears, combining with it instruction for the entirety of the monastic life. The hearers, through the appearance of their own tears, revealed that they understood the meaning and universality of the teaching. Many words were not necessary.

The gift of tears, this warmth of God's grace, most often visits ascetics during attentive prayer, being one of its usual fruits. To others, it comes during reading; to others, it comes during some active work. Thus, St Kyrill of Belozersk would begin to weep while cooking in the monastery kitchen. While looking at the material fire, he remembered the eternal fire of suffering and shed tears. St Kyrill, understanding that in silence his compunction and tears would increase, wanted to leave for the silence of his cell. According to the will of God, circumstances made this wish of his a reality, but what happened? With the removal of the reason for his compunction and tears, his tears dried up, and Kyrill asked the abbot to return him to the fires of the monastery kitchen.[36]

The Holy Fathers recommend that one remain in that labor that inspires tears, because tears are a spiritual fruit, and the point of monastic life is the gathering of such fruits in whatever ways that God finds necessary for us. One of the desert Fathers would say that

> he knew a monk who kept silent in his cell and would weave rope for his obedience. When this monk sat and wove rope, all the while

practicing the prayer of the heart, tears would fall. Then he would stand for prayer, but his tears would immediately dry up. The brother would again sit down and work at the rope, concentrating his thoughts inside himself, and the tears would come once again. Likewise, when he sat and read, the tears would fall. He would stand to pray, and again the tears immediately would cease. No sooner would he sit down to read, the tears would reappear.

Explaining this, St Theodore would say, "How fair is the teaching of the Holy Fathers that tears are the best teacher. They teach every person exactly what is useful for him."[37]

The saint would also say, "Every sin that a man does is outside the body, but he who commits sexual immorality sins against his own body"[38] because impurity pours out from the body, defiling it. In the same way, every virtue is outside the body, but he who weeps daily cleanses his body, because a tear that pours from above washes the body from its impurity.[39]

St John of the Ladder said, "A true repentant considers every day in which he did not weep to be wasted, even if he did good deeds during that day."[40] Further on, he writes, "No matter how exalted our life is, if we did not acquire compunction in our heart, our life is false and fruitless. It is necessary, truly necessary for the one who has defiled himself after the laver of regeneration (i.e., Holy Baptism) to cleanse his hands with constant fire in the heart and the mercy of God."[41] "We will not be denounced, O friends, after the release of our soul from the body, that we were not miracle-workers or theologians or that we did not see spiritual visions, but we will definitely have to answer to God for not weeping constantly,"[42] that is, were not in constant salvific sorrow for our sins and sinfulness. Even though sorrow is nearly always crowned with a greater or lesser amount of tears, some ascetics (as we see in the consolation offered to these ascetics by the Holy Fathers) suffer from heavy sorrow, either for their entire life or for a very long time, without the consolation and joy of tears. But they know that the essence of repentance is found in humility and a "heart that is broken"[43] when the spirit cries out because of extreme humility. The cry of the spirit, especially when physical strength is lacking for extreme ascetical labors and the actions of humility in the soul, replaces all these labors and actions, including tears.[44] Amen.

CHAPTER 37

Glory to God!

Glory to God! Glory to God! Glory to God! For everything that I see in myself, in everyone, in everything—glory to God!

What do I see in myself? I see sin, constant sin. I see the constant breaking of God's holy commandments. And my God sees my sins, He sees them all, He sees their countless numbers. When I, a limited creature, in my weakness similar to grass or a wildflower, more often look at my own sins, then they horrify me with their quantity and their quality. How must they look to all-holy and all-perfect God, Who sees everything?

Even so, He still looks at my sins with long patience! He still has not committed me to much-deserved suffering. The earth does not swallow me up, a sinner who is a burden even for the ground I walk on. The heavens do not burn me up, even though I have never heeded their commands. The waters do not rush to inundate me, who sin openly before all creation. They do not seize me and bury me in their dark pits and depths! Hell itself is restrained, it is not given the victim that it fairly demands, a victim who by all fairness belongs already to it!

Reverently and fearfully, I look at God, Who looks at my sins, seeing them more clearly even than my conscience. His miraculous patience amazes me and frightens me. I thank and praise this unutterable goodness. My thoughts become lost—I am completely overcome by gratitude and praise, and reverent silence descends on my mind and heart. I feel, think, utter only one phrase—*Glory to God!*

Where are you rushing, my thought? Look without turning away at my sins, force me to weep for them. I need to be purified by bitter tears, to be washed away by constant sorrow. But my uncontainable thought does not listen; it runs away, it stands on an incredibly high place! Its flight is like the flight of lightning, when it touches the two opposite sides of the sky at the same time. And my thought takes on the heights of spiritual contemplation, from where it looks at an astonishing, magnificent sight.

Before my thought stands the whole world, all the eras from the creation of the world to its end, all the events of the world, those that were and those that are and those that will be. My thought sees all the fates of every person in their infinite particularity.

It sees God, the Creator and omnipotent Lord of all creatures, Who sees everything, Who directs everything, Who gives to all things their goals and callings.

God allows man to see His direction of the world. But God alone knows the reasons for the fates of all things, the reasons for His commands. "For who has known the mind of the Lord? Or who has become His counselor?"[1] And the fact that man is allowed to see God in His providence, in His direction of creation, is a great benefit given to man, a source of great spiritual benefit.

The vision of the Creator and Lord of all things visible and invisible gives the viewer supernatural strength, and with this vision comes the realization of the limitless power of the omnipotent King over all creation. Even the hairs on our head, hairs so useless according to the weak wisdom of mankind, are counted in this limitless, all-encompassing wisdom, and are protected by Him.[2] Naturally, without His wish, no catastrophe can possibly occur in a man's life. A Christian, who looks to providence without turning away, preserves constant courage and unshakable firmness, even amid the worst tragedies. He says together with the Prophet David: "I foresaw the Lord always before me, for He is on my right hand, that I should not be moved."[3] The Lord is my helper; I will fear no evil circumstances, I will not give in to despair, I will not drown in the deep sea of unhappiness. For everything—Glory to God!

Endless submission to God is inspired by this vision of the providence of God. What if the slave of God is surrounded on all sides by various heavy sorrows? He consoles his wounded heart in this way: "God sees all this! If He, the all-wise one, knows of some reasons why such sorrows would not be beneficial and necessary to me, He would have prevented them, for His power is limitless. But He did not prevent them, and so it is His all-holy will that I suffer in this way. This will is precious to me, more precious than my own life! It is better to die than to reject the will of the Creator! In this will is true life! Whoever dies for the sake of fulfilling God's will, advances ever forward in the true life. For everything—Glory to God!"

This vision of God's providence inspires profound meekness and unchangeable love for one's neighbor, which cannot be disturbed or distressed by winds of temptation. For such a soul, insults, slander, and the evil acts of others simply do not exist. All creation acts according to the direction or the permission of the Creator. The creation is merely a blind instrument. In such a soul, the voice of humility becomes more pronounced, accusing the soul of countless sins, justifying one's neighbor as the tools of the just providence of God. This voice cries out joyfully in the midst of suffering, and brings calm and consolation. It quietly says: "I accept all this as fair because of my sins. It is better for me to suffer in this short life, rather than to suffer eternally in hell. My sins cannot go unpunished—this is required by God's justice. The fact that my sins are punished now, in this short earthly life, is proof of God's unutterable compassion. Glory to God!"

This vision of God's providence preserves and increases faith in God. He who sees the invisible and all-powerful hand, the Ruler of the world, will remain unfazed even in the worst storms that terrorize the sea of life. He believes that society, the Church, and the fates of all people are helped by the all-powerful and all-wise right hand of God. Gazing at the ferocious waves, at the terrifying storms, at the black clouds, he consoles and contents himself with the thought that God sees everything that happens. Man, that weak creature, is made for quiet, humble submission, reverent knowledge and contemplation of the judgments of God. May everything go along the lines drawn by God, according to the purposes determined above! For everything—Glory to God!

Before this vision of God's providence, not only do temporary sorrows flee but also the eternal sorrows that await a sinner beyond death. The consolation of grace that always comes to the one who has denied himself for obedience to God, dulls and destroys these sorrows. Even death is no longer frightening for the one who has denied the self and submitted to God's will, for the faithful servant of Christ gives his soul and eternal fate into the hands of Christ, gives himself up completely with firm faith in Christ, with an indomitable hope in His goodness and power. When the soul will leave the body, and the fallen angels will brazenly, shamelessly approach it, it will make them flee with the power of its self-denial.

"Go ahead! Take me!" the soul will say courageously. "Cast me out into the pit of darkness and flames, cast me into the abyss of hell, if this is my God's will for me, if this is what He wants for me. It is better to lose the sweetness of heaven, easier to bear the flames of hell than to reject the will and decision of the great God. I gave myself to Him, and I give myself to Him! He, not you, is the Judge of my weakness and sinfulness! You, even in your mad defiance, are still only the doer of His commands."

The servants of the prince of this world will stop in their tracks in apprehension, seeing this courageous, meek, submissive self-denial and trust in the will of God! They will flee in shame, and the soul will travel without hindrance to the place where its treasure is—to God.[4] There it will see Him face-to-face, Whom here on earth we only see through faith in His providence. And eternally we will cry out—Glory to God!

Glory to God! What powerful words! During our times of trouble, when the heart will be surrounded and embattled by thoughts of doubts, faintheartedness, lack of gratitude, and complaining, we must force ourselves to constantly, unhurriedly, and attentively repeat the words: Glory to God! Whoever will believe my advice in simplicity of heart and will practice it in actual fact, will see the miraculous power of the praise of God. He will rejoice in receiving such a beneficial new knowledge, he will rejoice in achieving such a strong and effective weapon against his spiritual foes. From the mere sound of these words, uttered during the attacks of dark thoughts of sorrow and despair, from the mere sound of these words, uttered even unwillingly, through forceful self-will, with the lips alone, the princes of the air shudder and flee in terror. All dark thoughts dissipate like dust in a strong wind. Heaviness and boredom leave the soul, and lightness, calm, peace, consolation, and joy settle there. Glory to God!

Glory to God! What triumphant words! Words that announce victory! Words that are the joy of all the faithful servants of God! Words announcing the defeat of all His enemies, and the destruction of all their weapons. These weapons are sin, a carnal mind-set, fallen human reasoning. They came about as a result of the fall, and have sin as its source, sin that is rejected by God, that constantly battles God, that is forever rejected by God. He who is wounded by sorrow is tended to in vain by all the wise of this world. Useless is their medicine of oratory and philosophy, useless is any effort by the sick one himself, if he wishes to untie the Gordian knot of his sorrows using his own reason. Very often, perhaps always, human reason is completely lost in the web of sorrow. Often, the sick man sees himself entangled, bound on all sides! Often, the very thought of deliverance seems impossible to him! And so, many perish under the unbearable heaviness of sorrow, they perish because of the fatal wound of sorrow, having found no earthly medicine strong enough to heal it.

Earthly wisdom exhausted all its methods, and they were all found to be powerless and insignificant. My beloved brother, avoid everything that God has forsaken. Lay aside all the tricks of your own reason! Use the weapon that is given you by the power of the preaching of Christ. The wisdom of man will derisively smile when it sees the weapon offered by faith; fallen reason, antagonistic to God in its very essence, will not fail to offer the most intelligent protestations, full of educated skepticism and irony. Pay no attention to these enemies of God, whom God has forsaken. In your sorrow, begin to utter from the depths of your soul, repeating the words "Glory to God," not allowing yourself to think. You will see a sign, a miracle. These words alone will banish sorrow and attract consolation into the heart. They will accomplish that, which the wisdom of the wise failed to do. This reason, this wisdom will be dishonored, but you, delivered, healed, believing with a living faith, proven to you by a miracle within you, will cry out, Glory to God!

Glory to God! Many saints loved to repeat these words often, for they had experienced the hidden power in them. When St John Chrysostom was speaking with his spiritual friends and brothers about some particular event (especially sorrowful ones), he always laid as his cornerstone the words: "Glory to God for everything!" He had a habit of beginning every sermon by slapping the forefinger of his right hand on the outstretched palm of the left with the words, "Glory to God for everything!"

Brothers! Let us also learn to frequently praise God. Let us run to this constant weapon against our sorrows. Through undying praise of our God, let us turn back and exterminate our invisible enemies, especially those that try to beat us to the ground with sorrow, faintheartedness, complaints, and despair. Let us cleanse ourselves with tears, prayer, and the reading of the Holy Scriptures and the Holy Fathers, so that we may become witnesses of the providence of God, Who sees all, Who is Master over all, Who directs all according to His inscrutable judgments, toward the goals that only He knows. Having become witnesses of God's lordship, let us be reverent and peaceful in heart, fully obedient in firm faith, and we will be amazed at the greatness of the unattainable God; we will praise him now and forever.

It is worthy and righteous for the creature to constantly praise You, O God the Creator, who summoned us into being from nothingness, only by Your endless, unattainable goodness, You Who have made us with the beauty of Your image and likeness, Who have led us into the blessedness and joys of heaven, for which an end has not been determined.

And yet, how did we repay our Benefactor? What did dust give in gratitude to the Creator who gave it life?

We cooperated with Your enemy, with the angel that rebelled against God, with the author of all evil. We listened to the words of blasphemy against our Benefactor. We decided to despise and envy the all-perfect Goodness, our Creator.

Alas, what darkness! Alas, what corruption of mind! From the heights of contemplation of God and true theology, our race, in the person of our forefather, in a moment fell into the abyss of eternal death.

The first to fall was Satan. The bright angel Lucifer became the dark demon. Having no body, he sinned with mind and word. Instead of praising God in pure joy with all the other holy angels, he was enamored of blasphemy. Hardly had he conceived this dark, death-dealing thought, hardly had he turned it into evil words, like the deadliest poison, than he became dark, transformed, and fell with unutterable speed from the heights of heaven to the earth. Of the swiftness of his fall we know from the witness of Scripture: "I saw Satan fall like lightning from heaven."[5]

Just as immediate was the fall of man, in emulation of the fallen angel. It began with the acceptance of a dark, blasphemous thought, after which followed the breaking of God's command. This disobedience was preceded already by secret disdain and rejection of God.

Alas, what blindness! What a terrible sin! What a horrifying fall! Compared with this sin, compared with this fall, no punishment is too great, not even exile from Eden, working for daily bread in the sweat of one's brow, the pain of childbearing, the return to the earth, from which the Creator formed our bodies.

But You, O eternal Goodness, what did You do? How did You answer our rejection of You, our answer to Your endless gifts? How did You punish us for our disobedience, for our lack of faith in You, for the acceptance of a horrifying blasphemy against You, against You who are goodness itself, perfection itself?

You gave us new gifts, even greater than the first! One of the divine Persons accepted humanity! You accepted, without sin, all our weaknesses that had become part of our nature after its fall. You appeared before our eyes, having covered the uncontainable power of Your divinity with a human body. Being the Word of God, You give us the word of God in the sounds of a human voice. Your power is the power of God! Your meekness is the meekness of an angel. Your name is the name of a man.

This all-holy name turns the heavens and the earth. How consoling and majestic is the sound of your name! *Jesus Christ!* You are the Lord of men, and a man also. How miraculously, how perfectly You united Your divinity with humanity! How marvelously You act! You are God and man! You are the Lord, and yet a slave![6] You are the High Priest and the sacrifice! You are the Saviour and the coming just Judge of the universe! You heal all diseases! You visit and accept sinners! You resurrect the dead! You command the waters of the sea and the winds of the sky! Marvelously, bread appears in Your hands, giving a harvest a thousand times over; in one moment, the incredible harvest is sown, harvested, baked, and broken, all at the same time! You hunger, so that we can be delivered from hunger. You thirst, so that our thirst can be quenched. You travel in the country of our exile with difficulties for Yourself, in order to return to us what we lost—the peaceful, heavenly essence, full of spiritual sweetness. And You pour out Your sweat in the garden of Gethsemane, so that we would cease sweating in the getting of our daily bread, so that we would instead pour out our sweat in prayers for the worthy communion of the Bread of Heaven.

The plants that were twisted into thorns by our corruption, You placed on Your head. You crowned and wounded your all-holy head with thorns! We were bereft of the tree of life and its fruit, which gave immortality to the one who ate it, but You, stretching Yourself on the tree of the cross, became that fruit that gives eternal life to those who eat Him. The tree of life and its fruit appeared on the earth, in the land of our exile. This fruit and this tree are greater than the ones in Eden; those gave immortality, but You give immortality and divinity. Through Your passion, You poured out sweetness onto our sufferings.

We reject earthly pleasures; we choose the fate of suffering, if only to become communicants of Your sweetness! As a foretaste of eternal life, it is sweeter and more precious than this temporary life itself! You fell asleep in the sleep of death, which could not hold You in its eternal sleep, You Who are God! You arose and awoke us from the cruel sleep of death; You gave us blessed and glorious resurrection! You raised our renewed nature to heaven and seated it at the right hand of the pre-eternal Father! You made Your Father our Father as well! You opened for us the path to heaven! You prepared mansions for us in heaven! You lead all faithful earthly wanderers to these mansions, You accept them, You console them, You give them rest after all the difficult travels on earth. All who call Your holy name, who fulfill Your holy commandment, who piously and properly serve You, who carry their own cross and drink of Your cup bravely, with gratitude and praise—all these will find mansions in heaven.

Glory to You, Creator of those who were in nonexistence! Glory to You, Redeemer and Saviour of those fallen and perished! Glory to You, our God and Lord! Allow us to praise, bless, and honor Your goodness both on earth and in heaven! Let us see with our uncovered faces Your awesome, unapproachable, magnificent glory, to see it eternally, to worship it, and to be blessed in it. Amen!

CHAPTER 38

The Praying Mind Seeks Union with the Heart

The doors of my senses have closed. My tongue is silent; my eyes are closed; my ears hear nothing that is outside me. The mind that is clothed in prayer, that has put away the weight of worldly thoughts, descends to the cell of the heart. The doors of the cell are shut; everywhere there is total darkness. The mind, in fear, begins to knock on the doors of the heart through prayer; it stands patiently at the doors, knocks, waits, knocks again, again waits, again prays. There is no answer there is no voice! The deathly quiet and dark are only answered by the silence of the grave. The mind leaves the doors of the heart, saddened, and crying bitterly it seeks consolation. It was not allowed to stand before the King of kings in the sanctum of the inner cell.

Why, why were you so rejected?

I am marked by sin. The habit of carnal thoughts distracts me. I have no strength within me, because the Spirit does not come to me for help, the all-holy and all-good Spirit, who reestablishes the union of mind, heart, and body that was severed by the terrible fall of man. Without the all-powerful, creative help of the Spirit, my own efforts are useless! He is most compassionate, He is eternally the lover of man, but my impurity does not allow Him access to me. I will wash myself in tears, I will purify myself through the confession of my sins, I will not give my body either food or sleep, which in excess only debilitate my soul. Robed in the cry of repentance, I will descend to the doors of my heart. I will stand there, or sit, like the blind man in the Gospels, I will bear the heaviness and boredom of the dark, I will cry out to the all-powerful One: *Have mercy on me!*

And I went down, and I stood, and I began to cry out with tears. I became like unto the blind man who cannot see the true, unsetting Light, like unto the deaf and dumb man who can neither speak nor hear spiritually. I truly felt that I was blind, deaf, dumb, standing before the gates of Jericho, the heart that is inhabited by sin. I wait for healing from my Saviour, Whom I cannot see, cannot hear, but to Whom I cry out, though it be a silent cry of my appalling state. I do not know His name, so I call the Son of God the son of David, because flesh and blood cannot give honor to God as God.

Show me the way, along which the Saviour walks! This way is prayer, as the Prophet said through the inspiration of the Holy Spirit: "The sacrifice of praise shall glorify Me; and there is the way, by which I will show him My salvation."[1] Tell me, what is the hour of the coming of the Saviour? Is it in the morning, midday, or the evening? "Take heed, watch and pray; for you do not know when the time is."[2]

The way is known, but the time is not! I will go outside the city, I will stand or sit at the gates of Jericho, as St Paul recommends: "Therefore let us go forth to Him, outside the camp, bearing His reproach."[3] The world is fading; everything in it is inconstant; it is not even called a city, but a camp. I will leave behind my attachment to money that is left behind after death, whether I want it or not, and often even before death. I will leave behind the accolades and honors that die with me; I will reject the pleasures of the flesh that make me incapable of the labors of the ascetic life. "For here we have no continuing city, but we seek the one to come,"[4] which will first reveal itself to me in my heart through the mercy and grace of God, my Saviour. Whoever will not ascend to the mystical Jerusalem with his spirit during this earthly life will have no sure way of knowing that even after the separation of his soul from his body he will be allowed to enter the spiritual Jerusalem. The first serves as the pledge of the second.[5]

Amen.

CHAPTER 39

A Vision of Christ

Do you want to see the Lord Jesus Christ? "Come and see," says His Apostle (John 1:46).[1]

The Lord Jesus Christ promised to be with His disciples "to the end of the age."[2] He is with them in the holy Gospels and the Mysteries of the Church.[3] He is not with those who do not believe in the Gospel—they do not see Him, blinded by lack of faith.

Do you want to hear Christ? He speaks to you through His Gospel. Do not ignore His saving voice. Turn away from your sinful life and be attentive to the teaching of Christ, which is eternal life.

Do you want Christ to appear to you? He tells you how to receive this vision. "He who has my commandments and keeps them, it is he who loves Me. And he who loves Me will be loved by My Father, and I will love him and manifest Myself to him."[4]

You are adopted as a son of God through the Mystery of holy baptism; you entered into a close union with God through the Mystery of the Eucharist. Keep this adoption alive, keep this union alive. With repentance, restore the purity and renewal given you in holy baptism, and feed your union with God through a life according to the Gospels and with frequent communion of the Holy Mysteries of Christ. "Abide in Me, and I in you. As the branch cannot bear fruit of itself, unless it abides in the vine, neither can you, unless you abide in Me. He who eats My flesh and drinks My blood abides in Me, and I in him."[5]

Keep yourself free of any fantasies that suggest that you already see Christ, that you can feel Him, touch Him. This is nothing more than the empty game of your bombastic, proud vanity. This is a pernicious self-deception.[6] Fulfill the commandments of Christ, and miraculously you will see the Lord in yourself, in your qualities. Thus did the holy Apostle Paul see Christ in himself. He insisted that all Christians must have the same vision; he considered those who did not have it as having not yet achieved the status of Christian.

If you live a life of sin, if you satisfy your passions and still believe that you love the Lord Jesus Christ, then the disciple who loved Christ, who reclined on his breast during the mystical supper, condemns you as one deceived. He says: "He who says, 'I know Him,' and does not keep His commandments, is a liar, and the truth is not in him. But whoever keeps His word, truly the love of God is perfected in him. By this we know that we are in Him."[7]

If you follow your own sinful will and break the commandments of the Gospel, then the Lord Jesus Christ will count you among those who do not love Him. "He who does not love Me," He says, "does not keep My words."[8]

Do not strive without reason to enter the bridal feast of the Son of God, to union with Him, without first looking intently at your old, filthy rags, even if you are called to this wedding, to which every Christian is called. The master of the house has such servants that will tie your hands and feet and cast you into the outer darkness, unknown to God.

These servants are the demons, the fallen angels, into whose power is given the brazen one not cleansed by repentance, the seeker for love and other exalted spiritual states, puffed up in his own conceit and self-importance. The outer darkness is the blindness of the human mind—a passionate, carnal state. Sin and the fallen angels reign over the person in such a state. He is deprived of moral freedom—his arms and legs are tied. The tying of his arms and legs signify the lack of ability to live a God-pleasing life and succeed spiritually. All those who deceive themselves are in such a state. In order to leave this disastrous state, one must recognize and reject this delusion and enter into a salvific life of repentance.

It is difficult to leave this delusion behind. At the door stands a guard; the doors are locked with heavy and firm locks; they are sealed with the seal of hell. The locks signify the pride of the deluded ones, a pride that hides deep in the heart; their vanity, which constitutes the source of their activity; their hypocrisy and deceit, with which they cover their pride and vanity, with which they put on a mask of good intentions and humility, even sanctity. The unbreakable seal is the acceptance of the fruits of this delusion as the fruits of divine grace.

Can the deluded one, who thrives on lies and deceit, be a doer of the commandments of Christ, whose true source is the Truth

Himself—Christ? Can the one who empathizes with lies, who finds sweetness in lies, who assimilates lies, who unites with lies in his soul empathize with the truth? No! He will hate it; he will become its maddened enemy and persecutor.

O miserable dreamers, what will be your condition, you who imagine that you have spent your entire earthly life in the embrace of God, when you will be shocked by the words of the Saviour: "I never knew you: depart from Me, you who practice lawlessness!"[9]

My sincere friend in the Lord! Go to the Lord Jesus Christ, come near Him on the path of the commandments of the Gospel; know Him through them; show and prove your love for Him by keeping them. He will reveal Himself to you in a day and hour known to Him alone. Together with this revelation, He will pour into your heart unutterable love for Himself. Divine love is not something that belongs by nature to fallen man—it is a gift of the Holy Spirit, sent by God alone to his vessels purified by repentance, to his vessels of humility and chastity.

Entrust yourself to the Lord, not to yourself—He is far more dependable. He is your Creator. When you allowed yourself to grievously fall, He took upon Himself humanity for your sake, He gave himself up to death, for you He shed His blood, to you He gave His divinity. What would He not do for you? Prepare yourself for His gifts by purifying yourself. That is your work. Amen.

APPENDIX I

A Short Biography of Bishop Ignatius (Brianchaninov)

The future Saint Ignatius was born on April 15/28, 1807, in the village of Pokrovskoye in the Vologda region of Russia. His given name at birth was Dimitry Alexandrovitch Brianchaninov. Of noble birth, his father was a wealthy provincial landowner. In due course the young Dimitry was sent to study at the Pioneer Military Academy in St Petersburg to be educated as a military officer.

Even before entering the Academy, Dimitry had aspired to the monastic life, but his family did not support these plans. Nevertheless, as a student, he was able to find some time to devote to prayer and the inner life and to find other students with similar aspirations. Remaining obedient to his parents, he remained diligent in his studies, winning the praise of his teacher and coming to the attention of the Grand Duke Nicholas Pavlovich, the future Tsar Nicholas I.

After graduating from the Academy, he took up his first commission in the army but soon became seriously ill. This made it possible for him to request an honorable discharge and having made a full recovery to at last embrace the monastic life. He was duly tonsured as a monk in 1831 and given the name Ignatius. His spiritual father was the revered Elder Leonid of Optina. Shortly after his tonsure he was ordained as a priest.

Meanwhile, his absence from the army had come to the attention of Tsar Nicholas. As soon as he was able to locate Fr Ignatius in his small monastery near Vologda, he ordered him back to the capital. So, at the age of only twenty-six, Fr Ignatius was made an Archimandrite and appointed as head of the St Sergius monastery in St Petersburg. He served faithfully in that capacity for the next twenty-four years.

In 1857 he was ordained to the episcopacy, serving as Bishop of Stavropol and the Caucasus. This period of his life lasted for only four years, after which he withdrew into seclusion at the Nicolo-Babaevsky monastery in the Kostroma region of Russia. Here he was able to devote the remaining six years of his life to spiritual writing and correspondence with his numerous spiritual children. He composed five volumes of *Ascetical Works*, the fifth of which, *The Arena*, has been translated into English.

Bishop Ignatius reposed on April 30/May 13, 1867. The Russian Orthodox Church canonized him at their local council in 1988 and his relics now reside at the Tolga monastery in the Yaroslavl region of Russia.

APPENDIX 2

My Lament

This text was written on January 7, 1847. Due to his ravaged health, Archimandrite Ignatius asked to be relieved of the responsibility of being the abbot of the Sergiev Hermitage and to be reassigned to the Nikolo-Babaevskii Monastery for his retirement. However, he was allowed only a short break, and rested in the aforementioned monastery for ten months.

What words will I write at this beginning of my lament? What will be the first of my sorrowful thoughts to put down in pen? They are all equally heavy. Each one, when it appears to the mind, seems the heaviest. Each one seems the most painful to the heart as it pierces it with remembrance. I have hoarded groans in my breast, and they are itching to be released. But instead of coming out, they keep returning to the breast and cause a strange hesitation inside me. Will I turn the eyes of my mind to the days that have passed? They are a chain of deceptions, a chain of sins, a chain of falls.

Will I turn my eyes to that part of life that still lies before me in this earthly wandering? I am filled with horror due to my weakness, proven to me by my countless experiences. Will I look at my soul? There is nothing consoling there! It is all covered in the wounds of sin; there is not a single sin it did not taste. There is not a single iniquity with which it has not been stamped!

My body, O my poor body! I smell the stench of you rotting. Corruption doth not inherit incorruption.[1] Your lot is the darkness of the coffin after death and the prisons of hell after the resurrection! What fate awaits my soul after its separation from the body? It would be good if a peaceful and bright angel stood before it and took it with him to the blessed mansions of Eden. But for what reason will he come to me? What virtues, what ascetic labors worthy of the inhabitants of heaven will he find in my soul? No! More likely, armies of dark demons, fallen angels, will surround my soul. They will find it related to them in its falls, its sinful qualities, its self-will, and its antagonism to God. They will lead it into their own dungeons, the places of eternal, cruel sorrows, the places of eternal darkness and the undying fire, the places of tortures and groans that never cease and never end.

I see myself thus, and I weep. Sometimes rare drops of tears, like dew, barely moisten my eyes; sometimes a deluge of tears falls from my cheeks to my robes or my bed; sometimes the tears dry up completely and only a bitter cry inundates my soul. I weep with my mind; I weep with my heart; I weep with my body; I weep with my whole being. I feel sorrow not only in my breast but in all the members of my body. Strangely and inexplicably they take part in my tears.

O my soul! Before the final, inexorable time of the passage into eternity, work on yourself. Come and unite yourself to the Lord with genuine, constant repentance, with a righteous life according to His all-holy commandment. The Lord is plentiful in mercy; He is eternally compassionate. He accepts all who run to Him; He cleanses the sins of the sinners; He heals their old, stinking, fatal wounds; He gives blessedness to all who believe in Him and submit to Him. Examine your earthly wandering from its very beginning, examine the great benefits given to you by God, entrust your fate to Him, seek to inculcate in yourself His holy will, submit to His all-good and wise commandments. The Apostle Paul mentions, "For if we would judge ourselves, we would not be judged.[2]

No one asked my Creator to bring me out of nothing into existence with His all-powerful command. The only intercessor for my existence was His coeternal goodness. I was born without knowing that I exist. I began to exist as though I did not yet exist. Alas! I was born fallen, and began life already as a dead man: "I was conceived in wickedness," and in the death of sin "did my mother bear me."[3] Life and death together were the beginning of my existence. I did not know or fully understand that I lived or that I was already dead in life, deceased in existence.

What a mystery is the birth of man in sin! How is he already dead, though he lives? How has he already fallen if he has not yet learned to walk? How has he sinned if he has not yet done anything? How are children, separated from the forefather Adam by thousands of years, partakers of his sin? My mind reverently gazes at the judgments of God, but I do not understand them. I dare not ask Him about them, but I see and marvel at them. I praise the unattainable, unknowable God.

My birth in sin was a calamity worse than nonexistence itself! How can it not be a calamity to be born for the sorrows of a short earthly life, and then to eternally exist in the darkness and sufferings of hell? There are no intercessors for me; I myself have no strength to pull myself out of the abyss of perdition. May the right hand of God rescue me from there! After giving birth to me through my parents for existence, He gives birth to me through Himself into salvation. He washes from me the stain of sin, He renews me with the Spirit in the waters of baptism, He accepts the vows of loyalty through my godfather, He gives me His name, He stamps me with His seal, He makes me a communicant of His divinity and an inheritor of His kingdom. Miracles are performed over me, and unutterable benefits are poured over me when I still can feel nothing, can understand nothing, not even the fact that I exist. You looked down on me, my Lord, when I was just a weak baby. What did I bring You, I who was wrapped in swaddling clothes, incapable of any actions or reason? How did You accept my oaths? How, having accepted them, did You grant me Your gifts? When I look at Your inconceivable goodness, I am overwhelmed. Even now I can do little more than what I was able to give You as a child—in silence of tongue and mind, I offer You my childlike cries and irrational tears.

What have I done in return for all these benefits given to me when I could not appreciate them? I continued to not recognize them or know them. My eyes were directed at the world; the honors and temporary service in the world seemed to me the true calling of a man. Death did not exist for me! The earthly life seemed eternal to me, so foreign to my mind was even the thought of death. Eternity! My eyes did not turn to contemplate her limitless paths.

I knew the dogmas and teachings of the Holy Orthodox Church; I believed in them, but my knowledge and my faith were dead. Of what consists the fall of man, what is his salvation, what are the signs, the proofs of the one and the other? I had no real, experienced knowledge of these things. I considered the commandments of God to be limited to the Ten Commandments of the Old Testament, and the commandments of Christ, His all-holy words, to be no more than moral teaching that was commendable and worthy of emulation but not inevitable for salvation. In this way, the unutterable gift of grace given to me at my baptism was hidden, like the talent in the parable, in the rag of ignorance that was deeply buried in the ground, that is, the worries regarding gathering ephemeral knowledge of the fading world. I buried this grace like ashes through my thoughts on earthly success and temporary pleasures, in service to vanity and the dark society of this vain age.

My childhood was full of sorrows. Even here I see Your hand, my God! I had no one to whom I could open my heart, so I began to pour it out to my God, began to read the Gospels and the lives of Your saints. For me, a veil covered the Gospel, only sometimes allowing glimmers of understanding, but Your Pimens, Sisoes, and Macariuses had a tremendous effect on me. My thoughts, often rising to God in prayer and reading, began little by little to bring peace and calmness to my soul. When I was a fifteen-year-old boy, an indescribable silence inundated my mind and heart. But I did not understand it; I thought this was the normal state of all people.

I entered the military service not by my own choice and desire. Then I did not dare, did not know how to want anything on my own because I had yet to find Truth; I did not see Him clearly enough yet to desire Him. Worldly sciences, the discoveries of a fallen human reason, became the main subjects that took up my attention. I aspired toward them with all the powers of my soul. Other pastimes and religious feelings remained secondary. I spent nearly two years in these earthly studies, and by then a kind of frightening emptiness had grown in my soul; I felt hunger, I felt unbearable longing for God. I began to bemoan my laziness, grieve over that forgetfulness to which I had abandoned my faith, shed tears over the sweet silence that I had lost, lament that emptiness that I had found, that was weighing me down, frightening me, filling me with a sense of abandonment, a lack of life! Surely this was the suffering of a soul that had separated itself from its true life, God. I remember how I walked the streets of St Petersburg in the uniform of a junior officer, and tears fell like a torrent from my eyes . . . Why do I not cry like that now? Now I need those tears! I have passed the halfway point of my life, and faster and faster flow the days, months, and years. They are rushing to the grave, from where I cannot return, beyond which there is no repentance or improvement.

I was already mature in my thoughts; I was looking for something definitive from religion. Involuntary religious feelings did not satisfy me; I wanted to see something clear, something sure—the Truth. During that time, various religious ideas entertained and worried the northern capital.[4] These ideas would tussle with each other, would fight each other. Neither one side nor the other appealed to my heart; it did not trust them, it feared them. My mind heavy with doubts, I took off my junior officer's uniform and put on the officer's. I missed my junior officer's uniform—in it, I could come to the church of God and stand in the crowd of soldiers, common men, and pray and weep to my heart's content. This young man had no time for worldly joys, entertainments! The world offered me nothing appealing; I was as cold to it as if the world truly was without any temptations. Truly, they did not exist for me. My mind was completely submerged in study while simultaneously burning with the desire to know where the true faith was hiding, where the true teaching was hiding, foreign to any dogmatic or moral deceptions.

In my mind, I already saw the limits of earthly knowledge. As I came up to these limits, I asked the earthly knowledge, "What do you give a person that he can keep for himself? A person is immortal; therefore, what he owns must also be immortal. Show me anything that you can give me that will not die, this true wealth that I will be able to take with me beyond the grave!"

All I see is knowledge given temporarily, which ends with the earth, which cannot exist past the separation of the soul and body. What is the purpose of studying mathematics? Its entire subject is created matter. It reveals the form of natural laws, teaches us to count and measure the world, to use these measures for the needs of our temporary life. It does point to the existence of infinity, but only as an idea beyond the limits of matter. An exact description of this idea is logically impossible for any reasonable but limited creature. Mathematics does show that some number and measure, either by their massiveness or minuteness, cannot be subjected to the study of man. It does point to the existence of knowledge to which man strives, but which he cannot understand with the methods of science. Mathematics only hints at the existence of objects beyond the ken of our senses.

Physics and chemistry reveal a different kind of natural law. Before the development of these sciences, mankind did not even know of the existence of these laws. Once revealed, they suggested the existence of still other countless natural laws, still undiscovered. Some of them have defied all attempts at description; others are simply indescribable due to the limits of the powers and abilities of mankind. When our excellent professor and orator Soloviev taught the introduction to chemistry,[5] he said that it seemed to him we study chemistry to understand that we know nothing and that we can ultimately know nothing, so great is the potential field of knowledge opened by this science! How insignificant are our own studies in this science! It proves and convinces us with blinding clarity that matter, which by definition is supposed to have definite limits, actually cannot be fully conceived or described by science because of its mass and for many other reasons. Chemistry describes the increasing subtlety of matter to a scale that is barely discernable to human senses, and in this microscopic state, it notices ever-increasing complexity and divisibility into constituent parts even smaller and more complex, even though this divisibility is technically impossible. In fact, man cannot see the end of the divisibility of matter or even the far limit of numbers or measures. He realizes that what is infinite cannot apply to matter, and at the same time, everything limited must apply by definition to matter. But this is an imprecise idea; what is definite is its reality. Furthermore, chemistry and physics focus only on matter, widening our understanding of its practical use for things of this earth, for the everyday needs of man and human society.

More harmful than the studies I have mentioned is philosophy, of which fallen man is especially proud. Natural sciences constantly base their ideas on material experiments through which they prove the validity of an accepted theory because without these experiments, a theory has no place in science. Philosophy lacks such a method of constant proof through experiments. There are many different philosophical systems that do not agree with each other, often contradict each other, and only prove the insufficiency of human "love of wisdom" when one does not have positive knowledge of the Truth. What free rein is given to philosophy to dream, imagine, and write down beautiful absurdities, none of which are possible in the exact sciences! Despite all that, philosophy is usually quite content with itself. Through its deceitful light, great arrogance, conceit, pride, vanity, and hatred for one's neighbor all enter into the soul. The blind world showers it with praises and honors since it belongs to the world. Whoever contents himself with the knowledge given by philosophy not only fails to acquire correct notions about God, himself, and the spiritual world, but he becomes infected with false knowledge that makes the mind diseased and damaged by delusion, incapable of communion with the Truth.[6] The Apostle Paul said, "The world through wisdom did not know God!"[7] "For to be carnally minded is death, because the carnal mind is enmity against God;

for it is not subject to the law of God, nor indeed can be,"[8] because this is impossible for the carnal mind. "Beware lest anyone cheat you through philosophy and empty deceit, according to the tradition of men, according to the basic principles of the world, and not according to Christ, in whom are hidden all the treasures of wisdom and knowledge."[9]

Philosophy, being the child of mankind's fall, flatters man's fallen state, masks it, preserves and sustains it. It is afraid of the teaching of Truth since it is condemned to death by Truth.[10] The state into which the spirit is led by philosophy is a state of self-deception, spiritual death, which is made very clear by the aforementioned words of Apostle Paul, who advises all who desire to acquire the true knowledge of God to reject the knowledge given by fallen man's so-called love of wisdom. "Let no one deceive himself! If anyone among you seems to be wise in this age, let him become a fool that he may become wise."[11]

True philosophy (i.e., "love of wisdom") is contained in the one teaching of Christ. Christ is the Wisdom of God.[12] Whoever searches for wisdom outside Christ renounces Christ, rejects wisdom, and acquires falsely named wisdom for himself, the inheritance of the fallen angels.

As for geography, geodesy, linguistics, literature, and all other studies and arts, it is not even necessary to mention them. They are all only for the world; the end of their necessity corresponds to the end of a person's earthly life, and more often than not, even earlier. If I waste all my life for the gathering of knowledge that ends with the earthly life, then what will I take with me beyond the reaches of this crude material world?

Human knowledge! Give me, if you can, at least one eternal, positive thing, something that is permanent and true, worthy to belong to man!

But human knowledge was silent.

For the only answer to this question that is satisfactory, necessary, pertaining to life is found in faith. But where are you hiding, O true and holy faith? I could not recognize you in fanaticism, which does not have the seal of Gospel meekness, but rather is inflamed with anger and self-righteousness. I could not find you in the self-willed teachings that separate one from the Church, that try to establish a new system, that vainly and pompously declare the discovery of a new, true faith in Christ, eighteen hundred years after the incarnation of God the Word! Oh! My soul was filled with such heavy doubts! How my soul suffered then! How it was buffeted by waves of doubt, arising from lack of trust in myself, out of suspicion toward everything that stormed and cried out around me—the general ignorance and blindness to the Truth.

And I began to beg God often, with tears, that He would not leave me a victim of delusion, that He would show the true path on which I could travel toward Him with my mind and heart. And immediately a thought came to me. My heart ran straight to that thought, as to the embrace of a friend. That thought told me to find the true faith in the sources—in the writings of the Holy Fathers. "Their holiness," this thought told me, "is proof of their veracity. Choose them as your guides." I listened. I found a way to obtain the works of the holy God pleasers; avidly, I began to read them, to study them deeply. Having finished one, I immediately began another. I would read, then reread and study. What was it that so affected me about the writings of the Fathers of the Orthodox Church? It was their agreement, their miraculous, majestic unanimity.

Eighteen centuries witnessed, from their mouths with one voice to the one teaching, the divine teaching! When I look at the clear sky on a bright autumn night, plowed with countless stars of such different sizes, all shining with the same light, I say to myself: even so are the writings of the Fathers. When I look on a summer day at the wide sea covered by a variety of ships with their sails unfurled like white swan wings, sailing with one wind to one common goal and harbor, I say to myself: even so are the writings of the Fathers. When I hear the blended sound of a large choir in which different voices sing one divine song in complex harmony, I say to myself: even so are the writings of the Fathers.

What teachings did I find there? I found a teaching repeated by all the Fathers, which says that the only path to salvation is to follow without fail the guidance of the Holy Fathers. Have you seen those who have been deceived by false teachings, those who perish from falsely chosen labors? Know this: they followed themselves, their own minds and their own opinions, not the teachings of the Fathers, which make up the dogmatic and moral traditions of the Church. The Church offers the teachings of the Fathers to its children as a priceless inheritance.

God, Who gives all good things, including the good thought, which is the beginning of every good thing, sent this thought to me. This thought was my first refuge in the land of Truth. Here my soul found rest from worries and contrary winds. It was a salvific, good thought! It was a gift without price from the all-good God, Who wants all people to be saved and come to a knowledge of the truth. This thought became the cornerstone for my soul's spiritual foundation! This thought became the star that led me through turbulent waters. It began to constantly illuminate the difficult, sorrowful, narrow, invisible path to God.

I looked at the religious world with this understanding in mind, and I saw that the source of all false teaching is ignorance, forgetfulness, and the absence of this thought.

Such were the gifts given to me by my God! Such an incorruptible treasure, leading to joyful eternity, was sent to me from the heavenly throne by God's mercy and wisdom. With what can I show my gratitude to my Benefactor? Only this—that I will dedicate my entire earthly life to the study and search for Him, to service to Him! But will I show gratitude this way? I will only invite new, greater benefits from Him. God Himself separated me from the vanity of the world. I lived in the world but remained apart from the wide and easy path. His good thought led me to a separate road, to living, cooling springs of waters, to countries where the harvest was plentiful along picturesque ways. But this road was also wild and dangerous, full of pitfalls, isolated from any human company. This is a road that a traveler rarely takes.

Reading the Fathers with complete clarity convinced me that salvation could be found within the Russian Church, which could not be said for the faiths of Western Europe, since they preserved in fullness neither the dogmatic nor the moral teachings of the Church of Christ. The Fathers showed me what Christ did for mankind, explained the fall of man, why the Redeemer was necessary, and the way of salvation that the Redeemer indicated and continues to indicate. They repeated to me: you must develop, experience, and see within yourself this salvation, without which faith in Christ and Christianity is dead—empty words without realization. They taught me to look toward eternity as an endlessness before which even the several thousand years of human history pale in comparison, let alone our own life, lasting only some half century or so. They taught me to use my earthly life in preparation for eternity, like a foreign envoy who waits in the anteroom, preparing to be admitted to the tsar's glorious chambers. They showed me that all earthly activities, enjoyments, honors, and advantages are little more than useless toys with which grown-up children play and then end up losing the blessedness of eternity.

What does everything earthly mean in comparison with Christ? Christ, the all-powerful God, gives Himself as an estate, an eternal gift, to man—a speck of dust. This visible world is not worth our service and our toil! How does it reward its servants? At first with toys, the murk of an unclear future, then with death, the grave, and the tears of one's dear ones and their quick forgetfulness. The servants of Christ have different rewards—they spend this life in the study of Truth, being formed in its light. Having been remade in it, they are sealed with the Holy Spirit, and they enter eternity already somewhat acquainted with it. They have already prepared a place of blessedness for themselves, since they were given the good news of salvation. "For the Spirit searches all things, yes, the deep things of God."[13] The Spirit gives knowledge of God's depths to those with whom he unites. This is described in vivid clarity by the Holy Fathers in their writings.

My heart grew cold to the world, to all of its great and sweet emptiness. I decided to leave the world, to dedicate my own life to knowing Christ, to acquiring Christ. With this in mind, I began to emulate the clergy both in the monasteries and in the world. This was difficult at first, especially considering my young age and inexperience. But I saw everything close-up, and after I entered the monastery, I found nothing new or unexpected. Many obstacles lay in my path toward the monastery! I will not mention them all. My own body was complaining to me: "Where are you leading me? I'm so weak and sickly. You've seen the monks, how they live. Their life is unbearable to you because of my sickliness, and because of your upbringing, and for a whole host of other reasons!" My own reason supported the conclusions of my body. But there was a voice, a voice in my heart—I think it was the voice of my conscience, or maybe my guardian angel—that always told me God's will, because the voice was determined and authoritative. It said to me, "To do this is your fundamental duty."

This voice was so strong that the seemingly logical and concerned arguments of my reason and body seemed pitiful. Without hotheadedness, without impulsiveness, and not as a slave who is perpetually tossed back and forth by the strong emotions of his heart, but rather through some inconceivable and inexplicable calling, I entered the monastery.

I entered the monastery like a bewitched person closing his eyes, turning off his thoughts, and jumping into the fire or into a gaping abyss. I was like a soldier who throws himself headlong into the bloody fray, into obvious death. My guiding star, that good thought, came to give me light in my solitude, in my silence, or rather in the stormy darkness of monasticism.

According to the teachings of the Fathers, the only kind of monastic life appropriate for our age is a life under the guidance of the Holy Fathers' writings with the advice of experienced, living monks. But even this advice must be checked against the writings of the Fathers. The Fathers of the first centuries of the Church suggested that one find a God-inspired guide and submit oneself to him in complete, unconditional obedience. They called this the shortest path, which it is, the surest, the one most beloved of God. However, the Fathers who lived a thousand years after the coming of Christ, while repeating the advice of the early Fathers, already complained about the scarcity of God-inspired guides and about the appearance of many false teachers. As a solution, they recommended a monk who was guided by the Scriptures and the Holy Fathers. The Fathers closest to our own time considered true God-inspired elders to be a thing of the past, and more decisively recommended the guidance of the Holy Scriptures and the carefully considered advice of contemporary monks, but only with the most careful scrutiny of their advice in light of the same Scriptures. I desired to be under obedience to an elder, but I could not find one who was an incarnation of the teaching of the Fathers, the kind of elder I most wanted. In general, I heard much that was useful and much that was absolutely essential, which served as a good beginning for my spiritual formation. May the Lord remember in a place of joy, peace, blessedness, and light these departed patrons of my soul! And may He give even greater spiritual progress and a blessed death to those who still wander and toil on the earth!

Here I will write a few words about Russian monasticism, based on many years of observations. Perhaps it will be useful to someone! In Russia, monastic life has become weak, as has the Christian life in general. It has become weak because it is intrinsically connected to the Christian world. If the world gives a monastery weak Christians, it cannot expect the monasteries to make strong monks similar to the ascetics of old, even if the Christians of old, living in the world, were crowned with a profusion of virtues and spiritual power. But monasteries, the foundlings of the Holy Spirit, do cast a bright light on Christianity—there is still food for the spiritually hungry; there is still the keeping of the commandment; there is still a strict, dogmatic, and moral orthodoxy. But how rare are those true tablets on which the Holy Spirit has carved the words of life! It is wonderful how all the spiritual flowers and fruits grew in those souls, which—far away from an external or internal knowledge of monasticism—still tilled the soil of their hearts through the reading of the Scriptures and the Fathers, with faith and love, inspired by their humble but overpowering repentance. Whoever has not tilled the soil has not seen any fruits.

What is the main work of the monastics, those for whom monasticism exists? It consists of the learning of all the commandments, all the words of the Redeemer, and their assimilation into the mind and heart. The monk becomes an observer of the two natures of man—the corrupted, sinful nature that he sees in himself and the renewed, holy nature he sees in the Gospel. The Ten Commandments of the Old Testament cut off the crude sins, but the Gospel heals our very nature, which is sickened with sin and striving for sinful qualities because of the fall. Through the light of the Gospels, the monk must enter the battle against himself, his thoughts, and the feelings in his heart; against a world that is antagonistic to the Gospel; against the powers of the world that try to keep man under their domination and imprisonment. The all-powerful Truth will set him free;[14] the all-good Holy Spirit seals and renews him who is released from the slavery to sinful passions and makes him an offspring of the New Adam.

Christian perfection is attained in monasticism, and monks are the light for their brothers who are busy and diverted by the cares and worries of the world and cannot delve deeply into the Gospels or enliven themselves in the full potential of the Gospels' teachings. Such a person can only imagine monasticism superficially or even with disdain; calling himself a Christian, he actually has only the most superficial and moribund understanding of Christianity.

In order for a monk to strengthen and mature in evangelical qualities, he must undergo suffering and temptation. His meekness must be tested. His humility must be tested. His patience and faith must be tested. He must test himself—are the Gospels, the words and commandments of Christ in which eternal life can be found, more precious to him than the benefits, comforts, and traditions of the world? Are they even more precious than his own life? The beginning of temptations always seem this drastic, but without them, it is impossible to learn the greatest and final commandments regarding treatment of one's neighbors—to forgive all offenses, to love one's enemies, to see in all things God's providence. If the inner man will not be formed by all the commandments, then he will not be able to become the dwelling place of the Holy Spirit. Without this descent of the Holy Spirit, there is no Christian perfection. Sorrows and temptations are considered by the Holy Scriptures and the Fathers as the greatest gift of God because they are the preliminary preparation for a life of hesychasm, in which a monk achieves the subtlest purification and, later, abundant illumination. The Fathers compare the sorrows of a monk that come before hesychasm with the passion of Christ before the cross. They compare hesychasm with the crucifixion on the cross itself and the burial, which is followed by resurrection.

I learned all this in good time from the writings of the Fathers. The holy order, the holy system that divine providence indicated for the servants of God, impressed me greatly. I was attracted with the love of my heart to contemplating this miraculous system. I especially loved St Barsanuphius the Great's teachings on the monastic life. It seemed as though he wrote for me, so quickly did my soul embrace his teachings.

"As you listen to the words of the Apostle: 'In everything give thanks,'[15] prepare to give thanks for everything," he wrote to one of his disciples, whom he was preparing in the coenobium for a life in seclusion,

> and whether you are in sorrow or in need or poverty or diseases or physical difficulties, thank God for everything. I hope that you will reach his peace for "we must through many tribulations enter the kingdom of God."[16] And so, never doubting in your soul, and never falling prey to laziness in your heart for whatever reason, remember the words of the Apostle: "Even though our outward man is perishing, yet the inward man is being renewed day by day."[17] If you cannot bear your suffering, then you will not be able to ascend your cross, but if you bear the sufferings from the beginning, you will enter the haven of peace, and you will live a life of silence without any cares, having a soul founded in the Lord, a soul attached to the Lord.[18]

Another brother expressed his desire for the hesychast life to the elder. The saint answered him:

> Brother, A person who still has debts to pay, if he does not pay them first, he will remain a debtor, no matter where he goes, no matter where he lives, either in the city or in the village. Nowhere will he find peace. When, thanks to his debts, he will be subjected to offences

from people, he will be forced in dishonor to find the money wherever he can. Then, having been freed from the debt, he can boldly choose to remain in the society of people or live alone in solitude. In the same way, the monk, when he is permitted to suffer (according to his strength) from offences, slander, envy, only then does humility and spiritual ascesis truly begin. For his humility and labor his sins are forgiven him, as it is written in Scripture: "Look upon my humbleness and hardship, and forgive all my sins."[19] Think of how much dishonor and pain our Lord Jesus Christ suffered before the cross. Having born them all, only then did he go up on the cross. Similarly, no one can attain true and fruitful hesychasm, no one can enter the holy refuge of perfection, if he does not first suffer with Christ and does not bear all of His offences, remembering the teaching of the Apostle: "if indeed we suffer with Him, that we may also be glorified together."[20] Don't be fooled—there is no other way to salvation. May the Lord help you, according to His will, to lay a firm foundation for your spiritual life on rock, as he commanded in the Gospels. For the Rock is Christ Himself.[21]

Soon after my entry into the monastery, many sorrows crashed down on me like purifying water. They included the invisible warfare, assorted diseases, poverty and need, and various shocks due to my ignorance, inexperience, and insufficient wisdom. Sorrows from men were still bearable. In order to fully appreciate them, I needed a new arena. By God's unfathomable providence, I was sent to the one place, near the northern capital, that I had never even wanted to look at, considering it completely unfit for my spiritual goals. In 1833, I was summoned to the Sergiev Hermitage and named its abbot. The monastery received me with hostility. In the first year of my new life, I was struck with one disease; the second year, another disease; the third year, yet another. They took away whatever I had left of my strength and weak health; they made me an invalid, constantly stricken by something. Here, I saw envy, ill will, slander; I was subjected to heavy, demeaning, lengthy punishments without a proper trial, without anyone bothering to investigate the truth. I was treated like a speechless animal, like a statue without feeling. Here, I saw the enemies who spewed forth unmitigated hatred and hunger to destroy me.

Here, the merciful Lord granted me the knowledge of joys and spiritual comfort that are indescribable in human terms. He allowed me to taste spiritual love and sweetness at the same time that I met my enemy who wanted my head, and in my eyes, the face of the enemy became the likeness of an angel. Through my personal experience, I understood the mystical meaning of Christ's silence before Pilate and the high priests of the Jews. What joy to be a victim like Christ! Or rather, what joy to be crucified near the Saviour, as the blessed thief was, and with the thief to confess, from the heart's deep conviction, "I have received what I deserved: remember me, O Lord, in Thy Kingdom."

Having reached age forty, completely ravaged by sickness, destroyed by many sorrows, weak and incapable of any sort of active lifestyle due to my physical state, what shall I say of my fate? I see no man whose life would be more desirable or preferable. I am a sinner, worthy of suffering both temporally and eternally; but no other person's lot is desirable to me. When I look at my sins, I am horrified; but even horrible sinners have a Redeemer.

O rulers of the temporal world, shepherds of the Church, fathers and brothers! I am no longer useful for service. What sort of work is left for one who is chained down by his illness to his bed, who cannot even leave his room? Cast me out; cast me out like a useless slave who is only a burden to you! I will not bother you with any requests for your continued solicitude. I do not need a garden with luxurious shadows and sweet-smelling flowers; I do not need many servants; a humble monk will serve me, a Christ lover will send me money for food and clothing. I do not need a large house or any kind of diversion belonging to this world. Let me go, who am sick and incapable of anything! I will find for myself a little-known solitary and silent refuge, far from the noise of the capital or any other city. There, in solitude, I will live out my days. My sickliness makes the silence of seclusion necessary for me. Would you like to know if I am hiding some sort of personal desires in my soul? I will satisfy your curiosity. I am a sinner, and I desire repentance.

I am leaving the society of people. They are but blind tools in the all-powerful right hand of providence. They bring to pass everything that He commands or permits. By thus applying to your compassion, I wanted to bring my humble payment of love and respect for my neighbor, a payment most pleasant and sweet for the heart of the one who pays. The world, busy with its business, worries, enjoyments, and honors, will not even pay attention to my words. The voice of the soul that feels a need for repentance and silence is strange, incomprehensible to the world.

O my unattainable, all-powerful, all-good, all-wise God and Lord, my Creator and Saviour! In sackcloth and ashes, this mote of dust, I, who have been called by You to existence, feeling, thought, desire! You see my heart. You see if the word that I dare to utter with my mind and lips is the same as the word hidden deep in my heart. You know what I ask even before I ask it. In Your judgments, You have already determined whether or not You will answer my petition. But You gave me my own will, and I dare to bring this request before You, this desire of my accursed, diseased, wounded heart! Do not listen to my heart; do not listen to the words of my prayer; do not do as I wish. Do that which is according to Your will, what You have chosen for me in Your all-holy wisdom. But I will still utter the desire of my heart; I will express with words the striving of my self-will!

Open unto me the doors of repentance, O lover of mankind! I have led a prodigal life, and I have come to the eleventh hour. All my strength is spent; I cannot fulfill Your commandments and service with my racked body. Allow me at least to bring my repentance, so that I do not leave the hostel of this world bereft of any hope. You see my weakness, the weakness of my soul and body! I cannot stand against the passions and temptations surrounding me! Lead me into a place of solitude and silence, so that I can submerge myself completely—mind, heart, and body—into repentance. I thirst for repentance!

Oh merciful Lord, satisfy my unquenchable, insatiable thirst and grant me repentance! You, Who have poured on me so many countless benefits, complete them with the gift of repentance! O all-holy Lord! Do not deprive me of this gift, for which I have, in my madness, begged You for so long, without even realizing what it is that I ask for, not knowing whether I am capable of receiving it, not knowing whether I will preserve if after receiving. One of your servants, sanctified and illumined by the Holy Spirit, said, "There is no true repentance outside of hesychasm."[22]

My sinful soul was astounded by these words, and they have rooted in my memory, continuing to pierce me like a sword every time I remember them. I see no repentance in myself, and I am overcome with worry. I force myself to repent, but I am unwillingly distracted by worries, diversions. They steal away my repentance! I cannot hold on to it among the noise and confusion; it slips away, leaving me with emptiness and lack of hope. O most merciful Lord! Give me the repentance gained only in silence, constant repentance, repentance capable of purifying my defiled soul and body, repentance that You give to all whom You choose and call to Yourself, whose names are written in the book of life, who have been chosen to eternally see Your glory and praise Your mercy. Give repentance to me, which is more precious and desirable than the riches of the whole world. Purified by repentance, let me see Your holy will, let me know the faultless paths to You, and I will tell my brothers of them!

You, my true friends, tied to me by bonds of friendship in the Lord, do not be sad, do not grieve at my leaving. I am going away bodily so that I can become closer to you in spirit. Outwardly I will be lost to you, but essentially you will find me. Leave me to my repentance, and it will return me to you purified, illumined, and I will give you the word of salvation, the word of God. Open unto me the doors of repentance, O Lord Who loves mankind, give me eternal salvation with all my friends, who have loved me for Your sake, so that all, in eternal blessedness, joy, and unutterable bliss, may praise the Father, the Son, and the Holy Spirit, one God in Trinity, who has revealed to the race of man His love and mercy, beyond all words, beyond all understanding! Amen.

Notes

All references to source material in the original text were to the classic Russian language editions. The author and translator followed a Russian cultural practice where one is not necessarily expected to provide all background detail and source material.

Chapter 1

1. John 12:26.
2. John 10:3–4.
3. John 10:9.
4. John 12:26.
5. John 1:1.
6. John 10:38.
7. 1 John 4:15.
8. Rev 3:21.
9. Mark 8:34–35.
10. Luke 14:26–27.
11. John 6:60.
12. Rom 8:6.
13. 1 Cor 1:18.
14. Matt 6:24.
15. Matt 6:24.
16. Isa 1:19–20.
17. Rom 8:6–7.
18. Luke 16:1–31.
19. Matt 19:16–30.
20. John 5:44.
21. Matt 10:16.
22. Matt 10:34–35.
23. Ps 39:13.
24. Luke 16:9.
25. Ps 118:105.
26. John 10:5.
27. 1 Pet 2:21.
28. Heb 1:3.
29. Matt 25:34.

Chapter 2

1. John 12:48.
2. Ps 118:18.
3. Luke 5:24.
4. John 9:39, 41.
5. Matt 9:13.
6. 2 Pet 1:21.
7. 2 Pet 3:16; 2 Cor 2:15–16.
8. Isa 66:2.
8. John 12:25.
9. *The Philokalia*, vol. 1, ch. 32.
10. 1 Cor 15:47.
11. John 12:36.

Chapter 3

1. Ps 17:26–27.
2. Luke 16:9.
3. 1 Cor 1:10.
4. Prov 11:15.

Chapter 4

1. "Let no one read the works of anyone who serves not God. If one reads such a book through ignorance, let him speedily remove it from his memory through reading the Holy Scriptures, especially those that will be most helpful in finding salvation in the spiritual state which he has already attained . . . Books that contradict this, one must never read. What good is it to accept into one's heart the spirit of darkness instead of the Holy Spirit? Whoever reads such works adopts the qualities of his reading, even if this is not evident to the inexperienced as it is to the experienced." St Peter of Damascus, *On Discernment, The Philokalia*, vol. 3.
2. According to the Book of Needs, a priest at confession must ask the penitent if he ever read heretical books.
3. 1 Cor 3:19.
4. Rom 8:7.
5. 2 Pet 3:10.
6. See, for example, the life of St Pachomius the Great.
7. 2 Tim 4:3–4.
8. 2 Tim 3:13.

Chapter 5

1. Matt 5:17.
2. John 3:21.
3. John 14:23.

4. John 15:10.
5. Acts 10, 14, and others.
6. Matt 21:31–32.
7. John 14:21, 23.
8. John 6:63.
9. Mark 1:15.
10. Matt 5:19.
11. St Mark the Ascetic, Homily 1 on repentance.
12. Matt 5:16.
13. Matt 6:1–19; Luke 21:17.
14. 1 Pet 4:10–11.
15. The footnote in the original says "1 Kings 2:30," which is following the Septuagint naming of books. In most English language bibles, this is 1 Sam 2:30.
16. John 12:26.
17. Matt 5:20.
18. St Mark the Ascetic, "On the Spiritual Laws," *The Philokalia*, pt. 1, ch. 32.
19. Ps 8:9.
20. Matt 5:21–22.
21. Matt 5:23.
22. Rom 12:18.
23. Matt 5:27.
24. Matt 5:28.
25. Matt 5:29–30.
26. Matt 5:31–32.
27. Matt 19:4–9.
28. Matt 19:11, 12.
29. Matt 5:33–37.
30. Matt 5:38–40.
31. Matt 5:44.
32. Col 3:12–13.
33. Matt 5:45.
34. Matt 6:18.
35. Matt 6:3.
36. Matt 6:14–15.
37. Mark 11:25.
38. Matt 6:19.
39. Luke 12:33–34.
40. Matt 6:22–23.
41. Matt 6:22–23; Luke 11:34–36.
42. Matt 6:24–34.
43. Matt 6:30, 25.
44. Matt 6:33.
45. Luke 6:37.
46. Matt 7:5.

47. Matt 7:7–8.
48. Luke 18:7.
49. Matt 7:11.
50. 1 Cor 2:9.
51. Luke 11:13.
52. St Isaac the Syrian, Homily 55.
53. Matt 7:12.
54. Luke 6:37–38.
55. Matt 7:13.
56. Matt 7:14.
57. Luke 12:32.
58. Luke 12: 35–36.
59. Mark 13:37.
60. Matt 7:15–16.
61. Luke 8:15.
62. Luke 21:19.
63. Matt 24:13.
64. Matt 11:28–30.
65. Mark 12:29–31.
66. Matt 22:40.
67. John 14:21, 23.
68. John 15:10, 4, 6.
69. Matt 11:12.

Chapter 6

1. This chapter is inspired primarily by St Peter of Damascus, *The Philokalia,* pt. 3.
2. John 3:6.
3. John 6:63.
4. Matt 5:3.
5. Ps 50:19.
6. Matt 5:4.
7. Matt 5:5.
8. Gen 3:19.
9. Ps 36:6.
10. Matt 5:6.
11. Matt 5:48.
12. Matt 5:7.
13. Matt 5:8.
14. St Isaac the Syrian, Homily 48.
15. Matt 5:9.

Chapter 7

1. See, for example, Thomas à Kempis, *The Imitation of Christ.*

2. Rom 10:17.
3. John 17:17.
4. Ps 118:86.
5. Ps 115:2.
6. John 8:31–32.
7. John 4:48.
8. John 3:2.
9. John 6:68–69.
10. John 8:31–32.
11. Luke 24:49.
12. John 16:13.
13. Genesis 3:5.
14. Matt 9:17.
15. Luke 18:7.
16. Gal 3:11.
17. Matt 8.
18. Exod 20:19.
19. Kempis, bk. 3, chs. 1–2.
20. Ps 88:8.
21. Isa 6.
22. Rom 10:14, 17.

Chapter 8

1. Mark 1:15.
2. Acts 20:21.
3. John 12:46.
4. John 3:16, 18.
5. John 3:20–21.
6. Matt 16:24–25.
7. Heb 11:6.
8. St Simeon the New Theologian, *The Philokalia,* pt. 1.
9. 1 Mark 24.
10. Jas 2:18.
11. St Simeon the New Theologian, Homily 3.
12. Saints Kallistos and Ignatius Ksanthopoulos, *The Philokalia*, pt. 2, ch. 16.
13. 1 Cor 6:19, 15, 20.
14. 1 Cor 15:45.
15. John 6:63.
16. Hebrews 10:38
17. Jas 2:17, 22.
18. Jas 2:21–23; Rom 4:1–3.
19. Rom 3:12.
20. Rom 10:9–10.
21. Numbers 20:10–12.

22. The Life of St Paisius the Great.
23. The Life of Martyr Philemon.
24. St Simeon the New Theologian, *The Philokalia,* pt. 1, ch. 1.
25. Heb 11:1.
26. John 11:25.
27. Rom 10:17.

Chapter 9

1. *Sayings of the Desert Fathers,* "On St Pimen the Great."
2. Matt 26:41.
3. Mark 13:37.
4. *Apophthegmata.*
5. Luke 21:34.

Part II

Reflection: The Sea of Life

1. Ps 103:25–26.
2. This exegesis is taken from an annotated Psalter published by the Kiev Caves Lavra in the nineteenth century.
3. John 15:19.
4. John 15:18.
5. 2 Tim 3:12.
6. Ps 44:25, Ps 43:26.
7. Here, the author plays on the Russian word *nebo*, which indicates both the sky and heaven.
8. Compare Matt 8:27.
9. Ps 8:9.
10. Ps 48:13.
11. *Sayings of the Desert Fathers.*
12. Job 41:34.
13. Add ref: The sixth irmos of the resurrectional canon in tone 6.

Chapter 10

1. Abba Dorotheus.
2. Eph 4:14.
3. Col 2:18.
4. Matt 24:12.
5. Ps 50:19.

Chapter 11

1. Matt 9:11.
2. Matt 9:12–13.

3. Matt 12:2.
4. Matt 12:7.
5. Luke 7:36.
6. Luke 7:39.
7. Luke 7:42.
8. Luke 7:47.
9. Luke 18.
10. Job 15:15.
11. Matt 5:3.
12. Luke 18:11.
13. Luke 18:14.
14. Matt 16:6.
15. Matt 23:16.
16. Matt 23:23–24.
17. Matt 23:33–36.
18. Isa 53:7.
19. Matt 16:6, Luke 12:1.
20. Matt 5:16.
21. Luke 16:15.
22. *Apophthegmata.*
23. John 5:44.
24. Matt 6:3.
25. Matt 10:38–39.
26. Matt 7:1–5.
27. *Apophthegmata.*
28. Ibid.
29. Inserted moved from main Titus 1:15
30. *Apophthegmata.*
31. St Isaac the Syrian, Homily 89.
32. Prov 25:8 [This has been translated directly from the Slavonic into English rather than matching the English version found in the Bible.]
33. *Apophthegmata.*
34. Ibid.

Chapter 12

1. St Seraphim of Sarov.
2. Abba Dorotheus, Instruction 13.
3. Ibid.
4. Ps 50:7.
5. Rom 7:14, 17, 20.
6. Rom 7.
7. Abba Dorotheos, Instruction 1.
8. Gal 5:24.
9. Abba Longinus.

10. St Isaac the Syrian, Homily 43.
11. St Macarius the Great, Homily 4, ch. 6.
12. Ps 34:13–14.
13. St Nilus of Sora called such falls "mental sins," Homily 3.
14. Prov 24:16.
15. 1 Chr 21:1.
16. St Nilus of Sora, Homily 3.
17. St Seraphim of Sarov.
18. Matt 5:8.
19. 1 Tim 2:4.
20. *The Philokalia,* pt. 1, ch . 4.
21. St Mark the Ascetic, *On the Spiritual Law*, ch. 32.
22. Abba Dorotheos, Instruction 13.
23. Ps 88:23.

Chapter 13

1. Eph 5:18. The Slavonic translation has the word *blud*, which means fornication, instead of "excess." St Ignatius obviously means the former to be understood in his use of the citation.
2. *Sayings of the Desert Fathers,* "On Abba Pimen," ch. 135.
3. St Isaiah the Egyptian Hermit, Homily 17, chs. 2, 8.
4. St Isaac the Syrian, Homily 89.

Chapter 14

1. Abba Dorotheos, Instruction 3, on the conscience.
2. Heb 10:22.
3. Matt 5:25, exegesis of Abba Dorotheos, Instruction 3.
4. Prov 14:25
5. *The Ladder of Divine Ascent*. New York: Paulist Press. 1982. Step 18.
6. Matt 25:12.

Chapter 15

1. Isa 1:6.
2. Gen 2:17.
3. Rom 7:23–24.
4. Gen 6:3.
5. 1 Cor 15:50.
6. Ps 50.

Part III

Reflection: Thoughts on the Shores of the Sea

1. Ps 30:21.

2. Ps 41:5.
3. Ps 55:12.

Chapter 16

1. Luke 16:15.
2. St Isaac the Syrian, Sermon 44.

Chapter 17

1. Matt 22:40.
2. John 1.
3. Matt 26:33–35, 74.
4. Matt 10:34–36.
5. *The Ladder of Divine Ascent*. New York: Paulist Press.1982. Step 15.
6. *The Ladder of Divine Ascent*. New York: Paulist Press.1982. Step 3.
7. 2 Kgs 13:15.
8. Prov 11:1.
9. Gal 3:27.
10. Luke 24:49.
11. Rom 13:14.
12. Matt 16:24.
13. John 17:21.
14. Ps 33:14.
15. Matt 25:40.
16. 1 John 4:20–21.
17. 1 John 3:14.
18. 1 John 4:16.

Chapter 18

1. 1 Sam 15:22.
2. St Pimen the Great.
3. John 14: 23–24.
4. Ps 118:127–28.
5. John 15:10.
6. John 3:6.
7. Heb 12:29.
8. *The Ladder of Divine Ascent*. New York: Paulist Press. 1982. Step 3&15.
9. Heb 12:28–29.

Chapter 19

1. Luke 21:34.
2. Luke 6:25.
3. Ps 22:5.

4. St Macarius the Great, Homily 1, ch. 4.
5. Matt 7:7.
6. Acts 13:2–3.
7. St Mark the Ascetic, Homily 8.
8. Ibid.
9. Gen 1:29.
10. Gen 9:3.
11. 1 Cor 10:23.
12. 2 Cor 6:17.
13. A popular drink in Russia traditionally made from fermented stale bread.
14. *The Ladder of Divine Ascent*. New York: Paulist Press. 1982. Step 14.
15. St Nilus of Sora, Sermon 5.

Chapter 20

1. *The Ladder,* preface to Step 28.
2. St Pimen the Great.
3. *The Ladder,* Step 28. ch. 7.
4. Ps 115:1.
5. Mark 11:24.
6. Luke 18:1.
7. Luke 18:3.
8. *The Ladder,* Step 7. ch. 11.
9. Luke 18:7.
10. Deut 3:26.
11. 2 Sam 12.
12. Jas 4:3.
13. 1 Sam 16:7.
14. Ps 88:8.
15. Mark 11:25–26
16. St Isaac the Syrian, Homily 89.
17. St John Cassian, *The Philokalia,* pt. 4.
18. St Isaac the Syrian, Sermon 85.
19. St Isaac the Syrian, Sermons 56–57.
20. St Simeon the New Theologian, sermon on the three images of prayer.
21. *The Ladder,* Step 28, ch. 17
22. St Gregory of Sinai, *On Spiritual Deception.*
23. St Simeon the New Theologian, on the three forms of prayer.
24. *The Ladder,* Step 28. ch 17.
25. St Seraphim of Sarov.
26. Rom 5:5.
27. St Isaac the Syrian, Sermon 55.
28. Answer 216, from *Answers of St Barsanuphius and the Prophet John.*
29. Ps 77:30–31.
30. 1 Cor 14:20.

31. Matt 6–8.

32. Luke 6:12.

33. St Seraphim of Sarov, a monk especially adept at prayer, spent a thousand days and nights standing on a rock, crying out to the Lord, "God, be merciful to me, a sinner!"

34. Acts 6:2, 4.

35. *The Ladder,* Step 28.

36. 2 Cor 3:18.

37. St Isaac the Syrian, Sermon 16.

38. Acts 10:11.

39. Acts 10:3.

40. Acts 22:21.

41. Matt 4:17.

42. Luke 17:21.

43. Luke 11:9–10, 13.

44. Luke 18:7–8.

45. St Macarius the Great, Homily 3, ch. 1.

46. *The Ladder,* Step 28, ch. 3.

47. Luke 1:17.

48. *The Book of Needs,* "The Rite of Confession."

49. Matt 18:17.

50. Matt 9:13.

51. Matt 5:23–24.

52. Matt 6:24, 21, 31, 33.

53. John 14:1.

54. Matt 6:6.

55. St Arsenios the Great.

56. St Isaac the Syrian, Sermon 41.

57. St John Carpathos, *The Philokalia,* pt. 4, ch. 13.

58. St Macarius the Great, Sermon 1, ch. 1, Sermon 7, ch. 1.

59. *The Lives of the Saints,* October 2.

60. *The Ladder,* Step 27. ch. 56.

61. St Isaac the Syrian, Sermon 56.

62. St Nilus of Sinai, "On Prayer," *The Philokalia,* pt. 4.

63. Job 1–2.

64. 1 Thess 5:18.

65. St Nilus of Sora, Sermon 3.

66. St Macarius the Great, Sermon 7, ch. 31.

67. 1 Pet 5:6–9.

68. 1 Cor 10:13.

69. St Macarius the Great, Sermon 4, ch. 7.

70. Rev 2:7; St Macarius the Great, Sermon 4, ch. 5.

71. St Macarius the Great, Sermon 4, ch. 6.

72. For example, St Justina's battle with passions of the flesh. *The Lives of the Saints,* October 2.

73. St Nilus of Sora, Sermon 3.
74. Luke 18.
75. Luke 17:4.
76. Jas 4:4–5.
77. Jas 1:8.
78. Rev 3:16
79. Luke 14:33.
80. Gal 5:24.
81. Ps 103:25.
82. Abba Dorotheos, Homily 11, on how to quickly cut off the passions.
83. Matt 19:21, 16:24; Mark 10:21.
84. St Nilus of Sora, "On Prayer," ch. 17.
85. St Macarius of Egypt, Homily 21, chs. 2–3.
86. Mark 8:35. Experience of such warfare and crucifixion is seen in the life of St Anthony the Great, St Macarius of Egypt, and other holy monks.
87. Mark 9:29.
88. Matt 6:17.
89. Col 3:12–13.
90. Luke 6:36.
91. Matt 5:48.
92. Matt 5:45.
93. St Isaac the Syrian, Sermon 21.
94. Rom 8:26.
95. Rom 8:27.
96. 1 Cor 2:11.
97. (John 14:26).
98. Rom 8:26.
99. St Simeon the New Theologian, Homily 6.
100. *Apophthegmata.*
101. St Sisoe the Great, *Apophthegmata*.
102. Answer 282, from *Answers of St Barsanuphius and the Prophet John*.
103. St Gregory of Sinai, "On Delusion."
104. Luke 11:9–10, 13.
105. Mark 13:35–36.
106. *The Ladder,* Homily 28, ch. 64. [This is not the same work as *The Ladder of Divine Ascent* or *The Ladder* that has been previously cited. This is a Russian language text with no equivalent text found in English.]
107. Matt 11:28–30.
108. *The Ladder,* Step 28, ch. 2.
109. Ps 33:11.
110. Ps 88:8.

Chapter 21

1. John 6:47.

2. i.e., Jesus Christ, the Son of God.
3. *The Lives of the Saints*, December 13.
4. Ps 49:7–8, 12.
5. 1 Cor 4:7.
6. Luke 12:48.
7. Ps 15:8.
8. 2 Sam 16:10–12.
9. Ps 25:2.
10. St Macarius the Great, Sermon 37, chs. 2, 4.

Part IV

Chapter 22

1. Mark 1:15; Matt 4:17.
2. St Macarius the Great, Homily 7, ch. 2.
3. Ezek 18:21–22.
4. Ezek 18:31.
5. Ezek 33:11.
6. Isa 1:16, 18.
7. Rom 2:4.
8. Rom 2:5–9.

Chapter 23

1. Matt 11:29.
2. *The Ladder,* Step 21, ch. 3.
3. Ibid.
4. St Isaac the Syrian, Homily 38.
5. Abba Dorotheos, Homily 2, on humble-mindedness.
6. Luke 18. Blessed Theophilact the Bulgarian's interpretation of St Luke's parable of the publican and the Pharisee.
7. Luke 18.
8. Matt 9:13.
9. See the first prayer in the morning rule by St Macarius the Great.
10. *The Philokalia,* pt. 3, bk. 1, art. 1.
11. Ps 142:10.
12. St Mark the Ascetic, "On Spiritual Laws." *The Philokalia,* pt. 1.
13. Matt 9:13.
14. St Nilus of Sora, "On Proud Thoughts."
15. *Sayings of the Desert Fathers.*
16. *The Ladder,* Step 4, chs. 23–24.
17. Answer 210, from *Answers of St Barsanuphius and the Prophet John.*
18. St Dorotheos of Gaza, Sermon 2.
19. Luke 16:15.
20. Isa 42:1–2.

21. 1 Pet 2:21, 23.
22. St Isaac the Syrian, Homily 89.
23. 1 Sam 24.
2.4 Luke 16.
25. *Apophthegmata.*
26. Ibid.
27. Answer 275, from *Answers of St Barsanuphius and the Prophet John.*
28. Matt 16:26.
29. cf. John 15:18–20.
30. Matthew 6.
31. St John of the Ladder, Sermon 4, chs. 82–83.
32. St Simeon the New Theologian, *The Philokalia,* pt. 1, chs. 70–72.
33. Luke 23:42.
34. Matt 10:38.
35. Ps 93:19.
36. John 14:1.
37. Answer 579, from *Answers of St Barsanuphius and the Prophet John.*
38. St. Pimen the Great, *Skete Paterikon.*
39. The last petition of the great ektenia.
40. The life of martyrs Timothy and Mavra (May 3). This is an incredible life! At every stage of their suffering, the martyrs never stopped insisting that their martyrdom was cleansing them of their sins. Illumined by the Holy Spirit, they greedily accepted this purification. The magnitude of their humility was united with overwhelming divine love. When Mavra was being led to be crucified, her mother stopped her, trying to convince her with tears to deny Christ. But the martyr, tearing herself from the arms of her mother, hurried to the cross, saying to her mother: "Why do you distract me from the cross, why do you not let me quickly feel the sweetness of my Lord by dying like He did?"
41. St Abba Dorotheos, Homily 2.
42. St Isaac the Syrian, Homily 48.

Chapter 24

1. Col 2:18.
2. Phil 2:5–8.
3. St Macarius of Egypt, Homily 7, ch. 4.
4. St Macarius of Egypt, Homily 8, ch. 5.
5. 2 Cor 9:13–15.
6. Luke 6:21, 25.
7. Thomas à Kempis, *Imitation of Christ.* bk. 3, ch. 2.
8. John 19:24.
9. Job 42:5–6.
10. Luke 23:41–42.
11. Matt 27:34.
12. John 7:24; Matt 7:16.
13. Kgs 17:21. [trans. from the Slavonic.]

14. Ps 88:21.
15. 1 Sam 16:7.
16. St Pimen the Great.
17. Luke 4:7.
18. *The Ladder,* Step 22, ch. 22.
19. John 19:10.
20. St Isaac the Syrian, Homily 33.

Chapter 25

1. St Elias, *The Philokalia,* pt. 4.
2. St Philotheos of Sinai, *The Philokalia,* pt. 2, ch. 13.
3. Matt 11:12.
4. *Apophthegmata*, "Of Archbishop Theophilus and Abba Dorotheos."
5. *Apophthegmata.*
6. Matt 7:5.
7. Abba Dorotheos, Homily 7, "On Self-Accusation."
8. Matt 10:29–30.
9. 1 Pet 5:6–7.
10. Dan 3:26–29. [From the Septuagint text.]
11. John 15:2.
12. Ps 18:10.
13. Ps 118:108, 175.
14. *Synaxarion* for January 26.
15. Heb 12:6.
16. Matt 19:21; Mark 10:21.
17. St Simeon the New Theologian, Homily 4.
18. Answer 304, from *Answers of St Barsanuphius and the Prophet John.*
19. Ps 15:8–9.
20. St Peter of Damascus, *The Philokalia,* bk. 1, pt. 3.
21. St Isaiah the Hermit, Sermon 8.
22. John 17:3.
23. Matt 24:13.

Chapter 26

1. 1 Cor 6:15.
2. Matt 15:19–20.
3. 1 Cor 6:16.
4. 1 Thess 4:3–5.
5. Matt 19:11–12.
6. Blessed Theophilact's exegesis on Matt 7:7–8.
7. St John of the Ladder, Homily 15, ch. 8.
8. St Isaac the Syrian, Homilies 43 and 38.
9. 1 Cor 6:17.

10. Matt 25:23.
11. St Isaac the Syrian, Homily 57.
12. *Apophthegmata.*
13. Ibid.
14. *Sayings of the Great Abba Pimen*, ch. 70.
15. St Macarius the Great, Homily 7, ch. 4.
16. Matt 7:21.
17. Ps 96:10.
18. *The Philokalia,* pt. 2, ch. 11.
19. 2 Cor 7:1.
20. Gen 3:15.
21. *Instructions for Those Rejecting the World,* ch. 37.
22. St Nilus of Sora, Sermon 8.
23. St John of the Ladder, Homily 7, ch. 31.
24. St Macarius the Great, Homily 5, ch. 14.
25. 2 Sam 11:2.
26. St Pimen the Great, *Apophthegmata.*
27. Ibid.
28. St Isaac the Syrian, Homily 2.
29. St. Agathon, *Apophthegmata.*
30. St Cassian of Rome, "On the Spirit of Fornication," ch. 5.
31. Abba Dorotheos, Instruction 13.
32. Answer 255, from *Answers of St Barsanuphius and the Prophet John.*
33. St Isaiah the Hermit, Sermon 27, ch. 2.
34. St Macarius the Great, Homily 21.
35. Abba Dorotheos, Instruction 13, "On the Patient Bearing of Temptations."
36. *Apophthegmata.*
37. Rom 7:23.
38. Matt 11:12.
39. St John of the Ladder, Homily 15, ch. 9.
40. Gal 5:24.
41. St. John Cassian. Book VI on the spirit of fornication, ch. 19.

Chapter 27

1. *The Philokalia,* pt. 2, chapters on St Philotheos of Sinai.
2. Isaac the Syrian, Homily 71.
3. 1 Tim 2:8.
4. Gen 39:9.
5. St Agathon the Great, *Skete Paterikon.*

Part V

Reflection: A Tree in Front of My Cell's Window During Winter

1. Ps 141:1, 142:1, 141:7.

2. Ps 141:6, 8.
3. Ps 141:7.
4. Ps 142:4.
5. Ps 114:3.
6. Ps 114:8.
7. Ps 15:5.
8. Ps 141:8.

Chapter 29

1. Luke 16:29.
2. Luke 16:31.

Chapter 30

1. St Isaac the Syrian, Homily 21.
2. Sir 7:39. [trans. from the Slavonic.]
3. Ps 33:21.
4. *The Ladder,* Step 6.

Chapter 31

1. *The Ladder of Divine Ascent*, Step 28, ch. 61.

Part VI

Reflection: The Garden During Winter

1. This cenobitic monastery is in the Orlov Diocese, between Sevsk and Dmitrovsk, about 27 miles from each.

Chapter 32

1. Matt 16:24.
2. Ps 119:38.
3. Gal 5:24.
4. Matt 11:30.
5. St Mark the Ascetic, "On Spiritual Laws," ch. 31.
6. *The Lives of the Saints*, May 3. [From a Russian calendar.]

Chapter 33

1. Matt 20:23.
2. Ps 115:4.
3. John 18:11.
4. Acts 14:22.
5. Phil 1:29.
6. Luke 23:41–42.

7. Matt 5:44.
8. Matt 11:12.
9. 1 John 3:15.
10. Acts 5:41.
11. Job 1:21.
12. Matt 26:53.
13. John 12:26.
14. St Isaac the Syrian, Homily 35.
15. Matt 26:39.
16. Matt 26:41
17. Rev 7:13–17.

Chapter 34

1. John 8:32, 44.
2. St Mark the Ascetic, *The Philokalia,* pt. 1.
3. St Peter of Damascus, *The Philokalia,* pt. 3.
4. 2 Thess 2:3.
5. *Apophthegmata Patrum* .
6. Luke 18:8.
7. Cor 6:17.
8. Abba Dorotheos, Instruction 1.
9. Cassiani Collatio XVIII, cap. V.
10. Lib. 11, *De Nocturnis orationibus,* Caput. V.
11. St Isaac the Syrian, Homily 55.
12. *The Life of St. Gordius*, January 3.
13. Matt 28:19–20.
14. Acts 20:20–21.
15. Col 1:27–28.
16. Jas 2:26.
17. Rom 10:17, 14.
18. Heb 6:1–2.
19. Heb 11, 12, 13.
20. John 14:21.
21. 1 Cor 7:32–33.
22. 1 Cor 6:17.
23. St John of the Ladder, Homily 2, ch. 9.
24. John 15:18–19.
25. John 3:36, 17:3.
26. Matt 19:17; Mark 10:19.
27. Luke 13:3, 5.
28. Abba Dorotheos, Instruction 1.
29. Matt 16:24; Matt 19:21; Luke 14:26.
30. Matt 16:24, 19:21; Mark 10:21; Luke 14:26–27, 33.
31. 2 Cor 6:16–18.

32. *The Ladder of Divine Ascent.*
33. Gal 5:24.
34. Eph 6:12.
35. St Simeon the New Theologian, Homily 2.
36. 1 Pet 4:10.
37. Job 1:5.
38. Matt 6:21.
39. Luke 12:33.
40. Matt 6:24–33.
41. Matt 14:22, 33.
42. St John of the Ladder, *The Ladder,* Step 4, ch. 43.
43. St Macarius the Great, Conversation 7, ch. 5.
44. St Isaac the Syrian, Homily 43, 48.
45. Gen 2:25.
46. Eph 5:32.
47. Luke 2:14.
48. *The Book of Needs,* wedding service.
49. Matt 19:12.
50. St Macarius the Great, Homily 1, ch. 13.
51. St John Cassian, bk. 4, ch. 5.
52. St Barsanuphius the Great, Answer 255, from *Answers of St Barsanuphius and the Prophet John.*
53. Matt 7:8.
54. *Histoire de Christianisme,* Fleury, livre 26, ch. 5.
55. Sir 6:18–19.
56. Eccl 11:9. Once again, the Slavonic Bible and the English Bible have readings of this verse with opposite meanings. The English has been adapted to correctly reflect the meaning in the Slavonic, the meaning given to this passage by the author.
57. Wisdom of Solomon 8:2–4.
58. Examples of such saints are St Savva the Sanctified, St Simeon of the Holy Mountain, and many others.
59. St Isaac the Syrian, Homily 47.
60. St John of the Ladder, *The Ladder,* Step 27, ch. 29.
61. Ibid., Step 1, chs. 18–19.
62. St John Cassian, Book 11, ch. 3.
63. St John of the Ladder, *The Ladder,* Step 1, ch. 4.
64. *The Rule of St. Nilus of Sora.*
65. Ibid.
66. Jas 5:16.
67. *The Philokalia*, pt. 4, "On the Holy Fathers of Sketis."
68. *Rule of St Nilus of Sora.*
69. Answer 603, from *Answers of St Barsanuphius and the Prophet John.*
70. Matt 13:29–30.
71. Matt 18:7.

72. Matt 24:12.
73. Matt 18:7.
74. 2 Tim 3:8, 5.
75. Heb 10:26.

Chapter 35

1. Much of this article is taken from St Macarius the Great, Homily 7, chs. 13–18.
2. Sir 2:1–2, 4. [Trans. from the Slavonic.]
3. 1 Cor 10:13.
4. Heb 12:8.
5. Rom 8:18.
6. 2 Cor 6:16.
7. St Macarius the Great, Homily 4, ch. 15.
8. Rom 12:19.
9. St Isaac the Syrian, Homily 37.

Chapter 36

1. Ps 83:6–8.
2. Ps 125:5–6.
3. We read this opinion in the dialogues of Severus Sulpicius, found in the complete works of the Church Fathers.
4. St John of the Ladder, *The Ladder,* Step 7; St Nilus of Sora, Sermon 8.
5. Ps 118:136.
6. Matt 5:3–4.
7. Answer 282, from *Answers of St Barsanuphius and the Prophet John*.
8. St Isaac the Syrian, Sermon 30.
9. Judg 1:15.
10. St Nilus of Sora, Sermon 8.
11. *The Ladder*, Step 7.
12. Ps 101:5–8, 10.
13. Ps 6:7.
14. St Nilus of Sora, Sermon 8.
15. St Nilus of Sora, in Sermon 2, calls prayer and the sorrow of the spirit "wise weeping and tears."
16. *The Ladder,* Step 7, ch. 60.
17. Ps 37:9.
18. 1 Thess 5:21.
19. St Isaac the Syrian, Sermon 89.
20. St Nilus of Sora, Sermon 8.
21. Matt 5:4.
22. Ps 114:5–7.
23. Ps 6:9–10.
24. St Macarius the Great, Sermon 4, ch. 19.

25. Lam 1:1.
26. Lam 1:2.
27. Answer 38, from *Answers of St Barsanuphius and the Prophet John.*
28. St Isaac the Syrian, Sermon 65.
29. Ps 79:6.
30. Ps 55:9.
31. Ps 41:4.
32. Ps 93:19.
33. Ps 125:1–2.
34. Jer 46:27.
35. *Apophthegmata Patrum* , ch. 33.
36. *The Lives of the Saints*, June 9.
37. *Apophthegmata Patrum* .
38. 1 Cor 6:18.
39. *Apophthegmata Patrum* .
40. *The Ladder,* Step 5, ch. 33.
41. Ibid., Step 7, ch. 64.
42. Ibid., Step 7, ch. 70.
43. Ps 50.
44. St Isaac the Syrian, Sermon 59; *The Ladder,* Step 7; St Nilus of Sora, Sermon 8.

Chapter 37

1. Rom 11:34.
2. Matt 10:30; Luke 21:18.
3. Ps 15:8.
4. St John Karpathos, *The Philokalia,* pt. 4, ch. 25.
5. Luke 10:18.
6. Luke 14:17, according to the interpretation of Blessed Theophilact the Bulgarian.

Chapter 38

1. Ps 49:23.
2. Mark 13:33.
3. Heb 13:13.
4. Heb 13:14.
5. St Hesychius, *The Philokalia,* pt. 2, ch. 4. All the other Fathers write the same.

Chapter 39

1. John 1:46.
2. Matt 28:20.
3. St Peter of Damascus says, "Christ is hidden within the gospel. He who wishes to find him, must sell all that he has and buy the Gospel, not only find Christ through reading, but to accept Him into his heart through His life's example. He who searches for Christ, says St Maximos, must find Him not outside, but inside himself, that is, he

must be both in body and soul like Christ, sinless as far as that is humanly possible" (*The Philokalia*, pt. 3).

4. John 14:21.

5. John 15:4, 10; 6:56.

6. This kind of self-deception is often mentioned by the ascetic Fathers. St John the Carpathian defines it thus: "Deception is a drunkenness of the soul on vanity and a carnal-minded blindness" (*The Philokalia,* vol. 4, ch. 49). The holy Apostle Paul has this to say about such deception: "Let no one cheat you of your reward, taking delight in false humility and worship of angels, intruding into those things which he has not seen, vainly puffed up by his fleshly mind" (Col 2:18). St Gregory of Sinai: "Those who speak from their thoughts before becoming pure have become beguiled by a spirit of deception. To such are the words of Proverbs addressed: 'Seest thou a man wise in his own conceit? There is more hope of a fool than of him'" (Prov 26:12; St Gregory of Sinai, *The Philokalia*, vol. 1, ch. 128).

7. 1 John 2:4–5.

8. (John 14:24).

9. Matt 7:23.

Appendix 2

1. 1 Cor 15:50.

2. 1 Cor 11:31.

3. Ps 50:7.

4. "The northern capital" is a reference to the city of St Petersburg.

5. Soloviev was a professor at St Petersburg University who taught physics in the entry-level officers' courses and chemistry in the upper-level courses of the Engineers' Technical School.

6. 2 Tim 3:8.

7. 1 Cor 1:21.

8. 1 Cor 1:21.

9. Col 2:8, 3.

10. 1 Cor 3:18.

11. 1 Cor 3:18.

12. 1 Cor 1:24, 30. "Without Christ there is no truth, there is no enlightenment, no redemption, and any wisdom without Christ is foolishness. Any wise man without Christ is a madman, and any righteous man without Christ is a sinner. Any pure man without Christ is impure . . . What do we have that truly belongs to us? Weakness, sickness, darkness, anger, sins."—St Tikhon of Zadonsk, Letter 11.

13. 1 Cor 2:10.

14. John 8:32.

15. 1 Thess 5:18.

16. Acts 14:22.

17. 2 Cor 4:16.

18. Answer 2, from *Answers of St Barsanuphius and the Prophet John.*

19. Ps 24:18.

20. Rom 8:17.
21. 1 Cor 10:4; Answer 342, from *Answers of St Barsanuphius and the Prophet John*.
22. St Isaac the Syrian, Homily 41.

Subject Index

Note: Citations in parentheses following page numbers refer to note numbers: for example, 214(n29) refers to text associated with note 29 on page 214.

Scripture Index

Note: Citations in parentheses following page numbers refer to note numbers; for example p, 248(n10) refers to text associated with note 10 on page 248.